America's Hundred Years' War

U.S. Expansion to the Gulf Coast and the Fate of the Seminole, 1763–1858

◇◇◇

EDITED BY

WILLIAM S. BELKO

University Press of Florida

Gainesville · Tallahassee · Tampa · Boca Raton

Pensacola · Orlando · Miami · Jacksonville · Ft. Myers · Sarasota

Copyright 2011 by William S. Belko
Printed in the United States of America on acid-free paper

First cloth printing, 2011
First paperback printing, 2015

Library of Congress Cataloging-in-Publication Data
America's hundred years' war : U.S. expansion to the Gulf Coast and
the fate of the Seminole, 1763–1858 / edited by William S. Belko.
p. cm.
Includes bibliographical references and index.
ISBN 978-0-8130-3525-3 (cloth: alk. paper)
ISBN 978-0-8130-6175-7 (pbk.)
1. Seminole Indians—Wars. 2. Seminole War, 1st, 1817–1818.
3. Seminole War, 2nd, 1835–1842. 4. Seminole War, 3rd, 1855–1858.
5. Seminole Indians—Government relations. 6. United States—
Territorial expansion. 7. Gulf Coast (U.S.)—History—18th
century. 8. Gulf Coast (U.S.)—History—19th century.
I. Belko, W. Stephen, 1967–
E83.817.A64 2011
973.5'7—dc22   2010024271

The University Press of Florida is the scholarly publishing agency
for the State University System of Florida, comprising Florida A&M
University, Florida Atlantic University, Florida Gulf Coast University,
Florida International University, Florida State University, New College of Florida, University of Central Florida, University of Florida,
University of North Florida, University of South Florida, and University of West Florida.

University Press of Florida
15 Northwest 15th Street
Gainesville, FL 32611-2079
http://www.upf.com

Contents

Illustrations

Introduction

WILLIAM S. BELKO

As Americans proudly celebrated their nation's 65th birthday—on July 4, 1841—how many of them at that moment could have anticipated that within the decade of the 1840s they would add to their Union a vast expanse of land, reaching from the Gulf of Mexico to the Pacific Ocean? Some, infected with that incubating germ of Manifest Destiny, could indeed envision an extensive territorial empire connecting the Atlantic to the Pacific, and a commercial one extending well beyond. On such a celebrated day, were they also aware of another story occurring off the Gulf Coast of Florida, several miles out from the Bay of Tampa—a powerful story directly connected to their passion for territorial acquisition, a tragedy unfolding in the name of their expanding Empire of Liberty? There, shackled on the quarterdeck of a U.S. transport vessel, stood the impressive Seminole leader Coacoochee—Wildcat, to those speaking only American—and a number of his warriors, captured months prior in the midst of the brutal and bloody Second Seminole War still raging throughout Florida. The irons around their feet enabled them to step a mere four inches at a time. Hanging their heads in silence, arrayed in order of their rank, they sat. Their manacled hands rested on their knees. The commanding officer of U.S. forces in the Florida war addressed them boldly. It was due time, declared Colonel William Jenkins Worth, that the Indian "felt the power and strength of the white man," and he followed with an ultimatum. Unless Coacoochee used his influence to convince the rest of his small band to surrender and accept emigration to lands west of the Mississippi, then "yourself, and these warriors now seated before us, shall be hung to the yards of this vessel, when the sun sets on the day appointed, with the irons upon your hands and feet." Such a deed, Worth concluded, "is for the benefit of the white and red man."[1]

Coacoochee rose to respond, as some of his warriors raised their hands to wipe away tears, their irons jingling in the action. "I was once a boy," he recalled, "then I saw the white man afar off." Yet, like the bear and the wolf, the white man came upon him, "horses, cattle, and fields, he took from me."

Despite assurances of friendship, the white man still came, and "too strong for us." He asked only for a small piece of land to cultivate and to live on, "a spot where I could place the ashes of my kindred, a spot only sufficient upon which I could lay my wife and child." But such the expanding Americans would never allow, at least not in Florida. "I feel the irons in my heart."[2]

Worth simply repeated his warning. "I say to you again, and for the last time, that unless the band acquiesce promptly with your wishes, to your last wish, the sun, as it goes down on the last day appointed for their appearance, will shine upon the bodies of each of you hanging in the wind." On the nation's birthday, as Americans cheered their independence, as they venerated their liberties, privileges, and immunities, the fate of other Americans proved considerably less sanguine. An American officer summed up the scene best: "Here was a chief, a man whose only offence was defending his home, his fireside, the graves of kindred, stipulating, on the *Fourth of July*, for his freedom and his life." Soon, a U.S. schooner moored nearby opened its batteries in a customary salute to the import of the day. Coacoochee heard the discharge, recognizing correctly that it was a "jubilee of freedom" emanating from his captors' vessels. "That flag," sardonically concluded the American officer recording the events before him, "waving from the mast-head of Coacoochee's prison-ship, symbolical of freedom, was saluted by the roar of artillery, announcing to the world the liberty of twenty millions of people, free, independent, intelligent, and happy." Not all in Florida, however, could hear the triumphant guns trumpeting the advance of American liberty. Most only heard the trampling of American soldiers, militiamen, and settlers, acquiring their lands.[3]

True to his word, Coacoochee secured the surrender of his band, and he did so within the requisite forty days. He chose five warriors to go deep into the wilds of Florida and convince those of his band to fight no longer and to accept removal to lands in the west. Before leaving the chains of their prison ship, Coacoochee implored his warriors to mind the solemnity of his words, and yet know that he would not die a coward if they failed. He gave them thirty nine sticks, one for each day, and a fortieth, much larger than the rest and with blood on it. "When the others are thrown away, and this only remains, say to my people, that with the setting sun, Coacoochee hangs like a dog, with none but white men to hear his last words. Tell my wife and child"—and here he could no longer speak, overcome with emotion as he thought of the two—the Seminole leader turned away to hide the tears streaming down his face. As the last of the five warriors passed over the side of the ship, Coacoochee managed some last words and a directive—he gave to his fellow warrior a silk handkerchief and a breastpin, "Give these to my wife and child."[4]

Coacoochee, (Wild Cat.)

Int.1. Coacoochee (Wildcat) (Florida State Library and Archives).

Also true to his word, Colonel Worth would not hang the Seminole leader from the yard arm of the prison vessel. Over the period of several weeks, Coacoochee's band turned themselves over to U.S. soldiers, and to the commanding officer's satisfaction. They were then ordered to board a transport vessel to be shipped via New Orleans, up the Mississippi River, overland through Arkansas, and finally destined to Creek lands in territory forever guaranteed to the Indians—the modern day state of Oklahoma. As they embarked for the vessel, the women bowed and kissed the earth, whispering curses to those forcing their departure. On October 12, 1841, Coacoochee and 211 others, his wife and child included, looked for the last time upon the only land they knew. No one spoke as they assembled on the deck. Coacoochee broke the silence: "I am looking at the last pine tree on my land." Sobs then emanated from the forced sojourners. "It was my home," sighed Coacoochee. "I loved it; and to leave it now, is like burying my wife and child. I have thrown away my rifle; have taken the hand of the white man, and now say to him take care of me." As an officer recalled, "the deck of the vessel was now substituted for the green turf of their native land." Before them lay a most uncertain expanse of water, either to swallow them or to carry them safely to new and unknown lands they knew not. Coacoochee's father, the great Seminole chief King Philip, had died two years earlier on his way west. His followers buried him on the banks of the Mississippi River just south of Baton Rouge, so far from his native land and yet so far from his destined one.[5]

As Florida slowly disappeared over the eastern horizon, Coacoochee's thoughts must have turned to the past. Maybe he recalled his capture early in the war, his subsequent imprisonment, and his daring escape. Maybe he remembered the several long years of the bloodletting that ensued, as he fled the advance of American soldiers, as he endeavored to keep his people alive to fight another day and to live free—albeit in fear—upon their native soil. Maybe he thought of the March day, in 1841, when he finally strolled into an American army camp and surrendered voluntarily. There, in the presence of Colonel Worth and his staff, his daughter, already a captive of the Americans, heard his voice, burst from her tent, and ran to the arms of her father. In his hands she placed some musket balls and powder she had secreted away while in captivity. Coacoochee, who believed his daughter no longer alive, wept. He thanked Colonel Worth and his officers—"the innate enemy of his race"—for protecting and returning his child, and then he evoked the last four years of his life, years where constantly he fought the advance of the Americans deeper into the peninsula of his home. "The white man comes," and with him only foreboding consequences. "The white men are as thick as the leaves in the hammock; they come upon us thicker every year." Most likely this is what came into his mind as the blue waters surrounding the ship swallowed all sight of land.[6]

Coacoochee indeed thought of the white men who had come to his lands in numbers too thick to resist. He recalled a dream he had before war came full upon his doorstep, a vision in which the spirit of his twin sister visited him. She had died years earlier, and her spirit Coacoochee now left behind. "In going from Florida," he declared, "I leave behind me the spirits of the Seminoles," yet when he died, he vowed to go and live with his sister. She had told him, in that dream, that in the spring of the Great Spirit all was peace. In some future day, Coacoochee vowed, he would go to her again. "I may be buried in the earth, or sunk in the water, but I shall go to her, and live with her. Game is abundant there; and there the white man is never seen." Indian country in the west, however, proved anything but the spring of the Great Father. Starvation, sickness, and death awaited them in the lands where the white man had sent them.[7]

Thus was the fate of the Seminole by the 1840s—a tragic consequence of U.S. expansion to the Gulf Coast during the late eighteenth and early nineteenth centuries—a story rarely told from the perspective of the vanquished, yet always colored in the perspective of the victor. The constant advance of Americans to the Gulf of Mexico made certain that Coacoochee's wish to cultivate his own plot of land, and there to bury the ashes of his kindred, his wife and his child, would never come true. Instead, it would be the Americans who would cultivate the plot of land and bury within their kindred. The unfortunate fate of the Seminole culminated from a long struggle with the young United States that commenced well before there was a United States of America—a fate that began in the Anglo-Spanish rivalry in the Southeastern borderlands, essentially sealed as a result of continual American incursions into Spanish Florida during the administrations of the Virginia Dynasty, intensified with the removal policy of the Jacksonian administrations, and sustained well into the twentieth century.

Yet U.S. relations with the Seminole have too long been viewed through the lens of an ethnocentric American history. Ever since the tragic events affecting Coacoochee and his people, scholars and students of American contact with the Florida Indians have traditionally directed their attention overwhelmingly to the Second Seminole War (1835–1842),[8] and only cursorily to the First Seminole War (1817–1818)[9] and even less to the Third Seminole War (1855–1858),[10] viewing these conflicts essentially as separate, unconnected episodes.[11] Even the dates provided for these conflicts reflect a distinct American perspective. Rarely has scholarship focused on the pivotal events and issues that spawned these violent episodes defining U.S.-Seminole relations during the first half of the nineteenth century. Even those few works that pay some scholarly tribute, albeit still abbreviated, to the last half of the eighteenth century—decades that proved crucial to the story of American contact with the Florida Indians— remain locked in a strictly American viewpoint that takes for granted the eventual Americanization and outright acquisition of Spanish Florida.[12] This indeed betrays a rather simplified and narrow approach to U.S.-Seminole interaction, a biased perspective that relegates this rarely peaceful relationship into abbreviated periods, with set dates, and often attributed to short-term causes. Such is not the case. The contentious contact between the expanding Americans and the retreating Florida Indians can only be described as one long unbroken struggle, commencing early in the eighteenth century and continuing well into the nineteenth. The traditional American dates provided for this conflict *certainly* fail miserably in assessing accurately the Seminole perspective. For them, the four decades from the War of 1812 to the eve of the U.S. Civil War proved to be a continuous fight for survival, an uninterrupted record of resistance, with no peace or rest in between—a history of conflict that commenced before American independence.

The chapters within this volume reassess the traditional periods provided for U.S.-Seminole relations, and, in this process, advocate a new approach to how we look at the relationship between American expansion and the adverse effects of such expansion on the Seminole people. Each essay, in its own way, lends support to the contention that the conflict between the young United States and the Seminole people transpired over a period of nearly a century, commencing in the decade prior to the American Revolution and ending in the decade before the U.S. Civil War. In the endeavor to reexamine the traditional line of thought that has previously defined the various confrontations between expansive and aggressive Americans and the retreating but resistant Florida Indians, each contributor uniquely expands the conventional views and periods of U.S.-Seminole contact, and each does so in a variety of manners—chronologically, geographically, culturally, politically, conceptually. Through such a lens as that provided by the essays herein, a new approach to U.S. expansion to the Gulf Coast and the consequent fate of the Seminole emerges, a fresh perspective that certainly requires more attention and additional study. The dates chosen for this volume, therefore—1763 to 1858—are not randomly selected. Rather, they indicate a more logical beginning and end to the bitter and protracted confrontation between Anglo-American and Seminole. These ten decades aptly delineate the unremitting U.S. expansion to the Gulf Coast and the consequent fate of the Seminole, making this struggle, as two Florida scholars have accurately titled it, "America's longest conflict"— indeed, it is America's own Hundred Years' War—and it modifies the traditional approach to how we view U.S.-Seminole relations.

The year 1763 most appropriately commenced the incessant conflict between Americans and the Florida Indians, for the pivotal events of that year set the stage for the tragic episode unfolding on the deck of a U.S. transport vessel off the coast of Tampa on that fateful day of July 4, 1841.[13] The year 1858, the end of the Third Seminole War, ultimately signaled the final defeat and removal of the Seminole. On the eve of the U.S. Civil War, a dramatic shift indeed occurred in the relationship between the United States and the Seminole, a change as portentous as that of 1763, and thus it stands as a fitting year for ending the long conflict. And, yet, even these dates fail to tell the complete story of Anglo-American expansion and Seminole resistance. The momentous changes wrought in 1763 had origins in the intense Anglo-Spanish rivalry in the North American Southeast during the seventeenth century,[14] and the bitter relationship between the United States and the Seminole continued well beyond the 1850s, into the period of the U.S. Civil War and Reconstruction, as the Seminole struggled to maintain their identity in the lands west of the Mississippi. But such an equally poignant story transpires in the West, in lands far from the Gulf Coast of Florida, from where the Seminole had nearly to a man been removed by the time of the Third Seminole War, and thus a narrative beyond the scope of this work.[15] Consequently, a more telling account, a more precise version, of U.S. expansion to the Gulf Coast and the fate of the Indians in Florida must be told within the decades from 1763 to 1858.

During this century-long conflict between American and Seminole, two pivotal dates emerge—1783 and 1812—revealing three distinct yet inextricable phases for America's Hundred Years' War. During the British period of Florida history—1763 to 1783—the Seminole emerged unwittingly as victims of an aggressive Anglo-American expansion, more commercial than territorial in nature, into the Gulf South borderlands.[16] Recognition of American independence in 1783 greatly accelerated this expansion, setting the stage for an unremitting push of white Americans southward towards the Gulf Coast and into lands restored to Spain. The year 1783 inaugurated an unprecedented period of policies and diplomacy, conducted by individual states as well as the new national government, and both territorial as much as commercial in nature, that pushed the Indian-white barrier right to the doorstep of Spanish Florida.[17] Beginning in 1783 and gradually intensifying until the outbreak of war between the United States and Great Britain in 1812, this unrelenting American expansion laid the groundwork for the ultimate destruction of the Seminole people—a fact that did not go entirely unnoticed by the Indians residing in Spanish Florida.

U.S. expansion to the Gulf Coast reached its zenith in the years following the War of 1812. During these decades the sword now accompanied, and in most cases, preceded the quill. Beginning in 1812 and continuing well into the 1850s, an American military presence combined with aggressive frontiersmen and settlers determined the fate of the Seminole more than any other factor. The Florida Indians had little, if any, respite during these four decades of incessant American aggression, decades that saw the United States finally wrest Spain from Florida, quell foreign intrigue and filibusters in the region,[18] essentially remove all Indians from the peninsula, and, ultimately, redefine the Florida landscape. An uninterrupted sequence of events, therefore, from 1812 to 1858—the Patriot War of 1812,[19] the War of 1812 in the South, the Creek War of 1813 to 1814,[20] the destruction of Negro Fort in 1816,[21] the First Seminole War of 1817 to 1818, the removal treaties of the 1820s and the 1830s, the Second Seminole War from 1835 into the 1840s, and the lingering Seminole resistance of the 1850s, and many lesser episodes in between—cannot stand alone; they all share the same causes, the same effects, the same objectives and the same results, and that is an unabated, aggressive American expansion to the Gulf Coast and a tragic outcome for the Florida Indians. When the Seminole perspective is taken into consideration, moreover, and given equal weight with the conventional American viewpoint, what emerges is indeed a century-long conflict for Americans, both Anglo-American and Native American, in the Gulf South frontier—a Hundred Years' War that primarily commenced in 1763, essentially ended by 1858, and no longer defined adequately by the traditional dates provided by an outdated, ethnocentric American perspective.

Rethinking traditional periodization is but one objective of this volume. Reassessing the historical import of U.S. expansion to the Gulf Coast and the consequent fate of the Seminole is the other purpose of these essays. The century-long conflict between Anglo-Americans and Florida Indians had a momentous impact indeed on the course of American history itself. Destroying, confining, or removing the Seminole in the wake of aggressive territorial expansion proved anything but an isolated incident, nor was it simply an episode restricted to set dates and occurring on the periphery of American history. The conflict between the United States and the Seminole significantly affected foreign and domestic issues and events seemingly distant from the tragic story unfolding in Florida. The chapters herein thus reshape our understanding of the periodization and reconsider previously established assumptions defining the relationship between the United States and the Florida Indians, and in so doing, hope to initiate a new round of research that generates innovative directions and a fresh look at a long and tragic story.

In the first essay, Susan Richbourg Parker illustrates how the 1783 Treaty of Paris reintroduced chaotic conditions along the border between American Georgia and Spanish Florida, a hostile environment directly and adversely affecting the Florida Indians. Since 1763, British ownership of both territories allowed for more efficient control over the region, thus keeping disorder to a minimum. But, once Florida reverted to Spanish control and Georgia became an independent republic, an international border once again separated the peoples residing in the area. The revival of international rivalry and jealousies among the powers of Britain, Spain, and the United States in the Gulf South borderlands heightened significantly after 1783, and lawlessness quickly pervaded the region. An enfeebled Spain maintained a weak grip on the Floridas, and, in order to retain the restored territory, Spanish authorities depended overwhelmingly on the support and loyalty of the Seminole. Americans only exacerbated volatile conditions as they pushed into Creek lands north of the Florida border. White settlement and ensuing Indian conflict in Georgia steadily drifted into East Florida, and the Seminole received their first taste of aggressive American expansion. Parker validates the year 1783 as a critical turning point in U.S.-Seminole relations, and thus demonstrates that the century-long conflict between the two peoples commenced well before the second decade of the nineteenth century.

James Cusick corroborates the need to rethink the traditional periodization that has long defined conflict between the United States and the Seminole. In the second essay in this volume, he, too, examines the reaction of the Seminole to the events unfolding in post-1783 Florida, as the Florida Indians attempted to remain neutral while Georgians, Creek, and Spanish clashed around them. From 1783 to 1812, the Seminole found themselves unwillingly entangled in these conflicts and steadily drawn into the geopolitical forces and alignments consuming the region of East Florida. The onset of war in 1812 between the United States and Great Britain changed everything, and the course of U.S.-Seminole relations entered an entirely new phase, one dominated by outright warfare accompanied by aggressive American territorial acquisition, and one in which the Seminole could not withstand. The fate of the Seminole, therefore, resides as much in the decades between the first Anglo-American war and the second, as it does in the years following the War of 1812.

The ratification of the Treaty of Ghent failed, however, to lessen international rivalry in the Gulf South borderlands, and this competition for mastery in the region continued to involve directly the Florida Indians and threaten their way of life. Certainly the Seminole proved anything but pawns in this game of international intrigue, nor were they unfortunate bystanders caught in the wake of larger powers jostling for control of the Floridas. The Southeastern Indians—the Seminole most of all—played an integral role in the turbulent game of commercial and territorial domination in the western hemisphere. The Florida Indians, from the very beginning, proved a formidable ally—as for Spain and England—or an equally fierce opponent—as for the United States. The Seminole undeniably helped shape the nature of the international competition in the Gulf South region, as much as they affected the outcome of the contest. They arguably prolonged the American advance to the Gulf of Mexico, as much as they precipitated it, and they quite possibly fostered, even intensified, foreign intrigue and intervention in Florida. In the end, the bitter conflict arising from such intense international rivalry may have hastened, ironically, the violent demise of the Seminole in the long run. Despite their active and heroic role, they arguably became victims of such rivalries and jealousies.

In the third essay, William S. Belko addresses how one facet of international rivalry in the Gulf South region ultimately determined the fate of the Seminole. This international competition significantly affected U.S. national security policy for the Gulf South region. The combination of Indian resistance and foreign influence compelled U.S. policymakers, through a number of means, to push harder to the Gulf of Mexico. Anxious aggrandizement characterized American expansion in the late eighteenth and early nineteenth centuries as much as it would the massive territorial expansion of the 1840s. For one, Americans in Washington and on the scene ardently believed that foreigners in the region, both officially and unofficially, instigated Indian resistance, which hampered the eventual American settlement of all territory south of the 31st parallel. Removing one factor necessarily eliminated the other. Belko thus argues that intense Anglophobia in America determined ultimately the nature of U.S.-Seminole relations in the wake of the War of 1812, and thus the effort to drive the British out of the region led directly to the eventual military destruction and removal of the Florida Indians. U.S. acquisition of Spanish Florida dampened, for the most part, fears arising from British influence in the Gulf South and set the course for American occupation of all of Florida— only the Seminole remained alone to combat the Americanization of the Gulf Coast. As such, the First Seminole War cannot adequately be defined by the years 1817 to 1818, but must be expanded to include at least a decade stretching from the years just preceding the War of 1812 to the years just following the Adams-Onis Treaty of 1819. In addition, the story of Seminole demise cannot be told apart from the intense Anglo-American rivalry of the early nineteenth century.[22]

The slavery issue likewise shaped, even intensified, the long conflict between the United States and the Florida Indians, as much, if not more, than fears of British influence. Nearly all of the chapters in this volume address the slavery issue in some form—for it was that pervasive, that imperative for U.S. national security in the region—but the chapter by Matthew Clavin clearly reveals more than any other contribution the intense fear harbored by Americans, especially those in the slaveholding South, of a massive slave rebellion originating from a concerted alliance of African and Indian in Florida. By focusing on literary accounts of the day, this essay looks at the Second Seminole War as a war against blacks as much as against Indians. By connecting the slave insurrection on the island of St. Domingo to the Nat Turner rebellion in the United States, whites throughout the American South feared that the events in Florida could indeed incite a substantial slave rebellion. Clavin convincingly shows that the fate of the Seminole joined with that of the African in Florida, and that the topic of slavery and of fugitive and free blacks among the Florida Indians cannot be dissected from the story of U.S.-Seminole relations, nor can it be confined simply to the traditional periodization for the Seminole wars of the nineteenth century.[23]

The next two chapters reveal the extent domestic American politics influenced and were influenced by Seminole resistance to U.S. expansion. Jeanne and David Heidler, in their essay on Jackson's 1818 invasion of Spanish Florida—the First Seminole War—and the immeasurable repercussions of that brief event, demonstrate how this conflict shaped the course of American political history. In 1819, both the Monroe administration and Congress spent an inordinate amount of their time and energy investigating the episode, even to the detriment of several prominent political issues facing the country at the same time, such as the Missouri question. Arguments for and against Jackson's actions continued well into the next decade, going so far as to convince President Andrew Jackson to anoint Martin Van Buren, rather than John C. Calhoun, as his successor to lead the Democratic Party. Beyond any doubt, the controversy surrounding the First Seminole War contributed directly to altering permanently the political landscape in Antebellum America, as the face of the Democratic Party followed that of Martin Van Buren and not John C. Calhoun. The Heidlers also show how Jackson's actions in Florida raised significant questions about executive authority and the war powers, provoking a constitutional crisis that went, for the most part, unresolved. The First Seminole War, furthermore, bolstered Jackson's remarkable military record, joining the crowning victories at Horseshoe Bend in 1814 and New Orleans in 1815, and jettisoned Old Hickory to the White House a decade after he handed Florida to the United States.[24]

The chapter by James Denham and Canter Brown also illustrates how another major political and constitutional crisis in Antebellum America—the Nullification Crisis—involved the long conflict between the United States and the Seminole. Following the outbreak of the Second Seminole War, Nullifiers used the conflict in Florida to ensconce their political power in South Carolina.

As a result of their dismal military record in the conflict, the Nullifiers quickly blamed the federal government for the military morass in Florida, which led to national controversy over the conduct of the war and a subsequent investigation of several prominent U.S. commanding generals in that theater. Nullifiers in South Carolina then succeeded in a concerted campaign to discredit Unionist elements within their own state, revitalize their reputation for challenging federal authority, and obtain statewide political power. The Nullifiers, in short, maintained their political ascendency in the Palmetto State primarily as a result of events in Florida; the demise of the Seminole in Florida ensured the vitality of a political faction in South Carolina. In light of the two previously discussed articles, conflict between the United States and the Florida Indians undeniably influenced American political development in the half century before the Civil War, as much as American politics determined the fate of the Seminole and the Americanization of Florida. Future research will most certainly reveal other ways in which the long conflict helped shape the course of antebellum American politics, and vice versa.

Much, if not most, of the scholarship on U.S.-Seminole relations has emphasized the military aspects, concentrating almost exclusively on the three traditional Seminole Wars. The Second Seminole War has received the most attention, and surface appearances would seem to preclude the need for any further research on this particular event. By reexamining the traditional periodization and rethinking basic assumptions about the import of U.S.-Seminole conflict on larger historical development, however, additional research may be needed in this arena above all others.

In his chapter on the Second Seminole War, Joe Knetsch reviews the rather deplorable conduct of the war by the United States, and, in so doing, raises questions about the lessons learned, if any, from this bloody confrontation. The United States was undoubtedly and completely unprepared for the conflict in Florida erupting in late 1835. Numerous factors provided little chance for a quick victory over the Seminole—a retrenchment-minded Congress drastically reducing military funding, a strategy and tactics that followed European-style fighting, a pervasive distrust of a professional military dominating the mindset of Jacksonian Americans, a defective supply system, outright ignorance of guerilla warfare, waning national interest in the conflict after 1836, and conspicuous and rampant disagreement between state authorities and the federal government, and between the army and those in Washington, over the direction of the war. These factors significantly undermined the ability of the United States to wage effective combat, and most of the blame for this can be directed at Washington and at Tallahassee. Little wonder, then, that the Florida campaign became the graveyard of commanding officers—seven in as many years as the United States defined the length of the war itself—all unable to bring an acceptable resolution to the conflict. This utter failure by the United States to adapt to the nature of warfare in Florida, to modify strategy, operations, and tactics in order to secure victory, and to overcome a glaringly arrogant and ignorant approach to Indian warfare only led to more bloodshed, more expense, more tragedy for the Seminole. Knetsch's analysis undoubtedly elicits further exploration into the Second Seminole War and its consequences for American strategy and tactics—to what extent, if any, did the conflict in Florida influence the U.S. approach to subsequent Indian wars erupting across the Great Plains, the Pacific Northwest, and the American Southwest? Did federal authorities ever correct the problems that significantly impaired the American effort to defeat the Seminole? Did the commanding officers of the Florida campaign likewise recognize failures and make the requisite corrections for use in future conflicts, such as the Mexican War (1846–1848), which immediately followed the Second Seminole War? How did many of these commanding officers—Winfield Scott, Zachary Taylor, William Jenkins Worth—fail so miserably in Florida, yet earn a distinguished service record in the war against Mexico?

One of the obvious limitations of existing studies focusing on the military facet is the lack of attention given to the Seminole perspective. Of course this cannot be an easy task due to the dearth of written records explicating the Seminole standpoint. An examination of a Seminole strategy for resisting American expansion is, nonetheless, critical for more fully understanding America's Hundred Years' War, and in a provocative essay by Sam Watson, such a refreshing approach is made. Watson examines to what extent, if any, a Seminole strategy existed to check aggressive white advance into the Gulf Coast region from the period 1812 to 1858. The Florida Indians conducted a lengthy and valiant resistance in the effort to remain on their lands, and Watson reveals several reasons for their stout defiance. But he also identifies a number of factors, most beyond the control of the Seminole, which eventually sealed their demise. Still, an exploration of Seminole strategy yields a tantalizing wealth of fresh considerations, all of which Watson admirably probes, subjects which permanently revise our approach to the long conflict between American and Seminole and beg additional inquiry—the national security concerns and policies of the Seminole, their use of negotiation as a weapon of war, a strategy of attrition that eventually undermined Seminole resistance in the end, how American dispersal of the Florida Indians prevented concerted attacks against whites, the damning effects of internal dissension resulting from the absence of a centralized political system, Seminole acuity for recognizing opposition to Indian removal in certain political quarters of the United States and exploiting this to their advantage, an underestimation of the power and determination of the Southern slave interest, the prospect that the Creek and Cherokee challenge to removal would prolong Seminole resistance, and the extent to which Seminole resilience actually unified the American effort to defeat and remove them. The Seminole perspective would indeed shed considerably more light on why the traditional periodization and basic assumptions about U.S.-Seminole relations should be reassessed. Seminole resistance to aggressive American expansion to the Gulf Coast during the eighteenth and nineteenth centuries, therefore, cannot be confined to specific dates in American history nor viewed as isolated episodes; it must be seen as one long, unbroken struggle.

The century-long conflict pitting aggressive and expansive Americans against an equally resilient and determined Seminole also cannot be told without the direct involvement of other native peoples. A number of Indian groups found themselves caught in the tidal wave of U.S. expansion to the Gulf Coast from the 1760s onward, and their perspective requires as much attention as that of the Seminole, for these Indians had a direct impact on the ultimate fate of the Florida Indians. In fact, a full account of America's Hundred Years' War necessitates the active participation of the Creek Indians. From 1763 to 1812, Anglo-American expansion to the Gulf Coast largely concerned the Creek residing in Georgia and future Alabama. To get to the Gulf of Mexico, Americans had to push first through the Creek before they ended with the Seminole. The Creek, then, not the Seminole, made the first stand against Americans penetrating the Gulf South borderlands. Yet the effects of the Creek retreat were just as destructive for the Seminole people, as the pivotal year of 1812 soon proved.[25]

In the final chapter of this volume, Brian Rucker shows how violence between white Americans and the Creek persisted in Florida well into the 1850s. A number of Creek remained in the Florida panhandle, roaming the countryside, committing depredations, attempting to escape detection; other Creek fled deeper into Florida and joined the Seminole cause. From the American perspective, then, a little-known Second Creek War coincided with the more publicized Second Seminole War, both occurring in Florida from the 1830s into the 1850s. From the Indian perspective, native resistance to U.S. expansion had long characterized life in the Gulf South region—a story of unremitting conflict that began in the late eighteenth century and continued well into the nineteenth.[26]

By 1858, about all that remained of the Native American presence in the Gulf South region was Coacoochee's Great Spirit and a handful of renegade Indians. The rest belonged to the Americans, a prize of war from a journey they commenced nearly a century before the one they forced on the Seminole. In the lands of the Great Spirit game was abundant and the white man was not. But in the new lands in the West, game was anything but plentiful and the white man still preyed too closely. Shortly after his arrival in Indian Territory, Coacoochee encountered conditions little removed from his last years in Florida. Here, in Indian country, the more powerful Creek, who hated the Seminole living among them, lorded over them with disdain, until a treaty in 1845 finally separated them. Here, in Indian country, the rivers flooded, crops rotted, and supplies of grain washed away. In an emotional appeal printed in an Arkansas newspaper in the spring of 1844, Coacoochee summed up the fate of the Seminole and the ultimate consequences of American expansion to the Gulf Coast:

> I have been at war with the United States. I defended the soil of my birth-place with my blood. It was dear to me, and to my people as our homes, and as our country of our fathers. But, that war is now ended. My people were overcome by a stronger party. What the sword did not destroy, your money bought. Like the rain that falls upon the earth from the Heavens, the memory of that war is absorbed and forgotten. We emmigrated [*sic*] to this country upon the faith of your people—promises were made us of another home, a separate and distinct soil, where we could gather again the fragments of a distracted and unhappy people. The hand that could conquer, should possess the heart to fulfill promises made to a subdued people. None knows our condition better than you do. Look at us! A distracted people, alone, without a home, without annuities—destitute of provisions, without a shelter for our women and children—strangers in a foreign land, dependent upon the mercy and tolerance of our Red Brothers, the Cherokee, transported to a cold climate, naked, without game to hunt or fields to plant, or huts to cover our poor little children— they are crying like wolves, hungry, cold, and destitute![27]

Conditions remained bleak in the new lands of the west, and little help arrived. But for white Americans, conditions could not have been more propitious. In the year following Coacoochee's 1844 appeal, Texas and Florida each added a white star to the blue canton of the Stars and Stripes—the very same flag that waved above the vessel on which Coacoochee found himself shackled only four years earlier. U.S. expansion to the Gulf Coast was now complete and the fate of the Seminole sealed. During the height of the Third Seminole War, in 1857, Coacoochee died of smallpox, in Mexico, far from Florida. In one last bit of tragic irony, the great Seminole leader finally went to the spring of the Great Spirit, sent there by a disease introduced by the white man. Coacoochee's story epitomized that of his people. His fate was that of nearly all Seminole—a fate determined alone by the insatiable and incessant expansion of the American people to the Gulf Coast.

Notes

1. John T. Sprague, *The Origin, Progress, and Conclusion of the Florida War* (1848; reprint, Gainesville: University of Florida Press, 1964), 287–88. For a study of Coacoochee's life, see John L. Elder, *Everlasting Fire: Cowokoci's Legacy in the Seminole Struggle against Western Expansion* (Edmond, Okla.: Medicine Wheel Press, 2004).

2. Sprague, *Florida War*, 288–89.

3. Ibid., 289–90.

4. Ibid., 291.

5. Ibid., 322, 323, 324.

6. Ibid., 259–60.

7. Ibid., 323, 328, 329.

8. The most comprehensive study of the Second Seminole War still remains John Mahon's *History of the Second Seminole War, 1835–1842* (Gainesville: University Presses of Florida, 1967), but also see Mark F. Boyd, *Florida Aflame: The Background and Onset of the Seminole War, 1835* (Tallahassee: Distributed by Florida Board of Parks and Historic Memorials, 1951), George S. Buker, *Swamp Sailors: Riverine Warfare in the Everglades, 1835–1842* (Gainesville: University Press of Florida, 1975), Joe Knetsch, *Fear and Anxiety on the Florida Frontier: The Second Seminole War, 1835–1842* (Dade City: Seminole Wars Historic Foundation, 2008), Milton Meltzer, *Hunted Like a Wolf: The Story of the Seminole War* (New York: Farrar, Straus and Giroux, 1972), and George Walton, *Fearless and Free: The Seminole Indian War, 1835–1842* (Indianapolis: Bobbs-Merrill, 1977). Numerous articles likewise address various aspects of the Second Seminole War.

9. For the First Seminole War, see David and Jeanne Heidler, *Old Hickory's War: Andrew Jackson and the Quest for Empire* (Baton Rouge: Louisiana State University Press, 2003); Dianne K. Deutsch, *Andrew Jackson's Invasions of Spanish Florida* (Coral Gables: privately published, 1971); Sean M. O'Brien, *In Bitterness and Tears: Andrew Jackson's Destruction of the Creeks and Seminoles* (Westport, Conn.: Praeger, 2003), chaps. 17–19; and Frank L. Owsley Jr. and Gene A. Smith, *Filibusters and Expansionists: Jeffersonian Manifest Destiny, 1800–1821* (Tuscaloosa: University of Alabama Press, 1997), chap. 8. As with the Second Seminole War, several articles address the First Seminole War.

10. For the Third Seminole War, see James W. Covington, *The Billy Bowlegs War, 1855–1858: The Final Stand of the Seminoles against the Whites* (Chuluota, Fla.: Mickler House, 1981).

11. A number of studies address all three conflicts and the interludes. See Joe Knetsch, *Florida's Seminole Wars, 1817–1858* (Chicago: Arcadia, 2003), John and Mary Lou Missall, *The Seminole Wars: America's Longest Indian Conflict* (Gainesville:

University Press of Florida, 2004), Virginia Peters, *The Florida Wars* (Hamden, Conn.: Archon Books, 1979), J. Leitch Wright, *Creeks and Seminoles: The Destruction and Regeneration of the Muscogulge People* (Lincoln: University of Nebraska Press, 1986), chaps. 7–9; Edwin C. McReynolds, *The Seminoles* (Norman: University of Oklahoma Press, 1957), chaps. 6–15. For other monographs addressing various aspects of U.S.-Seminole relations during the nineteenth century, see the "For Further Reading" section herein.

12. Traditional scholarship divides U.S.-Seminole relations into five distinct periods: the British period of Florida history (1763–83), the Confederation and Federalist period (1783–1800), the Jeffersonian period (1800–1821), the territorial period (1821–45), and the period of Florida statehood to the end of our story (1845–58). The British period of Florida history, 1763–83, witnessed a dramatic and rapid expansion and monopolization of the Indian trade by Anglo-American trading firms in the Southeast, from South Carolina and Georgia, to East and West Florida—all British provinces following the events of 1763. This, coupled with a number of Anglo-American land cession treaties with the Creek and the Seminole, resulted in a marked increase of white advance into the Gulf South region, both commercially as well as territorially. The American Revolution, however, changed everything. The disruption and dismemberment of the British empire in North America thoroughly and permanently altered the locus of the Indian trade, provoked sporadic yet intense violence along the border between Georgia and Florida, and, after the Spanish seizure of British Pensacola and the transfer of title of Florida from Britain to Spain in the 1783 Treaty of Paris, created an international boundary now recognized for its rampant chaotic conditions. The official recognition of American independence in 1783 inaugurated a new era in the relations between Americans and the Southeastern Indians (1783–1800), one that accelerated an era of violence, aggressive territorial acquisition and conquest, and the eventual demise of the Florida Indians. During the 1780s, Georgia took the lead in pushing white settlement into Indian lands of the Gulf South borderlands. By way of several treaties and outright intimidation, Georgia secured Creek lands and opened the way for the American advance towards the Gulf of Mexico. During the 1790s, the new U.S. government, under the aegis of the Federalists, continued what Georgia had started. In a series of treaties, both with Spain and the Indians of the Southeast, the United States acquired ownership of extensive territory that allowed them to push further into the Gulf borderlands. In the meantime, life along the border region between the United States and Spanish Florida remained in a state of chaos, fomenting foreign intrigue and filibusters. These treaties included the Treaty of Augusta (1786), Treaty of Shoulderbone (1786), Pinckney Treaty (1795), Treaty of New York (1790), Treaty of Coleraine (1796). For the various U.S. treaties with the Creek, see Claudio Saunt, *A New Order of Things: Property, Power, and the Transformation of the Creek Indians, 1733–1816* (New York: Cambridge University Press, 2003) and Kathryn H. Braund, *Deerskins and Duffels: The Creek Indian Trade with Anglo-America, 1685–1815* (Lincoln: University of Nebraska Press, 1993). The election of Thomas Jefferson in 1800 inaugurated the most aggressive period of U.S. expansion to the Gulf Coast, one instigating

outright conflict between expanding Americans and defensive Seminole. From 1800 to 1821, the Virginia Dynasty initiated a number of policies and employed a variety of means to acquire all of the Gulf Coast territory from Spanish Texas to all of Spanish Florida. No period of U.S.-Seminole relations proved as crucial to U.S. expansion and the ultimate fate of the Florida Indians, with both the Seminole and the Spanish emerging as victims of the rapid American advance southward. From the Louisiana Purchase (1803) to the annexation of the West Florida Republic (1810), from the Patriot War (1812), the seizure of Mobile (1813), the Creek War (1813–14) and the resulting Treaty of Ft. Jackson (1814) to the U.S. invasion of Spanish Florida (1818), the First Seminole War and the consequent Transcontinental Treaty (1819), the Jeffersonians brought Americans to the doorstep of the Seminole, and when the Stars and Stripes unfurled over all of Florida in 1821, the Seminole knew full well that their world had dramatically changed. Indeed, arguably no period stood so damning for the Seminole as that directed by the Virginians in the White House. Other major actions during this period include the Treaty of Ft. Wilkinson (1802), the building of the Federal Road (1807–11), the assimilation policies of U.S. Indian Agent Benjamin Hawkins, and the U.S. destruction of Negro Fort in 1816. The best treatment of the Jeffersonian period is Owsley and Smith, *Filibusters and Expansionists*; see also Wanjohi Waciuma, *Intervention in Spanish Floridas, 1801–1813: A Study in Jeffersonian Foreign Policy* (Boston: Branden Press, 1976). Both Wright, *Creeks and Seminoles*, and McReynolds, *Seminoles*, are good examples of conveniently placing U.S.-Seminole relations in the traditional American-centered periods.

13. In 1763, as a result of the negotiations ending the French and Indian War, Great Britain assumed ownership of the Floridas, which commenced the two-decade period of British control of Florida that one scholar has noted "witnessed the emergence of a unique Seminole cultural and political identity." The British period also inaugurated a wave of white migration into Indian lands of the Southeast, first involving the Creek and eventually damning the Seminole. Also in 1763, Parliament passed the notorious Proclamation Act, which, among its sundry provisions, drew a distinct northern boundary for East Florida, the region lying east of the Apalachicola River. All Indians residing below that line the American colonists labeled Seminole, separating them from the Creek situated above in Georgia and in the future state of Alabama. Other measures followed in 1763. Although British officials squabbled over how Indian lands should be disposed and just who should do the disposing, they agreed that Anglo-American colonization required some land cessions along the Gulf Coast. In 1763, British officials secured several small strips of land adjacent to St. Augustine and Pensacola, the capitals of East Florida and West Florida respectively. In the Augusta Treaty of 1763, the Creek ceded territory north of the upper Ogeechee River, which, combined with the East Florida and West Florida treaties in that same year, firmly created a dividing line between Anglo-Americans and native Americans from Georgia to West Florida. British officials expected that these imaginary and arbitrary—and permanent—boundaries would promote peaceful relations between white and red in the region. Instead this dividing-line approach destabilized relations between Anglo-

Americans and Southeastern Indians, and opened the flood gates to rapid white expansion into the Gulf South frontier. Parliament drew such lines (running from Canada, down the spine of the Appalachian Mountains, and to the Gulf of Mexico) in order to establish a permanent Indian country, one in which no white man could go. British citizens in South Carolina and Georgia (as well as in other colonies to the north), however, reckoned otherwise. Five years later, in 1768, the British government turned control over Indian matters to the colonial governments, thus beginning a policy that the soon-to-be independent states would continue, namely territorial and commercial expansion directly involving and adversely affecting the native peoples in their line of advance. Despite the acts of Parliament, far away in London, the British citizens of South Carolina and Georgia essentially established the policies that determined the fate of the Indians in the American Southeast, the Seminole among them. The Union Jack really meant Charleston and Savannah and the steady westward and southward push of Anglo-Americans across the southeastern frontier. These land cessions only beget more cessions, as the white wave of settlement into the lands of Creek and Seminole intensified during the decades after 1763. The year 1763 also commenced the period of the American Revolution, an event more than any other of the eighteenth century that permanently and adversely determined the fate of the Seminole.

14. During the late 1600s, Spain and its Indian allies, especially the Apalachee, from their base in Florida, frequently raided the English colony of South Carolina, but with no great success. To counter Spanish attack, the English colonists likewise relied on Indian allies, namely the Yamassee, who would, in turn, enslave the Apalachee. When the Apalachee well ran dry, the British enslaved some of the Yamassee, upon the pretext of covering debts owed to British traders. The Yamassee then joined the Creek, the Apalachee, and runaway black slaves and attacked South Carolina between 1714 and 1716. English colonists suppressed the Yamassee revolt, and the Yamassee wisely fled to Spanish Florida and thus became Seminole. The English also conducted unsuccessful assaults on St. Augustine, in 1719 and in 1728, and, to create a buffer zone between Spanish Florida and English South Carolina, they established the colony of Georgia in 1732. Thereafter, Georgians emerged as the greatest threat to the Seminole. This intense Anglo-Spanish rivalry in the southeast continued in the 1740s, with the "War of Jenkins Ear," as the British again made several unsuccessful assaults on St. Augustine. On Anglo-Spanish rivalry in North America, see J. Leitch Wright Jr., *Anglo-Spanish Rivalry in North America* (Athens: University of Georgia Press, 1971). The most decisive European influence on the culture of the Indians of the Southeast likewise originated during the decades preceding the fateful year of 1763, and this was the complete transformation of the Indian way of life. Europeans, and the British above all, permanently altered Indian economy and society by converting them from a culture based on agriculture to one completely driven by commercial hunting and droving. Deerskins replaced maize as the economic foundation of Indian culture. Trade, therefore, as much as treaties and tomahawks, played a central role in determining the ultimate fate of the Seminole. The prevalence of the Indian trade, moreover, set the stage for Anglo-American expansion, as debt consumed the Indians of the Southeast, and paying this

debt entailed ceding lands to whites advancing from the North and the East. Through-out the eighteenth and early nineteenth centuries, the British monopolized the Indian trade. Regardless of which flag flew above the Indians of the Southeast—Spanish, Brit-ish, American, even French—British traders, primarily Scots factors, controlled and expanded the Anglo-American presence in the Gulf South borderlands. Following the British acquisition of Spanish Florida in 1763, the epicenter of the Indian trade gradu-ally shifted from British South Carolina and Georgia into British Florida. On the In-dian trade, see Wright, *Creeks and Seminoles*, 41–71, and William S. Coker and Thomas D. Watson, *Indian Traders of the Southeastern Borderlands: Panton, Leslie & Company and John Forbes & Company, 1783–1847* (Pensacola: University of West Florida Press, 1986).

15. For the Seminole struggle to survive on the West during and after the years of re-moval, see Jane F. Lancaster, *Removal Aftershock: The Seminoles' Struggles to Survive in the West, 1836–1866* (Knoxville: University of Tennessee Press, 1994); see also Wright, *Creeks and Seminoles*, chapter 10, and McReynolds, *Seminoles*, chaps. 16–21.

16. From 1763 through the years of the American Revolution, the Seminole way of life arguably changed little, only the destination of their deerskins. It mattered little to the Seminole whether Florida replaced South Carolina and Georgia as the center of the Indian trade in the years following 1763. For those Indians south of the warring colonies to the north, life seemed good. The American naturalist William Bartram travelled throughout the Gulf South borderlands in the months leading up to Lex-ington and Concord and during the first three years of fighting, and he recorded in his journals the condition of the Seminole in Florida. Abundant game and plentiful fields, fat cattle and strong horses, great banquets within clean and sturdy abodes, and a contented people he described. The Florida Indians, Bartram wrote, "enjoy a super-abundance of the necessaries and conveniences of life, with the security of person and property, the two great concerns of mankind." These Indians appeared "free from want or desires" with "no cruel enemy to dread" and "nothing to give them disquietude, but the gradual encroachment of the white people." Contented and undisturbed, "they appear as blithe and free as the birds of the air, and like them as volatile and active, tuneful and vociferous," and in their deportment "form the most striking picture of happiness in this life" and "joy, contentment, love, and friendship" consume them to their last breath. Not even the debilities of old age prevented a "joyous simplicity," and when the sun set "a gladdening, cheering blush" remained on the western horizon. That blush on the western horizon appeared as only the calm before the storm, for the white man soon arrived from that "west." Mark Van Doren, ed., *The Travels of William Bartram* (New York: Dover, 1955), 167–70, 181–84.

17. The American Revolution indeed had a significant impact on the future of the Seminole. Following the opening salvos of the American War of Independence, nearly all of the Scotsmen controlling the Indian trade in the Southeast remained loyal to King George III. When South Carolina and Georgia proclaimed their independence and proceeded to defend it through the force of arms, these Loyalist Indian traders fled to East Florida and then into West Florida. When the smoke cleared, Pensacola had

replaced Charleston as the hub of the Creek and Seminole trade. Yet, in 1781, while the American Washington and the Frenchman Rochambeau defeated the Briton Cornwallis at Yorktown, Virginia, the Spaniard Bernardo de Galvez captured Pensacola and ejected the British from the West Florida capital. Because of these battles (and other events around the globe), the negotiators at a table in Paris then recognized the independence of Virginia and returned the Floridas to Spain, all in 1783. But Spain could not conduct the Indian trade nearly as well as the Scots Loyalists and thus to the satisfaction of the Indians amongst them, so they reluctantly turned to the British traders and allowed their trading empire to continue, even strengthen. Following the Revolution, the British firm of Panton, Leslie and Company monopolized the Indian trade until its demise following the American acquisition of all of the Gulf South borderlands in the early nineteenth century. Panton and his associates would play a leading role in American expansion to the Gulf Coast. The Revolution may have cost the Americans control of the Indian trade with the Creek and Seminole, but it also set into motion an aggressive American diplomacy that would soon influence these Loyalists Indian traders to return their allegiance to the Americans. The year 1783 also ushered in an equally aggressive American expansion into Indian lands of the Gulf South borderlands. As for Bartram's contented Seminole, their fate commenced with the period of the American Revolution, and so it was that the consequences of the 1783 Treaty of Paris quickly spurred the demise of the Seminole. See Coker and Watson, *Indian Traders*, chaps. 1–3. It should be noted here that some of the most savage partisan warfare of the American Revolution, especially during the years from 1775 to 1778, occurred along the frontier between Georgia and East Florida. See J. Leitch Wright, *Florida in the American Revolution* (Gainesville: University of Florida Press, 1975).

18. For the various filibusters and foreign intrigues in Spanish Florida, see Owsley and Smith, *Filibusters and Expansionists*, chap. 7.

19. The seminal study of the Patriot War is James Cusick's *The Other War of 1812: The Patriot War and the American Invasion of Spanish East Florida* (Gainesville: University Press of Florida, 2003); see also Owsley and Smith, *Filibusters and Expansionists*, chap. 4.

20. On the War of 1812 in the South and the Creek War of 1813–14, see Frank L. Owsley, Jr., *Struggle for the Gulf Borderlands: The Creek War and the Battle of New Orleans, 1812–1815* (Tuscaloosa: University of Alabama Press, 1981), Benjamin W. Griffith Jr., *McIntosh and Weatherford: Creek Indian Leaders* (Tuscaloosa: University of Alabama Press, 1988), Robert Remini, *Andrew Jackson and His Indian Wars* (New York: Viking, 2001), and O'Brien, *In Bitterness and Tears*.

21. On Negro Fort, see Owsley and Smith, *Filibusters and Expansionists*, chap. 6; Mark Boyd, "Events at Prospect Bluff on the Apalachicola River, 1808–1818." *Florida Historical Quarterly* 16, no. 2 (October 1937): 55–96; and Nathaniel Millett, "Defining Freedom in the Atlantic Borderlands of the Revolutionary Southeast," *Early American Studies* 5, no. 2 (Fall 2007): 367–94.

22. Economic considerations likewise determined U.S. national security policy for the Gulf South region, for commercial expansion necessarily accompanied territorial

expansion. Here, again, the Florida Indians played an integral part as Americans sought to ply the waters from the Mississippi to the St. Johns. American policymakers from the 1780s to the acquisition of Florida in 1821 desired to open more markets across the globe to American goods, and a key to this goal were the rivers that emptied into the Gulf of Mexico. The Mississippi River was, obviously, the central artery, but other rivers proved as important as Old Man River. River systems from the Pearl to the Apalachicola were essential transportation and communication avenues for Americans moving into the southwestern areas of U.S. territory: parts of Tennessee, Georgia, Mississippi, and Alabama. But as long as the current of these rivers ended in Spanish territory, American settlers encountered substantial difficulty in getting their produce and goods to markets. Diplomacy between the United States and Spain eventually opened these rivers to American commerce, but similar efforts with the Indians of the American Southeast turned violent. In the pursuit to connect the American hinterland with the Gulf of Mexico, U.S. policymakers pushed the Creek and Seminole to their limit. Indian resistance to the constant American incursions into their lands erupted in outright bloodshed in the years after 1812. The story of U.S. expansion to the Gulf Coast and the fate of the Seminole cannot be addressed adequately, therefore, without taking into consideration the desire for American commercial expansion in the late eighteenth and early nineteenth centuries. Both subjects—U.S.-Seminole relations and U.S. commercial development in the South—irrevocably shaped each other, ultimately determining the very course of American history in the Gulf South region. More research into this potential connection between American commercial objectives and the role of the Florida Indians is needed.

23. The subject of slavery had long been a critical concern in the region, for it had accelerated Anglo-Spanish rivalry in the Southeast since the late 1600s, as slaves from British Georgia and South Carolina fled to Spanish Florida, there to be protected by royal edict. Slaves from the American South continued to find Spanish Florida a haven well into the nineteenth century. An intense fear of widespread slave rebellion throughout the slave states ensued, and events in Florida merely exacerbated these fears. British officers trained, armed, and employed former slaves against Jackson's forces in the South during the War of 1812, for the very purpose of ravishing the southern United States. Americans continued to view runaway slaves, seeking harbor among and even joining with the Seminole, as a pretext for taking direct action along the U.S.-Florida border in the years after the War of 1812. Even the nature of Seminole slavery itself distressed Southern slaveholders, for it appeared to Americans that fugitive Africans were not really property of the Florida Indians at all, that they intermarried, and that blacks maintained an undue influence over the Seminole. For American military officers of both the First and the Second Seminole Wars, the evidence indeed seemed to confirm this last charge. The progress of the Antislavery movement also parallels the various conflicts in Florida. Abolitionist forces vehemently denounced U.S. actions in and policies toward the Seminole in the decades after 1812, seeing them as nothing more than a slavepower conspiracy to enslave free blacks in Florida and to add more slave territory to the Union. The Second Seminole War above all became embroiled

directly in the public and private debates agitating the slavery question in the 1830s and 1840s. For studies that address the role of Black Seminoles, see Kenneth W. Porter, *The Black Seminoles: History of a Freedom-Seeking People* (Gainesville: University Press of Florida, 1996) and Bruce E. Twyman, *The Black Seminole Legacy and North American Politics, 1693–1845* (Washington, D.C.: Howard University Press, 1999).

24. The long conflict between the United States and the Seminole also affected the development of the Second American Party system. U.S.-Seminole relations, specifically the years from 1812 to 1858, influenced partisan rivalry in the United States in ways that have yet to be more fully explored. The rise of the Whig Party in Florida, the intense antagonism between U.S. regulars and the various state militias fighting in Florida, the equally bitter hostility expressed by Floridians for the Seminole policy of the U.S. military and the federal government, the division within federal ranks over the future of the Seminole in Florida—these political affairs originated and developed solely within the context of the Seminole wars occurring within the four decades after the War of 1812. Stiff Seminole resistance to removal even brought into question the efficacy of the government's removal policy itself, as the officer corps in Florida, supported by the U.S. Indian Agent, supported a separate reservation for the Seminole in Florida. Federal officials in Washington refused to countenance this quite reasonable request, especially considering the cost in both manpower and money being expended to remove the Florida Indians, and argued that the success of the entire Indian removal policy depended on defeating the Seminole. Several other Indian conflicts in opposition to removal surfaced during the 1830s, but certainly none to the extent and ferocity of the Seminole challenge. Growing nationwide Whig opposition to the Florida war during the 1830s also helped defeat the 1840 reelection of President Martin Van Buren. Political rivalry and partisanship indeed colored the "Seminole war," as much as the conflict shaped American political development.

25. During the War of 1812, American troops in the South engaged Indians first—in the bitter Creek Civil War of 1813–14—before facing British regulars. Following a series of devastating victories over the Red Stick faction, General Andrew Jackson forced the Creek, in the 1814 Treaty of Fort Jackson, to surrender to the United States 23 million acres of land—more than half of the remaining Creek domain, which encompassed nearly three-fifths of Alabama and Georgia. In one stroke, Jackson effectively removed Creek obstacles to American expansion, opening up a vast domain for American migration to the Gulf Coast. For Americans, the Creek Civil War began with the massacre at Fort Mims in 1813 and officially ended with Jackson's victory at Horseshoe Bend and the subsequent Treaty of Fort Jackson in 1814. For the Creek and the Seminole, however, the Creek Civil War had not commenced at Fort Mims nor had it ended at Horseshoe Bend or in the Treaty of Fort Jackson. The Creek who escaped Jackson's knife fled to Spanish Florida, there to take up arms and continue the resistance against American expansion to the Gulf Coast; most of the Indians Jackson chased through Florida during the First Seminole War were actually renegade Creek.

26. The Creek specter continued to haunt U.S.-Seminole relations long after the Creek War and the First Seminole War. During the 1820s and 1830s, for example,

a chief reason for Seminole opposition to removal was the completely unacceptable stipulation that they would live on lands governed by the Creek and be subject to laws promulgated by the Creek National Council. Both Creek and Seminole promised an Indian civil war if such an arrangement transpired, for bad blood had existed for some time between the Seminole and the Creek—Creek, that is, who had sided with the Americans in annihilating the Red Stick faction and the Seminole in turn. In May 1832, U.S. commissioners and an unrepresentative group of Seminole leaders agreed to the Treaty of Payne's Landing, which provided for the removal of the Seminole to lands in the west. The details of this plan proved anything but conducive to Seminole identity, as they would become part of the Creek Nation, reside on land given to the Creek Nation, and receive their annuities from a sum appropriated for the Creek Nation alone.

27. *Arkansas Intelligencer*, 30 March 1844.

1

So in Fear of Both the Indians and the Americans

SUSAN RICHBOURG PARKER

William Pengree, a former British loyalist, fled to Spanish East Florida in 1786, feeling "so in fear of both the Indians and the Americans." He was seeking asylum from the Lower Creeks and from his patriot neighbors. Lewis Fatio, Pengree's neighbor in Florida and also a loyalist, received a warning the following year from his own friend in Georgia that Fatio was "particularly in danger from the Americans."[1] Indian groups feared other Indians and the Americans, and bandits threatened everyone. In the years immediately following the American Revolution, every resident of south Georgia or northeast Florida probably had his or her own list of perceived perpetrators.

Fear and upheaval was a daily feature of life in northeast Florida and along the border formed by the St. Mary's River, where unsettledness and the need for self-preservation set the tone for social and diplomatic relations in the region. Spanish officials in East Florida fashioned relationships with Indian groups as well as whites in this context of chaos. In the immediate postrevolutionary period, whites exhibited the factionalism and sense of autonomy that had so long characterized Creek groups. But unlike the Creeks, whites did not aim to achieve consensus.

Little has been written about the problems along the border between Spanish East Florida and the new United States, where factionalism and personal enmities were important elements in the shaping of the region. Military and civil officials of Spanish East Florida documented life along the border in correspondence that was archived in the governor's office in St. Augustine. White and Indian residents signed petitions, usually with X marks, that were forwarded to the Spanish governor's office. The reports and pleas from the countryside illustrate that confusion and chaos for all was an inextricable part of relations among Indian groups and for nations headed by Europeans or Euro-Americans.[2]

The American Revolution had ended, and treaties were signed to resolve issues from the war. But for the Georgia-Florida border, the high-level arrangements made in Paris brought uncertainty and loss of assets from forced evacuation and from theft. Perhaps what the border residents had most in common in the years following the 1783 Peace of Paris was a sense that they had been deprived—of their homes, possessions, and especially their safety. Too many countered by showing little restraint in depriving others of possessions (and, if possible, land) to offset what they believed were their own losses.

In 1784, St. Mary's River became an international boundary that separated the territories of Spain and the new confederation of the United States. The river's role as international border did not necessarily suit the needs of many living along its banks, who probably saw the river as an innocuous and familiar natural feature rather than an international limit drawn on a map. Until 1763 the St. Mary's had been just another river in the southeast. For almost a century following the founding of Charleston in 1670, the English and the Spanish made territorial claims that overlapped. Carolina's claims reached far south of St. Augustine. Spanish Florida's extended into the area that the English considered to be Carolina. The watershed of the St. Mary's lay within what historians would aptly call "the debatable lands." And Indian groups continued to claim the land as their own. For slaveholders in the English colonies north of Spanish Florida, this was the area where escaping slaves hid from their pursuers as the runaways headed for the tantalizing idea of freedom in Spanish Florida. Not only did the Spanish hold out the lure of possible freedom for slaves who fled the English colonies. They also wooed and sheltered Indians who had fought or at least threatened the Carolinians. Residents of Carolina and Georgia were quite accustomed to having their way in this area. From the northwest, the Creek Indians moved in to fill the Indian-population vacuum created by Spanish-English dueling. Privateers and pirates lurked along the coastal islands. In the 1750s terrestrial bandits were able to establish their own settlement of New Hanover south of the Altamaha River. With the governors of both British Georgia and Spanish Florida condemning and condoning the bandits' activities, the highwaymen went unchecked. In 1763 Spain turned over its Florida colony to Great Britain.[3]

James Grant, first governor of British East Florida, advocated in 1763 that the St. Mary's River become the boundary between the colonies of East Florida and Georgia. The boundary reflected Grant's success in arguing that East Florida's northern riverine region be retained as part of Great Britain's new colony rather than be included in Georgia. Grant considered this area the most valuable part of Britain's new province. In East Florida investors and settlers created the King's Road to link the British colonies of East Florida and Georgia in a seamless route. Thirty-five miles upriver from the Atlantic

1.1. Colonel Lachlan McIntosh (Library of Congress).

Ocean, a ferry connected the route at a point where the St. Mary's River was "not more than a pistol shot" in width.[4] For a dozen years the new boundary was peaceful. But when East Florida did not join its fellow colonies to the north in rebellion, the St. Mary's became the demarcation between warring polities. In the late spring and early summer of 1776, revolutionary patriot invaders from Georgia pillaged plantations on the St. Mary's, grabbing cattle and slaves. For a while Colonel Lachlan McIntosh's militia from Georgia had almost free rein between the St. Mary's and St. Johns rivers. British Floridians reciprocated and further disrupted the frontier. When the diplomats who met in Paris in 1783 formally elevated the status of the St. Mary's to that of an international boundary, they created a multinational situation in an area inhabited by residents who had no such broad perspective or understanding.

The treaty arrangements of 1783 forced Great Britain to depart and return the Florida colonies to Spanish control, bringing even more factionalism and disruption into an area that was already characterized by justice handled at the informal and extralegal personal level. Seminole Indians in Spanish Florida and Lower and Upper Creeks in American Georgia faced intrusions from white settlers and consequently from other Indian groups displaced by the white settlers. In 1784 British loyalists faced the decision of whether or not to relocate yet again. The loyalists had escaped to British East Florida when Americans who supported the cause of the Revolution threatened and maimed their neighbors who chose not to rebel. Loyalists who returned to Georgia after the Revolution, such as William Pengree, found that animosities from the war were still alive. And there were loyalists who chose to remain in East Florida under Spanish rule. The more fortunate among them had been able to build homes and clear forests to plant fields.[5] Many of these were merely squatters and clamored for the Spanish government to make a decision on the status of land ownership or its availability. Half of the approximately twelve thousand wartime refugees from Carolina and Georgia had been enslaved blacks brought by their owners and had little input into the decisions about their lives. With the change in East Florida to Spanish rule, the slaves might find themselves evacuees again and forcibly relocated once more. Or relocation might be even more rudely imposed when evacuating and remaining whites captured slaves.

Perhaps the least disturbed and disrupted group at this time was the Seminoles. Arriving Spanish officials became the beneficiaries of the good relationships that the British had established with the Seminoles. The British had formally restricted white settlement to the northeastern part of the peninsula and mostly to the east of the St. Johns River. The disruptions brought by the Revolution had pretty much stalled British development and white expansion in East Florida. Whites wishing to acquire farmsteads had no need to move farther inland and away from waterways that led to the Atlantic Ocean in order to acquire farmsteads. Thus there had been little pressure on Seminole lands by whites. Spanish governor Vicente Manuel de Zéspedes moved quickly to continue the peaceful status with the Seminoles.

The two governments divided by the St. Mary's River faced the same problem for different reasons in 1784; both Spain and the United States lacked the soldiers needed to keep the peace. As the last decade of the eighteenth century began, decisions that were made far from Florida and at the highest levels brought definite and noticeable change to the region. Problems derived from the relations within and among the states of the U.S. Confederation. Individual U.S. states acted as autonomously as the various Indian groups.

Scuffles among the residents arose also over the problem of access to markets and material goods. Such matters concerned even those who seemed to be beyond "civilized society," far inland from ocean ports and entrepôts. Sharp metal tools, firearms, and cloth had become an integral part of Indian life. Indian groups could see that the supply of manufactured goods from the British was changing and might possibly be cut off. Both the Indians and the settlers worried about how to get their own products to markets and who would supply their needs for manufactured goods and processed food. Great Britain lurked literally just off shore in hopes of doing so. In the Bahamas, the islands' governor, John Murray, Earl of Dunmore, and his cohort planned how they might control trade in the southeast without the expense of defending territory—the best of all possible worlds. The British were far from ready to leave the southeast.[6]

Loyalist refugees had thought that Great Britain would surely maintain East Florida as a home for King George's loyal subjects and as a buffer against bumptious Americans. After all, British soldiers and militiamen had succeeded in maintaining East Florida's territorial integrity throughout the war. But again, as in 1763, Florida's residents learned that diplomatic ink in Paris was mightier than musketballs and bayonets in the local swamps and forests. The undefeated East Florida colony was ceded to Spain, a victor in the recent war.[7]

British residents of East Florida had until March 19, 1785, to leave for other British locales and dispose of what property they could not carry away with them. Evacuee Hugh Rose lamented that he had believed that East Florida "offered a safe and not unpromising asylum for people in his unfortunate situation," and he had settled on the St. Johns River, where "he invested what little remains of fortune was left him."[8] The St. Mary's harbor was chosen as the main point of debarkation for the departing British, and evacuees began gathering there in the spring of 1785. The harbor was an excellent port, but located at the border with the United States. The area moved into a period of a "convulsed state," and existence was hand-to-mouth for the remaining settlers as well as the waiting evacuees.[9] Chairs, tables, clocks, cooking utensils, and clothing of the emigrants blanketed the shores of the harbor. English sailors vengefully set fire to houses to prevent the Spanish from using them. Folks destined for the Bahamas brought their dismantled dwellings, outbuildings, and hardware to the harbor to transport to a location where construction materials were scarce. The loyalists' claims for compensation abound with accounts of housing materials denied cargo space and left on the shore of the St. Mary's harbor. Tempers flared when Spanish officials embargoed the timber recently cut by the evacuees to use for building materials at their destination or to sell to the arriving Spanish for boat repairs.[10] Ambulatory assets added to the dockside chaos. Evacuees became desperate to sell their cattle and tried to keep them in their control until a sale at a reduced price.[11] Some slaves fled into Indian territory rather than relocate to British colonies. The temptation of so many slaves, horses, and cattle amassed in the uncontrollable environment of the evacuation center at the St. Mary's harbor led to altercations, conflicting ownership claims, pistol whippings, thefts, and arrests. Bandits helped themselves to the horses and slaves of both the departing and remaining whites. Desperate victims subsequently claimed other persons' slaves and horses as replacements or as retribution against their suspect of the moment.[12]

The problems at the evacuation staging area composed a microcosm of Governor Zéspedes's colonywide problems: conflicts over slave ownership, Indians' fears, the flight of lawbreakers to the American side of the river, an inadequate military force, the inability of the provincial government to protect the inhabitants and their property, and no experience or guidance for dealing with the weak and fractious U.S Confederation. Zéspedes knew from the start that he needed the support of the Seminoles in East Florida. Helen Hornbeck Tanner stated that Zéspedes "understood that in numbers alone, their [Seminole] warriors could easily match the strength of the Spanish garrison." Zéspedes held a congress with the chiefs and head warriors of the Seminoles on September 30, 1784, in St. Augustine. Presented as a minor item in Zéspedes's talk was a major matter. Zéspedes attributed a shortage of "all the things I should like to give you" to his recent arrival, but the persistent and systemic lack of gifts and trade goods was indeed a major impediment to peace with the Indians. Two months later Seminoles and Lower Creeks came for a second meeting held in the capital. Governor Zéspedes had invited Alexander McGillivray, whose leg injury provided an excuse for not attending the congress. Neither Mad Dog nor other Upper Creek chiefs attended the December conclave. This later time the governor addressed Indians' concerns about hunting and trading. He promised goods and gifts, but in words almost identical to his September talk, he explained that the gifts "are very few because of my recent arrival here."[13] Spain's tactic was to depend on the Indians to be "the human border" (la frontera humana) and, in the words of modern Spanish scholar Elena Sánchez-Fabrés Mirat, "the living barrier" (la barrera viviente). Governor Carondolet of Spanish Louisiana remarked that "not only will Spain always make the American settlements tremble by threatening them with the Indians, but she has no other way of molesting them."[14]

With the Revolution over, settlers moved in ever-growing numbers into lands in Georgia occupied by the Indians. The most desirable lands lay between the Ogeechee and Oconee rivers. The Indians resisted the immigration, and hostilities moved southward, closer to Spanish East Florida. Although Upper Creeks began the attack, Georgians retaliated by turning on Lower Creek towns.[15] Frightened and panicky south Georgians found Spanish East Florida preferable to angry Indians. At the Florida border, the Spanish magistrate, "Judge" Henry O'Neill, had to inform fleeing families that official Spanish policy permitted only settlers who "embraced the Catholic religion."

Nevertheless, Americans seeking asylum were often given permission to settle in East Florida for a period of refuge, but some stayed many years. However great was the need for settlers in the East Florida hinterland, until 1790 the Spanish Crown's insistence that all new subjects be Roman Catholics remained a major impediment to immigration. The only non-Catholics admitted were those fleeing from the Georgia-Indian wars.[16] Indian activities were no doubt exaggerated by land-seeking, non-Catholic persons to provide a justification to enter East Florida and squat on vacant land in hopes of future ownership. Spanish officials suspected that the plea for asylum was used also to bring cattle into Florida as quickly as possible and to avoid the fee for importation. Otherwise, to bring cattle into East Florida, the drover or owner had to produce a passport from a Georgia magistrate, then wait at the border for the governor of Florida, residing in St. Augustine, to grant permission for the cattle to be brought in. This required written communication from Amelia Island to St. Augustine and back.[17] And the Spanish wished to prevent stolen cattle from coming into Florida because the animals' deprived and angry owners might not be far behind. Men intended to "have satisfaction" whether that be retrieving their own cattle or stealing the cattle of another. They did not intend to return to Georgia empty-handed.

In his quandary about the mostly Protestant applicants, O'Neill sent them on to St. Augustine for the governor to handle, but realized that many would melt into the countryside and steal horses rather than go to the capital. O'Neill feared that Indians were being blamed for thefts "when it is probably those [refugee] Crackers that doeth the mischief." Writing in August 1787, O'Neill expressed his fear that if the Georgia-Indian war ended, anger would be directed to the south side of the St. Mary's.[18] Indians too fled into Florida. An Indian man and woman were found at Little Bar at the mouth of the St. Mary's. The two had left Indian lands and relocated to an area that was undisputedly white. When the Spanish officer at the Amelia Island post offered to return them to their nation, they refused. What threats in Indian lands had caused them to prefer a barrier island inhabited by whites?[19]

Rumors "ran the rivers" about Indian strikes against the Americans, and Florida's border residents requested instructions from their governor in May 1787. With no experience, precedents, or instructions for diplomacy with head-strong individual states (Georgia in this instance), Zéspedes responded to the fretful residents with weak and contradictory platitudes. He advised that the residents had nothing to fear, but they should prepare to defend themselves. He counseled that "divine and human law" permitted meeting force with force and that "any vassal of His Catholic Majesty ha[d] the right to defend himself, and to mete out death if met with resistance." But five months later he replied quite differently to the distraught settlers' petition for the governor's assistance in the face of more threats from the Georgia-Indian war. From the safe distance of St. Augustine, Zéspedes informed the settlers that they had nothing to fear because Spanish subjects were "neutral in whatever takes place between Georgia and the Creek Nation. . . . Now, as in the past, Spain finds itself at perfect peace and friendship with the United States."[20]

The following spring the governor reiterated his homily about perfect peace and friendship, adding a prohibition against the pursuit of raiders, whether Indian or white, across the St. Mary's into American territory. He promised "to proceed heartily in proper channels" to rectify the residents' problems. What Zéspedes could not promise was a show of military might that would force either Georgians or Creeks to respect East Florida's territorial integrity. Spanish soldier Gregorio Castillo, after returning from Cumberland Island in Georgia, reported that 150 armed men were expected at that barrier island; that he was subjected to inquiries from the Americans regarding "Spanish" feelings about the Georgians' war with the Indians; and that he met two "commissioners" who were organizing a town sixty miles up the St. Mary's. This last incident would be further encroachment into Indian lands.[21] Zéspedes's decision at this time to move the main warehouse for the frontier from Amelia Island at the border to St. Johns Bluff on the eponymous river must have suggested to the residents the governor's concern for attacks by either Indians or Americans.[22]

Residents of East Florida could cause as much contention and fear as those who lived outside of the colony. In the spring of 1788, Richard Lang spearheaded complaints about Henry O'Neill's administration of justice on the St. Mary's and created new contentions among the residents over this issue. Soon afterward, O'Neill was shot while at Cumberland Island and died within a few days. Margaret O'Neill accused Lang of complicity in the deed, saying that on his deathbed her husband had "laid the blame to two or three men on this side of the St. Mary's" as much as to the man already jailed for the crime in Georgia. In midsummer, the body of another murdered resident was found lying on the Georgia side of the St. Mary's. Nevertheless, the governor appointed Lang to replace O'Neill as magistrate in spite of Mrs. O'Neill's assertions.[23]

With Lang, the judgeship took on a venal character, for he intended to enjoy more perquisites than the Spanish government provided. He repeatedly requested that the governor award him a portion of recovered stolen or contraband items. Denied official consent, Lang presumed to reward himself, appropriating property of incoming refugees for nominal safekeeping. Lang was less discriminating than O'Neill about the actual admission of refugee Georgians or their cattle. For a price, Lang would delay informing the governor of a refugee's presence until some period of time had passed. Lang waited four months, for example, to write the governor about the entry of the Mazell family with their cattle and pigs. Lang allowed a man without even permission to be in East Florida to act as bailee of the horse of a suspected smuggler. By the time Lang wrote the governor about newcomers, they were established and their immigration to East Florida was a fait accompli. Lang's actions, in practice, nullified royal orders, and new settlers who did not readily qualify to immigrate entered East Florida with their possessions. Zéspedes chastised Lang for being "remiss," but did not replace him.[24]

Meanwhile, Indian problems that were fomented in central Georgia continued to move farther into East Florida and intensify the level of threat. After plantation slaves provided Indians with transportation across the St. Johns River to Julington Creek (despite orders to the contrary), the Indians then headed downriver to the home of the ferry operator at the Cow Ford (San Nicolás to the Spanish). The ferry operator had earlier refused to carry these very Indians across the river. At the ferryman's home, the Indians broke household items and threatened the ferryman's wife with knives. Even more frightening was the treatment given a "Mr. Clark," who had been a visitor at the home of Margaret O'Neill. The Indians burned out Clark's eyes, saying that he "was a Virginia man and it was good to kill him." While the Indians exacted personal-level justice, the river residents worried about how the governor would wish them to act in such threatening situations, "whether there can be no stop put to these evils; whether we must stand in our own defenses or give entirely up to the savages to destroy our livings?"[25]

In 1790 when American troops began to gather along the border, both Florida white residents and the Indians turned to Governor Zéspedes for assistance or at least guidance. The settlers wanted protection, the Indians information about American intentions that they thought the governor might have learned from diplomatic communiqués. The settlers saw themselves as bystanders and the ultimate victims of Indian anger that had been instigated by Americans. But Zéspedes sent no additional Spanish soldiers to the border, only orders to be kept informed of any developments. To the Indian chiefs, the governor provided no answers, only remarks about the right of the United States to maneuver its soldiers within its own borders. The settler's earlier question about "giving up to the savages" continued to haunt them.[26]

Although a little known personage, James Allen fomented much of the trouble between all parties in the region. Allen was an Indian trader who lived on the "upperest" part of the St. Mary's River. Although officially restricted to working for Panton, Leslie & Company, Allen's isolated location allowed him to trade at will for his own benefit, dealing in the goods and property of anyone and with little care of how the items were acquired. James Allen was known to few whites at the time, and he mostly disappeared from history. Daniel McGirt is better known than Allen, and in the region's history he appeared as the most notorious bandit of the time. With antics and pronouncements befitting the protagonist of a ballad, Dan McGirt had plagued the countryside before the British evacuation. He continued into the second Spanish period to appease his appetite for other people's horses and kept the region astir, crossing the international river boundary at will. The posse that assembled to capture him brought almost as much havoc to the region as did its prey.[27] The chaos caused by McGirt was indeed important, but Allen's activities were more insidious, intrusive, and influential. Allen was the destination for stolen property, especially horses and cattle. He had the support of Creek Indians and with Indian assent lived near or within Indian land. His location was almost out of reach for officials. In 1789, however, it seems that Allen made an uncharacteristic appearance in the settled area in order to be counted in a census.[28]

Some of the Lower Creek leaders sided with and defended Allen. When Richard Lang, in his role of magistrate, "sent two men to deal with James Allen," Allen balked and challenged that "as I [Lang] had more business with him than he had with me, that I was to come to him." Lang asked the governor for guidance in the face of disdain by "such men that fly in the face of authority." Lang fretted that confidential correspondence with St. Augustine was not secure. "My letters from Your Excellency have arrived broken open." Lang declared that Allen "breaks the law every day by selling horses and cattle to a man who then ships them to Cumberland Island (Georgia)." When the Spanish officials tried to remove Allen from his lair in East Florida, he refused to comply, and his Creek friends came to his defense. Creek leader Jack Kanard signed a letter written to Lang complaining that Lang and others had taken a good deal of property from Allen, "some that he had bought from the people of this land." The "chiefs of the towns" told the Spanish that they "gave Allen the privilege to settle there and want to know why he cannot stay there in peace. He has been a good friend and he supplies us with our needs." The chiefs did not want someone else settling there to replace Allen.[29]

Zéspedes's replacement, Juan Nepomuceno de Quesada, inherited the problem with James Allen. The new East Florida governor sent two interpreters in November 1791 to present the official's words to John Kanard, whom the intermediaries addressed as *Amigo y Hermano* (friend and brother). The talk laid out Allen's offenses: he had threatened almost everyone on the St. Mary's with either ejection or killing; robbed Florida residents of cattle to sell in Georgia and vice versa; Allen was neither Spanish nor American and deceived both and the "red people" as well. The spokespersons-interpreters asserted that Allen lied and "breaks the chain of friendship that unites the Indians and the Spanish. What he sells to the Indians he has stolen from the Spanish and the Americans."[30]

Governor Zéspedes had offered platitudes and little else to the settlers of the rivers and rattled only a verbal sword at the Lower Creeks; however, he was able to make a show of force and decisiveness to pacify complaints and demands from the Seminoles. Zéspedes overstepped his authority within the colonial hierarchy in order to deliver quick satisfaction to the Seminoles for a crime committed by a man of Spanish origin. Lorenzo Barreto was a convict laborer assigned to serve his sentence in St. Augustine. Barreto killed a Seminole and wounded another. Zéspedes reported that Barreto confessed and the governor convened a tribunal in St. Augustine that condemned Barreto to death—a move that was beyond the governor's purview. The prisoner was executed quickly. Zéspedes let "Seminole justice" outweigh Spanish colonial judicial procedures, which would have required review by higher officials located beyond East Florida. Claudio Saunt points out that traditional Creek justice required having satisfaction as a personal matter, not the state's carrying out justice and punishment.[31] With threats of attacks along the northern border from Georgians and from Lower Creeks, Zéspedes could not afford to lose the support of the Seminoles. If the governor could not get active support from the Seminoles, then he badly needed the Seminoles to remain peaceful toward the Spanish. If Seminoles went on the attack from the west and perhaps from the south, Zéspedes could face a two-front war, which would have been deadly for the settlers in rural East Florida and the townspeople of St. Augustine. Zéspedes bowed to traditional Indian practices in this matter to achieve his immediate goal and kept the trial and sentence within East Florida, where the Seminoles could observe the outcome.

Spain's invitation to slaves in rival nations to seek refuge and possibly freedom in Florida added to the animosities along the border. Formalized in 1693 by King Carlos II of Spain, the slave sanctuary policy had been suspended when Florida became a British colony. In 1784 Governor Zéspedes reluctantly reinstituted the sanctuary policy when Spain returned to the peninsula. The governor thought that the escapees invoked the desire of conversion to Catholicism as a guise for their true motive, which was freedom. Canoes carrying fleeing blacks arrived from Frederica, Savannah, and as far away as Charleston. One particularly large party of twenty-one escapees "was hurled" in their boat across the bar at the mouth of the St. Johns River. Spanish officials, always in need of canoes for their own transportation, usually confiscated the slaves' escape vessels and put the boats into the service of the Spanish government.

American claimants who came to Florida with hopes of retrieving at least the weapons and boats brought by the slaves were further angered when they received inferior canoes from the Spanish "fleet" as substitutes while soldiers kept the Americans' better vessels for themselves.[32]

Americans frustrated by Spanish imperial policies and by local decisions turned their wrath on the settlers who lived in Spanish Florida. From the American side came the message that there would be raids on the Spanish detachment at Amelia Island and upon the Florida river residents "to carry off all the Negroes they can." In formal retaliation against Spanish practices, angry Georgia administrators refused to admit Floridians who did not have a pass from Georgia officials. Spanish Florida residents were subject to arrest and fine in Georgia and restricted from bringing goods out of that state. The Georgians felt that the blacks came into Florida "in such numbers that everyone from Florida" was suspect. Georgians tried to kidnap the slaves who accompanied Florida resident George Aarons on a shopping trip to Cumberland Island. Richard Lang reported that the Georgians "will have satisfaction or say it will become disagreeable for those of us who live on this frontier."[33]

The year 1790 brought important changes that were decided far from the Florida-Georgia border: a treaty agreement between the Creek leaders and the United States, the end of Spain's slave sanctuary policy, and the inception of homestead land grants in Spanish East Florida. All residents, with their chaos, complaints, pleas, and flouting of directives, had played a role in shaping the need for and the details of the formal arrangements.

The signing in New York City of a treaty between the United States and the Creeks ended Georgia's attempts to negotiate its own treaties and land acquisitions with the Indians. The first treaty to be signed under the U.S Constitution, the Treaty of New York, denied the validity of state treaties and made it clear that only the federal government could make such agreements. As for the effect on Floridians, the Treaty of New York put the disrupted backcountry at a farther remove from the locus of treaty decision and lessened the role of immediate and nearby fear and anger in negotiations. For the Spanish government the move clarified the diplomatic situation, which had been a major concern for officials in East Florida. Along the border, however, Georgians continued to act with little concern for federal directives and often with disregard or in defiance of orders. In 1794 and 1795 the U.S. secretary of state thought that federal officials would have to intervene to control Georgians' military-like activities along the Florida border.[34]

On May 17, 1790, Spain and the United States reached an agreement to end Spain's offer of refuge to runaway slaves who fled from U.S. territory. The news of the decision was transmitted from Havana to St. Augustine on July 21, 1790. Henceforth, black runaways who asked for asylum in Spanish East Florida would be returned to the United States. Contentions continued, however, about the issue of escapees who entered Florida before the agreement and remained in the Spanish colony. For the Americans, the suspension of sanctuary did not compensate for their loss of enslaved workers and the boats, firearms, and other items that the runaways had brought into Florida. But slaves in Georgia and Carolina faced much less benefit after 1790 to run to Florida, and Americans seeking to compensate themselves for losses now had fewer reasons to violate the border or to attack Floridians coming into Georgia.

In 1790 the Spanish government began offering free grants of land to settlers who occupied, planted, and fulfilled homesteading requirements. Land grants were available as well to those who were not Roman Catholic, although the open practice of any other religion was still forbidden. Squatters could claim the land that they had been occupying or perhaps could relocate to better tracts. Many settlers along the St. Mary's used the opportunity to move to lands farther from the border in hope of a safer location. Those who wished to move into Florida no longer had to fabricate danger or exaggerate threats to their lives to make a case for immigration.[35]

Even these three important changes did not turn the Florida-Georgia border into a peaceable kingdom. But these policies and agreements did result in fewer factions, codify decisions, regularize procedures, and thus solidify the strength of the governments in the region. The formalities provided rules and procedures to officials, where previously too much had been left to the officials' discretion and the influence of immediate problems. Threats or perceived threats from Lower Creeks diminished in East Florida. Spanish officials now dealt more with the Seminoles than with the Creeks. The new problem on the horizon was the arrival of more land-hungry Americans. The Spanish in East Florida would soon find themselves the target of schemers wanting to acquire Florida lands.

Notes

1. William Irwin to Governor Vicente Manuel de Zéspedes, October 17, 1786; Lewis Fatio to Governor of Florida, November 1, 1787, East Florida Papers (EFP), Library of Congress Manuscript Collection (microfilm copies). The East Florida Papers are the Spanish government archives that were impounded by the U.S. government in 1821.

2. Kenneth Coleman, *A History of Georgia* (Athens: University of Georgia Press, 1977), 92–95. Coleman does not mention Indian troubles in southern Georgia or problems between Georgian settlers and Spanish Floridians along their common border.

3. Robert L. Gold, *Borderland Empires in Transition: The Triple Nation Transfer of Florida* (Carbondale: Southern Illinois University Press, 1969), 127–29.

4. Charles Loch Mowat, *East Florida as a British Province, 1763–1784* (Gainesville: University of Florida Press, 1964), 10–13; Nicolas Grenier, November 10, 1784, cited in Joseph Byrne Lockey, *East Florida, 1784–1785* (Berkeley: University of California Press, 1949), 306–11.

5. Some of the departing loyalists reported abandoning land in East Florida that they already had cleared and ditched for rice culture. Wilbur Henry Siebert, *Loyalists in East Florida, 1774–1784* (Deland: Florida State Historical Society, 1929), vol. 2; J. Leitch Wright Jr., *Florida in the American Revolution* (Gainesville: University Presses of Florida, 1975), 125–26; census returns, EFP.

6. J. Leitch Wright Jr., *Anglo-Spanish Rivalry in North America* (Athens: University of Georgia Press, 1971), 143–45. Wright notes that Dunmore was among "a number of prominent figures in one fashion or another" involved in a grandiose design for control of most of North America.

7. Wright, *Florida in the American Revolution*, 121–24.

8. Siebert, *Loyalists in East Florida*, 2: 105.

9. Helen Hornbeck Tanner, *Zéspedes in East Florida* (Coral Gables: University of Miami Press, 1963), 61; Henry O'Neill to Carlos Howard, April 17, 1785, EFP.

10. Siebert, *Loyalists in East Florida*, 2:36; Henry O'Neill, EFP; Samuel Kelly, *Samuel Kelly: An Eighteenth-Century Seaman Whose Days Have Been Few and Evil, to Which Is Added Remarks, Etc., on Places He Visited during His Pilgrimage in This Wilderness* (New York: Fredrick A. Stokes, 1925), 118–19.

11. Tanner, *Zéspedes*, 62; Siebert, *Loyalists in East Florida*, vol. 2.

12. Nicolás Valderas to Zéspedes, October 27, 1785, EFP.

13. Tanner, *Zéspedes*, 56–57; Zéspedes, September 30, 1784, and December 8, 1784, in Lockey, *East Florida*, 280–82, 428–29.

14. Baron Carondelet cited in Frederick Jackson Turner, "The Diplomatic Contest for the Mississippi Valley," *Atlantic Monthly* 93 (1904): 678; Elena Sánchez-Fabrés Mirat, *Situación histórica de las Floridas en la segunda mitad del siglo XVIII (1783–1819)* (Madrid: Ministerio de Asuntos Exteriores, 1977), 11, 111.

15. Coleman, *A History of Georgia*, 92–95; Tanner, *Zéspedes*, 100; Henry O'Neill to Zéspedes, August 1, 1787, EFP. Coleman does not mention any Indian troubles in southern Georgia or problems between Georgian settlers.

16. Carlos Howard to Henry O'Neill, April 14, 1788, EFP.

17. Richard Lang to Zéspedes, June 16, 1790, EFP.

18. Henry O'Neill to Zéspedes, August 1, 1787, EFP.

19. José María Solves to Governor, September 5, 1785, EFP.

20. Zéspedes to Henry O'Neill, May 3, 1787; Zéspedes's reply to residents' petition, October 27, 1787, EFP.

21. Zéspedes to Richard Lang, May 18, 1787; Henry O'Neill to Carlos Howard, October 21, 1787; Gregorio Castillo to Zéspedes, October 30, 1787; Howard to O'Neill,

November 2, 1787; Gregorio Castillo to Zéspedes, November 15 and 16, 1787, 137, 138, EFP.

22. Zéspedes ordered that "the Bluff, so called by the English," would henceforth be named San Vicente Ferrer. Ostensibly the basis for his decision was the bluff's more central location with relation to the various posts, a larger storage area, and the fact that the new site would diminish the potential for illicit trade that the border location provided. Zéspedes, Instructions, October 24, 1787, EFP.

23. Jaime McTernan to Zéspedes, April 11, 1788, and May 2, 1788; Margaret O'Neill to Carlos Howard, May 1788; Joseph Tasso to Zéspedes, June 12, 1788; James Woodland to Commander of Spanish Galley, June 12, 1788, EFP.

24. Zéspedes to Richard Lang, May 2, 1787; Lang to Zéspedes, July 17, 1788, Carlos Howard to Lang, January 21, 1789, EFP.

25. Richard Lang to Zéspedes, July 13, 1789; Residents of the St. Johns River to Zéspedes, October 8, 1789, EFP.

26. Residents of the St. Johns River to Zéspedes, October 8, 1789; Zéspedes to Joseph Tasso, April 25, 1790; Richard Lang to Zéspedes, May 21, 1790; Zéspedes to Lang, May 25, 1790, EFP.

27. James A. Lewis, "Cracker-Spanish Florida Style," *Florida Historical Quarterly* 63 (1984): 184–204. During Zéspedes's administration McGirt was evicted three times from East Florida and had been suspected of involvement with the shooting of Henry O'Neill. Tanner, *Zéspedes,* 189, 225. For the cattle trade, see Susan R. Parker, "The Cattle Trade in East Florida, 1784–1821," in Jane G. Landers, ed., *Colonial Plantations and Economy in Florida* (Gainesville: University Press of Florida, 2000), 150–67.

28. Allen listed in the census a wife and five children and two boarders, one hundred head of cattle, twenty horses, and eighty pigs. Residents of the St. Mary's and Nassau rivers, and Amelia and Talbot islands, December 1789, signed by Pablo Catajal, December 10, 1789, EFP.

29. Richard Lang to Governor, June 19, 1790; Jack Kanard to Lang, July 10, 1790, EFP.

30. Talk, Governor Quesada to "Friend and Brother Juan Canard [*sic*]," November 24, 1791.

31. Zéspedes remarked that he proceeded without a hangman because there was none available, suggesting another irregularity in the interest of haste. Zéspedes to Antonio Portier, October 28, 1789, and Portier to Zéspedes, April 18, 1790, EFP; Claudio Saunt, *A New Order of Things* (New York: Cambridge University Press, 2003), 90–93.

32. Blas de Bouchet to Zéspedes, September 24, 1788, doc. 223; Manuel Otero to Zéspedes, September 25, 1788; José Trujillo to Zéspedes, September 25, 1788; Zéspedes to Trujillo, November 12, 1788, EFP; Jane Landers, *Black Society in Spanish Florida* (Urbana: University of Illinois Press, 1999), 76.

33. Fernando del Postigo to Governor, March 17, 1787, and Richard Lang to Governor, July 17, 1788, EFP.

34. J. Leitch Wright Jr., *Creeks and Seminoles: The Destruction and Regeneration of*

the *Muscogulge People* (Lincoln: University of Nebraska Press, 1986), 136–40; Richard K. Murdoch, *The Georgia-Florida Frontier, 1793–1796: Spanish Reaction to French Intrigue and America Designs* (Berkeley: University of California Press, 1951), 122.

35. Historical Records Survey, *Spanish Land Grants in Florida* (Tallahassee: State Library Board, 1940), 1: xx.

2

◇◇◇

King Payne and His Policies

A Framework for Understanding the Diplomacy of
the Seminoles of La Chua, 1784–1812

JAMES CUSICK

The Seminoles of the La Chua area of north central Florida (today's Alachua County) tend to attract only minor consideration in histories of the Creek Confederation. This is not due to historical oversight. The towns of Alachua—which consisted first of La Chua and Cuscowilla and later of Paynes Town and Bowlegs Town—can be regarded as far outliers in the nexus of Seminole settlements in Florida that were loosely affiliated with the Lower Creeks. This essay presents a preliminary study of the dynamics between the Seminoles of Alachua and their neighbors. In particular, it examines the policies of King Payne, headman of Alachua from 1784 to 1812, as he attempted to maintain a stance of neutrality with the three powers in the region: the Spaniards, the Georgians, and the Lower Creeks.[1]

During the second half of the eighteenth century and the opening of the nineteenth century, various bands of Hitchiti-speaking peoples moved into northern Florida and established towns, hunting grounds, grazing lands, and modest economies based in trade and subsistence agriculture. The group occupying Alachua came from the Georgia tidewater, and they are sometimes identified in documents as Oconees, although usually as Seminoles. They were a small group—estimates put their population at 450 people in the 1760s—but they found themselves strategically placed. Of all the Seminole and Creek towns in northern Florida, theirs were nearest to areas of fairly dense white settlement. They also occupied the lands between these settlements and other Seminole towns further west, such as Talahasochte on the Suwannee River and Miccosukee (by the lake of the same name). Over time the Seminoles of Alachua became major breeders of cattle and horses and participated in the deerskin trade. This gave them some economic influence with their neighbors, both as trading partners for whites and as trading middlemen to other Indian towns.

Although this group of Seminoles first moved into the Florida peninsula when it was under Spanish rule, their sympathies were with the British. Cowkeeper (or Ahaye), the principle *micco* over the various groups in Alachua, pledged support to the governor of Georgia, James Oglethorpe, in 1740 and aided his attacks on Spanish strongholds. Cowkeeper's people remained hostile to the Spaniards for the next twenty years and then became firm friends with the new British regime that controlled Florida from 1763 to 1784. By the time of Cowkeeper's death, in that same year, the Seminoles of Alachua were probably better known to the white settlers of Florida than any other Native American group in the area.[2]

Indeed, the naturalist William Bartram based many of his conclusions about the Seminoles in general on his observations of this group. From his visit to Alachua in 1774 and also from his visit to another band of Seminoles at Talahasochte, he later wrote: "The Siminoles [are] but a weak people, with respect to numbers, all of them I suppose would not be sufficient to people one of the towns in the Muscogulge. . . . Yet this handful of people possesses a vast territory, all East Florida and the greatest part of West Florida, which being naturally cut and divided by thousands of islets, knolls, and eminences, by the innumerable rivers, lakes, swamps, vast savannahs and ponds, form so many secure retreats and temporary dwelling places, that effectually guard them from any sudden invasions. . . . Thus they enjoy a superabundance of the necessaries and conveniences of life, with the security of person and property."[3]

This "security of person and property" was Cowkeeper's most important legacy to his successor as *micco*, a Seminole sometimes identified as his son, sometimes as his nephew, and usually recorded in documents as Payne or King Payne. Unlike many other Seminole or Creek headmen, Payne does not seem to have been of mixed blood. He did, over the course of his years in leadership, show definite signs of acculturation: he eventually built himself a plantation-style house in Alachua, made frequent visits to St. Augustine, and communicated in a basic, if stilted, English when required. Unlike Cowkeeper, he does not seem to have been a war leader, and he usually favored mediation with others over the warpath. His chief goal, according to one source, was to keep "a peaceful conduct with everybody and to be friendly to all comers."[4]

This proved to be a challenging philosophy for Payne to follow. He lived at a time when his people faced increasing threats from outsiders. When he assumed the position of *micco*, at the conclusion of the American Revolution, his people's traditional and preferred trading partners, the British, had been expelled from the region. The Florida peninsula once again came under Spanish control, and it now bordered a new and rapidly expanding American republic. For most of the years between 1784 and 1812, the Seminoles of

Alachua would find themselves unwillingly embroiled in disputes between Spanish East Florida, the state of Georgia, and the Lower Creeks.

Payne's efforts to deal with this situation, although radically different from Cowkeeper's in method, were not so different in overall goals. Like Cowkeeper, Payne placed a high priority on maintaining his people's access to trade. Without British help, it was pointless to foster a continued enmity against the incoming Spanish colonial regime in St. Augustine. By necessity, the Seminoles of Alachua had to make their peace with whatever power controlled St. Augustine and the St. Johns River. These were crucial trading points for a people who were otherwise land-locked and far from the trading posts that dotted the territory of the Creek Confederacy. Moreover, Spanish officials, beginning with Governor Vicente Manuel de Zéspedes, were anxious for the goodwill of Payne's people. They viewed the Seminoles of Alachua not only as potential allies against American or British encroachments into Florida but also as a buffer between St. Augustine and Creeks and Seminoles further west who were openly hostile to a Spanish presence in Florida. This laid the groundwork for a change in local alignments. Anxious to maintain trade, and apparently pleased that Spain would allow a British firm, Panton, Leslie & Co., to operate under Spanish license, Payne adopted a conciliatory posture toward the new regime. In doing this, he guaranteed his people easy access to trade goods; but he also made them potentially unpopular with other Seminoles, such as those at the town of Miccosukee, who frequently raided Spanish settlements and were disinclined to trade through Panton, Leslie & Co. Payne's affiliation with the Spaniards also meant his people could potentially end up on the wrong side of any military conflict between Spanish East Florida and the state of Georgia. These were the risks of choosing a path that isolated Alachua from other allies.[5]

It should therefore come as no surprise that Payne was as much an advocate for peace as his predecessor, Cowkeeper, had sometimes been for war. Peace was essential to the well-being of Alachua. The Seminoles there were too small a population to be a military power, and they lived just a few days' march from the Spanish military garrison at St. Augustine, the frontier militias of Georgia, and the war parties of the Lower Creeks and Seminoles. In times of tranquility, Alachua was a crossroad for trade, a ranching heartland, where livestock dealers from Georgia and Florida frequently traveled in search of cattle and horses. In times of war, however, Alachua was a battleground for retaliatory strikes, with all of its wealth in livestock, deerskins, and crops open to pillage. To protect his people, Payne often faced the thankless task of being a peacemaker in an era that was prone to border raids and other conflicts.[6]

Through most of his years of leadership, Payne tried to keep his people out of hostilities with neighbors. As early as 1793, he met with Indian commissioners in Georgia to talk about a possible alliance with American interests. He stopped short, however, of any formal treaty or promise of military aid. In 1795, when an attempted rebellion against Spanish rule in Florida stirred up fighting on the Georgia-Florida border, the Alachua Seminoles refused to take sides. At other times Payne had to put down trouble caused by his own hotheaded warriors. In 1800, for example, he personally intervened to recall nearly one hundred warriors and two chiefs from raids on the settlements along the St. Johns River. He was described as "much disgusted" with their actions. "I have according to your desire done Everything in my power to keep Peace and a clean path Between you and us," he told Governor Henry White of St. Augustine. "I have told my young people of their Error in being rash in taking to bad talks." By the same token, he seems to have maintained great distance, both geographically and politically, between himself and quarrels among the Lower Creeks and Seminoles. For instance, he did not get involved in the disputes over a cession of lands to Forbes & Co. that caused great dissension in the Creek Confederacy in 1804.[7]

This policy of neutrality protected Alachua from some of the upheavals of the times, but it came at a cost. In order to keep a connection to St. Augustine, Payne often had to put up with Spanish officials who held the Alachua Seminoles responsible for any breach in the peace. Governor White, Spain's chief administrator in East Florida between 1796 and 1811, frequently blamed Payne for raids or troubles that were actually caused by other Seminoles further to the west. Between 1802 and 1807, for example, White shut down trade with Alachua, accusing Payne's people of hostilities that were stirred up by Seminoles from the town of Miccosukee in the Red Hills area. Payne had to petition White repeatedly, explaining that he had no authority over Miccosukee, before the governor finally admitted his mistake and reopened trading posts on the St. Johns River.[8]

Perhaps the best illustration of the problems facing Payne come from his stormy relationship with William Augustus Bowles, a British agitator, and Bowles's close ally, Kinache (rendered phonetically as *Kin-odgy* in Spanish records), the principle *micco* of Miccosukee. Bowles, a former British Loyalist from the American Revolution, was constantly probing the strength of Spanish control over Florida. In 1788 he embarked on plans to attack Panton, Leslie & Co.'s trading posts on the St. Johns River. These plans received no sympathy from Payne, whose people relied heavily on the posts, and Bowles was forced to retreat from the area around Saint Augustine when half his men deserted and it became clear that Payne's people would not assist him. A few years later, however, his overtures to Seminoles further west were better received.

2.1. William Augustus
Bowles (Florida
State Library and
Archives).

In 1792, he was gathering adherents along the Apalachicola River, promising
them British aid and a trading post dedicated to their interests if they would
first destroy the Panton, Leslie & Co. operation near Fort St. Marks. After raiding this store, Bowles once again had to retreat. He was captured, and then he
disappeared from the region for a while. But in 1799 he was back. This time his
powerbase was at the town of Miccosukee. From then until his capture again
in 1803, Bowles waged a steady war of harassment against Spanish interests.[9]

The problems between the Seminoles at Alachua and those at Miccosukee became especially acute at this time. Howard Cline, in his ethnohistorical
study of the Florida Seminole, noted that these two groups of Hitchiti-speaking Seminoles rarely cooperated with each other and were usually opposed
in their political sympathies. Kinache, the key headmen at Miccosukee, was
avowedly anti-Spanish and encouraged his people to raid plantations in Spanish territory. As the leader of the largest Seminole town in Florida and an
influential *micco* among the Lower Creeks, Kinache also regarded himself
as the spokesman for all Seminoles. He looked upon Payne as a subordinate

headsman or at least as a markedly less important one, and treated him with great disdain. Although Payne often visited the town of Miccosukee, one of his few regular points of contact with the Seminoles in the Red Hills area, he never met with a welcome reception.[10]

Several episodes of trouble with the town of Miccosukee illustrate the dilemmas that Payne, and at times his half-brother Bowlegs, faced when acting as intermediaries for officials or settlers near St. Augustine. At the turn of the nineteenth century, the Seminole of Miccosukee, prompted by Bowles and Kinache, raided deep into Florida, carrying off slaves and families as captives. In August 1801, the powerful East Florida family of Francis Philip Fatio reported to Governor White that a band of raiders, later identified as being from Miccosukee, had stolen thirty-eight slaves from the Fatio plantation on the St. Johns River. Bowlegs went to Miccosukee to try to intercede for the return of these slaves, but he was treated dismissively. Payne then offered to go to the town in company with Francis Philip Fatio Jr. and to guarantee his safety. What happened next is told through the lens of Fatio's hostile report back to his father.[11]

Payne, he complained, proved absolutely useless at Miccosukee. He took with him, Fatio said, "only an old Indian and two boys. He never expressed himself to obtain the return of either the negroes or my horse, which the Mikasouky Indians also stole from me. He never spoke a word in their Public Assembly but told me to explain my own business. In all his conduct whilst there he betrayed evident signs of fear and indifference."[12]

What lies behind these harsh words about a sixty-nine-year-old chief who apparently went to great lengths to accompany Fatio? Any interpretation must be speculative. But it is worth noting that Payne's chief responsibility to Fatio was as a protector. He had no influence at Miccosukee and claimed none. To directly challenge Kinache or Bowles would have accomplished nothing; Payne had no means of backing up threatening words, and it was not in his interests to make Alachua a target for their raids.

In fact, Payne honored his role as mediator and made at least two additional trips to Miccosukee, negotiating not only in this matter but in another involving the kidnapping of members of the Bonelli family from East Florida. His clear purpose was to avoid getting Alachua caught up in retaliatory strikes between Kinache's people and the Spaniards. In May 1802, for example, he intervened to stop a war party from leaving Miccosukee for the Spanish settlements. He was also quick to make sure Spanish officials disassociated Alachua from the actions of more hostile Seminoles. "You may depend on it, our design to make peace with you," he told Governor White. "We have nothing to say to the Mikasuky Indians, we are a people to ourself."[13]

Ultimately, Payne did not have sufficient authority to move Kinache, and the colonial government in St. Augustine appealed matters directly to the Lower Creeks. Again, Payne served as an intermediary. He and nine other headmen from Alachua accompanied a Spanish representative, John Forrester, to the Flint River in Georgia in July 1802. Here they sought the aid of John Kinnard, headmen of the Hitchitis.[14]

Payne's role in subsequent negotiations was a minor one. It was Kinnard who rallied a host of Creek chiefs and four hundred warriors and went to Miccosukee to deliver what amounted to an ultimatum to Kinache. This show of strength and the release of a leading Miccosukee from Fort St. Marks were sufficient to establish a truce. Payne's delegation then managed to obtain the release of Mrs. Bonelli and three of her children, along with seventeen of the slaves stolen from the Fatio family, plus four other slaves and four free blacks.[15]

Although Payne's efforts at peaceful diplomacy did not make him the most admired of the Seminole *miccos* in Florida, he did, despite all, keep Alachua free of conflict. It took a major war—the War of 1812—to defeat him. When American troops put East Florida under military occupation in 1812, it was once again Payne, at eighty years of age, who tried to restrain his warriors from becoming involved. In this, he eventually gave way to Bowlegs and others, and his people proceeded to ally themselves with Spanish interests and strike American outposts. The result was one Payne might have predicted but probably could not have prevented.[16]

On Sunday, September 27, 1812, a war party heading east from Alachua for a conference with the Spaniards at St. Augustine met a detachment of Georgia militia headed west to attack them. The Seminoles won this engagement, forcing Colonel Daniel Newnan and his expedition to limp back to the St. Johns River. But the Seminoles, momentarily victorious, paid a heavy price. Payne lay mortally wounded. Within a few months a much larger American force drove into Alachua to seize the Seminoles' livestock, destroy their crops, and burn out their towns. The Seminoles would not be there to oppose them. Under the direction of Bowlegs, their war leader, they took refuge to the west near the Suwannee River. In the future they would only return to their old home territory of Alachua to hunt. Micanopy, successor to Payne and Bowlegs, would eventually settle his principal town somewhat to the south.[17]

The fate of Alachua underscores the difficulties that all native leaders faced in defending the lands and culture of their people in competition with the early American republic. In the ever changing, ever unstable Southeast, *no* set of policies and *no* economic or military ties guaranteed long-term security. For twenty-five years, Payne followed a fairly successful path of diplomacy that kept his people out of war with whites or other Indians. But his ability to remain neutral was predicated on two things: a close affiliation with a potential power—such as Spain—and a geographical buffer zone between his people and the military power of Georgia. These things collapsed with American military intervention in East Florida in 1812. The Seminoles of Alachua became the first people of that name to be *forced* into war with American frontiersmen intent on taking their territory. A struggle that began for them in 1812 would soon engulf all people called Seminole, leading to what we now know as the First, Second, and Third Seminole wars, and to a major reworking of Seminole self-identity during the nineteenth and twentieth centuries.

Notes

1. The most complete assessment of La Chua, its history, towns, and headmen, is Howard Francis Cline, "Notes on Colonial Indians and Communities in Florida, 1700–1821," *Florida Indians I* (New York: Garland, 1974). See also Howard Francis Cline, "Provisional Historical Gazetteer with Location Notes on Florida Colonial Communities," *Florida Indians II* (New York: Garland, 1974), and Charles H. Fairbanks, "Ethnohistorical Report on the Florida Indians," *Florida Indians III* (New York: Garland, 1974), esp. 127–36, 149–81, 213–14. The career of King Payne is traced in James F. Doster, *Creek Indians and Their Florida Lands, 1740–1823*, 2 vols. (New York: Garland, 1974). General background on the Seminoles of Alachua is covered in the opening chapter of J. Leitch Wright Jr., *Creeks and Seminoles* (Lincoln: University of Nebraska Press, 1986), 1–40, and more specifically by Gregory A. Waselkov and Kathryn E. Holland Braund, *William Bartram on the Southeastern Indians* (Lincoln: University of Nebraska Press, 1995), 49–72. See also James W. Covington, *The Seminoles of Florida* (Gainesville: University Press of Florida, 1993), 12–22; Brent Richards Weisman, *Like Beads on a String: A Culture History of the Seminole Indians in Northern Peninsular Florida* (Tuscaloosa: University of Alabama Press, 1989), 1–13, 59–81; Brent Richards Weisman, *Unconquered People: Florida's Seminole and Miccosukee Indians* (Gainesville: University Press of Florida, 1999), 13–15; Brent Richards Weisman, "Plantation System of the Florida Seminole Indians and Black Seminoles during the Colonial Era," in *Colonial Plantations and Economy in Florida* (Gainesville: University Press of Florida, 2000), 138–41. General and useful background on the era comes from Benjamin W. Griffith, *McIntosh and Weatherford, Creek Indian Leaders* (Tuscaloosa: University of Alabama Press, 1988); Frank Lawrence Owsley, *Struggle for the Gulf Borderlands: The Creek War and the Battle of New Orleans, 1812–1815* (Gainesville: University Press of Florida, 1981); Charles A. Weeks, *Paths to a Middle Ground: The Diplomacy of Natchez, Boukfouka, Nogales, and San Fernando de las Barrancas, 1791–1795* (Tuscaloosa: University of Alabama Press, 2005).

2. Cline, *Florida Indians I*, 78–87, dates the advent of the Alachua Seminoles between the Diego Peña expedition of 1716 and the arrival of the Oglethorpe expedition

in 1740; by that time, Cowkeeper was already established in La Chua and was offering assistance to the Georgians. In discussions with officials in Georgia, Cowkeeper seems to have defined his territory as La Chua and south rather than west. See also James W. Covington, *British Meet the Seminoles; Negotiations between British Authorities in East Florida and the Indians, 1763–1768* (Gainesville: University Press of Florida, 1961); Covington, *Seminoles,* 17–18; Wright, *Creeks and Seminoles,* 4; Weisman, *Unconquered,* 15–21; Fairbanks, *Florida Indians III,* 149. Cowkeeper's band was estimated at 450 people for the early 1760s; Payne was able to throw about 300 warriors in the field in 1812, suggesting a total population of close to 1,000 persons.

3. Waselkov and Braund, *William Bartram,* 57. On the deerskin trade, Kathryn E. Holland Braund, *Deerskins and Duffels: The Creek Indian Trade with Anglo-America, 1685–1815* (Lincoln: University of Nebraska Press, 1993), 62–63, 65: "The Latchoways and other East Florida villagers hunted all along the Florida peninsula, even as far south as the cape. During the long winter hunting season, Creek hunting parties could be found from Tampa Bay to the Cumberland River valley."

4. Covington, *Seminoles,* 29; Doster, *Creek Indians,* 1:50.

5. On the succession, see Covington, *Seminoles,* 17, 22; for an example of negotiating with Georgia, see Janice Borton Miller, *Juan Nepomuceno de Quesada, Governor of Spanish East Florida, 1790–1795* (Washington, D.C.: University Press of America, 1981), 103–7. La Chua was just one point in a widespread network of trade with St. Augustine. Indeed, in the 1780s, the newly reestablished Spanish government made every effort to disperse monthly gifts to a wide variety of Creek and Seminole towns in an attempt to win goodwill. These were purchased from Panton, Leslie & Co. at the expense of the Real Hacienda. Ships or supply caravans regularly left St. Augustine with foodstuffs, cloth, tools, guns, powder, rum, and other goods. Much of this traffic was destined for key towns located near the northwestern limits of East Florida, from Chiaha on the Flint River to Ocmulge and Eufala on the Chattahoochee, Tallassee on the Tallapoosa, and Miccosukee near Lake Miccosukee. Other towns frequently mentioned include Techitas, Palichocle, Natelaiga, Useechee, Laguna Grande, and Puebla Viejo. Not surprisingly, though, the towns of Cuscowilla and La Chua, only a few days' travel from St. Augustine, were regular recipients of gifts. In 1786, Chief Payne himself appears in the accounts of the Real Hacienda, first in an account of goods sent to La Chua and Old Town and then in conjunction with goods dispatched to La Chua and Miccosukee. Besides the expected shipments of guns, powder, and ball, Panton, Leslie & Co. regularly arranged for bread, rice, salt beef, salt pork, sugar, salt, and rum to go west. Accounts of Presents to the Indians, 1785–1788, East Florida Papers, hereinafter cited as EFP. For town names, see also Georgia Historical Society, *Letters,* 220, and Cline, "Provisional Historical Gazeteer," *Florida Indians II.* Payne communicated constantly with Spanish officials in St. Augustine but rarely appeared in any councils among the Lower Creeks. American contemporaries—such as the influential agent for Indian affairs, Benjamin Hawkins—rarely alluded to La Chua. Georgia Historical Society, *Letters.* See also Doster, *Creek Indians,* 1:52. The Indian agent James Seagrove, stationed at Colerain, never even met Payne prior to 1793. Payne took a more active

role in events to the west starting in 1800, and he sent a delegation of fourteen chiefs to the August 19, 1802, conference in Apalachee with Spanish officials. Cline, *Florida Indians II*, 109, 112. Although Doster argues throughout his work on the Creeks that all Seminoles in Florida were subject to the Confederacy and acknowledged its authority, both Cline and Fairbanks, in their research on the Seminoles, asserted that the Alachua Seminoles were an early breakaway group. Here is one of numerous statements to this effect by Fairbanks, *Florida Indians III*, 203: "The Alachua settlements were more separate from Lower Creek authority." On Zéspedes, see Helen Hornbeck Tanner, *Zéspedes in East Florida, 1784–1790* (Coral Gables: University of Miami Press, 1963), 93–102.

6. Alachua was a center of Spanish ranching in the late 1600s and continued to be excellent grazing land throughout the eighteenth century. Charles W. Arnade, *Cattle Raising in Spanish Florida, 1513–1763* (St. Augustine Historical Society, 1965), 5, 9–10; Weisman, *Unconquered*, 24; Waselkov and Braund, *William Bartram*, 53, 61–63. The Seminoles of Alachua were quick to enter ranching. William Bartram noted that Cowkeeper slaughtered prime steers for a feast at Cuscowilla; in contrast, a feast at Talahasochte on the Suwannee River featured bear and game. Both towns were noted for raising horses. Benjamin Hawkins also described Florida as fine rangeland in *A Sketch of the Creek Country* (New York: Kraus Reprint, 1971). Doster, *Creek Indians*, 1:191. Braund, *Deerskins and Duffels*, 76: "The Seminole leaders Ahaye (Cowkeeper) and Wolf thus differed from their Creek brethren in becoming major keepers of livestock." Beef-on-the-hoof was an especially important asset for the Seminoles of Alachua because they had no river access. Trade was over land. See Burke G. Vanderhill, "The Alachua Trail: A Reconstruction," *Florida Historical Quarterly* 55 (1977): 423–38, and "The Alachua–St. Marys Road," *Florida Historical Quarterly* 66 (1987): 50–67. Florida Cracker cattle, who moved in follow-the-leader formation, were fairly easy to drive. The purchase agents for cattle (typically free blacks or slaves who knew one or more native languages) were also trained cowpokes, so the responsibility for driving the cattle often became the responsibility of the buyer and his agent rather than the Seminoles. Most ranching families in Florida bought their breeding stock from the Seminoles. The family of Manuel de Solana, for example, owned nearly 1,600 head of cattle and purchased more annually from the Seminoles in order to replenish the herd. Cattle commanded a good price, bringing $6 to $7 a head if sold to middlemen and $12 to $15 a head at market. There was also no monopoly over cattle, which prevented a single entity, such as Panton, Leslie & Co., from controlling the terms for trade. Covington, *Seminoles*, 29–30; James G. Cusick, *The Other War of 1812: The Patriot War and the American Invasion of Spanish East Florida* (Gainesville: University Press of Florida, 2003), 195, 216–17; Susan R. Parker, "The Cattle Trade in East Florida, 1784–1821," in *Colonial Plantations and Economy in Florida*, ed. Jane G. Landers (Gainesville: University Press of Florida, 2000), 153–55, 158, 160–61; Weisman, *Beads*, 67.

7. Payne's earliest negotiations with Americans seem to date to 1793, when he accepted the invitation of Indian commissioner James Seagrove to a meeting in Colerain. Correspondence at this time emphasizes that Payne would take no responsibility for

the actions of Indians outside Alachua and that he intended to remove his people temporarily to Cape Florida if there were trouble. Payne to the Governor, 8 May 1793, EFP; Doster, *Creek Indians*, 1:147–50; Fairbanks, *Florida Indians III*, 202. Doster takes this as evidence that Payne considered himself under the jurisdiction of the Creek Confederation; in fact, it argues just as strongly that he was following Cowkeeper's policy of independent action. Again, in fending off Spanish requests for military assistance against Georgia in 1794 and 1795, Payne alluded to the official Confederacy policy of neutrality. But in refusing to engage in hostilities, he was following a course he had set in 1784 and would maintain until 1812. Governor to Payne, 21 January 1794, Payne to Governor, 31 January 1794, King Payne to Governor of Florida, July 1795, EFP; Doster, *The Creek Indians*, 1:169–71. Late in 1795, Philatouchie tried to involve the Creeks and Payne's people on the Spanish side; the trouble was over before this became necessary. Philatouchie to the Governor of Florida, 22 October 1795, EFP. In any case, Payne stayed out of the fight. Doster, *Creek Indians*, 1:180. Payne's actions to maintain peace in 1800 can be partially attributed to the fact that his territory lay immediately between Bowles's strongholds and the East Florida plantation district; any military action would devastate Alachua. John Forrester to the Governor, 17 June 1800, and Payne to the Governor, 29 July 1800, EFP. Forrester concluded, "I really think Payne desires some encouragement and a present for his services now and formerly, he has always proved himself a great friend of our Government and has always been very faithful." See also Doster, *Creek Indians*, 1:214–15. Payne did send a delegation of fourteen chiefs, and he may have attended a conference with Spanish officials in Apalachee on August 19, 1802. Cline, *Florida Indians II*, 109, 112. However, he does not appear to have attended either of the meetings pertaining to the deeds of cession for the Forbes Grant, one at Prospect Bluff on August 22 and the other at Pensacola on December 3. His name does not appear on the deeds. He first signed a deed pertaining to this cession of land in 1810. Doster, *Creek Indians*, 1:255–61, 2:11.

8. Doster, *Creek Indians*, 1:147–50; Junta de Guerra, 18 June 1807, "Proceedings of the Juntas de Guerra (Councils of War), 1790–1820, and Various Documents, 1771–1817," EFP. Henry White exhibited a frequent distrust and belligerence toward Payne. He was quick to blame Payne for hostilities caused by the Seminole of Miccosukee. In this particular junta, he admitted to his advisors that closing down trade with Alachua unfairly punished a group of Seminole who supported Spanish interests.

9. William S. Coker and Thomas D. Watson, *Indian Traders of the Southeastern Spanish Borderlands: Panton, Leslie and Company and John Forbes Company, 1783–1847* (Gainesville: University Press of Florida, 1986), 149–51; Covington, *Seminoles*, 22–24; Doster, *Creek Indians*, 1:86–87; J. Leitch Wright, *William Augustus Bowles, Director General of the Creek Nation* (Athens: University of Georgia Press, 1967), 139–69.

10. According to Cline, *Florida Indians I*, 101, Miccosukee was pro-Spanish between 1740 and 1770 when La Chua was pro-British. When La Chua moved into alliance with the Spaniards in the 1780s, Miccosukee moved into alliance with the British (via Bowles) and later the Americans. Hence these two groups of Seminoles seemed to have been habitually on opposite sides. This did not preclude an active commerce

between them, however. The Alachua Seminole used their access to St. Augustine and to trading posts on the St. Johns River to become middlemen in funneling goods west to Miccosukee. On Kinache, see Covington, *Seminoles*, 25: "Leader from 1770 to 1818 of the largest American Indian village in Florida, Kinache was possibly of mixed white and Native American ancestry." See also Wright, *Creeks and Seminoles*, 126–27. For evidence of Payne's visits to Miccosukee, see the following footnotes. Spanish records place him there in 1801, 1802, and 1803. On his stance vis-à-vis Kinache, he was certainly on the opposite side regarding Bowles, and he seems to have taken a neutral stance on the running of the new boundary line from the Treaty of San Lorenzo (1795). Kinache actively agitated against the survey team running the line. Doster, *Creek Indians*, 1:206.

11. Doster, *Creek Indians*, 1:221. Fatio Jr. was offended by the offer, apparently feeling that Payne should go himself and rectify matters. Major James Seagrove to John Kinnard, king of Hitchiti tribe, Creek Nation, 10 Sept. 1801, made 26 Sept. 1801; Francis Philip Fatio Jr. to his father, 2 Oct. 1801, made 3 Oct. 1801; and report of Francis Philip Fatio Jr. on this trip to Miccosukee, 12 Nov. 1801, EFP.

12. Report of Francis Philip Fatio Jr., 12 Nov. 1801, EFP. The absence of any warriors in his party was, within Creek tradition, an indication that his mission was peaceful.

13. Rogers C. Harlan, "A Military History of East Florida during the Governorship of Enrique White, 1796–1811" (master's thesis, Florida State University Tallahassee), 151; Payne to the Governor [Henry White], 22 May 1802, and Payne to the Governor, 5 June 1802, EFP, John Forrester to the Governor, 7 Sept. 1802, EFP; Doster, *Creek Indians*, 1:223–24. Payne was probably under some pressure to intervene with Kinache, as White was threatening to cut off trade with La Chua unless Payne cooperated.

14. As it happened, several Creek chiefs were already upset with the Seminoles of Miccosukee, seeing their alliance with William Augustus Bowles as a threat to the overall well-being of the Confederation. Doster, *Creek Indians*, 1:225–28.

15. The journey to the Flint came at an opportune time, close on the heels of a general Creek council with Benjamin Hawkins and other commissioners from the United States. The various Creek leaders had therefore been discussing Bowles at length. Doster, *Creek Indians*, 1:229–32; John Forrester to the Governor, 7 Sept. 1802, EFP. These incidents concerning the Fatio slaves and the Bonelli family indicate that Payne, as much as possible, sought to pursue a role as neutral middleman between the Spaniards on the one hand and Kinache and Bowles at Miccosukee on the other. He was, perhaps, playing a weak hand in this, mostly as an auxiliary to more powerful Creek headmen such as John Kinnard, but his involvement gained him the continued goodwill of the authorities in St. Augustine. "Payne and his people, who went with me," John Forrester noted in his report, "behaved extremely well." John Forrester to the Governor, 7 Sept. 1802, EFP; Governor to Jacobo Debrevil, 3 Oct. 1803, EFP. Later that same year, when Cuban fisherman killed a party of Indians at Tampa Bay, including Kinache's brother, Payne again interceded on behalf of Spanish interests.

16. Doster, *Creek Indians,* 2:49–52; Rembert Wallace Patrick, *Florida Fiasco: Rampant Rebels on the Georgia-Florida Border, 1810–1815* (Athens: University of Georgia Press, 1954), 185.

17. The episode with Newnan is covered in Patrick, *Fiasco,* 195–210, and it quickly found its way into standard texts such as Covington, *Seminoles,* 29–31, and Weisman, *Unconquered,* 24; see also Cusick, 240–43; Doster, *Creek Indians,* 2:52, 55–56. Wolf Warrior, in a talk recorded by Benjamin Hawkins, offers another contemporary observation that Alachua was far out on the Creek periphery and prone to isolation: "One thing has been against the Alachua people: they are 300 miles from our nation and could not conveniently get the talks of the Nation, and the young people have become headstrong and foolish." From the perspective of Wolf Warrior, Alachua's distance from the Creek heartland was not an advantage but the cause of its downfall. Doster, *Creek Indians,* 2:57. Other Creeks also seemed to regard the Alachua Seminoles as outcasts. They warned the Miccosukees not to go to their aid. Doster, *Creek Indians,* 2:52: "They are a great way from you" were the words from the Nation. "They have throwed themselves away and must abide by the consequences." In 1813, John Kinnard and Kinache did use their influence to broker a respite for Alachua from retaliations out of Georgia.

3

Epilogue to the War of 1812

The Monroe Administration, American Anglophobia, and the First Seminole War

WILLIAM S. BELKO

On a cold and wet morning in early March 1818, a sizeable contingent of U.S. regulars, militia, volunteers, and Creek warriors under the direct command of Major General Andrew Jackson departed Fort Scott in Georgia and crossed into Spanish Florida. The First Seminole War had commenced. Jackson's ample force worked its way down the Apalachicola River, with the objective of pursuing the hated Seminole Indians deep into the interior of East Florida. Over the next three months, Jackson's army destroyed several major Indian towns—burning homes and confiscating supplies and livestock, capturing men, women, and children of Indian and African background, executing several Indian leaders, and ultimately scattering the Seminole deeper into the peninsula of Florida. In the process of temporarily destroying Seminole resistance to U.S. expansion in the region, Jackson also seized several Spanish settlements and forts and captured and executed two British citizens—viewed by most Americans as the instigators of this Indian war. With the Spanish surrender of Pensacola, the capital of West Florida, and nearby Fort Barrancas, in late May 1818, Jackson returned to his home in Nashville, Tennessee, leaving behind an adequate force to occupy and protect the newly acquired posts in Florida—and ultimately handing over Spanish Florida to the Monroe administration. The First Seminole War had ended, barely three months after its commencement.

This seemingly brief episode in the volatile and fabled history of U.S. expansion was anything but an isolated incident. It proved more than a simple expedition outfitted solely to punish hostile Indians; it was as much, if not more, a campaign to purge the British from the Gulf South borderlands, an objective launched several years prior—it was, in short, an epilogue to the War of 1812. The fate of the Seminole in 1818, therefore, had as much, and in some cases more, to do with widespread American Anglophobia, with the intense fears of British influence and activity in Spanish Florida. Qualms about redcoats more than redskins spawned the First Seminole War. Seminole hostility certainly played a factor, but the apparent intervention of the British in such activities required far more immediate attention and response than mere Indian depredations on or near American territory. The specter of the British presence in North America—always a mantra of antebellum Americans—coupled with sensitive fears about national security in the Gulf Coast region continued unabated after 1815 and provided a powerful impetus for Americans to seize the Floridas. Removing this specter demanded more immediacy, more energy, than merely disciplining hostile Seminole, and to this the United States succeeded in 1818. In the end, however, it was the Spanish and the Seminole who paid the heavy price—the former simply lost an untenable territorial possession, whereas the latter lost their homes and an untold number of lives in a tragic story that unfolded for nearly a century after Jackson's 1818 invasion.

Certainly other factors caused the First Seminole War, and many were as pertinent as fears of British influence—precontact ethnic rivalry among the Muscogulge people (exacerbated by European contact), land hunger on the part of frontier Americans, border depredations between whites and Indians that resulted from this expansionistic tendency, inability of Spain to police its side of the border as stipulated by treaty, commercial expansion on the part of Americans seeking access to the river systems running from U.S. territory through Spanish territory to the Gulf of Mexico, concerns of slaveholders as their slaves sought refuge across an international border and received succor from the Seminole, rivalry over the cattle industry between whites and the Seminole, an extension of the Creek War (1813–14) as Red Stick Creek who had fled to Spanish Florida continued their resistance to the United States, and, of course, intense American Anglophobia. This essay focuses on the intense American Anglophobia and the consequent quest to secure U.S. national security in the Gulf Coast region, namely, in the Floridas. And what better way to demonstrate this than to focus on the perspectives, policies, and actions of the three powerful men who directly and indirectly represented the Monroe administration—President James Monroe, Secretary of State John Quincy Adams, and Major General Andrew Jackson. These three also played leading roles in the War of 1812—then Secretary of State James Monroe, then U.S. Minister to England John Quincy Adams, and Major General Andrew Jackson—thus setting the stage for their consistent viewpoints and behavior from 1815 to 1818. Through their eyes and in their actions, the First Seminole War emerges as an epilogue to the War of 1812.

Well before the outbreak of war between the United States and England in

1812, Americans along the Gulf South frontier continually suspected British designs in Spanish Florida. No matter what event or activity occurred south of the 31st parallel, the shadow of the British specter seemed always to be lurking. When "citizens" of Baton Rouge revolted against Spanish rule in 1810 and created their own state—the West Florida Republic—Americans along the border with Florida worried about potential British influence infecting that new "nation." Writing about the situation in this new West Florida Republic, the governor of the Mississippi Territory, David Holmes, informed the U.S. secretary of state that the "friends to a connexion with Great Britain are numerous intelligent and active, their endeavors to gain proselytes are unremitting and the arguments brought forward in support of their Opinions are of an impressive and operative Nature." Holmes feared the ability of the British "to afford the best Markets for the productions of the province and to promote in other respects the pecuniary Interests of the Inhabitants [which] are Urged as powerful inducements for forming a connexion with that nation." The territorial judge of Mississippi, Harry Toulmin, agreed and warned Americans not to interfere with events in the new republic as it could induce the inhabitants to gravitate toward a British orbit: "Should we encroach upon a neighbouring province without their sanction; the misguided adventurers would find no refuge from the necessary severity of our own government,— but in the protection of Great Britain:—and if this should be even granted; it would only be with a relinquishment of the fruits of a long & bloody revolutionary war. Instead of being Independent Americans,—they would become British colonists." Fortunately for the American cause of national security, the citizens of the West Florida Republic—all recent residents of the nation to the north—desired to enter the American union and not the British empire. To preclude British intervention, President Madison quickly annexed the new republic. (Of course, the United States already possessed title to this region according to the terms of the Louisiana Purchase, so that made taking possession relatively easy.) Thenceforward the citizens of the region looked to the United States to afford them with the best markets for their productions and to promote their pecuniary interests.[1]

The following year, the Madison administration again took action to thwart British intrigue in the remaining portion of Spanish Florida. In 1811, rumors reached the Madison administration that Great Britain claimed Spanish Florida. The president again quickly maneuvered to counter such unnerving reports. He sent to Congress documents that revealed official British intention to acquire some portion of Spanish Florida, and in a special message to Congress, the president stated in no uncertain terms that a British Florida must be prohibited. "I recommend to the consideration of Congress," appealed Madison, "the seasonableness of a declaration that the United States could not see without serious inquietude any part of a neighboring territory in which they have in different respects so deep and so just a concern pass from the hands of Spain into those of any other foreign power." Ironically, then, the "Monroe Doctrine" originated not with Monroe's enunciation in 1823 but with Madison's in 1810, with fears of British possession of Spanish Florida pressing the American nerve of national security.[2]

Congress listened, as it, too, shared the sentiment of its countrymen residing along the border with Spanish Florida. The Spanish empire in the Americas was crumbling, as Spain's colonies revolted from 1808 to 1821, one by one securing their independence. As a result, Spain's grip on Florida—the backwater of the Spanish empire—faltered. She was unable to maintain control of the Floridas, a fact obvious to the United States. In the name of national interest—of military and commercial security—Florida could never fall into the hands of any foreign power, namely, Great Britain. So, in January 1811, Congress confirmed the "Monroe Doctrine" expounded by Madison and enacted the "No-Transfer Resolution."

> Taking into view the peculiar position of Spain and her American provinces; and considering the influence which the destiny of the territory adjoining the southern boundary of the United States may have upon their security, tranquility, and commerce: Therefore, *Resolved, by the Senate and House of Representatives of the United States of America in Congress assembled,* that the United States, under the peculiar circumstances of the existing crisis, cannot without serious inquietude see any part of the said territory pass into the hands of any foreign Power; and that a due regard to their own safety compels them to provide under certain contingencies, for the temporary occupation of the said territory; they, at the same time, declare that the said territory shall, in their hands, remain subject to a future negotiation.

The phrase "under certain contingencies" obviously applied to a single contingency, and that was British intervention. Beyond any doubt, the entire resolution applied to Great Britain. Americans could hardly envision Spanish Florida and the U.S. borderlands without the haunting British presence. It underpinned all their actions, all their perspectives, all their policies about the nation's security in the Gulf Coast region—and the Indians in this country would pay the ultimate price for this chronic Anglophobia.

Prior to the War of 1812, James Monroe solidified his opinion that Spanish Florida must become American Florida and not Anglo-Florida. Long before assuming the presidency in 1817, Monroe had established a record for promoting the acquisition of Florida for reasons of U.S. national security. Great Britain figured directly into his arguments. Shortly after the conclusion of the treaty with France for the purchase of the Louisiana Territory, Monroe wrote Secretary of State Madison about the importance of acquiring the Floridas from Spain. He assumed that England would be indifferent or unopposed to U.S. acquisition of the Spanish territory, and, quite possibly, England would even wish such an event, as it would, in Monroe's estimation, weaken her enemies Spain and France and open new markets for her manufactures. "Should we not however acquire this territory of Spain at this period, there is danger of its falling into the hands of some other power hereafter; a circumstance which might give us much trouble, as it commands the mouths of several of our rivers, and gives a right to the navigation of the Mississippi." The acquisition of the Floridas, Monroe continued, "is an important object with our government." Monroe then departed immediately to Spain to pursue the purchase of the Floridas.

Monroe assumed that American acquisition of Spanish Florida would not face opposition from the British. After talking with Lord Hawkesbury, Monroe concluded that the British had no intention of interfering in the Floridas. "I do not think that G. Britain is desirous of adding to her possessions on the American Continent," he told Madison. "I am satisfied she will not attempt it at the expense of a collision with us."

The collision came nonetheless, and British activities, both real and perceived, in North America were a direct cause of that collision. The War of 1812 changed Monroe's mind, as British activities in Spanish Florida during the war merely intensified American fears of a British-owned Florida.[3]

The United States made several unsuccessful attempts to acquire the territory from Spain prior to the outbreak of war with Great Britain in 1812. Most of these were diplomatic overtures to purchase the territory outright or to acquire it to cover claims made against Spain. Some were military ventures, such as the West Florida Revolt in 1810 and the Patriot War of 1812. The former event resulted in U.S. acquisition of Florida territory from the Mississippi River to the Perdido River—but that was not a stretch for the Madison administration, as the Jeffersonians ardently believed that this territory had been included in the Louisiana Purchase. The remainder of Spanish Florida, they knew, was clearly Spanish title. What diplomacy could not achieve, military force might, and in 1812, the U.S. government essentially sanctioned the seizure of East Florida by U.S. troops. Tennessee volunteers also entered the fray by invading deep into the Alachua region of north central Florida. Here again, fears of British acquisition of Florida played a central part. Efforts to take Florida by force failed in 1812. But Spanish Florida continued to be a major battleground between the United States and Great Britain throughout the war, and in this struggle, Indians hostile to the United States played a leading role.[4]

Beyond any doubt, British activities in Florida during the War of 1812 served as the foundation for U.S. policy and actions regarding that Spanish territory and the Indians therein for the years up to the First Seminole War. Following Jackson's crushing defeat of the Red Stick Creek in the Creek War of 1813–14, the British intervened to rescue and rejuvenate the Red Stick that had fled to Florida. They armed, trained, and supplied them as allies in the war against the United States. Red Stick leaders Josiah Francis and Peter McQueen had intended to surrender to U.S. authorities before the British arrived with their full support, but, bolstered by British officers and marines, the renegade Creek and some of their Seminole allies turned from peace and toward war. Even Creek leaders allied with Jackson during the Creek War flirted with the British. Big Warrior, albeit always lukewarm in his support of the United States, would have led his friendly Creek to British lines if the redcoats had taken New Orleans and Mobile. British influence in Florida indeed spurred Indian hostilities against frontier Americans, thus greatly threatening national security in the Gulf region, and this the Americans could not and would not forget.[5]

For the war between the United States and Great Britain in the Southern theater, the opening salvo came in the summer of 1814 about sixty miles south of the U.S.-Florida border, at a site overlooking the Apalachicola River known as Prospect Bluff. The British trader William Hambly, working as an associate of John Forbes & Company, the successor firm to the famed Panton, Leslie & Company, had opened a store at the site in 1804. Prospect Bluff acquired a new importance during the War of 1812, however, when British Admiral Lord Cochrane ordered British Captain George Woodbine ashore to arm and train Indians and blacks in Florida for use as allies in the war against the United States. Within a very short time, British Lieutenant Colonel Edward Nicholls joined Woodbine. Nicholls assumed command of the activities at Prospect Bluff and prepared an army of Indians and blacks for an invasion of the Southern states. The British government had authorized Nicholls to recruit five thousand blacks from the South to form provincial regiments, which were to be bolstered by Southeastern Indians hostile to the United States, primarily Red Stick Creek and Seminole bands. The British constructed a massive fort at Prospect Bluff, built in the British grand style and essentially impregnable from attack by land or river. Sitting on a cliff on the eastern side of the Apalachicola River, the fort boasted an earthen parapet 120 feet in diameter, 15 feet high, and 18 feet thick, with a double row of logs serving as a palisade. A moat, 14 feet wide and 4 feet deep, surrounded the fort, with a swamp to its west, a large stream to its north, and a smaller stream to its south. British arms and munitions flowed into the fort. From here, Nicholls, with the aid of Woodbine, indeed armed and trained renegade Creek, who had already informed U.S. authorities that they fully intended to continue their fight against the Americans. The frontier would be aflame with Indian warfare, and frontiersmen knew fully who to blame—the British.[6]

Nicholls's next maneuver further outraged Americans in the South and West. In August 1814, the British officer beseeched the residents of the Louisiana Territory and the states of the Ohio Valley to unite under his standard and thus liberate themselves from their "faithless and imbecile Government." How little Nicholls understood the rabid patriotism of these American citizens and the bitter hatred they harbored for everything British. He even praised the Indians—a people frontiersmen detested as much as Britons. Nicholls also urged the infamous pirate Jean Lafitte to join his cause and make war against the United States.[7]

When Nicholls learned of more Red Stick refugees gathering at Pensacola, he accepted the unauthorized invitation of the Spanish governor to occupy Pensacola and protect it from a supposed American invasion. From Prospect Bluff, Nicholls and his force boarded Royal Navy vessels, sailed on, and occupied Pensacola in September 1814. Within days, nearly seven hundred Creek and Seminole warriors came to the aid of Nicholls and Woodbine, who gladly armed and trained them. Under cover of fire from the British navy, Nicholls sent one hundred British marines and three hundred Indian allies under the command of Woodbine against American Fort Bowyer at Mobile Point. Jackson had already occupied Mobile and repaired, supplied, and garrisoned Fort Bowyer. The British proved no match for the American defenders. Withering musket volleys and devastating cannonading from Fort Bowyer sent the British running, back to Pensacola, with over thirty dead and forty wounded. U.S. losses stood at four dead and five wounded. Wasting little time, General Jackson, now commanding a force of over 4,000 American troops composed of regulars, Tennessee militia, Mississippi dragoons, and Choctaw warriors, took the offensive. In early November, 1814, Old Hickory seized Pensacola. The British quickly withdrew, returning to their post at Prospect Bluff, preparing to fight another day. Jackson withdrew as well, marching to New Orleans, preparing to repulse a massive British invasion.[8]

If any figure epitomized the Anglophobic American residing in the South and the West, it was the very figure that pursued Nicholls into Florida—Andrew Jackson. His view of the situation regarding the British threat, Indian hostilities, and Florida reflected the typical American viewpoint of the day—and this perspective remained consistent from 1813 to 1818. Indeed, Jackson's objective of suppressing Indian warfare by eliminating the native's British instigators who roamed freely in Spanish Florida defined his military actions during the Creek War in 1813, the campaign along the Gulf Coast in 1814 and early 1815, and the First Seminole War in 1818. U.S. national security demanded the removal of British influence among the Indians and for all of Florida to come under the Stars and Stripes. Of all the individuals that dominated the scene from 1813 to 1818, Jackson alone secured these objectives which many Americans in the South and the West and in Washington pursued.

During the summer of 1814, following his crushing defeat of the Red Stick Creek, General Jackson received regular intelligence of a massive British force collecting in Florida, arming blacks and Indians, and preparing for an attack on Mobile and New Orleans, which, if successful, would allow the British and their Indian allies to ravage the Southern and Western frontier, from the Mississippi to the St. Johns. There was no need for the Spanish governor of West Florida, when he alerted Jackson to the British activities there, to mention that this army existed solely for the "manifest design of enabling the Creeks to renew a sanguinary war against the United States." Jackson and most Americans knew this fact since the days of the Revolution, and 1814 was no different. "The British are using every art to draw them [Indians] to their standard," Jackson declared, and to the governor of West Florida he labeled the Indians hostile to the United States as "murderous rebellious Banditti who have not only embrued [*sic*] their hands in the innocent blood of our helpless women and children, but raised the exterminating Hatchet against their own nation, who had been excited to these horrid deeds of butchery by an open enemy great Britain." The epicenter of this British invasion? The very seat of the Spanish governor of West Florida, Pensacola. Little wonder, then, that Jackson made this strategic Spanish settlement his ultimate project in 1813, in 1814, and in 1818, and argued consistently for its seizure in the years between. Many Americans in the South and the West and in Washington agreed with the Old Hero. Little wonder, then, that he emerged as the most popular man in America during these years.[9]

Jackson notified Secretary of State Monroe in the fall of 1814 that "I have been induced to determine to drive the British and Indian force from that place [Pensacola], possess myself of [Fort] Barrancas, (which I expect to find occupied by the former) and all other points that may be calculated to prevent a British fleet from entering Pensacola Bay. This will put an end to the Indian war in the South, as it will cut off all foreign influence." The sole purpose for capturing Pensacola, therefore, was to "give security to this section and put down an Indian war." To his wife, Rachel, he surmised that "by driving the British from the shores & harbor [*sic*]," it would convince the Indians "that there was no safety in British protection."

After pursuing the British from Mobile to Pensacola and seizing the Spanish settlement following the British retreat, Jackson again wrote to Monroe:

> I flatter myself that I have left such an impression on the mind of the Governor of Pensacola, that he will respect the American character, and hereafter prevent his neutrality from being infringed. Should he suffer the British again to occupy his Town, and the Indians to return, this district [Mobile] cannot be protected, unless they are (as you have expressed in your letter of the 7th. Septr.) promptly expelled. . . . I need not again mention to you the geographical situation of that place [Pensacola], the goodness of the harbour, and the ease with which our enemy can thence attack any point on the coast, either in the 6th. or 7th. Military Districts; and keep up their constant intrigue with the Indians.

National security thus necessitated the expulsion of British influence from the Gulf Coast. It was the only way to suppress Indian hostilities in that volatile region. After making these assertions to U.S. officials in Washington, Jackson departed the Spanish settlement, turned westward, and hastened to New Orleans, where he orchestrated the valiant defense of the Crescent City in the winter of 1814–15. Within a short time, he would return to Pensacola and for the exact reasons he had done so in 1814. Americans in the South and West loved him for it, and regardless of what some scholars argue, the Monroe administration condoned it as much as the Madison administration had acquiesced in it.[10]

Despite ordering Jackson not to attack Pensacola in 1814, for Monroe the British occupation of that settlement changed the situation. He told Old Hickory that if he had already taken the town by receipt of his order, the general should withdraw his troops immediately from Spanish territory, but when doing so to declare "that you had entered it for the sole purpose of freeing it from British violation." Seizing a Spanish Pensacola was obviously very different than seizing a British one. Still, the U.S. acquisition of Spanish Florida in order to prevent it from becoming a British Florida was a primary objective of U.S. policymakers. During the early years of the war with England, Monroe, then serving in the cabinet of President Madison, continued his arguments on behalf of U.S. acquisition of Florida on the basis of national security. In May 1813, Monroe had received indirect word, based on "respectable sources," that Spain had sold the Floridas to the British government, and "that it had done so under a belief that we had or should get possession of it." Monroe argued that if the United States acquired the Floridas, it would facilitate substantially U.S. negotiations with the British over the sensitive issues that fueled war between the two nations. If the United States would "push our fortunes in that direction"—Spanish Florida—it would send a message to British negotiators that the U.S. government refused to yield on any issue concerning American expansion into its borderlands. The United States would not, however, retain Pensacola in 1814, but Monroe and Jackson nonetheless continued to pursue American ownership of that place, which in their eyes would end the threat of British intrigues and Indian wars and thus guarantee national security along the Gulf Coast—together, they would succeed in 1818. Nicholls and his successors in Florida, meanwhile, did everything in their power to stimulate Monroe and Jackson's cherished goal.[11]

Ample precedent for intense Anglophobia existed following the ratification of the Treaty of Ghent in February 1815, and British activities in Spanish Florida throughout that year merely intensified this preoccupation with the British in the Gulf Coast region to a near rabid status for Americans in the South and in the West, as well as for many in Washington. A menacing British military presence remained just south of the U.S. border, and that military presence openly promoted Indian resistance to the United States, ultimately provoking a continuation of the Indian wars that had commenced in 1813. Nicholls employed all his energy in a concerted effort to realize such an end, and British officials seemed to support it. After hearing of the Treaty of Ghent, Admiral Cochrane ordered Nicholls to remain at Prospect Bluff with a contingent of British troops. The British strengthened the fort and continued to supply, arm, and train the more than one thousand Creek warriors and the steadily growing number of blacks fleeing bondage north of the 31st parallel. All the while, Nicholls promised the Indians that King George would protect them, and the Indians counted on such protection.[12]

British justification for remaining at Prospect Bluff centered on one article of the Treaty of Ghent, Article IX, which stipulated that all Indian allies of Britain still at war with the United States at the time of the signing of the treaty would have their lands restored to 1811 status. The United States, however, interpreted this article differently than the British. U.S. officials, Jackson primarily, insisted that the 1814 Treaty of Fort Jackson preceded the signing of the Treaty of Ghent, and thus the Creek were not at war with the United States and thus exempted from Article IX. No Creek lands would be returned. British authorities obviously cried foul and protested loudly. As for Nicholls, he immediately drafted a formal treaty with the Florida Indians hostile to the United States. According to the terms of this treaty, Great Britain would recognize the Indians in Florida as an independent nation and as allies of King

George and continue to supply them with arms and goods; in turn, the Indians would cut any and all ties with the United States and Spain. In the summer of 1815, Nicholls persuaded Josiah Francis, one of the Indian leaders Americans loved to hate, to accompany him to England in order to campaign on behalf of the alliance proposed by Nicholls. American officials watched warily as these events unfolded.[13]

But Nicholls did not stop there. He established a pseudo-protectorate over the Florida Indians and initiated a very antagonistic and threatening correspondence with the powerful and well-connected U.S. Indian agent to the southeastern tribes, Benjamin Hawkins. Throughout the spring of 1815, the British colonel unleashed a barrage of statements that merely reinforced the American belief that all the Indian troubles originated with British intrigues in Spanish Florida. Nicholls informed Hawkins that any efforts to survey the Treaty of Fort Jackson line would be met with Indian violence, that captured slaves had been sent to British colonies and there freed, that Article IX of the Treaty of Ghent was binding on the United States and that it would be enforced (signed by a number of Creek and Seminole leaders), and that he had advised the natives to take defensive measures against Americans by putting to death anyone who molested them. To ensure such violence, Nicholls supplied the Indians with the requisite arms and ammunition. Of course, Hawkins ably responded. He considered Nicholls's activities in Florida to be a violation of the treaty of peace between their two nations and warned Nicholls that the United States would never tolerate British machinations along its borders, especially when it produced Indian hostilities. The correspondence between Hawkins and Nicholls also infuriated Georgians, those most vulnerable to hostilities along the border with Florida, and those most willing to commence hostilities along that imaginary line. British interference into matters that should be left to the United States and Spain inflamed Georgian Anglophobia most of all.[14]

Further evidence of Nicholls's influence over the Creek and Seminole arrived in Washington during the late spring of 1815. General Edmund Pendleton Gaines informed the secretary of war about the British in Florida supplying the Indians there in the months following the ratification of the Treaty of Ghent. To support his charges, Gaines included a sworn deposition of a British marine sergeant recently stationed at Prospect Bluff. The deposition, which U.S. authorities obviously believed, included all the damning activities that both frightened and angered Americans:

> [T]hat the English colonel (Nicholls) had promised the hostile Indians at that place a supply of arms and ammunition, a large quantity of which had been delivered to them a few days before his departure, and after the news of a peace between England and the United States being confirmed

had reached Apalachicola; that, among the articles delivered, were, of cannon, four 12 pounders, one howitzer, and two cohorts; about three thousand stand of small arms, and near three thousand barrels of powder and ball; that the British left with the Indians between three and four hundred negroes, taken from the United States, principally Louisiana; that the arms and ammunition were for the use of the Indians and negroes, for the purposes, as it was understood, of war with the United States; that the Indians were assured by the British commander that, according to the treaty of Ghent, all the lands ceded by the Creeks, in treaty with General Jackson, were to be restored; otherwise, the Indians must fight for those lands, and that the British would in short time assist them.[15]

Fortunately for Americans along the Gulf South borderlands, the British government had had enough of Nicholls's activities in Florida. In the summer of 1815, British authorities refused to endorse Nicholls's treaty (and few even knew of the treaty), ordered his departure from Florida, and refused to receive any of his letters concerning Indian affairs. They likewise sent Francis back to Florida with nothing but a hollow commission in the British army and a fancy red uniform to accompany it. The British government informed the Royal Navy not to bring any more Indians to England, and the Prince Regent let the hostile natives know that peace with the United States was their wisest option. Both the War Office and the Foreign Office surrendered to the U.S. position on Article IX of the Treaty of Ghent. Yet, all that Americans could see was what Nicholls had wrought in Florida—a formidable fort containing a well-armed and supplied contingent bent on resisting by force any American advance, and a bitter Red Stick refugee with a fancy red uniform and a commission in the British army. Americans also concentrated not on the official British disavowal of Nicholls's activities but on the charges levied against the U.S. government by Admiral Cochrane and Lord Bathurst, secretary of war for the colonies, charging that the United States had violated the Treaty of Ghent by enforcing the Treaty of Fort Jackson and that Great Britain should come to the defense of the Indians. As a result, by the end of 1815, the first full year of peace between the United States and England in quite some time, the connection between the British and the Indians in Florida still existed for most in the South and the West and in the White House and in Congress. This intense Anglophobia was kept alive by the specter of a British-controlled Florida just over the horizon.[16]

Yet, even after Nicholls's departure from Florida, U.S. policymakers still felt the pangs of his activities. Both Monroe and Adams quizzed British officials about Nicholls's real intent in the "southern part of the United States" and whether the British government sanctioned his "proceedings." The U.S. government was "peculiarly interested" in the events in Florida "because they appeared to be marked with unequivocal and extraordinary marks of hostility." Adams attested that the southern Indians, both in the United States and in Florida, "still threatened hostilities." But these hostile Indians "would certainly be disposed to tranquility and peace" with the United States, unless they "should have encouragement to rely upon the support of Great Britain." British officials informed Monroe and Adams that the British government expressed "unequivocal marks of displeasure" toward Nicholls, that they would not countenance his proposed treaty with the Florida Indians, that any Indians brought to England by Nicholls would be sent back to America, and that the Indians there would be advised to make terms with the United States. Most Americans remained unconvinced of British assurances of nonintervention.[17]

One reason for American skepticism was that rumors and charges of hostile British influence continued to circulate throughout American and Spanish circles during the year following the ratification of the Treaty of Ghent, even after Nicholls had departed the scene. Folks living near Florida reported "Indian allies of His Britannic Majesty" destroying cattle, stealing horses, and absconding with American slaves (April 1815) and that the British were erecting a fort near the forks of the Flint River and another on the Apalachicola, with a "number of British landed there" (December 1815). Spanish citizens also complained as late as February 1816 of certain British officers in Florida. Most damning, however, was the fact that Francis had returned to Florida in 1816 and, invigorated by winks of British sympathy for his cause, soon inspired the renegade Creek and the Seminole to take up the tomahawk against the United States. Such reports undoubtedly drifted into the hands of high-ranking U.S. officials, simply more evidence of what most Americans already believed—the British in Florida intended to continue Indian hostilities against the U.S. Gulf borderlands.[18]

That Americans indeed found it difficult to shake off British intervention in Florida during the War of 1812 and in the several months thereafter became evident in postwar negotiations with Spain over the potential transfer of Florida to the United States. Secretary of State Monroe continually mentioned to the Spanish minister to the United States, Don Luis Onis, the fact that British troops and agents "had been introduced" into Florida during the war and that they maintained active communication with and support of Indians hostile to the United States. Adams, too, evoked British activities in Florida in his correspondence with the Spanish minister. Spain, he charged, had breached its neutrality in the war between the United States and Great Britain by permitting, even possibly authorizing, British troops and British agents to operate freely in Florida, arming and inciting Indians, all "to the great injury of the United States." No American official negotiating with Spanish authorities over the future ownership of Florida could let this issue die. They reminded Spain of it every chance they had.[19]

But more damning than the presence of British troops and a potential Indian alliance with Great Britain were reports circulating in high places in the United States that Spain harbored other plans for Florida, plans that excluded any peaceable transfer of the territory to the itchy neighbor to the north. The intentions of the Spanish government, therefore, may have been more menacing for U.S. national security in the Gulf Coast region than Nicholls and Woodbine, but such intentions proved so threatening precisely because they included the British. In the months following the War of 1812, U.S. authorities received word that Spain intended to cede the Floridas to Great Britain. The Spanish government desired British mediation in resolving the widespread revolt of Spain's American colonies, and as payment for such services, Spain was willing to allow the Union Jack to wave permanently over Florida. Another consideration predominated as well—Spain's hold on Florida was quite tenuous, to say the least, and some other power would certainly take possession in the very near future. The United States had already started whittling away portions of Florida, from the Mississippi to the Perdido, and had invaded Florida on several occasions and with considerable ease. Spain could do nothing to halt this process, but England could. Spain obviously preferred an English Florida over an American Florida, as this would establish "a barrier against the encroachments of the United States." Under this plan, England would also guarantee to Spain "Louisiana and the Island of New Orleans," possessions already owned and guarded jealously by the United States. England rejected the overture, however, as such a proposal "must necessarily occasion a war between the United States and Spain." Regardless of the failure of Spain's design to hand Florida to England, even the talk of such a scheme alarmed Americans, and U.S. officials grilled Spanish and British authorities about the proposal.[20]

In late 1815, months after the ratification of the Treaty of Ghent, Monroe raised the issue with Adams. Reports continued to arrive in Washington that Spain had indeed ceded the Floridas and Louisiana to the British. Rumors even indicated that Great Britain had outfitted an extensive expedition to the Gulf Coast region. "Ten thousand men it is said," Monroe recounted, "are likely to be sent from Great Britain and Ireland and it has been intimated that some foreign troops will be taken into British pay and employed in the expedition." So large a body of men sent a single message to American officials: Britain meant to take Florida and to do so by force. If the British government accepted the cession of Florida, or Louisiana, or both, the U.S. government clearly could not let such a perilous event occur, as it obviously jeopardized U.S. national security in the South and West. Monroe comprehended best the full extent of a British invasion of the Gulf Coast:

> As well might the British Government send an army to Philadelphia or to Charlestown as to New Orleans, or to any portion of Louisiana westward of the Perdido, knowing as it does the just title of the Unites States to that limit. To send a considerable force to East-Florida even should the British Government state that it had accepted the cession of that province only, could not be viewed in a friendly light. Why send a large force there if Spain has ceded and is ready to surrender the Province unless the British Government has objects in view, unjust in their nature, the pursuit of which must of necessity produce the war with the United States? East-Florida in itself is comparatively nothing but as a post in the hands of Great Britain it is of the highest importance. Commanding the Gulph of Mexico and all its waters including the Mississippi with its branches and the streams emptying into the Mobile, a vast proportion of the most fertile and productive parts of this Union, on which the navigation and commerce so essentially depend, would be subject to its annoyance, not to mention its influence on the Creeks and other neighboring Indians.[21]

When negotiations between Onis and Adams broke down in early 1816, Monroe could not help but blame Great Britain. He informed Adams that a "strong suspicion is entertained here by many that the Spanish government relies on the support of the British, if it is not instigated by it." The secretary of state, likewise, could not help but think that Onis's equivocation in negotiating with the United States over possession of Florida merely veiled an intention to transfer ownership of Florida to Great Britain. Indeed, any negotiations (or the failure thereof) with Spain over Florida entailed for most Americans a threatening British influence.[22]

Such "strong and confidant intimations" received by U.S. officials of a cession of Florida by Spain to Great Britain, Adams informed Lord Castlereagh, justified the vociferous U.S. reaction to Nicholl's activities in Florida, namely his proposed treaty with the Indians there. The two could not be a coincidence, so Adams continued to pepper the British ministry. He remarked to the British minister that the U.S. government thought "that with dominions so extensive and various" as the British empire, Great Britain "could not wish for such an acquisition of Florida, unless for purposes unfriendly to the United States, and hence it was that these rumors had given concern to the American government." Despite ardently denying any cession of Florida, even going so far as to declare that British journals suggesting such a transfer were "addicted to *lying*," Castlereagh admonished Adams that the United States should likewise observe the same moderation when it came to Florida. "If we shall find you hereafter pursuing a system of encroachment upon your neighbors," he warned, "what we might do *defensively* is another consideration." Such a response could not have pacified Adams and Monroe. Although Adams eventually accepted the British disavowal of a Florida cession, reports of such continued to arrive in Washington, further undermining negotiations between Spain and the United States and continuing the rampant Anglophobia along the Gulf Coast region and in the nation's capital.[23]

Many Americans believed that the pursuit of Florida by either the United States or Great Britain would eventually result in war with either Spain or its ally Great Britain, or both. Adams, for example, suggested that war with Great Britain was indeed more than a possibility. A few months after the ratification of the Treaty of Ghent, he opined to his father that "we must not flatter ourselves with the belief that the restoration of peace by compact with Great Britain has restored either to her government or people pacific sentiments toward us." During his negotiations with British officials over the Convention of 1815, Adams commented to Monroe about the hostile posture of the British government: "So many simultaneous acts of British officers at various stations and upon both elements, indicating a marked spirit of hostility, were calculated to inspire serious doubts with regard to the pacific, not to say the amicable dispositions of the British." Although he assumed that the British government would never sanction any act of open hostility, it was still evident from his discussions "that the animosities of the condition from which the two nations had lately emerged had very little subsided."

War with Britain, most Americans believed, could recommence at any time and for just about any reason—the most accepted *casus belli* being Florida. Even a full year after Jackson's drubbing of British forces south of New Orleans, Adams stated to Monroe that should the United States and Spain go to war over Florida, "we may take it for granted that all the propensities of the British Government will be against us. Those of the Nation will be so, perhaps in equal degree; for we must not disguise to ourselves that the national feeling against the United States is more strong and more universal than it ever has been," and in a bout of Anglophobia inherent to Americans of the day, Adams finished by saying that "there is no Nation with which a War would be so popular as America." Any discussion of every "question of difference" between the United States and Spain, Adams concluded, must necessarily include Great Britain, and, as such, U.S. policymakers "must always take it for granted that the British feeling and policy will be against us." Few Americans disagreed with him. Even the Anglophile Daniel Webster could see the potential for hostilities continuing between the United States and Great Britain over the ownership of Florida: "The closest connexion exists of course between England & Spain. There is reason to apprehend, therefore, that some arrangement has been made between them, ceding Florida to England;—if so the quarrel about the division line between West Florida & Louisiana will probably be a serious obstacle to peace." For that matter, even Spanish officials warned of some form of an alliance with Great Britain. Onis and the captain general of Cuba, Juan Ruiz Apodaca, both argued that an Anglo-Spanish alliance would infuriate the United States, resulting in war.[24]

Ironically, one of the avenues facilitating negotiations between the United States and Spain over Florida included Great Britain. The British government actually offered to mediate. The invitation proved tempting for the Monroe administration, but, in the end, no one in the Executive Mansion in his right mind would accept such an offer. The president and his cabinet feared the reaction of the American public more than the British, and declined the goodwill gesture summarily, as it would certainly inflame public opinion in the United States. Even the slightest hint that the British were involved in the negotiations would cause "ill will and irritation" in Americans and "awaken jealousy and revive animosity against the mediating power." In his "Memorandum on the British Offer to Mediate between the United States and Spain," Adams surmised that the American people "would be still more aggravated, if in the course of such a mediation, any concession should be suggested or recommend to the United States to which they would not readily agree by the means of a direct negotiation with Spain alone. That the public opinion would in that case attribute the concession to the interference of the third power, and the strong censure which would fall upon the American government for having asked the interposition of any third power, would be mingled with irritation against Great Britain, who would be represented as influenced by motives unfriendly to the United States." Spanish officials also knew the Americans would never allow British mediation, but they hoped that if the British would press the issue, it could intensify the animosity between the United States and Great Britain and thus potentially benefit Spain. Anglophobia frequently influenced diplomacy between the United States and Spain over Florida.[25]

The United States whittled away at and violated the sovereignty of Spanish Florida during the Madison years—the annexation of the Republic of West Florida in 1810 (completed with the military seizure of Mobile in 1813), the Patriot invasion of 1812, Jackson's brief occupation of Pensacola in 1814. This pattern of occupying or violating Florida territory every two years revealed a preoccupation on the part of U.S. policymakers with national security in the Gulf South borderlands. If the pattern held, then the year 1816 would see another step taken. Such an act indeed occurred: another invasion, another violation of Spanish Florida—the reduction of Negro Fort.

After the British had fled their well-built and well-armed fort at Prospect Bluff in the summer of 1815, they left the post in the hands of another entity as intolerable and as feared by Americans as redcoats—runaway slaves. By 1816, fugitive black farmsteads surrounded the fort, extending for miles along the Apalachicola. Approximately 350 men, women, and children occupied the fort, under the leadership of the free black Garcon. About fifteen hostile Choctaw and their chief joined the well-fortified contingent. Now widely known throughout the United States as Negro Fort, this bastion was situated along a key navigable waterway, commanding transportation and communication routes into Georgia and the Mississippi Territory, and it was within close range of the Southern slave states, fueling fears of potential slave rebellions.

The U.S. government adamantly demanded that Spain eliminate the fort, but when Spanish authorities—who also desired the elimination of the fort— admitted they were too weak to do so, Jackson ordered Gaines to reduce it. In July 1816, a small contingent of U.S. infantry, more numerous allied Creek warriors, and a few U.S. naval gunboats arrived on the scene and asked to parley. Negro Fort's commander responded that he would sink any vessel on the river flying the Stars and Stripes. He then defiantly raised the Union Jack and the red flag of no surrender above his ramparts. This combination of rebellious former property of U.S. citizens, hostile Indians bent on killing U.S. citizens, and the flag of the British Empire made the next step quite easy. The besieging force was only too delighted to honor the fort's red flag of no surrender.

One of the U.S. gunboats succeeded in blowing the fort sky high with a single hot shot directed toward the fort's powder magazine. Few survived. Burning and blackened bodies covered the entire area, dangling from treetops, strewn in the river, and mixed with debris of all kind. Indian survivors (and Garcon himself) faced vengeful Creek tomahawks, and any hostile Indians within earshot of the explosion wisely fled. Raising the Union Jack proved no isolated act of defiance, however, as the fort's residents still believed in the promises made to them by Nicholls the previous year. The Americans who sent the force to destroy the former British bastion and those sent to do the dirty work also believed that King George would honor the promises of Nicholls. Yet, in the end, the destruction of Negro Fort demonstrated that, even with British arms, the Florida Indians and their black allies were no match for the United States.

British aid to the Seminole proved illusory in 1816, but no matter, as the

United States would not tolerate any British influence—real or perceived—along its Southern border. Events during the following year confirmed for many Americans that the British threat remained in Spanish Florida. The two-year pattern of entering Spanish Florida thus required American action in 1818, so the year 1817 had to be filled with episodes of British intrigue and Indian hostility that scared the Anglophobes north of the 31st parallel.[26]

With the arrival of 1817, U.S. interest in Spanish Florida obviously had not abated in the slightest. In order to stave off potential British acquisition of Florida, the United States stepped up its diplomatic efforts with Spain to acquire the territory via purchase. Spain, however, proved reluctant to release its title. The longer the negotiations dragged on, the greater the American fear of British intervention. Spain maintained a tenuous grip on Florida. It could not control the Indians on its side of the border as required in the 1795 Pinckney Treaty, and it lacked the manpower and the munitions to repulse an invasion.

Florida was ripe for the taking, and a number of adventurers indeed succeeded in 1817, in East Florida, at Amelia Island—Gregor MacGregor in the summer and Luis-Michel Aury in the fall. Both adventurers received extensive financial support from American citizens and even the unofficial consent of the newly inaugurated Monroe administration. American veterans of the War of 1812 eagerly joined the ranks, and both MacGregor and Aury depended on the expertise and leadership of two well-connected American businessmen. Both ventures eventually failed, however, and for a number of reasons, and neither of the men ever succeeded in taking their ultimate objective—St. Augustine, the capital of East Florida. To the consternation of the Monroe administration, Amelia Island quickly emerged as a haven for pirates, smugglers, and armed black troops—all considered threats to national security.

These events in East Florida only heightened American anxiety along the southern border and continued the resolve to acquire the Floridas. Those in Washington likewise felt the angst. "If we don't come to an early conclusion of the Florida negotiations," Secretary of State Adams admonished Spanish Minister Onis, "Spain won't have the possession of Florida to give us." That was in January 1818. Movements in the United States were already underway to prove the accuracy of Adams's prediction, and a combination of episodes in 1817 in both East and West Florida—and involving British intrigue and Indian incitement—ensured that the two-year pattern of taking action in Florida would remain intact.[27]

Before Jackson's 1818 invasion of Spanish Florida, evidence of British machinations among Florida Indians hostile to the United States merely fed the American perception that their old nemesis was still up to no good along the

American frontier. Although Woodbine had departed Florida in early 1817, American authorities and pro-American traders at the scene could not have been too sanguine, as prior to his departure, Woodbine had summoned Kinache, leader of the formidable Mikasuki, to Tampa Bay for one last meeting. Kinache complied, and Woodbine left him one last promise of British aid: Colonel Nicholls would return, and he would do so sometime in February of that year.

Within the first week of February, the governor of Georgia wasted little time in reporting the rumored return of Woodbine and the shadow of British influence among the hostile Florida Indians. "You, no doubt, have already been informed that the notorious Woodbine has recently made his appearance again at the mouth of the Apalachicola," he reported to the commanding officer along the Florida border, Brigadier General Edmund Pendleton Gaines, "and that he has an agent now among the Seminole Indians and negroes in that quarter, stirring them to acts of hostility against this country; and that Woodbine himself has gone, in an armed vessel, to some part of the West Indies for supplies . . . which may serve as an intimation of the future conduct of these people, when once in the possession of the supplies which it is said they expect on the return of Woodbine." Additional intelligence arrived in Washington about supposed British intrigues in Florida. U.S. Indian Agent David Mitchell informed the secretary of war a month later that he had received information "that a British agent is now among these hostile Indians, and that he has been sending insolent messages to the friendly Indians and white men settled above the Spanish line." Although he believed this Briton most likely an adventurer rather than an official representative from Great Britain, this agent, continued Mitchell, was nonetheless "charged with stimulating the Indians to their present hostile aspect." Mitchell also warned General Gaines of renewed British influence south of the border. Gaines informed the War Department that British operatives were again up to no good in Florida. The general warned U.S. authorities of a British agent in Florida giving the Indians powder, lead, tomahawks, knives, and a drum for each town—all with the "royal coat of arms" painted on them.[28]

Gaines and Mitchell were only half correct. According to U.S. authorities, *two* notorious British agents operated in Florida throughout 1817, inciting Indians to hostility against American citizens along the Florida frontier. The first was the aged Scots trader, Alexander Arbuthnot. The Scotsman had been trading with the Creek and Seminole from the Bahamas, but soon moved to Florida in order to replace traders of the Forbes Company who Arbuthnot believed had joined the Americans and thus betrayed the Indians' best interests. Arbuthnot's activities in Florida greatly worried U.S. officials, as the

British trader quickly took over the role once played by Nicholls. Arbuthnot corresponded regularly with British officials, from the British governor of the Bahamas to the British minister in Washington, and even to "a person of rank in England" and to that hated British officer himself, Colonel Nicholls. The content of such letters was consistent and clear. Arbuthnot requested that the British government take official steps to protect the interests of the Florida Indians. He pleaded for supplies, arms, and ammunition. He asked that an official British agent be assigned directly to the Indians. Most damning for U.S. officials, however, was Arbuthnot's ardent efforts to enforce Article IX of the Treaty of Ghent and thus see Creek lands taken by Jackson in 1814 returned. As proof that the Scotsman was stirring the Florida Indians to violence, U.S. authorities pointed to the fact that the Red Stick Creek and the Seminole had officially recognized Arbuthnot as their agent authorized to represent them in their concerted effort to receive aid and protection from the British government. The Indians even gave him power of attorney, signed by twelve Creek and Seminole chiefs, several of whom were most wanted fugitives in the United States.[29]

Of course officials in the United States were quite aware of Arbuthnot's behavior. Arbuthnot sent letters to them as well, to Gaines, to Mitchell, and to William Hambly, now a Florida trader attached to the American interest. The Scotsman declared that the Florida Indians hostile to the United States had appointed him their official representative, that Great Britain was "the especial protectors of the Indian nations," and that the English government disagreed with the U.S. contention that the Red Stick and their Seminole allies in Florida were outlaws. This merely intensified Anglophobic sentiment throughout the South and the West and in Washington. As early as March 1817, Arbuthnot informed General Gaines that the British government would not tolerate American intrusion into Creek and Seminole lands, even into lands taken in the 1814 Treaty of Fort Jackson, territory entirely within U.S. boundaries. If the American government refused to return such lands, or if they made further encroachments, then the chiefs "have only to represent their complaints and the aggressions of the Americans to the Governor of New providence, who will forward them to England, or get them conveyed to the British minister at Washington, who has orders from the King of England to see that the rights of the nations above mentioned are protected, and the stipulations contained in the treaty [of Ghent], *in their favor*, are faithfully carried into execution." Imagine the import of such words when they reached the ears of Jackson and other high-ranking officials in the U.S. government.[30]

The U.S. government obviously considered Arbuthnot public enemy number one. But another British agent and former military officer, Robert Christie Ambrister, stood a very close second to the Scotsman. Ambrister had been recruited in the West Indies by Woodbine and sent to Florida with a contingent of black troops to aid in MacGregor's efforts to seize Florida from the Spanish. The redcoat officer, like Arbuthnot, regularly requested of British officials arms, ammunition, and supplies for Indian resistance to Americans along the Florida border. His correspondence, like Arbuthnot's, reached British officials and included missives to Nicholls. If any figure fueled Indian defiance in Florida, it was Ambrister, not Arbuthnot. Although Arbuthnot and Ambrister were not working cooperatively, and Arbuthnot even detested Ambrister, U.S. officials saw them as two peas in a pod. Arbuthnot and Ambrister had simply replaced Nicholls and Woodbine. Nothing had changed in Spanish Florida from the War of 1812 to the eve of the First Seminole War. The British presence seemingly lurked as dangerously as ever.[31]

For U.S. officials, the activities of Arbuthnot and Ambrister in Florida and among Indians hostile to the United States may have been more tolerable if not for the increased depredations committed by both whites and Indians along the Florida border. Instances of Indian atrocities filled Georgia newspapers during 1817. The notorious and brutal murder of Mrs. Garrett and her two young children infuriated Americans, prodding them to take vengeance upon any Indian anywhere in the vicinity of the Florida line. Reports continued of Indian attacks on American settlers, and horse and cattle theft was a common complaint. Florida Indians, of course, protested loudly against similar activities perpetrated by American citizens. Little wonder, then, that the Creek and Seminole in Florida regularly sought British intervention. As a delegation of Lower Creek beseeched the British governor of the Bahamas, "without the interference of the English, we shall soon be driven from the land we inherited from our forefathers." Indeed, Americans (namely Georgians) committed far more acts of violence than the Indians in Florida. Indian victims of American aggression definitely stood on the defensive and desired to avoid any confrontation with aggressive American frontiersmen. Of course, the United States took the opposite view. General Gaines blamed Kinache's Mikasuki for the murdering, the pillaging, and the thieving. He admonished the Seminole leader to deliver up the guilty and to refrain from further hostility toward American citizens, or else punishment would be swift and certain. Gaines also warned Kinache about Seminole carousing with the real enemy on the scene, the real instigator of violence along the Florida border, and the real reason why the United States would discipline the errant: "But there is something out in the sea—a bird with a forked tongue—whip him back before he lands, for he will be the ruin of you yet. Perhaps you do not understand who or what I mean—I mean the name of Englishman." For U.S. officers on the scene, Indian hostilities originated directly from British aid and influence.[32]

Indian resistance to U.S. expansion continued, and the violence finally escalated into a confrontation. In November 1817, at the village of Fowltown, situated across the Flint River in the vicinity of Fort Scott just north of the Georgia-Florida line, the first official action of the First Seminole War unfolded. The town's chief, Neamathla, warned General Gaines that American troops were not to enter his land for any reason. Gaines considered the land in question as part of the territory ceded to the United States in the 1814 Treaty of Fort Jackson. Neamathla vehemently disagreed. Conflict came on November 21, after the Mikasuki chief refused to attend a conference called by Gaines. Gaines then dispatched Major David Twiggs, with 250 troops, to bring in Neamathla. The Mikasuki fired on the advancing troops but, heavily outnumbered, quickly fled, and the Americans entered the town. Two days later, a larger force, led by Lieutenant Colonel Mathew Arbuckle, returned to seize Neamathla. Arbuckle's force was again fired on by about sixty warriors hidden in a nearby swamp. Again, the Indians fled. Unsuccessful in finding Neamathla, U.S. troops burned the village and the surrounding fields.

In the immediate aftermath of the Fowltown attack, U.S. troops found in the house of Neamathla a British uniform coat, complete with gold epaulettes, and a certificate by a captain of the British marines on behalf of Colonel Nicholls, stating that the chief had always been a true and faithful friend of the British. Additional intelligence provided by Creek allies trickled in to Gaines's tent as well. The hostile Indians in Florida, they apprised him, "have been promised . . . assistance from the British at New Providence [Bahamas]," and that this promise "is relied on by most of the Seminole Indians." In words echoing his commanding officer back in Nashville, Gaines confidently presumed that as soon as the Seminole discovered that "their hopes of British aid to be without foundation," they would quickly sue for peace.[33]

For the Indians of Fowltown, a state of war existed, commenced by the United States, and they took their revenge nearly two weeks later. After the events at Fowltown, the Apalachicola River became a treacherous avenue for Americans, as vengeful Indians roamed the river's banks awaiting the unfortunate white soul that came ashore or ran aground. In order to supply Fort Scott, provisions had to be shipped from New Orleans and Mobile via the Gulf of Mexico and thence up the Apalachicola River. After learning that the supply convoy had reached the mouth of the Apalachicola, General Gaines dispatched Lieutenant Richard W. Scott and forty men downriver to inform the convoy's commander, Major Peter Muhlenburg, that the river's depth would allow safe passage to Fort Scott. Scott reached the convoy several days prior to the U.S. attack on Fowltown. A week after this affair, Muhlenburg ordered Scott back up the Apalachicola, in advance of the supply convoy. Scott was warned of a hostile party of Indians converging just south of Fort Scott and determined to attack any boats ascending the river. To make matters worse for Scott, Muhlenburg kept twenty of the lieutenant's healthy men and switched them for twenty of the major's sick; seven women also accompanied Scott's ill-fated party upriver. Scott's vessel stayed to the middle of the river, for safety's sake, but about a mile south of the conjunction of the Flint and Chattahoochee, a sharp bend and a swift current in the river forced Scott's party too close to the shore. Indians ambushed them. The first volley downed Scott and most of the soldiers. The attackers then rushed the boat to complete their grisly task, using the tomahawk and scalping knife instead of the musket. Two soldiers, who fell overboard at the initial volley, survived, swimming to safety and then to Fort Scott to report the fate of their unfortunate comrades. Indians butchered six of the women and took one as a prisoner.

In the aftermath of the Scott massacre, Gaines addressed the chiefs of Indians south of the Florida border and west of the Apalachicola, who remained, as of yet, neutral in the affair, or leaning at least toward helping the United States discipline the hostile Seminole. He said but little, but deemed it necessary "to endeavor to counteract the erroneous impressions by which they have been misled by pretended British agents." The greatest Briton- and Indian-slayer in American history, General Andrew Jackson, was already en route to the Spanish line to render justice, Gaines informed them. Beware of the siren that lured the Seminole. The hostile parties in Florida, Gaines concluded to the chiefs, "pretend to calculate upon help from the British! They may as well look for soldiers from the moon to help them. Their warriors were beaten, and driven from our country by American troops. The English are not able to help themselves: how, then, should they help the old 'Red Sticks,' whom they have ruined by pretended friendship?" Indeed, for most Americans along the Gulf South borderlands, talk of hostile Creek and Seminole accompanied reference to British influence and intrigue; they could rarely be separated. By the end of 1817, therefore, blood flowed freely between white and red along the Florida border. Georgia and the Alabama Territory screamed for federal aid. Jackson, back in Nashville, screamed with them. For the Old Hero, the solution was obvious: to suppress Indian warfare in the Gulf South region, the United States must eliminate British succor and seize Florida.[34]

Gaines adamantly supported an invasion of Florida. "The laws of nature," Gaines wrote Jackson, "sanction such a measure of self-preservation." Ironically, Gaines wrote this phrase not in 1817 or 1818, but in 1815, when he supported a U.S. seizure of Pensacola. He reiterated the same phrase in December 1817. The dire situation along the Florida border necessitated an invasion "when self defence is sanctioned by the privilege of self preservation."

Jackson and other U.S. officials had used such language before. In July 1814, for example, Secretary of War John Armstrong wrote to Jackson, informing the commanding officer of U.S. forces fighting in the South that if the Spanish in Florida aided or cooperated with the British and hostile Indians in any manner, the United States would retaliate "on the broad principle of self-preservation." By the time the letter arrived at Jackson's headquarters, the general had already seized the Spanish capital of West Florida, Pensacola. Four years later, Jackson arrived in Pensacola for the second time, taking the Spanish capital on the grounds that it had aided and abetted hostile Indians in their attacks across the Florida border. Jackson informed the Spanish governor, Jose Masot, that his reasons for invading Spanish Florida in March 1818—the First Seminole War—were "justifiable on the immutable principles of self-defence."

This very phraseology pervades Old Hickory's public and private correspondence during his 1818 invasion and in the months thereafter. President Monroe used this same language on a number of occasions when referring to the First Seminole War. The United States possessed the right to pursue the enemy into Florida on the "principle of self-defense . . . this great and sacred right of self-defense," he told Congress in March 1818, shortly after ordering Jackson to enter that territory. Secretary of State Adams likewise argued that the situation unfolding in Florida impelled the United States to take action "from the necessities of self-defence." In all of these instances—1814 and 1818—and to all of these men, "self-preservation" had clear meaning—it meant U.S. national security. The greatest threat to that security emanated from one source more than a combination of any others—Great Britain. Obviously the British had posed a grave threat to Americans well before the War of 1812 and the First Seminole War, and in most instances, American Anglophobia was well justified. How little things changed from Jackson's first invasion of Spanish Florida to his second one.

Continued evidence of British intrigue substantiated in the minds of many postwar Americans the need to seize Florida in the name of national security, of self-preservation, of self-defense. Similar events along U.S. borderlands had fueled Southerners and Westerners to war in 1812; such events would inflame them again in 1817 and propel them into war in 1818. The Monroe administration listened in 1818 as had its predecessor, the Madison administration, in 1812.[35]

While hostilities along the Florida border intensified during 1817 and into early 1818, the Monroe administration faced continued rumors of a Spanish transfer of Florida to Britain. In the fall of 1816, for example, Thomas Sydney Jesup, the commanding officer of U.S. troops stationed in New Orleans, apprised both Jackson and Monroe that he had received information from a person in the confidence of the Spanish consul in New Orleans that "a secret negociation is going on between the Courts of Madrid and London for the purpose of transferring to Great Britain the Floridas and the Island of Cuba, for which it is understood, she is to assist in reducing to Subjection the revolted Colonies of Spain." The gravity of such an event did not escape Jesup. "Should Great Britain obtain Cuba, she will give law to all Western America, and in the event of war with the United States, her first blow will be at New Orleans, and if she obtain possession, she will never relinquish it, for as she will be able to obtain supplies by Sea, she may render it impregnable."

The Spanish foreign minister had indeed proposed a transfer of Florida to Great Britain in the summer of 1817, in a memorandum to the Spanish Council, and when rumors that U.S. negotiations with Spain had once again broken down, in January 1818, Americans believed that Florida had indeed been ceded away to their archenemy. With the War of 1812 still fresh in their minds, such continued evidence of British intrigues greatly influenced Monroe's cabinet. The combination of Indian depredations and the attack on Scott's party, British agents operating freely in Florida, and evidence that Florida could fall into the hands of Great Britain proved too much for the Monroe administration. On the eve of the new year, 1818, the lesson for many Americans remained unchanged; it was identical to what they had learned in 1812 and, for that matter, as far back as to the days of the Revolution. The southern frontier would remain aflame if the other red menace was not removed entirely. Redcoats again incited redskins, and something had to be done. Enter Andrew Jackson, Monroe's agent.[36]

Jackson maintained a clear and consistent course regarding Florida after 1815. He had conceived his plan for remedying the whole matter as he departed Nashville to crush the Red Stick Creek in 1813: move through Alabama territory, annihilate the Red Stick, and seize Pensacola, the source of all Indian hostilities along the Gulf Coast region. Jackson saw the whole Creek War as nothing short of British intrigue, and he was far from alone in this sentiment. Most Americans, namely those in the South and West and those directly affected by the Red Stick uprising, believed the British ultimately pulled the strings of the Red Stick and the Seminole. Captured documents found among the Red Stick convinced Americans that the British were the instigators of

Indian warfare. Indeed, preventing foreign influence among the Indians in the South was one of the reasons for the massive cession of Creek lands in the 1814 Treaty of Fort Jackson. Old Hickory saw in the events of 1817 the same thing he had since the War of 1812, and he proposed the same remedy. Throughout the last weeks of December and into the first months of 1818, Jackson beseeched Monroe to take action, to strike the wolf in his den. Destroy British succor, Jackson argued, and the Creek—and all other Indian resistance in the South— would end. To do that, Florida must come into American hands. His solution was simple: seize Florida before more Indians killed more settlers, and more settlers killed more Indians, and the territory itself ended up in British hands while the United States did nothing. By seizing Florida, he told Monroe, "it puts all opposition down, secures our Citizens a compleat indemnity, and saves us from a war with Great Britain, or some of the Continental Powers combined with Spain." Negotiations proved unsuccessful; other, more direct means became necessary.

Jackson's 1814 correspondence differed little, if at all, from that of 1817 and 1818. But then why should it? The situation had not changed from 1813, when Jackson commenced his project, to 1818, when Jackson completed it. And all the while, Monroe and Adams were part and parcel to this project. Florida was finally to be invaded (again). The British demon must be exorcised and the Seminole disciplined for their devotion to this evil spirit, and the only man capable of pulling it off without a hitch—Andrew Jackson—was ordered to the scene to see it done. In March 1818, Jackson led U.S. forces into Spanish Florida. The First Seminole War had commenced. The two-year pattern remained intact.[37]

U.S. troops serving under Jackson during the First Seminole War shared a common sentiment that the British were the real instigators of Indian hostilities. Captain Hugh Young, Jackson's topographical engineer, commented in his official report that "spirited on by G. Britain," the Florida Indians "had carried on for years a system of depredation and cruel outrage on our southern border." Jackson's aide-de-camp, Captain Richard Call, spoke of the "Seminole war, that waged so relentlessly between the United States and the Indians of Florida, aided and abetted in the first instance by Spaniards and Englishmen." One of the regulars entered into his diary that Arbuthnot had been "busy in stirring up the savages" and that Ambrister was in his employ. Indeed, Jackson and his entourage desired the heads of Britons Arbuthnot and Ambrister as much as they did the heads of the fugitive Red Sticks Francis and McQueen. Within two months after the invasion of Spanish Florida, they would have the heads of three of the four.[38]

Evidence of British collusion could not escape Jackson's eye in his campaign through Florida. He could not see an instance in which his longtime nemesis did not have some role of instigation. He was there to chastise Seminole, but he was also there to remove the source of Indian hostilities—British operatives. During the 1818 U.S. invasion of Spanish Florida, Jackson employed William Hambly and Edmund Doyle, agents of the John Forbes Company and longtime residents of Florida who knew of the affairs in that quarter. Just prior to Jackson's campaign, the two men had been seized by the Seminole, sentenced to death by Arbuthnot, but eventually released to the Spanish at Fort St. Marks. When U.S. troops seized the Spanish post in April 1818—taken because "foreign agents, who have been long practicing their intrigues and villainies in this country, had free access into the fort"—Hambly and Doyle spilled everything they knew to Captain Isaac McKeever, commanding the small flotilla of U.S. naval vessels in the bay. The Indians expected supplies from England "to enable them to undertake a war with the frontier settlements of Georgia," and that if McKeever would yank the Stars and Stripes and raise the Union Jack, he would see the truth of their intelligence.

The ruse worked. As soon as McKeever hoisted the Union Jack, a canoe carrying several Indians approached the vessel, unaware of its true national origin. American seamen netted quite a catch, Josiah Francis and Homothelimico, two of the most wanted Indians who had escaped death or capture during the Creek War, two of the leading instigators of Seminole depredations along the American border with Florida, two signatories to Arbuthnot's power of attorney. They were brought onshore where Jackson had them summarily executed—hanged from the very yardarm of the vessel that captured them, an example to all Indians who sought protection from the British.[39]

Another prize of war awaited U.S. troops at Fort St. Marks: Alexander Arbuthnot. Here was the man behind it all. Here was the active defender of hostile Florida Indians. Here was the man who railed against the Treaty of Fort Jackson and enticed Indians to resist it by force, the man who actively sought British arms, munitions, and supplies in order to equip Indians in their defiance against the United States and to serve as faithful allies when King George returned, the collaborator of Nicholls, Woodbine, and Ambrister, the competitor of the pro-American trading firm of Forbes & Company, the facilitator of the capture of Hambly and Doyle and the one responsible for trying and sentencing them to torture by the few survivors of Negro Fort.

Ambrister's capture followed in April, in the wake of Jackson's attack on Bowlegs Town on the Suwannee River. The British agent and his aide wandered into Bowlegs Town after nightfall, assuming the fires were those of the

friendly Seminole and their blacks, finding instead the fires were those of occupying American troops and their friendly Creek allies. When taken to Jackson, who questioned them extensively, Ambrister "replied in the tone of con-
scious innocence . . . stating his connection with Arbuthnot as his clerk," and
that he was there only with the purpose of supplying the Indians with trade
goods and ammunition for hunting purposes. Jackson as coolly replied that if
Ambrister's statement proved correct, then he had nothing to fear. "But if as I
have heard," Jackson sternly admonished his British captive, "you are engaged
in keeping alive the hostility of the Indians to the United States, and inciting
them with the negroes to commit depredations upon the frontier, I can give
you no hope." Hope indeed failed to save both Ambrister and Arbuthnot.[40]

Now with the two most wanted Britons in all of North America in irons and
their Indian pawns beaten and driven deeper into the wilds of Florida, Jackson
proceeded to punish his captives for their crimes against America. "I owe to
Britain a debt of retaliatory Vengeance," Old Hickory had once promised his
wife. "Should our forces meet I trust I shall pay the debt." He had made that
promise in August 1814, and he carried it out in Pensacola in 1814, at New
Orleans in 1815, and now he would do so again, at the now American Fort St.
Marks, in 1818. In April 1818 a special court, composed of American officers
with Gaines presiding, assembled at Fort St. Marks to investigate the charges
against Arbuthnot and Ambrister. The court charged Arbuthnot with enticing
the Creek to war against the United States, acting as a spy, supplying enemies
of the United States, and encouraging the Indians to murder William Hambly
and Edmund Doyle. It charged Ambrister with aiding, abetting, and comfort-
ing enemies of the United States, namely, providing military intelligence to
the Seminole and their black allies and leading Lower Creek into battle against
Americans. The most damning evidence brought against the two Britons came
not from the men testifying against them but from the documents found on
the two men when captured. Here was all the proof needed of British collusion
with Indians hostile to the United States, laid out for the whole world to see,
and what damning evidence it proved to be—Arbuthnot calling the English
government the "special protectors of the Indian nations, and on whom they
rely for assistance"; Arbuthnot's numerous requests for official British intervention on behalf of the Florida Indians and his official appointment as their
representative to England; Ambrister's calls for arms, ammunition, and supplies to fight the Americans; Ambrister's desire to see the return of Nicholls
to Florida; Ambrister sending out warriors to fight the invading American
army.[41]

The one document that certainly sealed Arbuthnot's fate was a memorandum on the back of a letter to the British minister in Washington, which listed

3.1. Trial of Ambrister (Florida State Library and Archives).

Seminole manpower arrayed against the American invaders and a substantial quantity of arms, ammunition, powder, knives, tomahawks, and other supplies needed for conducting effective warfare. It remains unclear whether this was a list of what the Seminole already possessed or a wish list presented to British officials on behalf of the Seminole. But for the American court, it obviously meant the latter. Ample evidence of regular Creek and Seminole requests for such aid from the British government provided the justification for reading the list as such. "To the English we have always looked up as friends, as protectors," petitioned the Red Stick faction in Florida, "and on them we now call to aid us in repelling the approaches of the Americans." Success in resistance required "the interference of the English."

One of the most prominent Seminole leaders fighting the United States stated in a letter to the governor of the Bahamas everything that American officials had adamantly believed for years—the dangerous existence of an unswerving alliance between the British and Indians hostile to the United States. "Our sinews of war are almost spent," Boleck informed the British governor, "and harassed as we have been for years, we have not been able to lay by the means for our extraordinary wants; and to whom can we look up to for protection and support, but to those friends who have at all former times held forth their hands to uphold us, and who have sworn in their late treaty with the Americans to see our just rights and privileges respected and protected from insult and aggression."

Both recent history and the promises of Arbuthnot and Ambrister convinced the Seminole that such support and protection was coming. The Florida Indians called King George their "good father," and reminded British authorities of promises also made to Francis by those in the British government that whenever the Indians needed ammunition, it would be supplied in order "to enable us to protect our just rights." How could rabid Anglophobes interpret the evidence before them in any other light? The succession of years and events in Florida from the War of 1812 to the First Seminole War, from 1813 to 1818, convinced the Americans that the British specter haunted the U.S. borderlands.[42]

The court found Arbuthnot guilty of two charges and sentenced him to death. He was hanged from the yardarm of his own vessel, which had been captured earlier by U.S. troops at the mouth of the Suwannee River. As for Ambrister, the court found him guilty on all charges, but after sentencing him to death, they considered his plea for mercy and changed the penalty to a number of lashes and hard labor. The court then forwarded its decision to Jackson, who was already returning to Fort Gadsden. When Jackson learned of the court's change of penalty regarding Ambrister's sentence, he chose to enforce the previous sentence of death. Ambrister, stunned by the turn of events, nobly accepted his death. He was executed by firing squad on April 29. Both Arbuthnot and Ambrister were placed in unmarked graves, just as their Indian allies, Francis and Homothelemico, had been after their execution. Jackson had achieved his vengeance, and Americans loved him for it.

For Jackson, the invasion of 1818 was a complete success. The objectives for entering Spanish Florida had been realized. He had caught the two most wanted Britons in all of North America, public enemies one and two, labeled by Old Hickory as the true ringleaders of the Indian wars in the South, the "foreign agents" that roamed Spanish Florida freely, the "exciters of this savage and negro war," undermining U.S. national security in the Gulf Coast region. Jackson consistently called Arbuthnot "the instigator of this war" and Ambrister as "successor to Woodbine." Spanish posts in Florida had become "the hot beds" from where "Woodbine's British Partizans" and "British agents," supported by the Spanish officers, "excited the Indians to massacre & plunder" and "to enrich their own coffers by purchasing the plundered property at a reduced price." He even blamed the "British agents," rather than Spain, for the "negro establishments on the Apalachicola and St. Juan rivers." The "immutable laws of self-defence," Jackson consistently exclaimed, thus "compelled the American Government" to take possession of Florida. In so doing, U.S. forces "divided and scattered" the Seminole, and thus "cut [them] off from all communication with those unprincipled agents of foreign nations who have deluded them to their ruin."[43]

But had these two British agents acted alone? Jackson believed not. The evidence collected for the trial of Arbuthnot and Ambrister obviously pointed to the two men as "instigators of this savage war," but it likewise, "in some measure," involved "the British Government in the agency." Jackson informed the secretary of war that, on the commencement of his operations in early 1818, "I was strongly impressed with the belief that this Indian war had been excited by some unprincipled foreign or private agents." He believed that the renegade Red Stick and the Seminole had neither the manpower nor the will to fight the United States, and therefore he was "firmly convinced" that "succor had been promised from some quarter," and this he had to ascertain.

Following the trial of Arbuthnot and Ambrister, Jackson believed he had the answer. The British government "is involved in the agency." "If Arbuthnot and Ambrister are not convicted as the authorized agents of Great Britain," he told Calhoun, "there is no room to doubt but that Government had a knowledge of their assumed character, and was well advised of the measures which they had adopted to excite the negroes and Indians in East Florida to war against the United States. I hope the execution of these two unprincipled villains will prove an awful example to the world, and convince the Government of Great Britain as well as her subjects, that certain, though slow retribution awaits those unchristian wretches who, by false promises, delude and excite an Indian tribe to all the horrid deeds of savage war"—spoken like a true Anglophobe in the years following the War of 1812, and, again, Americans in the South and West loved him for it.[44]

But how would the British government and her subjects react to the public execution of two of its citizens? For that matter, just what was the official British position regarding its relations with the United States and with the Indians in Florida after 1815? How justified was American Anglophobia in the years following the War of 1812 and leading up to the First Seminole War? While the American perception of British policy remained relatively unchanged from 1815 until 1818, the official British policy toward the United States changed substantially after the War of 1812. The British government's negative reaction to Nicholls's machinations in Florida in 1815 hinted at the change in attitude toward the United States. Conciliation marked official British policy after 1815; peace and appeasement regarding the United States prevailed. As a result, official British postwar policy, under the direction of Castlereagh, precluded any involvement in the Floridas. Did the British government desire to see Spain retain possession of Florida, thus keeping it out of American hands? Certainly. Would the British government undertake policies after 1815 actively to attain such a desired end? Certainly not. In no way would the British government jeopardize its amicable and profitable relationship with the United States in order to keep Florida from falling into American hands—an event British officials saw as inevitable after 1815. Neither would the British government sacrifice its new relationship simply to defend Indians against U.S. expansion—a fate British officials knew full well after 1815.

A number of instances testify to the changes in British postwar policy. The British government's response to Nicholls's activities in the summer of 1815 has already been stated, but other examples of British conciliation and cooperation prove more convincing. A commercial convention in 1815 helped address some of the disagreements that led to war in 1812, establishing a healthy precedent for a series of successive conventions over the next decade. The Rush-Bagot Agreement in 1817 demilitarized the Great Lakes, resulting in what would evolve into the longest, most peaceful border in the world, and precluding an arms race that could erupt into another Anglo-American war along the Canadian front. But one of the best examples of the change in official British attitude came in the wake of the First Seminole War, after Jackson had tried and executed two of its citizens. Not a single protest emanated from the British government when it learned of the death of Arbuthnot and Ambrister. Not a peep. The British government even went so far as to avoid asking for Arbuthnot's belongings. Yes, the British public screamed bloody murder and demanded reprisal. But when the U.S. minister to England showed Castlereagh the court proceedings and other evidence about the activities of the two Britons in Florida, the foreign minister quickly dismissed it without even saying a word. "This leaves me to infer, for the present," the U.S. minister to England informed the U.S. secretary of state, "that no exception is taken by this court to any of them. The names of Arbuthnot and Ambrister were only glanced at, and that incidentally." In fact, the British government proceeded to endorse, in October 1818, one of the most important Anglo-American accords to date, the Convention of 1818, which established the 49th parallel as the border between U.S. territory and British Canada west of the Great Lakes and to the Oregon territory. As for Oregon, they decided that people of both nations could settle there unmolested by either of the two powers. Greater peace, not war, resulted in 1818, and this after the execution of two British citizens in Spanish Florida.[45]

But for those Americans living along the border with Spanish Florida—from the Mississippi River to the Atlantic Ocean—the threat of British intervention and influence could not have been more real. Despite the official stance of the British government not to interfere in the affairs of Spanish Florida and to leave the Florida Indians to their fate, many in the United States still applied

3.2. Jackson in the First Seminole War (John Frost, *Pictorial Life of Andrew Jackson*, 1847).

ulterior motives to the British government. A half century of mistrust had developed between the two powers, and they had engaged in two general wars within that time. The British government may have disavowed the activities of its citizens in Florida, but Americans saw this as only smoke and mirrors for a more dastardly covert British policy to check American expansion, both territorial and commercial. American suspicions—more times justified than not—of British designs could not be suppressed easily, if at all, and American policy—both official and unofficial—reflected this fact. The Creek War and the First Seminole War were both, at the root, conflicts ultimately to counter British intrigues in the Gulf South borderlands. It did not matter to Americans whether these British intrigues were real or perceived, for they could not distinguish reality from perception. The Seminole and the Creek paid the price for this American failure.

In the weeks following the end of the First Seminole War, Monroe feared that, instead of eliminating the British presence—whether official or unofficial—in Florida, Jackson's actions could actually heighten such activity. He wrote to Jackson in July 1818, suggesting that if the United States retained the Spanish posts and settlements that he seized, then Spain would in all probability declare war. In such a scenario, Monroe surmised, "the adventurers of Britain" would hide behind the Spanish flag and plunder American commerce. Other leading republicans agreed with Monroe. Calhoun surmised that a war with Spain alone "would be nothing," but such a war "would not continue long without involving other parties, and it certainly would, in a few years, be an English war." Albert Gallatin, too, believed that the "most dangerous consequence [of Jackson's invasion] would be the use which England may make of this event to regain her influence over Spain." Indeed, the potential reaction of Great Britain, more than that of Spain, preoccupied American officials in the wake of the First Seminole War.[46]

Yet, by the end of 1818, the leading spokesman for the official U.S. policy regarding the recent events in Florida was not the aged Virginia planter from Ash Lawn, nor was it the warrior general from Nashville. Rather, it was the erudite statesman from Braintree. In his official correspondence, Secretary of State Adams stated at length, and in a considerably more refined and succinct manner, the arguments expounded by most Americans throughout the South and the West and in Washington. He focused on the long train of incidents that resulted in the First Seminole War, and he began with the events of the summer of 1814, when British forces under the command of Nicholls and Woodbine used Florida to invade the United States. Such an episode could be excused during a general state of war, but when hostilities terminated, Nicholls remained with his "parti-colored forces in military array." The British officer refused to let the peace between Great Britain and the United States halt his "military occupations" and his "negotiations with the Indians against the United States." Nicholls had recruited hostile Red Stick and Seminole, persuaded them that they were entitled to all the Creek lands taken in the 1814 Treaty of Jackson, promised them the support of the British government in retrieving their lands, drafted a treaty of alliance with the Indians in Florida, and even "embarked for England with several of the wretched savages."

Adams then recalled the events at Negro Fort, pointing to the fact that the bastion was "blown up with an English flag still flying as its standard." Next came the most recent unforgiveable manifestations of British hostility against the United States. Adams branded Arbuthnot as the "successor of Colonel

Nicholls in the employment of instigating the Seminole and outlawed Red Stick Indians to hostilities against the United States," the "firebrand by whose touch this negro-Indian war against our borders had been re-kindled," and the "mover and fomenter of the war" that without his interference "never would have happened." As for Ambrister, he was simply the "agent of Woodbine, and the subaltern of MacGregor," who had delivered arms and ammunition to hostile Indians and actually led them in war against U.S. troops. Indeed, Adams concluded, "the connection between Arbuthnot and Nicholls, and between Ambrister, Woodbine, and MacGregor, is established beyond all question" by the evidence presented at the court-martial. Their "principal purpose" was to act as the agents of Indians hostile to Americans, to obtain the support of the British government, and thus to commence their "murderous incursions" against the United States. The cause which they espoused "was the savage, servile, exterminating war against the United States." Adams finished his "exposition of the origin, the causes, and the character of the war with the Seminole Indians and part of the Creeks" by declaring that the various Indian wars since 1815 were simply a legacy of the war started by Nicholls, which then passed to his heirs, Woodbine, Arbuthnot, and Ambrister—an uninterrupted conflict in which Great Britain itself shared the blame.

> It is thus only that the barbarities of the Indians can be successfully encountered. It is thus only that the worse than Indian barbarities of European impostors, pretending authority from their governments, but always disavowed, can be punished and arrested. Great Britain yet engages the alliance and cooperation of savages in war; but her government has invariably disclaimed all countenance or authorization to her subjects to instigate them against us in time of peace. Yet, it so happened, that, from the period of our established independence to this day, *all* the Indian wars with which we have been afflicted have been distinctly traceable to the instigation of English traders or agents. Always disavowed, yet always felt; more than once detected, but never before punished.

In this official letter alone, Adams had indeed coalesced all the arguments for going into Florida in 1818. He most ably had put into a single document what all other Anglophobes had been thinking and saying since the War of 1812 and even before.[47]

Of course, Adams also openly shared this viewpoint with the Spanish government and with fellow leading republicans. In a missive to Gallatin, the former secretary of the treasury, Adams again labeled Arbuthnot "the mover, instigator and conductor of the Indians in their war against the United States." He went on to wax eloquently that the "Indian wars that we have suffered by the instigations of such characters, the hundreds and thousands of our citizens, of either sex and of every age, butchered with every horrible aggravation of savage cruelty, under the stimulus of these disavowed and unauthorized agents, are also to be considered. The necessity of a signal example was urgent and indispensable. It has been given; and if its operation should be, as we trust it will, to deter unauthorized foreign intruders from intermeddling between the United States and the Indians, it will be the greatest benefit ever conferred by a white man upon their tribes." Certainly the Spanish had a hand in fomenting Indian hostilities, whether directly or indirectly, Adams told Gallatin. But he never once mentioned Francis, or McQueen, or Kinache, or any other Red Stick Creek or Seminole leader. These were mere puppets, and the puppet master was none other than John Bull himself. Jackson could not have agreed more with Adams's position, and he could not—and did not—capture in words the American mind-set better than Adams.[48]

Jackson's 1818 invasion of Spanish Florida undoubtedly caused a stir in Washington—mainly for the *manner* in how he took Spanish Florida and not for the fact that he *took* Spanish Florida. The Monroe administration found itself in quite an awkward position. Debate continues whether or not Jackson had received authorization, but the Monroe administration did have a direct hand in the events that unfolded in 1818. Calhoun ordered Gaines to cross the Florida line to punish the Seminole, but more effective means were needed for success. They needed the direct intervention of General Jackson, and they authorized him to do whatever it took to accomplish the mission. Monroe knew exactly who he was sending into Florida, and he was fully cognizant of what Jackson could, and did, accomplish—the acquisition of Florida. Still, the Monroe administration would take the heat, and in order to distance themselves from any apparent overt complicity with Jackson, they held a secret cabinet meeting to plan their extrication from the now unsavory affair—and to determine the fate of Andrew Jackson. The Monroe administration flirted with the idea of reprimanding Jackson for his "unwarranted" use of power in his invasion. Calhoun led the charge (and paid the price for it in 1831); Adams fought it outright (and still paid the price for it in 1828). Other cabinet members waffled (fearing Jackson's wrath and his popularity), and Monroe simply hid behind plausible denial. In the end, the administration caved both to popular opinion and the fact that they were finally a step closer to acquiring Florida and thus decided it wise to leave Jackson alone.

But some effort to appease Spain had to be taken. Spain threatened to terminate negotiations with the United States if their demands for justice went unmet. So Monroe weakly disavowed Jackson's authority to do what he did, and to placate Spain, he returned the posts taken by U.S. forces, greatly angering

Jackson and his supporters. Many U.S. officials believed that Jackson's actions undermined peaceful diplomacy as a means for acquiring Florida. Adams disagreed, obviously, and he used Jackson's invasion to badger Onis into reinvigorating their negotiations. For the New Englander, Jackson had aided the cause of securing possession of Florida through peaceful rather than military channels. The damage had been done.

The United States easily ran all over Spanish Florida and, with as much ease, simply took it. Sell us Florida, Adams hinted, or a "third invasion" should give us Florida altogether. This time Onis listened. In 1819, Adams and Onis drafted a treaty for the U.S. acquisition of Florida. According to the terms of this treaty, the United States acquired all of Florida, relinquished any title to Texas, resolved American claims against Spain, and drew to the Pacific Ocean an official boundary between Spanish North America and the United States. The Transcontinental Treaty of 1819 stands as a triumph of U.S. territorial expansion. The U.S. Senate quickly ratified the treaty, despite significant opposition from nascent Jacksonians who believed Texas had been part of the Louisiana Purchase and thus its transfer nonnegotiable. Jackson himself never recognized that part of the agreement with Spain.[49]

Despite any unease he may have harbored about how the United States acquired the Floridas, President Monroe gladly took credit for securing the nation's southern border from foreign intrigue. On his tour of the United States in 1819, Monroe regularly received praise in the South and the West for his handling of the Florida affair. The citizens of Nashville, for example, represented the sentiment of their frontier brethren when they applauded the president: "To your administration do we trace the acquirement of the Floridas, a territory which heretofore has involved us in difficulties and whence danger might in future be looked for, if left in possession of a foreign power." Monroe agreed completely. Replying to the adulation heaped on him by the residents of Charleston, Monroe commented that from the moment the acquisition of Florida was completed, "our southern frontier may be considered as essentially secure against regressions and troubles of the kind, with which it has heretofore been visited." These difficulties and dangers, these regressions and troubles, obviously referred to British intrigues and incitement of Indian hostilities. To the citizens of Augusta, Georgia, the president proudly declared that "experience has shewn that while [Florida] was held by another power, we could never be secure against Indian hostilities in their worst form, and that our interior was exposed, more particularly the neighboring States to every other species of annoyance which could have proceeded from savage neighbors, liable to be practiced on, and seduced, by indigent and grasping adventurers, from every country." Madison had said essentially the same in his 1812 war message to Congress. President Monroe, then, faced in 1818 the same situation along the American frontier that his predecessor in the executive mansion had in 1812—British provocation of Indian warfare. Nicholls and Woodbine were no different than Arbuthnot and Ambrister.[50]

While Adams defended Jackson, lectured England, harangued Spain, and secured a treaty for the cession of Florida, and while Monroe forgave Jackson, appeased Spain, toured America, and relished the acquisition of Florida, Congress turned out to be the main theater of action in 1819 over Jackson's invasion of Spanish Florida. In November 1818, President Monroe sent to Congress all the documents related to the campaign in Florida, whereupon the House and the Senate quickly convened committees to investigate the court-martial of Arbuthnot and Ambrister and the conduct of the war against the Seminole. The rancorous debates over Jackson's actions in 1818 consumed the greatest part of Congress's time in 1819—a pivotal year in American history, one that witnessed America's first significant depression, the Panic of 1819, its first Supreme Court case signaling the rise of Jacksonianism, *McCulloch v. Maryland*, its first hint of the divisive power of the slavery question, Missouri's official request for statehood, and, of course, its official acquisition of Florida, the Transcontinental Treaty. Jackson still took center stage, as Congress could think of little else.

After all of the debating, Congress essentially adopted the position of the Monroe administration and refused to take action against the Old Hero, despite the majority reports scolding Jackson for his transgressions in Florida. The American public roundly supported his actions in Florida, as did most of the representatives of that public. Regardless of which side of the aisle a congressman found himself—haranguing Jackson for his deeds, or praising him for his actions—and despite their sundry approaches to this singular event—constitutional, political, diplomatic, military, even economic—the congressional debates clearly revealed a preoccupation with British influence in Spanish Florida. Congressmen consistently commented on the treacherous operations of foreign agents upon the Florida Indians. Anglophobia was alive and well on Capitol Hill as much as it was in the White House. The official committee reports, like the correspondence delivered to them by the executive, regularly referred to "foreign incendiaries, instigating the savages," and that the "two principal foreign instigators" were none other than Arbuthnot and Ambrister—the former labeled "the successor of the notorious Colonel Nicholls" and the latter as "the successor of Woodbine of notorious memory." The savages, said many in Congress, conducted their cruel war against American citizens and U.S. troops solely as a result of the "deceptive representations of foreign nations" and promises that "they would receive assistance from the

British." Even the majority reports condemning Jackson's behavior in Florida recognized that the "influence of foreign emissaries" spawned Indian hostility against the United States.[51]

Jackson, obviously infuriated over the congressional scrutiny and the half-hearted support from his administration, responded accordingly. In a lengthy memorial presented to Congress in 1820, he reiterated all the reasons for his actions two years past. Of course, the British played a central role. "British emissaries," aided by Spanish officers, incited Indian hostility against the United States, he vehemently maintained. Since the War of 1812 and continuing through the years prior to the 1818 invasion, British agents such as Woodbine, Arbuthnot, and Ambrister, acting as the "chiefs of the negroes and Indians," committed numerous acts of atrocity and thus became identified with "these monsters—*associates* in the war." Here were the "principal authors of the hostilities of the ferocious savages," shunning the rules of civilized warfare, never giving quarter, engaging in unlawful war, soliciting and supplying arms and ammunition. Some of the guilt must reside with the British government, as "Great Britain would not interfere to prevent those miscreants from instigating the fugitive negroes and the Indians from burning, and pillaging, and scalping, the inhabitants of Georgia and Alabama." Jackson's memorial, however, was more an endeavor to defend his honor and reputation than it ever was an ardent appeal for Americans to espouse his viewpoint. They already had, as far back as the War of 1812.[52]

Although a spirited defense of things that had already occurred, Jackson's memorial also indicated the American state of mind in the several years after the First Seminole War. Anglophobia still infected Americans. Americans could not shake their fear of the British presence threatening their security in the Gulf Coast region. Even after Jackson had supposedly exorcised British demons in Florida, rumors of the phantom redcoat menace still surfaced in Washington. The commanding officer of the U.S. garrison stationed at Fort St. Marks reported in late 1818, for example, that an English trading vessel had been seen at Tampa and two more near Snake Island near the mouth of the Suwannee River. "Some provisions and ammunition were procured from her by the enemy," reported the U.S. officer. "Thus, there can be but little doubt of the Seminoles being now well supplied with ammunition and provisions."[53]

Even after the Adams-Onis Treaty, American fears still flared over the possibility that Spain would relinquish Florida to Great Britain. When the Spanish government delayed its ratification of the treaty, rumors spread widely through the American press that the British government had intervened to oppose the cession of Florida to the United States. Even U.S. officials believed such talk. In his efforts to secure Spanish ratification of the treaty, for example,

John Forsyth, U.S. minister to Spain and future secretary of state for President Andrew Jackson, mentioned the "danger of a British occupation of Florida to forestall action by the United States."[54]

Of course, proceedings in Great Britain only fueled such rumors in the United States. The British press angrily denounced the pending U.S. acquisition of Florida, as such an event would threaten British possessions in the Caribbean. Some in Parliament also questioned the potential transaction and asked the ministry why they had not prevented the cession of Florida to the United States. An American Florida, they charged, undermined British interests if war erupted with their transatlantic rival. Some British officials suggested seizing Spanish Cuba in order to counteract an American Florida. Despite sentiment to see Florida remain in Spanish hands, the British ministry adopted a more moderate position and admonished the Spanish government to settle affairs with the United States as quickly as possible. Great Britain would never pursue possession of Florida, nor would it go to war to prevent the cession of that territory to the United States, and delaying ratification of the Adams-Onis Treaty would inevitably result in another American military takeover of Florida. Castlereagh also responded to American suspicions that the British government was responsible for Spanish dawdling. Monroe listened and accepted the British disavowal of any intrigues. Spain listened as well and ratified the treaty in 1821. In the summer of that year, the Stars and Stripes flew permanently over Pensacola and St. Augustine.[55]

Despite the Monroe administration's acceptance of Castlereagh's assurances of British nonintervention, most Americans remained skeptical. Even if the status of Florida was no longer in question, Americans feared that other Spanish possessions in the Gulf region could end up in British hands as a result of the U.S. possession of Florida. Cuba also emerged as a national security threat, a direct result of the chatter emanating from across the Atlantic. During Monroe's presidential tour in 1819, the *Missouri Gazette* reported that the president had left Nashville for Washington "in consequence of the accounts having been received, that the late Spanish treaty ceding the Floridas had been rejected by the Spanish government, and that Cuba has been ceded to Great Britain." Such news, continued the paper, if true, was "of the greatest political importance to the U. States, and particularly to the western states." The U.S. minister to the Netherlands, Edward Everett, informed Adams that the Transcontinental Treaty was "a measure which seems to have awakened [British] jealousy in a considerable degree" and that the British would seek the cession of Cuba as compensation. Secretary of War Calhoun could not help but reveal his Anglophobic side about the future of Cuba either. He agreed with Jackson's assessment regarding the "importance of Cuba to our country":

It is, in my opinion, not only the first commercial and military position in the world, but is the Key stone of our Union. No American statesman ought ever to withdraw his eye from it; and the greatest calamity ought to be endured by us, rather than it should pass into the hands of England. That she desires it, and would seize it, if a fair opportunity presented itself, I cannot doubt; and that, such an event would endanger our union, is to me very manifest. These are my fixed opinions. Should our relation with Spain end in a rupture, we ought to be prepared immediately, at the very commencement of hostilities, to seize it, and to hold it for ever. On the contrary, I think there are strong reasons, why we ought, at first, to limit our operations to Florida, and rest there for the present, unless Spain should choose to come to a rupture with us; or that the designs of England on Cuba should become sufficiently manifest.

Obviously, for those in and around the Monroe administration, the British lurked everywhere the American eagle spied.[56]

For that matter, the Gulf Coast was not the only American borderland where U.S. officials feared British intrigues. In the late spring of 1819, while Congress debated Jackson's actions in Florida, Jackson notified U.S. army officer Henry Atkinson to be always vigilant for Indian attack along the western frontier, as British traders on the Missouri River "will no doubt excite the Indians to hostility." In words reminiscent of his days in Florida, he asserted angrily that these British agents "ought in my opinion be hung, where ever they are found among the Indian Tribes within our Territory," and "a few exampled would be sufficient and the Commanding Officer of the Troops is the proper authority to judge of their Guilt and Order their execution." But the lesson he learned over the Arbuthnot and Ambrister affair had made some impact, as he concluded to Atkinson that "the over cautious policy of the Executive, has directed that they only be arrested and reported to him. . . . This instead of putting down the influence of British emissaries I fear will have a different effect."

Atkinson never found an Arbuthnot or Ambrister along the Missouri frontier. Despite the continuation of American Anglophobia well into the 1840s, Jackson had removed the threat of any such emissaries along the Gulf Coast in 1818—at least for the portion of territory east of the Mississippi River, the Floridas. Texas remained to further incite intense Anglophobia, as Americans in the South and in the West and in Washington feared an ominous British presence in the Lone Star Republic, again threatening U.S. national security in the borderlands. But Jacksonians succeeded in removing any such dangerous emissaries there by the year of Jackson's passing in 1845.[57]

In the final analysis, many Americans in the South and West claimed that Indian depredations resulted from British intrigues, that the British menace must be eliminated in both Canada and Spanish Florida, and that this would be the only way to achieve peaceful relations with the Indians. This strong belief underpinned the War of 1812, the Creek War, and the First Seminole War. British influence had indeed played a significant, if not a primary, role in kindling the Indian wars during the administrations of Madison and Monroe. When President Madison asked Congress for a declaration of war against England in the summer of 1812, he included British influence among the Indians along the American frontier as one of the enumerated grievances for going to war. "In reviewing the conduct of Great Britain toward the United States," Madison declared, "our attention is necessarily drawn to the warfare just renewed by the savages on one of our extensive frontiers—a warfare which is known to spare neither age nor sex and to be distinguished by features peculiarly shocking to humanity. It is difficult to account for the activity and combinations which have for some time been developing themselves among tribes in constant intercourse with British traders and garrisons without connecting their hostility with that influence and without recollecting the authenticated examples of such interpositions heretofore furnished by the officers and agents of that Government." President Monroe could have said the same in the summer of 1818—Andrew Jackson and John Quincy Adams actually did.

Following the ratification of the Treaty of Ghent in the month following the resounding defeat of British arms by Jackson's motley crew just south of New Orleans, American desire to secure its borders along the Gulf Coast continued unabated. If anything, the British occupation of Spanish Pensacola, its use of that place to make an unsuccessful attack on Mobile, and its massive invasion of Louisiana via the Gulf of Mexico—all in 1814—convinced Americans that its southern and western frontier still remained vulnerable to British influence. In short, the British represented a direct threat to U.S. national security in the Gulf region. The acquisition of Spanish Florida thus became a prime concern. As one noted historian described the Floridas, "In the hands of any foreign power they were a pistol pointed at the heart of the future Continental Republic. East Florida was the butt of the pistol. Pensacola the trigger-guard, and the 'panhandle' of West Florida was the horizontal barrel with its muzzle pressed against the nation's life-artery, the Mississippi River, just above New Orleans. Spain had been too feeble to load the pistol and pull the trigger, but not her ally England, nor her enemy Napoleon if he could lay hands on the weapon."[58]

Those in the Madison and Monroe administrations, or in the lower Mississippi valley, or along the Gulf South borderlands, or in the Hermitage, could

3.3. John Quincy Adams (Library of Congress).

not have put it any better. Indeed, if the War of 1812 revealed anything to those residing along the southern U.S. border, it was how easily England had intervened in Spanish Florida, and thus how easily she threatened Mobile, New Orleans, and the entire Deep South frontier, especially when it came to arming and fueling the Southern Indians. The other blatant revelation was the utter weakness of Spain's grip on the Floridas. Someone other than Spain would obviously occupy the Floridas within a very short time, and for the United States, only two choices existed after the War of 1812—the United States or Great Britain. The acquisition of Florida, therefore, was a logical end to defeating the British in the Gulf region once and for all, an end not met at Chalmette in January 1815 or by the ratification of the Treaty of Ghent the following month. The U.S. invasion of Spanish Florida in 1818—the First Seminole War—and the official acquisition of Spanish Florida in 1821 clearly manifested an uninterrupted quest to promote national security in the South and the West. In the end, the ultimate expulsion of the British from the Gulf Coast region came not south of New Orleans in January 1815; rather, it came two hundred miles to the east, at Pensacola, in the summer of 1818. Or, more correctly, the official removal of the British menace from the Gulf South borderlands came not with the ratification of the Treaty of Ghent in 1815 but with the Adams-Onis Treaty in 1821. As for the fate of the Seminole, it may have been sealed more due to U.S. insecurity and international rivalry in Florida than for any other reason. The Seminole were indeed pawns in a larger game of chess between a superpower and an emerging one. They were victims of a long rivalry between the United States and Great Britain. They were simply in the way of the U.S. pursuit to remove British influence from its borderland regions. In this light, the First Seminole War was undeniably an epilogue to the Creek War of 1813–14 and to the War of 1812.

Notes

1. David Holmes to Secretary of State, 12 September 1810, Judge Toulmin to the Captains of Militia, Washington County, 4 November 1810, in Clarence Carter, ed., *Territorial Papers of the United States: Mississippi Territory* (Washington: Government Printing Office, 1934–), 6:116, 131.

2. James Madison, Special Message to Congress, 12 December 1810, in James D. Richardson, ed., *A Compilation of the Messages and Papers of the Presidents, 1789–1897* (Washington: Government Printing Office, 1896), 1:488.

3. Monroe to Madison, 18 May, 31 August 1803, in Stanislaus M. Hamilton, ed., *The Writings of James Monroe* (New York: G. P. Putnam's Sons, 1901), 4:25, 26, 70–71, hereinafter cited as *Monroe Writings*. Monroe's reasons for acquiring the Floridas from Spain were that (1) West Florida was clearly part of the Louisiana Purchase and (2) he wanted restitution for Spanish depredations committed against American shipping during the war between Britain and France and in violation of the 1795 Pinckney Treaty. See Monroe to Talleyrand, 8 November 1804, *Monroe Writings*, 4:266–74.

4. During the War of 1812, in response to the British threat in the Gulf region and as a logical conclusion to the acquisition of Spanish West Florida from the Mississippi to the Perdido, U.S. regulars seized Mobile without a fight. It was a common assumption among U.S. policymakers that West Florida, from the Mississippi River to the Perdido River, was clearly within the bounds of the Louisiana Purchase. Monroe, for example, in his negotiations with France over the Louisiana Purchase, argued that the United States demanded the acquisition of West Florida as a "moderate recompense for spoliations," again, a common approach by U.S. officials. See Monroe to John Taylor, 10 September 1810, *Monroe Writings*, 5:124.

5. Frank L. Owsley Jr., *Struggle for the Gulf Borderlands: The Creek War and the Battle of New Orleans, 1812–1815* (Tuscaloosa: University of Alabama Press, 1981), 28–29, 87, 92–93.

6. For an excellent study on British activities in Spanish Florida during the War of 1812, especially the British recruitment of blacks and Indians and how this threatened the American sense of racial order in the Deep South, see Nathaniel Millett, "Britain's 1814 Occupation of Pensacola and America's Response: An Episode of the War of 1812 in the Southeastern Borderlands," *Florida Historical Quarterly* 84 (2005): 229–55.

7. Edwin C. McReynolds, *The Seminoles* (Norman: University of Oklahoma Press, 1957), 63–64; letter by Lieutenant Colonel Edward Nicholls, 29 August 1814, in *American State Papers: Foreign Relations*, 4:548, hereinafter cited as *ASPFR*.

8. McReynolds, *Seminoles*, 64–67; Frank L. Owsley and Gene A. Smith, *Filibusters and Expansionists: Jeffersonian Manifest Destiny, 1800–1821* (Tuscaloosa: University of Alabama Press, 1997), 95–98.

9. Jackson to Rachel Jackson, 16 July 1814, Jackson to William C. C. Claiborne, 21 July 1814, Manrique to Jackson, 26 July 1814, Jackson to John Hickman, 2 August 1814, Jackson to John Reid, 27 August 1814, Jackson to Claiborne, 30 August 1814, Jackson to Manrique, 9 September 1814, Jackson to Monroe, 27 September 1814, 10 October 1814, Jackson to Daniel Patterson, 14 October 1814, in Harold D. Moser, David R. Hoth, Sharon Macpherson, and John H. Reinbold, eds., *The Papers of Andrew Jackson* (Knoxville: University of Tennessee Press, 1991), 3:89, 91, 96, 102, 124, 126, 131, 150, 155, hereinafter cited as *Jackson Papers*.

10. Jackson to Monroe, 26 October 1814, Jackson to Rachel Jackson, 15 November 1814, Jackson to Monroe, 20 November 1814, *Jackson Papers*, 3:173, 187, 191–92.

11. Monroe to Gallatin, 6 May 1813, Monroe to Jackson, 7 December 1814, *Monroe Writings*, 5:259, 301.

12. J. Leitch Wright Jr., "A Note on the First Seminole War as Seen by the Indians, Negroes, and Their British Advisers," *Journal of Southern History*, 34 (November 1968): 569; Owsley and Smith, *Filibusters*, 98–99.

13. Owsley and Smith, *Filibusters*, 98–102.

14. Ibid.; McReynolds, *Seminoles*, 69–71; Peter Early to Sebastian Kindelan, 1 June 1815, in *The Papers of the Panton, Leslie and Co.*, Special Collections, John C. Pace Library, University of West Florida; Wright, "Note," 568, 570. For the Hawkins-Nicholls correspondence, see *ASPFR*, 4:548–51.

15. Gaines to Secretary of War, 14 May 1815, Deposition of Samuel Jarvis, 9 May 1815, *ASPFR*, 551.

16. Wright, "Note," 572; Owsley and Smith, *Filibusters*, 114–16.

17. Adams to Monroe, 19 September 1815, 8 February 1816, in Worthington C. Ford, ed., *Writings of John Quincy Adams* (New York: Macmillan, 1913–17), 5:377, 378, 385, 386, 502, hereinafter cited as *Adams Writings*.

18. Timothy Barnard to David Blackshear, 2 December 1815, Edmund Doyle to Robert Gamble and Captain Spencer, 6 April 1815, Pedro Cevallos to Fernan Nunez, 29 February 1816, in *Papers of the Panton, Leslie and Co.*

19. Onis to Monroe, 22 February 1816, in William R. Manning, ed., *Diplomatic Correspondence of the United States Concerning the Independence of the Latin-American Nations* (New York: Oxford University Press, 1925), 3:1897–98; Adams to Onis, 19 January 1816, in *British and Foreign and State Papers, United States and Spain, 1815–16*, 3:117–18; Onis to Adams, 22 February 1816, ibid., 4:322; see also Erving to Don Pedro Cevallos, 26 August 1816, ibid., 4:358.

20. Charles R. Vaughan to Viscount Castlereagh, 16 November 1815, in C. K. Webster, ed., *Britain and the Independence of Latin America, 1812–1830: Select Documents from the Foreign Office Archives* (New York: Octagon Books, 1970), 344; Bradford Perkins, *Castlereagh and Adams: England and the United States, 1812–1823* (Berkeley: University of California Press, 1964), 283, 284.

21. Monroe to J. Q. Adams, 10 December 1815, *Monroe Writings*, 5:301.

22. Perkins, *Castlereagh and Adams*, 284.

23. Adams to Monroe, 8 February 1816, Adams to William Eustis, 29 March 1816, Adams to George William Erving, no date, *Adams Writings*, 5:502, 503, 547, 6:37.

24. Adams to Monroe, 22 January 1816, *Diplomatic Correspondence*, 3:1434; Adams to Monroe, 19 September 1815, *Adams Writings*, 5:377, 378, 6:22; Webster to William F. Rowland, 11 January 1815, in Charles M. Wiltse and Harold D. Moser, eds., *The Papers of Daniel Webster: Correspondence, 1798–1824* (Hanover, N.H.: University Press of New England, 1974), 1:181; Owsley and Smith, *Filibusters*, 92.

25. "Memorandum on the British Offer to Mediate between the United States and Spain," *Adams Writings*, 6:295; Perkins, *Castlereagh and Adams*, 287, 288.

26. Owsley and Smith, *Filibusters*, 106. For the most complete study of Negro Fort's pivotal role on the history of the southeastern borderlands, see Nathaniel Millett, "Defining Freedom in the Atlantic Borderlands of the Revolutionary Southeast," *Early American Studies* (Fall 2007): 367–94.

27. Owsley and Smith, *Filibusters*, 118–40; entry of 14 January 1818, in Charles Francis Adams, ed., *Memoirs of John Quincy Adams, Comprising Portions of His Diary from 1795–1848* (Philadelphia: J. B. Lippincott, 1874–77), 4:42.

28. Edmund Doyle to John Innerarity, 28 January 1817, Panton, Leslie Papers; Governor of Georgia to General Gaines, 5 February 1817, Mitchell to Gaines, 5 February 1817, Mitchell to Secretary of War, 30 March 1817, Gaines to Secretary of War, 3 April 1817, in *American State Papers: Military Affairs*, 1:681, 683, 748, hereinafter cited as *ASPMA*.

29. Arbuthnot to Nicholls, 26 August 1817, Arbuthnot to Charles Bagot, no date, Arbuthnot to Governor of Havana, no date, "Power of Attorney from the Indian Chiefs to A. Arbuthnot," no date, Arbuthnot to a Person of Rank in England, 30 January 1818, *ASPFR*, 4:578–9, 585, 588–89, 589, 607.

30. Arbuthnot to Gaines, 3 March 1817, Arbuthnot to Hambly, 3 May 1817, Arbuthnot to Mitchell, 19 January 1818, *ASPFR*, 4:588, 591, 610–11.

31. Ambrister to Governor Cameron, 20 March 1818, Ambrister to Nicholls, no date, *ASPFR*, 4:594.

32. Petition of the Chiefs of the Lower Creek nation to Governor Cameron, no date,

ASPFR, 4:590; Gaines to Seminole Chief [Kinache], no date, *ASPMA*, 1:723; Gaines to Jackson, 6 April 1817, *Papers of Jackson*, 4:460.

33. Gaines to Jackson, 21 November 1817, *Papers of Jackson*, 4:150.

34. Gaines to Secretary of War, 2 December 1817, *ASPMA*, 1:687.

35. Armstrong to Jackson, 18 July 1814, Gaines to Jackson, 14 May 1815, *Jackson Papers*, 3:90, 356; Jackson to Masot, 23 May 1818, *ASPMA*, 1:713; Monroe to Congress, March 25, 1818, *Messages and Papers of the Presidents*, 2:31, 32; Gaines to Secretary of War, 2 December 1817, *ASPMA*, 1:687; Adams to Erving, 28 November 1818, *Adams Writings*, 6:475, 487.

36. Jesup to Monroe, 3 September 1816, Thomas Sydney Jesup Papers, Letterbook, 1816–17, Duke University; Jesup to Jackson, 5 September 1816, *Jackson Papers*, 4:444; Charles C. Griffin, *The United States and the Disruption of the Spanish Empire, 1810–1822: A Study of the Relations of the United States with Spain and with the Rebel Spanish Colonies* (New York: Octagon Books, 1968 reprint), 84, 162; William Wirt to Monroe, 28 February 1818, Monroe Papers, Library of Congress.

37. Wright, "Note," 565, 566; Owsley and Smith, *Filibusters*, 95; Jackson to Monroe, 6 January 1818, in John S. Bassett, ed., *Correspondence of Andrew Jackson* (New York: Kraus Reprint, 1969) 2:345.

38. Hugh Young, "A Topographical Memoir on East and West Florida with Itineraries of General Jackson's Army, 1818," *Florida Historical Quarterly* 13 (July 1934): 96; Richard K. Call Journal, Florida State Archives, 179; April 6 and 18 entries, Edward Brett Randolph Diary, Southern Historical Collection, University of North Carolina.

39. Jackson to Calhoun, 8 April 1818, Affidavit of Isaac McKeever, 5 June 1818, *ASPMA*, 1:700, 763; Call Journal, 202.

40. William S. Coker and Thomas D. Watson, *Indian Traders of the Southeastern Spanish Borderlands: Panton, Leslie & Company and John Forbes & Company, 1783–1847* (Pensacola: University of West Florida Press, 1986), 314, 316.

41. Jackson to Rachel Jackson, 5 August 1814, *Jackson Papers*, 3:105; An Officer, *A Concise Narrative of the Seminole Campaign* (Nashville, 1819); Note of Indian Talks, no date, Arbuthnot to Nicholls, 26 August 1817, Ambrister to Cameron, 20 March 1818, Ambrister to Nicholls, no date, *ASPMA*, 1:724, 732, 733. For the complete minutes and testimony of the Ambrister and Arbuthnot court martial, see *ASPMA*, 1:721–39.

42. Arbuthnot to Bagot, 27 January 1818, Cappichimicco and Boleck to Governor Cameron, no date, Petition of the Chiefs of the Lower Creek Nation to Governor Cameron, April 1818, *ASPMA*, 1:723, 724, 728.

43. Jackson to Monroe, 6 January 1818, 2 June 1818, *Jackson Papers*, 4:167, 214; Jackson's Proclamation, 29 May 1818, Jackson to Calhoun, 20 April 1818, 5 May 1818, *ASPMA*, 1:701, 702, 720.

44. Jackson to Calhoun, 20 April 1818, 5 May 1818, *ASPMA*, 1:701, 702. Despite his success in Florida in 1818, in the months following the campaign Jackson still warned the Monroe administration that "as long as there are Indians in Florida, and it is possessed by Spain, they will be excited to war and the indiscriminate murder of our citizens, by foreign agents and Spanish officers." Florida must, therefore, be taken by

the United States in order to guarantee national security in the lower Mississippi Valley. "If possession is given of the points now occupied by our troops, and a war ensues, an attempt will no doubt be made to penetrate our country by the Apalachicola, and, by the aid of the Indians, to reach the Mississippi at or above the Chickasaw Bluffs [Memphis]. Should this be done with a formidable force, in our unprepared state, it is highly probable that the enemy might reach the banks of the Mississippi." American occupation of Florida would prevent such a catastrophe. Jackson to Calhoun, 10 August 1818, *ASPMA*, 1:745.

45. Benjamin Rush to Adams, 3 August 1818, *Diplomatic Correspondence*, 3:1448, 1453; Perkins, *Castlereagh and Adams*, 289, 290, 292.

46. Monroe to Jackson, 19 July 1818, in James P. Lucier, ed., *Political Writings of James Monroe* (Washington: Regnery, 2001), 504; Calhoun to Jackson, 8 September 1818, *ASPMA*, 1:745; Gallatin to John Quincy Adams, 10 August 1818, *Diplomatic Correspondence*, 2:1384.

47. Adams to Erving, 28 November 1818, *Adams Writings*, 6:474–502. See also Adams to Erving, 2 December 1818, *ASPFR*, 4:546–47.

48. Adams to Gallatin, 30 November 1818, *Adams Writings*, 6:512–13.

49. In his justification of Jackson's invasion to Onis, Adams mentioned only the threat of Indians and black depredations along the U.S. frontier; he never mentioned the threat of England in Florida. Adams only referred to British influence in Florida to other Americans. See Adams to Onis, 23 July 1818, *Adams Writings*, 6:386–94.

50. Daniel Preston, ed., *Papers of James Monroe: A Documentary History of the Presidential Tours of James Monroe, 1817, 1818* (Westport, Conn.: Greenwood Press, 2003), 1:601, 649, 672.

51. For the voluminous debates on the First Seminole War, see the *Annals of Congress*, 15th Cong., 2nd sess., 1818–19. For the committee reports, see *ASPMA*, 1:735–43.

52. Jackson Memorial, *ASPMA*, 1:756, 757.

53. Major A. C. W. Fanning to Gaines, 27 November 1818, *ASPMA*, 1:752.

54. Griffin, *Disruption*, 200, 209–10.

55. Ibid., 209–10, 224; Perkins, *Castlereagh and Adams*, 294–96.

56. (St. Louis) *Missouri Gazette*, 30 June 1819, in Preston, *Presidential Tours*, 1:744; Everett to Adams, 8 August 1819, *Diplomatic Correspondence*, 3:1711–12, Calhoun to Jackson, 23 January 1820, *Jackson Papers*, 4:352.

57. Jackson to Atkinson, 15 May 1819, *Jackson Papers*, 4:298.

58. Samuel F. Bemis, *John Quincy Adams and the Foundations of American Foreign Policy* (New York: Alfred A. Knopf, 1949), 302.

4

◇◇◇◇◇◇◇◇◇◇◇◇◇◇◇◇◇◇◇◇◇◇◇◇◇◇◇◇◇◇◇◇◇◇

Mr. Rhea's Missing Letter
and the First Seminole War

DAVID S. HEIDLER AND JEANNE T. HEIDLER

In March 1818, Major General Andrew Jackson, commander of the Southern Department of the United States Army, invaded Spanish Florida. He had instructions from President James Monroe's War Department to chastise Florida's Seminole Indians who had raided the Georgia and Alabama Territory and others who had attacked the U.S. Army ascending the Apalachicola River toward southwestern Georgia. Most Seminoles fled before Jackson's army: a collection of regulars, Tennessee and Georgia militia, and allied Creek Indians.

Jackson consequently found few Indians to fight. Instead, he led his army to St. Marks, a Spanish fort on the Gulf of Mexico. After forcing the small Spanish garrison to surrender, Jackson headed east to destroy Seminole villages near the Suwannee River. Seminoles there fought rearguard actions to help noncombatants to escape, but Jackson burned their towns and food stores before returning to St. Marks. After a brief rest, he headed west to occupy Pensacola, the Spanish capital of West Florida. From start to finish, it took Jackson about eight weeks to eliminate Spanish control of West Florida and raise the American flag in its capital. He had killed a few dozen Seminoles, razed villages, appropriated livestock, destroyed food stores, executed two British subjects, and taken possession of Spanish forts as well as His Most Catholic Majesty's provincial capital. As he returned to his home near Nashville, he sent reports about these remarkable exploits to the War Department, but disturbing rumors about them had already reached the government. The administration was not pleased; in fact, by the time Jackson's official reports arrived, it was in a state of rising panic.

Contemporaries called Jackson's two-month invasion of Florida the Seminole War, an event later dubbed the First Seminole War to distinguish it from subsequent conflicts with those Indians, but despite its name, it had little to do with Indians. Their role as *casus belli* would soon become a relatively minor part of the violent storm Jackson's invasion caused at home and abroad. Spain understandably protested it, and Jackson's killing of British subjects was likely to excite London. In the United States, nobody could dispute that Jackson at least had mounted his campaign under the authority of his government, but his behavior in Florida had been nothing short of astonishing. In fact, Monroe's administration grimly weighed the meaning of the assaults on Spanish forts and Pensacola, projects not only beyond the scope of Jackson's orders but explicitly prohibited by them. Quite obviously Jackson had made war on a foreign power without congressional approval. Congress was sure to bristle on that basis alone, and as Monroe's cabinet struggled to frame a response that would placate foreign and domestic critics, it was hectored by Secretary of War John C. Calhoun, incensed by Jackson's rank insubordination.

Jackson insisted that he had done nothing wrong. His orders, to his thinking, had not barred him from attacking Spaniards if restoring peace to the Florida border required it. Of course, Jackson's thinking on this matter was filtered through the prism of his egocentrism, allowing him to interpret his orders as he saw fit, even if that interpretation was directly contradictory to what those orders had said. In the months following the invasion, Jackson's imperturbable denial of the facts, his unassailable popularity as the Hero of New Orleans, and his legendary temper were enough to see him through the controversy, and he stuck to his story about the ambiguity of his orders through it all. It is important to keep that in mind when weighing what happened thirteen years later when, in the midst of political battles, he radically changed his defense: not only had his orders not forbidden his attack on Spanish posts, he claimed, but President Monroe had explicitly authorized him to do so. The prism of his egocentrism was again bending the truth to shape it as he saw fit, recasting a series of events that unfolded in the Florida wilderness as he had made war on Spaniards, Seminoles, and Creek refugees. His behavior at first caused a constitutional crisis, and finally it transformed the entire affair into an ugly political squabble. The story of how all this occurred is as complicated as the consequences were profound.

Andrew Jackson's role in the story started with the Creek War of 1813–14. Jackson ended that war by defeating Red Stick Creeks at Horseshoe Bend on the Tallapoosa River in March 1814, but the victory set into motion events that led to his Florida invasion four years later. Many Red Sticks were killed at the Horseshoe, but many of those who survived fled with their families to Spanish Florida. The subsequent Treaty of Fort Jackson in August 1814 took from the entire Creek Nation more than half of its lands and increased Indian animosity toward the United States throughout the region, but especially on its southern border where Red Stick refugees and Florida Seminoles were persistently hostile and occasionally aggressive.

Into this fragile situation came a flood of white settlers, lured into the Creek cession by the land's potential for growing cotton. These squatters were eager to scarf up the best lands even before the government could survey them, but they were also a lawless bunch who saw Indians as obstacles and their property as plunder. Soon they were traipsing into Florida to steal anything they found of value, especially Indian cattle. The Florida Indians retaliated.

Those Indians who lived closest to the United States were Seminoles, many descended from earlier immigrants from Georgia and Alabama. The Seminoles who had lived in Florida for generations were now joined by Red Stick Creeks, recently in flight from their war with the United States. Communities of maroons (fugitive slaves and their descendents) lived amid both groups, but primarily in proximity to Seminoles. White Americans tended to call all these people "Seminoles," mindless of the variety they represented. More important, white Americans were acutely aware that the alliance between Indians and African Americans made maroon communities havens for runaway slaves. A series of incidents in 1815 and 1816 included an American military raid to destroy just such a refuge called Negro Fort on the Apalachicola River, but the foray worsened rather than eased tensions.[1]

Finally in November 1817, Brigadier General Edmund Pendleton Gaines received orders to pacify the unruly border. He responded to Indian complaints about the increased military presence in the region by demanding that Creek leaders meet with him at Fort Scott. When the suspicious Indians refused, Gaines sent troops to burn one of their principal villages, Fowltown. Dispossessed Fowltown Creeks rapidly allied with Seminoles below the Florida border to retaliate by slaughtering Lieutenant Richard Scott's party of soldiers and their families as it ascended the Apalachicola. Gaines's efforts to calm the situation had obviously failed.

He was soon called away, in any case, to deal with a developing predicament on the eastern end of the Florida border. Pirates and mercenaries had set up shop on Amelia Island just off the Florida coast, and the U.S. government saw them as a threat requiring attention. The War Department told Gaines to take a detachment of his soldiers to oust the banditti from Amelia, which meant that when Washington heard about the Scott massacre, no senior officer was in southwestern Georgia to deal with the rising crisis. The government in Washington, in fact, was not in the best shape to deal with a military crisis anywhere because Secretary of War John C. Calhoun had just assumed his post, a position Monroe had found exasperatingly difficult to fill.

Calhoun hit the ground running because he had to, but haste and urgency likely made everything a blur during those crucial days. In early December 1817, he fired off letters to his commanders in the field. To keep Jackson informed about operations in his department, Calhoun always sent Jackson copies of Gaines's orders.[2] Calhoun was unaware of the Scott massacre when he sent this information, but that grim news finally reached Washington to make Gaines's operation against Amelia Island supremely irrelevant. The new secretary of war quickly reassessed his southern deployments. On December 16, he told Gaines that if the Seminoles were unwilling to redress this latest outrage, he was to cross the Florida border and chastise them, with the significant exception of those who sought to "shelter themselves under a Spanish post."[3] The following day he sent copies of these orders to Jackson at the Hermitage, his home near Nashville. But Calhoun was apparently unsure about Gaines's location. So nine days later, he instructed Andrew Jackson to take most of his division to the Florida border and request militia reinforcements from southern governors if necessary. In this December 26 letter, Calhoun did not tell Jackson to cross into Florida, but since he had copied to him what he had sent to Gaines on December 16, he remained under the impression that those orders, which did direct the army to cross the border and included instructions not to attack Spaniards, were understood by everyone in the region, Jackson included.

Although Jackson did not receive Calhoun's December 26 letter until January 11, 1818, he had long believed that the Florida border was a problem in need of a permanent solution.[4] Gaines's report about the Scott massacre reached him on December 31, validating for him his repeated warnings to Calhoun's predecessor, Acting Secretary of War George Graham, that the sanctuary provided by Spanish territory only emboldened Florida Indians to greater aggression.[5] Now with this latest violence as additional evidence, Jackson wrote President Monroe a remarkable letter on January 6, 1818, five days before his orders from Calhoun arrived.

In this letter, Andrew Jackson acknowledged Calhoun's December 17 message that copied his December 16 order to Gaines authorizing a foray into Spanish Florida to attack Seminoles as long they did not take shelter with Spaniards. Jackson, however, strenuously objected to this restriction, arguing that any victory Gaines achieved would be made meaningless when the Indians scampered behind the walls of St. Augustine or Pensacola. Worse, the Indians would likely join with Spaniards and British freebooters to annihilate American forces. This was no time for half measures, he insisted. Instead, the United States should seize East Florida, including Amelia Island, and hold it as a surety against further aggression by the Seminoles. Jackson assured Monroe it all could be done without implicating the government. All the president had to do was send word through an intermediary, and Jackson would place Florida in American hands within sixty days. He suggested Tennessee congressman John Rhea act as Monroe's liaison.[6]

Jackson probably chose Rhea because he was both a personal friend and a member of John Overton's powerful Tennessee political faction. Born to Scots-Irish parents in Londonderry, Ireland, in 1753, Rhea came to colonial Pennsylvania with his parents when he was sixteen. Nine years later he moved South to the part of North Carolina that would become eastern Tennessee. After fighting in the Revolution, he became active in politics, participating in Tennessee's 1796 constitutional convention, serving in its state legislature, and finally commencing in 1803 a twenty-year career in Congress. At the time Jackson recommended him to convey Monroe's consent to make war on Spain, Rhea was elderly and nearing what he likely thought would be a quiet retirement. He had no idea how eventful the last years of his life would be.

Jackson's January 6 letter to Monroe crossed Calhoun's December 26 letter. By both the evidence and the behavior of everybody at the time, Calhoun's letter was the last communication relating to Florida that Jackson received before his campaign, which is to say that the standing orders—those to Gaines on December 16—were not to attack Spaniards. Neither the evidence nor anyone's behavior in the months that followed indicates that Jackson ever received a direct answer from Monroe or an indirect response from Monroe through John Rhea that would have altered the instructions in the December 16 orders.

And yet the administration's handling of Jackson's January 6 letter when it arrived in Washington was anything but orderly. Unfortunately, the administration's conduct regarding this letter from the time it first appeared was so slipshod that later speculation about the government's motives and the president's integrity was made almost certain. Because Monroe was ill in bed when the letter arrived, he did not read it, he later recalled, but he did show it to Calhoun and Secretary of the Treasury William H. Crawford. Calhoun and Crawford read the letter and would remember doing so, although Crawford's memory of the event became less crisp in later years, another problem that would trouble the official version of this episode.

In fact, the administration's version of this episode borders on the fantastic, which at least has the advantage of suggesting that nobody in his right mind would make it up expecting it to be believed. Calhoun told Monroe upon first reading the letter that it should be answered, but it never was, according to them, and that decision, while unwise in retrospect, probably made sense at the time. Jackson had, after all, fresh orders from Calhoun's desk, and it possibly seemed best to let them speak for themselves and ignore the letter with its

4.1. William H. Crawford (Library of Congress).   4.2. John C. Calhoun (Library of Congress).

alarming suggestions. By the end of January 1818, though, as Jackson was well along with his preparations to invade Florida, Monroe was haunted by gnawing worry verging on full-scale fear that more would be occurring in Florida than the administration bargained for. He told Calhoun to repeat to Jackson that he was not to attack Spanish posts. Calhoun did not do this, evidently because he did not feel it necessary. He had already made such instructions clear with the copies of his orders to Gaines that had been forwarded to Jackson. In addition, Calhoun was new to his job and was probably reluctant to repeat instructions to the prickly Jackson that even slightly implied that Old Hickory might not obey orders. As it turned out, it would have been much better to try Jackson's temper and have the administration's position on record with the documents neatly filed.[7]

As noted, Jackson received the December 26 orders from Calhoun five days after writing his January 6 letter to Monroe. Jackson sent word for Georgia militia to muster (actually, many Georgians were already in the field) and for the Tennessee militia to be ready to march in a few weeks. At the end of January, he started south through Alabama and Georgia, arriving at Fort Scott on March 9, 1818. The extreme shortage of food at the fort compelled Jackson to put his force of Georgia militia, regulars, and allied Creeks on the march right away. He moved into Florida toward the Gulf of Mexico in the hope that the navy would supply him.[8]

Jackson did in fact receive food from navy gunboats on the Apalachicola. He also built a supply base on the ruins of Negro Fort before moving east to strike the Miccosukee villages. It was at this point that he veered south toward the Spanish fort at St. Marks; the navy had instructions to stand off in the gulf until Jackson's army arrived.[9] On the evening of April 6, Jackson demanded the fort's surrender. The outnumbered garrison had no choice but to comply.[10]

Jackson hoisted the United States flag at Fort Marks both to take possession and to signal the navy, which soon sent ashore two Red Stick leaders captured through the subterfuge of the American gunboats flying the British flag. Jackson ordered them hanged. In addition, Jackson arrested Alexander Arbuthnot, an elderly Scottish trader who was visiting the Spanish fort. Arbuthnot had acted as an interpreter for the Red Sticks and Seminoles, even writing letters to U.S. officials on their behalf.

Jackson then marched to the Suwannee River to destroy Seminole and maroon towns there, but as before, the Indians were aware of his approach, and most fled while scattered warriors fought rearguard actions. As the army spent several days rounding up Seminole livestock and burning Indian villages, two white men stumbled into its camp, to everybody's surprise. Arbuthnot employee Peter Cook was traveling with thirty-one-year-old Robert Chrystie Ambrister, formerly of the British Royal Marines. Apparently Ambrister, otherwise unemployed, had turned to the risky occupation of mercenary; he was in Florida to recruit Seminoles and maroons for an uprising against Spaniards in Florida and possible other Latin American colonies as well. Andrew Jackson, however, considered the arming and training of Indians and maroons an outrage, no matter who their prospective targets might be. He clapped Ambrister in irons and took him back to St. Marks.[11]

Jackson selected the tribunal that tried Arbuthnot and Ambrister on charges of making war on the United States by aiding the Seminoles. The court found both men guilty and ordered Arbuthnot hanged. Ambrister, however, pleaded for mercy with such sincerity that the court reduced his sentence to lashes and imprisonment. Jackson would not have it. He overturned Ambrister's sentence and ordered him killed with Arbuthnot. Accordingly, American soldiers hanged Alexander Arbuthnot from the yardarm of his own trading schooner; a firing squad shot Robert Chrystie Ambrister dead.[12]

Jackson was already marching west toward Spanish Pensacola. He later defended taking St. Marks with the claim that it was in danger of falling to the Indians, and he concocted the same rationale for Pensacola, insisting that there were hundreds of hostile Indians taking shelter in the town while planning murderous incursions into the United States. At the end of May, Jackson traded a desultory fire with Spaniards at Fort Carlos de Barrancas before accepting the surrender of Pensacola. He raised the American flag and established an American customs house before heading home, continuing to compose en route the reports that shocked the diplomatic community and stunned the Monroe administration to its foundations. Jackson evidently had no idea of the coming storm.[13]

The first dispatches from the campaign arrived at the War Department early in May 1818. They described the seizure of St. Marks. The Arbuthnot and Ambrister executions had not yet occurred when Jackson sent these reports, but Secretary of State John Quincy Adams recorded in his diary on May 4 that Jackson had mentioned the hanging of the two Red Sticks "without due regard to humanity" and that he had taken Arbuthnot prisoner and "appears half inclined to take his life."[14] Jackson, however, had not disclosed any plans to move against Pensacola, and Monroe waited as he hoped for the best. Possibly Jackson had finished chastising Seminoles and was already on his way home.

As Monroe soon discovered, the best had not happened at all. Official news of the campaign's most disturbing events arrived weeks later, but newspaper reports preceded official dispatches, filling the capital with rumors that Jackson had done far more than take an isolated Spanish fort. When the report about taking Pensacola finally did arrive, it raised more questions than it answered. Monroe was lucky that Congress was not in session, but foreign diplomats, particularly the Spanish and British ministers, were already asking discomfiting questions. Beginning in mid-July Monroe and his cabinet held daily meetings to frame a response about Jackson's actions. Almost everyone agreed that Jackson had exceeded his instructions, but Secretary of State Adams focused on how to turn events to the government's advantage and achieve the purchase of Florida from Spain. Calhoun remained intractable about the event itself, especially its author. He argued that Jackson had set a dangerous precedent by disobeying orders, particularly by making war on his own authority, and he must be publicly reprimanded. The other cabinet members and the president were not so sure about that.

What is most interesting about these disagreements is that they occurred at all. Nobody mentioned Jackson's January 6 letter, indicating that the administration had forgotten about it or did not think it pertinent to the current crisis. Correspondingly, nobody mentioned anything about Monroe giving his consent to General Jackson through Congressman John Rhea to take Florida from Spain. Such an executive directive would have made all arguments about Jackson's campaign pointless; in fact, it would have made the feverish cabinet meetings unnecessary. Instead, the cabinet decided to undo the very thing that Monroe would have authorized had he agreed to Jackson's January 6 proposal: the United States would return both St. Marks and Pensacola to Spain.[15]

The cabinet thus finally agreed (Calhoun quite reluctantly) to adopt the "politically astute position of having it both ways: Jackson was justified in and should be congratulated for his assault on the Spaniards. His actions, however, neither reflected the administration's policy nor would receive the executive's endorsement."[16] No one expected this stance to satisfy anyone with objections about what had happened in Florida, but at least it bought time while the administration tried to gather more evidence. There was always the chance that Jackson had good reasons for his actions.

First Monroe on July 19 wrote to Jackson. Taking Pensacola, he said, had been imprudent because Jackson was well aware of Gaines's orders not to molest Spaniards. Monroe also gently explained that Jackson would have to take responsibility for exceeding those orders. Attacking a foreign post was an act of war. Only Congress could authorize war and was likely to take offense at Jackson's presumption. To keep Congress from taking action as well as to mollify Great Britain and Spain, Jackson had to provide more evidence supporting his extraordinary activities.[17]

Perhaps Jackson really did not think that his activities in Florida had been so extraordinary. He certainly was not aware that he had put Monroe and the cabinet into a panic. Instead, he alerted Calhoun that gaining respect abroad and security at home required the army to have at Spain again, this time to take St. Augustine in East Florida.[18] A few days after making this remarkable suggestion, though, Jackson received Monroe's July 19 letter. This first intimation that his campaign was being discussed as irregular sent him into one of his legendary rages. He insisted that he had not violated his orders. He had shown over many years his willingness to make any sacrifice for his country, he thundered, but the current circumstances did not require him to take any blame because he had simply done nothing wrong. His orders had not precluded anything he had done, he said. He was told to pacify the border, and because his orders had not expressly forbidden him from taking Spanish posts or towns (or executing British subjects, for that matter), his discretion to pacify the border in the way he saw fit trumped everything. Jackson then split hairs. Calhoun's December 26 letter had not explicitly bound him to orders previously sent to another officer, nor did it limit him in any way as to terminating the conflict. How could Monroe, Jackson sputtered, now say that he transcended those orders? He concluded with a promise to provide the government with proof that Spanish officials in Florida were hostile to American interests and that national security justified his actions.[19]

As with the cabinet discussions, what is missing from Monroe and Jackson's exchange is its most interesting feature. Nowhere is there any mention of Monroe's authorizing Jackson's actions. Clearly, the final communication Jackson had from anyone in the government before he invaded Florida was Calhoun's December 26 letter, because Jackson based his entire argument on the discretion he had presumably inferred from that message. The most charitable interpretation for Jackson can only rise from his possible confusion about what that message really meant, despite what it said. He had written his January 6 letter to Monroe before he received Calhoun's December 26 letter, but possibly he interpreted Calhoun's message from the perspective of the aggressive January 6 proposal. Because he heard nothing beyond the December 26 orders, which only told him to take command at Fort Scott and proceed to the border, perhaps he believed that the administration had tacitly come around to his way of thinking about Florida. If this were the case, Jackson's anger over Monroe's little constitutional lesson becomes understandable.

But even presuming that everything was merely an awkward misunderstanding does not justify what happened in Florida or the events that followed. Jackson remained silent about his January 6 letter (which we know existed) as well as any response to it from Monroe, undoubtedly because such a response did not exist. Jackson's silence persisted as the controversy intensified with Great Britain and Spain and as Congress prepared to convene in November 1818 with the obvious intention of asking pointed questions. Instead, Jackson spent those months collecting testimony to prove that Spanish officials in Florida had been conspiring with Seminoles and Red Sticks against the United States. At the same time, Adams tried to contain the diplomatic crisis while Monroe and Calhoun soothed Jackson, nonetheless trying to convince him that his version of events did not square with the documents. Congressional curiosity increased as the November session approached, but Jackson refused to budge, finally irritating an already frustrated president.[20] Monroe told Calhoun to make Jackson understand the gravity of what he had done. At last refusing to bow to Jackson's bluster, the administration parsed the orders to show that his reading of them made no sense. How could Jackson argue, Monroe asked Calhoun in exasperation, that Gaines's orders did not apply to him? If that had been so, Jackson had not possessed authority even to invade

Florida. Calhoun's December 26 orders had only told Jackson to repair to the border and, if necessary, request militia reinforcements.[21]

The parsing seems to have jogged Calhoun's memory about Jackson's January 6 letter. He mentioned it to Monroe. The president later said that he had forgotten all about it at the time. Now he read it for the first time and immediately began to worry. The congressional session had brought John Rhea to town, and without revealing what he was referring to, Monroe asked Rhea if he had at any time earlier in 1818 shown him or even mentioned to him a letter from Jackson. Rhea said that he had not.[22] Despite this reassurance, James Monroe nervously prepared his annual message to Congress.

Congressmen had already been asking troubling questions in their home districts, and the president knew that the session would be turbulent for the administration. Speaker of the House Henry Clay and many like him were unlikely to accept evasive or half-baked explanations. It was odd then that Monroe included in his message a vague and half-baked explanation, placing it in the middle and prefacing it with a grossly inaccurate statement: "Our relations with Spain remain nearly in the state in which they were at the last session." After noting how Spain's authority in Florida had completely broken down to allow lawless Indian bands to raid the United States, he casually mentioned that Jackson had occupied Spanish posts to prevent their cooperation with the Indians. All was now calm, Monroe declared, and the administration would return the posts to Spain.[23]

The explanation satisfied only Jackson's friends and the administration's firmest supporters. The House of Representatives immediately divided into pro-Jackson and anti-administration (and, by association, anti-Jackson) factions. Initially, anti-administration members of Congress gained momentum by raising the embarrassing matter of the Constitution, especially if the president had authorized the invasion of a foreign country without congressional consent.[24] As if Monroe did not have enough trouble, Andrew Jackson reacted to even implied criticism by threatening to come to Washington and personally take care of his detractors.[25]

On January 12, 1819, the House Committee on Military Affairs delivered a critical report of Jackson's actions in the trial and execution of Arbuthnot and Ambrister, setting off a debate that turned rancorous early.[26] A minority report favorable to Jackson returned fire, and twenty-six days of speeches followed, exploring every aspect of the invasion. Amid numerous addresses condemning Jackson's behavior in Florida, Henry Clay fluently stated the constitutional problems with Jackson's actions.

This famous Clay performance had an enduring legacy that shaped later events and helped to stoke Jackson's lasting antagonism. Politics motivated

Clay, but veins of principle marbled his effort as well, especially because he had much to lose by attacking a fellow westerner and military hero. When Clay spoke on January 20, 1819, he injured himself more than he did Jackson. He also alienated a man famous for being an implacable, relentless enemy.

Clay carefully avoided attacking President Monroe. Instead, he began by criticizing Jackson's 1814 treaty with the Creeks. Because Clay had been in Europe negotiating the end of the War of 1812 at the time, he had not read the Treaty of Fort Jackson until now, and he was appalled by its terms. "A more dictatorial spirit he had never seen displayed in any instrument," he cried.[27] Moreover, this unjust treaty caused the Seminole War. He condemned as barbarism the execution of the two Red Sticks who had fallen into Jackson's hands through subterfuge rather than capture in battle. The laws of civilized nations abhorred the killing of unarmed captives.[28] Yet even this act paled before the extreme irregularities surrounding the matter of Alexander Arbuthnot and Robert Ambrister. It was one thing to presume their guilt, Clay argued, but the U.S. military's assumption of jurisdiction over them was more than objectionable. No civilized nation could contrive a legal basis for executing those men, and to justify their deaths, as some congressmen had done, by saying it would discourage others from riling Indians and consorting with America's enemies was an artful deceit. Clay flatly stated to the House that "it is not always just to do what may be advantageous."[29] The legality of the executions could only obtain if one acknowledged Jackson's right to establish the court that passed the sentences. Clay reminded Congress that only it could authorize war, appropriate the money for war, and establish "the rules and articles of war." Congress had the example for this authority in its having established tribunals to try spies in time of war, a procedure meant to shield suspects from the whimsy of any officer with an itch to form a firing squad. Why were Arbuthnot and Ambrister not entitled to these congressionally sanctioned protective measures? Clay proclaimed that "no man could be executed in this free country without two things being shown; 1st. That the law condemns him to death; and 2dly. That his death is pronounced by that tribunal which is authorized by the law to try him." To violate either or both of these principles "was the very definition of tyranny itself." Possibly Jackson had not intended to violate the nation's laws, Clay said, but his possible ignorance did not make them any less violated.[30]

For Clay, though, the gravest issue struck at the very core of the nation's constitutional government. He believed that "of all the powers conferred by the Constitution of the United States, not one is more expressly and exclusively granted than that is to Congress of declaring war."[31] The Framers had reserved that power exclusively to the people's representatives to prevent the vanity, anger, and ambition of single individuals from placing the nation into that most perilous of situations. The entire Florida war might have been avoided, he said, if Congress had been consulted as the Constitution required. In a March 25, 1818, message to Congress, President Monroe had declared that the military had orders not to assault Spanish posts. Clay pointed out the strange coincidence that on that same day, Jackson had written from Florida that he planned to assault the Spanish post of St. Marks. He then seized Pensacola from the Spanish governor of West Florida; no other description could be used for Jackson's actions but war. Jackson, under orders not to make war on Spain, had done so without any constitutional authority. Clay urged the House to challenge this dangerous precedent.[32]

Clay's address framed the constitutional and legal issues raised by Jackson's actions, but the political wisdom of condemning a popular war hero gave Congress pause. Those who defended Jackson rarely touched on the constitutionality of his assaulting Spaniards, and most avoided the disconcerting Arbuthnot and Ambrister executions. Instead, they emphasized the savagery of Indian warfare and argued that it occasionally required extraordinary measures. John Rhea took this position.[33] In a rambling speech that traced the history of United States–Indian relations since the Revolution, Rhea defended Jackson's actions in Florida, but he never mentioned Jackson receiving authorization for them. Rhea based Jackson's defense solely on the need to protect American security from the threat posed by Florida's Indians. "Jackson was authorized by the supreme law of nature and nations," Rhea declared, "the law of self-defence."

Rhea did not mention any executive authorization because he knew of none. In a private letter to Jackson on December 18, 1818, Rhea spoke of the controversy likely to result from the impending congressional investigation. He assured Jackson that he had read all of the documents supplied by the administration and had concluded that he could support Jackson's actions in Florida. Even in this private letter that specifically referred to the debate over the campaign, Rhea made no reference to any covert authorization from James Monroe to seize the province.[34]

In fact, the only public mention during the entire 1818–19 controversy of anything even remotely connected to the subject of authorization was a single reference to Jackson's January 6 letter. It was made by Jackson's camp, and rather than supporting the contention that Rhea was enlisted to convey the president's blessing, it refutes Jackson's later statements about the matter. In an attempt to help Jackson, an anonymous letter signed "B.B." appeared in the Philadelphia *Aurora* in December 1818. The letter was the work of Jackson henchman and hanger-on William B. Lewis, who certainly wrote with

Jackson's permission and likely with his help. Lewis argued that Jackson could not be blamed for anything he did in Florida because President Monroe had been negligent in *not* answering Jackson's request for permission to seize the province. Lewis even said that by not answering the letter, Monroe had tacitly approved Jackson's actions, a position deeply flawed in itself as a constitutional vindication: Monroe as president could not authorize Jackson to make war, something that continued to trouble many in the branch of government that did have the constitutional power to declare war.[35]

On January 30, Congressman William Lowndes addressed that subject with cool detachment. Admired for his fairness and judicious temperament, Lowndes was frequently mentioned as presidential timber, especially because he seemed immune to ambition.[36] Everybody listened when William Lowndes spoke because he always said something worth hearing.

On this occasion, he said a mouthful. Lowndes began by conceding that the government had the right to cross the Florida border to chastise Seminoles, and if making war on Spain were necessary to protect the nation's interests, the United States had the right to declare it under proper constitutional prescriptions. Yet Lowndes quietly recommended that the House confine its deliberations to questions at hand: "Had General Jackson the right to take possession of St. Marks and Pensacola? Had the President of the United States the right? The rights of his subordinate officer were not greater than his own." Lowndes reminded the House of Georgia congressman John Forsyth's resolution from the previous spring that had urged seizing Florida. No one could have believed that by defeating that resolution the House was leaving the decision to seize Florida to President Monroe or to General Jackson. Lowndes calmly asked how some could now "justify a General in taking what the Congress of the United States had determined not to take?"[37]

Warming to his work, Lowndes forcefully stated that "the power of declaring war is given to Congress. To employ the army of the nation for the purpose of taking possession by force of the territory, the towns, and even the forts, of a foreign state, seems to fulfil every condition which can be necessary to constitute an act of war."[38] Lowndes pointed out that Monroe obviously recognized the plain constitutional facts of the matter in the orders issued before the invasion that no Spanish posts be molested and subsequently by directing that Spain's territory be restored.[39]

From this distance, Lowndes seems irrefutable, but at the time his case fell prey to Jackson's colossal popularity, which was the deciding factor in the House as it defeated the censorious majority report. The Senate, however, was another matter. The Senate select committee investigating Jackson's actions, headed by Pennsylvanian Abner Lacock, methodically gathered and sifted evidence, impassive to the histrionics of the volatile House. Jackson arrived in the capital on January 23, 1819, and smoldered from the start. The Senate's methodical deliberation infuriated him even more than any of the House speeches, even Clay's. The general's handlers tried to keep him calm, and in public, Jackson obliged them. In private, however, he was a thundering volcano, raging that he would challenge Clay to a duel and cut off Lacock's ears, threats that alarmed his friends but left his potential targets unmoved. Despite the Senate committee's condemnation of Jackson's actions in Florida, Clay was only snubbed and Lacock kept his ears. Thanks to Jackson's invasion, in fact, John Quincy Adams concluded a treaty with the Spanish minister to cede Florida to the United States. The Senate never voted on the committee report.[40]

The controversy regarding Florida quickly died down as other matters such as the economic Panic of 1819 and the crisis over Missouri's admission to the Union preoccupied Congress and the nation. Old Hickory emerged from the debates more admired than ever, and he set his sights on the presidency in 1824. Jackson won the popular vote in that contest, yet a crowded field of candidates deprived him of the necessary majority in the Electoral College. The election was thrown into the House of Representatives where John Quincy Adams was made president on the first ballot. Jackson and his followers were outraged that they had won the election only to lose it in the legislature, something they blamed on Speaker of the House Henry Clay, who supported Adams and persuaded others to follow him. When Adams selected Clay as his secretary of state, the charge that it was a "Corrupt Bargain" became a constant Jackson refrain. Adams took office on March 4, 1825, but the campaign for 1828 was already under way.

Andrew Jackson was determined to right the wrong he thought Adams and Clay had done to him. During the next three and a half years, Jackson and his people worked tirelessly to discredit opponents and fend off attacks. By 1827, Jackson was at odds with James Monroe, an argument that briefly resurrected the controversy over Jackson's unauthorized seizure of St. Marks and Pensacola. It started at a dinner party when Secretary of the Navy Samuel L. Southard casually observed that then Secretary of War James Monroe deserved more credit for the American victory at New Orleans in 1815 than he had been given. A reasonable man would have dismissed Southard's remark for the idle social chatter it was, yet when Jackson heard from a partisan an imprecise version of Southard's remarks that made them sound even more critical, he exploded. Worse, he gradually became convinced that Monroe was behind an attempt to diminish Jackson's role in defending the Crescent City. Soon the Jackson machine was in full roar, smearing Monroe as a negligent secretary of war and lauding Jackson for winning the Battle of New Orleans in spite of Monroe, not because of him.[41]

Monroe was old and ailing and wanted nothing more than to be left alone in retirement, exempt from the political squabbling he had always found distasteful. By the end of 1827, though, the storm over the Battle of New Orleans had grown to include charges about Monroe's role in the Seminole War. Jackson and his operatives here for the first time flirted with the lie they would brazenly tell four years later in the midst of another feud. They were in the process of inventing the myth that Monroe had authorized Jackson through John Rhea to seize Florida.

Monroe was bewildered by it all. He could not understand why the man he had protected in 1818 would now treat him this way. Seeking to defend himself, Monroe turned to his former secretary of war, John C. Calhoun, who was now vice president. Monroe knew that Calhoun had become Jackson's political ally, but his detailed knowledge of the events of 1818–19 would be all the more helpful coming from someone in Jackson's camp. Calhoun doubtless wanted his 1818 opinion about Jackson to remain a secret, but it is likely that Jackson already knew much of what had occurred during those cabinet meetings following his Florida campaign. Monroe confided to Calhoun his hurt and anger over the effort to build up Jackson by personally attacking Monroe's record. He had defended Jackson's clear disobedience to "an order of the War Dept." in taking Pensacola, "contrary to order," Monroe repeated for emphasis.[42]

In a letter two days later, Monroe asked Calhoun if he could reveal without breaking a confidence who was the author of these attacks. It was in this note that he mentioned Jackson's January 6, 1818, letter. Monroe reminded Calhoun that he had not read the letter until after Jackson had returned from Florida and that he had later queried Rhea about any authorization, even an inadvertent one. Rhea, Monroe remembered, had assured him there had been none.[43]

That was as far as the matter went in 1827, and it would not surface again until four years later when Jackson's target became Calhoun. Yet the events of 1827 were telling in another regard. One of Jackson's harshest scholarly critics believed that it was perhaps this clash in 1827 that prompted Jackson to invent a letter from John Rhea authorizing him to seize Florida. In a 1936 article, Richard Stenberg cited circumstantial evidence suggesting that instead of 1819 it was during the 1827 dispute that Jackson wrote in the margin of his letterbook next to the copy of his January 6, 1818, letter to Monroe, "Mr. J. Rhea's letter in answer is burnt this 12th April 1819."[44]

By 1828, Calhoun was a resolute Jackson ally, and the South Carolinian's supporters were positioning him to become Old Hickory's successor at the close of a Jackson presidency. These maneuvers troubled Martin Van Buren, whose own ambitions were soon to pit him against Calhoun. Van Buren began gathering evidence apparently with the purpose of driving a wedge between Calhoun and Jackson. Van Buren operative James Alexander Hamilton tried to pry information from Monroe's secretary of the treasury and Calhoun's enemy, William H. Crawford, about Calhoun's insistence during the 1818 cabinet deliberations that Jackson should be arrested for violating his orders.

The wily Hamilton also tried to wheedle information out of Calhoun, claiming that he was gathering information to defend Jackson. Calhoun smelled a rat, especially after he learned that Monroe's September 9, 1818, letter to him had been removed from his papers and given to Jackson. This letter mentioned the cabinet deliberations in vague terms, but it did indicate both Monroe's and Calhoun's disapproval of Jackson's actions. Calhoun tried to smooth over matters, exchanging several letters with Jackson before the 1828 election and winning reelection to the vice presidency, but the trouble continued after Jackson took office.[45]

Jackson was soon more than disenchanted with Calhoun. Several issues converged to ruin the vice president's standing in the administration by the end of 1830. Jackson and others later claimed that Jackson had suddenly discovered Calhoun's disloyalty to the general during the 1818 cabinet discussions, but that is highly unlikely. As early as 1827 and perhaps before then, Jackson had learned of Calhoun's position during those cabinet meetings but had chosen to ignore it.[46] Instead, Jackson blamed Calhoun for the social storm over Margaret Eaton that rocked the early days of the administration.[47] By early 1830, Jackson also saw Calhoun as the leading force behind South Carolina's threats to nullify the federal tariff. Eager for evidence to destroy Calhoun's credibility completely, Jackson was primed when William Crawford offered it. Only by chance did it relate to the old business of the Seminole War in Florida.

Crawford had despised Calhoun, sometimes cordially, since their days together in Monroe's cabinet. On April 30, 1830, Crawford wrote to his friend John Forsyth, but the letter was clearly meant for Andrew Jackson. In it, Crawford detailed the cabinet deliberations of the summer of 1818 to cast Calhoun in the worst possible light. Crawford was careful to conceal his own part in the affair by stating that Jackson's January 6 letter had been revealed to him for the first time in those discussions and had convinced him to oppose a reprimand. Because Monroe had not answered the letter, Crawford recalled having said that Jackson could have misunderstood and thought he had permission to seize Spanish territory.[48]

Crawford's indirectly aimed dart was only slightly delayed in finding its target. Forsyth quickly put the letter in Jackson's hands, and the president just as quickly sent it to Calhoun with a demand for an explanation. For good measure, Jackson snarled that he had never exceeded his orders. In yet another instance, though, what Jackson did not say is the most interesting part of this latest correspondence about what by now was an old dispute. Not once did Jackson mention that he had received authorization from Monroe to seize Florida. Instead, he still insisted, as he had done for more than a decade, that he had simply not exceeded the orders issued by Calhoun in December 1817.[49]

After telling Jackson that he would compose an appropriate response soon, Calhoun said that he was glad to have everything at last out in the open.[50] Possibly that was true, for Jackson's vague but obvious disfavor at least now had tangible form that Calhoun felt he could challenge with evidence. He diligently set about gathering it. He asked Monroe for his recollection about the January 6 letter, and the request at long last rendered a complete recounting of the events of 1818. The story was not pretty, but it was too incredible not to be true.

Monroe reminded Calhoun that he was "sick in bed" when Jackson's letter arrived and was unable to read it. Instead, Monroe had given the letter to him, Calhoun, who read it and said it required an answer. Shortly after this exchange, Crawford appeared and was shown the letter as well, giving the lie to his claim that he had first learned about it during the summer cabinet meetings. As he convalesced, Monroe had forgotten the letter until Jackson's actions in Florida came to light. Monroe had no recollection of Jackson's January 6 letter ever being discussed by the cabinet that summer. He did not think he would have forgotten that.

Either Crawford's memory or Monroe's was faulty, or one of them was lying. Calhoun soon visited Monroe to confer about the events of 1818. Neither could remember the January 6 letter ever being discussed in the cabinet, a recollection confirmed by Monroe's attorney general, William Wirt, who went even further. Until Calhoun queried Wirt about the letter, he had never heard of it. Monroe reassured Calhoun that Jackson would never make the January 6 letter part of his attack because it was more damaging to Old Hickory than anyone else. Monroe hoped that a soft answer would turn away wrath and retire the entire dispute. He counseled Calhoun accordingly, but he could not have been more wrong.[51]

Calhoun, however, adopted that strategy, apparently hoping that cool logic and calm words would heal the breach with Jackson. Obviously, he said, a difference of opinion over Jackson's orders in 1817 had created this current misunderstanding. At the time, the entire cabinet had agreed, Calhoun said, that Jackson had exceeded those orders, and Calhoun did not believe he should now have to apologize for having done his duty. Yes, the president and his cabinet had decided not to punish Jackson, Calhoun concurring, but he cited Monroe and Wirt's statements as proof that the January 6 letter was never discussed by the cabinet. Calhoun explained that the letter was not brought up even privately until November 1818 when he had reminded Monroe about it. The president then had read it for the first time.

So far, so good. It was certainly likely to give Jackson's strategists something to mull over. But then Calhoun made the dreadful mistake of telling Jackson what was good for him. The January 6 letter, he said, "greatly weakens your defense."[52]

Jackson almost certainly never had any intention of letting the matter drop, but Calhoun's admonishment struck him as intolerable effrontery. Goaded by Calhoun's enemies, Jackson was persuaded that Monroe was just as untrustworthy as the Carolinian. He was easily convinced that Monroe's entire administration had always been against him and that now Calhoun was in league with Henry Clay, one of Jackson's many bêtes noires, to ruin his presidency.[53]

By the end of 1830, Jackson was determined to brand both Calhoun and Monroe as liars, even if he himself had to lie to do so. We will likely never know if he invented Monroe's response to his January 6 letter in 1830 or in 1827, but it was certainly an invention, a means to what he regarded as the justifiable end of ruining Calhoun.

Calhoun returned to Washington from South Carolina at the end of 1830 and discovered that the controversy he had tried to end had taken on greater life. William H. Crawford had been pressing others, including an ailing Monroe, to support his version of the cabinet meetings in the summer of 1818: Calhoun had condemned Jackson, Crawford had supported Jackson, and the January 6 letter had been discussed.[54] Crawford had not persuaded anyone to revise his memory, but his apparently relentless campaign against Calhoun was troubling. Jackson and his circle had turned frosty toward Calhoun, evidence that Crawford was influencing at least some people.

Calhoun was confident about his memory and knew that Crawford was lying. He also pondered the irrationality of Jackson's blaming him after all these years for something that happened in 1818. Righteous indignation combined with the dread of a cornered animal can drive a man to folly. During the early months of 1831, Calhoun, feeling both righteously indignant and backed into a corner, did something foolish. Jackson and his advisors were arranging his ouster and seeking to destroy his political future in the process.

He became convinced that only by disproving all the lies in his dispute with Jackson could he hope to salvage that future. In February 1831, he published all of his correspondence with Jackson as well as letters corroborating his version of events. Jackson was enraged. He resolved to prove to the world that the Monroe administration had given prior approval to everything he had done in Florida.[55]

Even before Calhoun published the letters, Jackson was ready for the last phase of this fight. He wrote to John Rhea, now an old man in rapid decline, to remind him how Monroe had asked Rhea in early 1818 to give Jackson the president's consent to seize Florida. Jackson also reminded Rhea that when Jackson came to Washington in early 1819, they had discussed Rhea's letter and that Rhea had asked Jackson, as a friend and "brother Mason to burn" it. Jackson said that he had done as Rhea asked but that he also had noted the destruction of the letter next to the copy of his January 6 letter to Monroe. Now, however, he wanted Rhea to substantiate Jackson's version of events because Monroe was saying it had never happened. He closed by urging Rhea to do as he asked because it "[is] important to me."[56]

Rhea did not know what Jackson was talking about. He responded that he had no memory of the events Jackson described beyond that provided by his papers, which only reminded him that Jackson indeed had been in Washington in early 1819. It was possible, he sadly confessed, that the press of other business had caused him to forget meeting with Jackson then. He needed something to jog his memory, but he preferred that his name not be used publicly. Short of that, he promised to help Jackson in any way he could.[57]

Yet this was really no help at all. Jackson asked longtime friend John Overton to say that he had seen Rhea's 1818 letter, but like Rhea, Overton was obviously puzzled by the request. And like Rhea, he asked Jackson to jog his memory. Jackson obliged with a more elaborate story, and Overton crafted a vague statement, as though he remained reluctant to say he remembered something he clearly did not, that he had seen something that never existed. In fact, Overton recommended that Jackson drop the entire matter. Let Calhoun and Crawford fight it out, he suggested, likely hoping that such a prospect would be too tempting for Old Hickory to pass up.[58] Instead, Jackson told John Rhea that Overton supposedly had seen the letter that Rhea could not recall writing. The old man now pathetically asked Jackson to tell him what that letter had said and when he had written it. He also wanted a copy of Jackson's January 6, 1818, letter to help him with the particulars. On June 2, 1831, Jackson essentially told John Rhea what he needed for him to say, or at least he enlisted his secretary of war, John Eaton—who was convinced that Calhoun was behind the social snubs of his wife, Margaret—to tell John Rhea how best to craft the lie. By then, Rhea had come to Washington. The following day, June 3, 1831, Jackson got what he wanted. Suddenly remembering everything in vibrant detail, Rhea wrote to James Monroe that Monroe had shown him Jackson's January 6 letter in early 1818 and had authorized Rhea to convey to Jackson the authority to take Florida. Rhea also now remembered that in January 1819 Monroe had asked him to have Jackson burn that letter. It took months of wheedling, but Jackson had finally coaxed what he needed from a doddering old man eager to please him. When Rhea died less than a year later, relatives contested his will on the basis that his last years had been for him a haze of mental incompetence.[59]

Rhea requested a reply from Monroe, but the former president never answered him, at least directly. When Monroe received Rhea's message, he lay dying in the New York home of his son-in-law, Samuel L. Gouverneur, and was physically unable to write a response. His former attorney general, William Wirt, however, advised him that a response was necessary. Monroe devoted his fading energy to dictating an affidavit that denied every part of Rhea's letter. He signed his deposition on June 19, 1831. Two weeks later, on July 4, 1831, James Monroe died.[60]

The deposition was not sent to Rhea, but Gouverneur discreetly made its existence known, and that apparently prevented Jackson from publishing the letter he had coaxed out of Rhea. John Quincy Adams received a thick packet of documents, including Monroe's deposition, as he prepared his eulogy of the dead president. Adams had always been vaguely contemptuous of James Monroe, regarding him as a plodding intellect and ditheringly indecisive, but he read through the paper record of what had been done to Monroe in his last days with growing disgust. "There is a depth of depravity in this transaction at which the heart sickens," he wrote in his diary, "a total disregard to truth is chargeable upon so many men of the very highest standing." That Jackson had fabricated this transparent lie by taking advantage of the "dotage of a political parasite" like Rhea was beyond contemptible.[61]

Jackson at least was persuaded that Monroe's deposition and especially his death shortly afterward made Rhea's recent letter useless. But he never completely abandoned his quest to cast Calhoun as the villain in the Seminole War and its aftermath.[62] Through it all, he refused to consider that his seizure of Spanish posts in Florida in 1818 violated the Constitution, even if Monroe had authorized it, the absence of congressional consent being the key problem with the legitimacy of his actions. Yet Jackson was no fool. He may recklessly have thought himself exempt from the essential prescriptions of the U.S. Constitution, but he knew that a large part of the nation coveted Florida and embraced territorial expansion. Just as his exploits during the War of 1812 had made him The Hero, his foray into Florida further polished his luster among a people who smiled at his impetuosity. Seizing St. Marks and Pensacola, killing Red Sticks and wandering Britons, and insisting on the purity of his motives throughout it confirmed him as a man of action, a bright contrast to the professional politicians who were governed by dry words and complicated statutes rather than "the supreme law of nature" of which Jackson was a genuine force. The luster could be bright enough to blind many of the people of his time as well as some historians to Jackson's penchant for the petty smear and the outright lie, the darkest arts of the political class.

Notes

1. Negro Fort was an abandoned British fortification left from the brief British occupation of the area during the War of 1812. The fort had been turned over to Seminoles and maroons, and by 1816 it was a refuge for runaway slaves from the United States and Spanish Pensacola. The British had left artillery and small arms in the fort, and its existence as a fortified runaway slave refuge was viewed by American military forces along the border as a threat. Therefore, U.S. Army and Navy forces, working together in the summer of 1816, destroyed the fort.

2. Calhoun to Jackson, December 11, 1817, *Papers of John C. Calhoun*, 28 vols., ed. Robert L. Meriwether et al. (Columbia: University of South Carolina Press, 1959–86), 2:10; Roger J. Spiller, "John C. Calhoun as Secretary of War, 1817–1825," PhD diss., Louisiana State University, 1977, 79. Jackson had taken angry exception to the War Department's occasional practice of issuing orders directly to his subordinates. Calhoun was careful not to repeat the policy that had sparked Jackson's ire.

3. Calhoun to Jackson, December 26, 1817, in *American State Papers, Military Affairs*, 7 vols. (Washington: Gales and Seaton, 1832), 1:690 (hereinafter cited as *ASPMA*); Calhoun to Gaines, December 16, 1817, Calhoun, *Papers*, 2:20.

4. Endorsement of Calhoun's December 26, 1817, letter to Jackson, in Sam B. Smith et al., eds., *Papers of Andrew Jackson*, 7 vols. (Knoxville: University of Tennessee Press, 1980–2008), 4:163.

5. Gaines to Jackson, December 2, 1817, Jackson to George Graham, December 16, 1817, Jackson, *Papers*, 4:153–54, 161.

6. Calhoun to Gaines, December 16, 1817, *ASPMA*, 1:689; Calhoun to Jackson, December 17, 1817, Calhoun, *Papers*, 2:24; Jackson to Monroe, January 6, 1818, in *Monroe Papers*, New York Public Library. Copies of the letter can be found in the published collections of Jackson's papers, though since this document was marked "confidential" and therefore considered personal correspondence, it was not included in the papers concerning the invasion that were supplied to Congress during its investigations in 1819.

7. Monroe statement, *Monroe Papers*, New York Public Library; Harry Ammon, *James Monroe: The Quest for National Identity* (New York: McGraw-Hill, 1971; reprint,

Charlottesville: University Press of Virginia, 1990), 416–17; William P. Cresson, *James Monroe* (Chapel Hill: University of North Carolina Press, 1946; reprint, Hamden, Conn.: Archon Books, 1971), 304–7.

8. Jackson to Calhoun, March 25, 1818, *ASPMA*, 1:698.

9. Jackson to McKeever, March 26, 1818, *Niles' Weekly Register*, March 20, 1819.

10. Jackson to Luengo, April 6, 1818, Luengo to Jackson, April 7, 1818, *ASPMA*, 1:704, 705; J. Leitch Wright Jr., *Creeks and Seminoles: The Destruction and Regeneration of the Muscogulge People* (Lincoln: University of Nebraska Press, 1986), 205.

11. Jackson to Calhoun, April 20, 1818, Jackson, *Papers*, 4:195; William S. Coker and Thomas D. Watson, *Indian Traders of the Southeastern Spanish Borderlands: Panton, Leslie & Company and John Forbes & Company, 1783–1847* (Gainesville: University Presses of Florida, 1986), 320; Edward Brett Randolph Diary, Southern Historical Collection, University of North Carolina, Chapel Hill, April 18, 1818.

12. Minutes of the Special Court, April 28 1818, General orders, Adjutant General Robert Butler, April 29, 1818, Butler to Park, *ASPMA*, 1:704, 730, 734; Wright, *Creeks and Seminoles*, 207.

13. Jackson to Calhoun, May 5, 1818, Jackson to Monroe, June 2, 1818, Jackson, *Papers*, 4:199–200, 213–15.

14. Diaries of John Quincy Adams, May 4, 1818, 30: 344, Digital Collection, Massachusetts Historical Society.

15. Cresson, *Monroe*, 312; Diaries of John Quincy Adams, July 15–19, 1818, 30: 373–76.

16. David S. Heidler and Jeanne T. Heidler, *Old Hickory's War: Andrew Jackson and the Quest for Empire* (Baton Rouge: Louisiana State University Press, 2003), 185.

17. Monroe to Jackson, July 19, 1818, Jackson, *Papers*, 4:224–27.

18. Jackson to Calhoun, August 10, 1818, Jackson, *Papers*, 4:232.

19. Jackson to Monroe, August 19, 1818, Jackson, *Papers*, 4:236–38.

20. Monroe to James Madison, July 20, 1818, Monroe to Thomas Jefferson, July 22, 1818, Stanislas Murray Hamilton, ed., *The Writings of James Monroe*, 7 vols. (New York: G. P. Putnam's Sons, 1898–1903), 6:61, 63.

21. Monroe to Calhoun, September 9 and 12, 1818, Calhoun, *Papers*, 3:113–14, 121.

22. Monroe to Calhoun, December 28, 1827, Calhoun, *Papers*, 10:325.

23. Monroe's State of the Union Message, November 17, 1818, in Fred N. Israel, ed., *The State of the Union Messages of the Presidents, 1790–1866*, 3 vols. (New York: Chelsea House Robert Hector), 1:157–61.

24. *Annals of Congress of the United States*, 42 vols. (Washington, D.C.: Gales and Seaton, 1834–56), 15th Cong., 2nd sess., 374–75.

25. John Henry Eaton to Jackson, November 20, 1818, Jackson to John Coffee, January 4, 1819, Jackson, *Papers*, 4:248–49, 266.

26. House Committee on Military Affairs Report, *ASPMA*, 1:735.

27. *Annals of Congress*, 634.

28. Ibid., 640–41.

29. Ibid., 641–43.

30. Ibid., 644–47.

31. Ibid., 647.

32. Ibid., 648–55.

33. Ibid., 855–70.

34. John Rhea to Jackson, December 18, 1818, in John Spencer Bassett, ed., *Correspondence of Andrew Jackson*, 7 vols. (Washington, D.C.: Carnegie Institute of Washington, 1926–35), 2:403.

35. Ammon, *Monroe*, 416; Diaries of John Quincy Adams, December 17, 1818, 30: 373–76; Monroe to Adams, March 11, 1831, and Monroe to Calhoun, May 19, 1830, Hamilton, ed., *Writings of Monroe*, 7:227, 209–10.

36. Lowndes was regarded as a serious contender for the presidential election of 1824 until his untimely death in 1822.

37. *Annals of Congress*, 914.

38. Ibid., 914.

39. Ibid., 915–16.

40. Jackson to William B. Lewis, January 30, 1819, Jackson, *Papers*, 4:268–69; Lacock to Calhoun, February 3, 1819, Lacock to Calhoun, February 8, 1819, Calhoun to Lacock, February 20, 1819, Calhoun, *Papers*, 3:240–41, 556, 596; Herbert Bruce Fuller, *The Purchase of Florida: Its History and Diplomacy* (Gainesville: University of Florida Press, 1964), 264–65; Heidler and Heidler, *Old Hickory's War*, 219–20. The British wanted to solidify amicable relations with the United States and consequently dropped their objections to the Arbuthnot and Ambrister executions.

41. Ammon, *Monroe*, 558–59. James Monroe in part became involved in this dispute because of efforts by Adams administration partisans, Southard prominent among them, to enlist the former president's support in the 1828 election. See Michael Birkner, *Samuel L. Southard, Jeffersonian Whig* (London and Toronto: Associated University Presses, 1984), 82–87.

42. Monroe to Calhoun, December 26, 1827, Calhoun, *Papers*, 10:323.

43. Monroe to Calhoun, December 28, 1827, Hamilton, ed., *Writings of Monroe*, 7:138–39.

44. Richard R. Stenberg, "Jackson's 'Rhea Letter' Hoax," *Journal of Southern History* 2 (November 1936): 490.

45. Hamilton to Forsyth, January 29, 1828, Forsyth to Hamilton, February 8, 1828, Hamilton to Calhoun, February 25, 1828, Calhoun to Hamilton, March 2, 1828, Calhoun to Monroe, March 7, 1828, Calhoun to Jackson, April 30, 1828, Calhoun, *Papers*, 10:342, 345, 354–56, 357–58, 378–79; Jackson to Calhoun, May 25, 1828, Jackson, *Papers*, 6:461–63.

46. Jackson, *Papers*, 6:463.

47. The Eaton Affair stemmed from the awkward social situation surrounding Secretary of War John Eaton's recent marriage to Margaret O'Neal Timberlake, a young widow of questionable reputation. The other cabinet wives refused to socialize with Mrs. Eaton, and Jackson was led to believe that Calhoun's wife had encouraged their

behavior. The ensuing discord put a considerable strain on Jackson's cabinet and eventually brought about its dissolution.

48. Crawford to Van Buren, October 21, 1828, Crawford to Forsyth, April 30, 1830, Calhoun, *Papers*, 10:430, 11:160–61.

49. Jackson to Calhoun, May 13, 1830, Calhoun, *Papers*, 11:159–60.

50. Calhoun to Jackson, May 13, 1830, Calhoun, *Papers*, 11:162–63.

51. Calhoun to Monroe, May 17, 1830, Monroe to Calhoun, May 19 and 21, 1830, Calhoun to Monroe, May 26, 1830, Wirt to Calhoun, May 28, 1830, Calhoun, *Papers*, 11:164–66, 169, 171–72.

52. Calhoun to Jackson, May 29, 1830, Calhoun, *Papers*, 11:173–87.

53. John Coffee to Jackson, June 16, 1830, Bassett, ed., *Correspondence of Jackson*, 4:151–52. Clay was actually in retirement in Lexington, Kentucky, and had no contact with Calhoun during these events. He would not return to Washington until he was elected to the Senate in 1831.

54. Crawford's motives in this affair have never been adequately explored. His dislike for Calhoun was certainly common knowledge, and he had had a falling out with Monroe toward the end of Monroe's term. In 1830–31 he continued in bad health, problems that began when he suffered an attack, perhaps a stroke, in 1823. However, by 1830, he was obviously contemplating a political comeback, and perhaps his attempt to work his way into Jackson's good graces was part of that effort. Crawford to Henry Clay, March 31, 1830, Henry Clay, *The Papers of Henry Clay*, 11 vols., ed. James F. Hopkins et al. (Lexington: University of Kentucky Press, 1959–92), 8:185–86.

55. Charles M. Wiltse, *John C. Calhoun, Nullifier, 1829–1839* (Indianapolis: Bobbs-Merrill, 1949), 94–96.

56. Jackson to Rhea, January 4, 1831, *Andrew Jackson Papers*, 1820–36, Perkins Library, Duke University.

57. Rhea to Jackson, January 4, 1831, Bassett, ed. *Correspondence of Jackson*, 4:221–22.

58. Overton to Jackson, February 3, 1831, Bassett, ed., *Correspondence of Jackson*, 4:236–38.

59. Rhea to Jackson, March 30, 1831, Jackson to Rhea, June 2, 1831, Rhea to Monroe, June 3, 1831, Bassett ed., *Correspondence of Jackson*, 4:238, 254–55, 288–89; Stenberg, "'Rhea Letter' Hoax," 483–84.

60. Bassett, ed., *Correspondence of Jackson*, 4:289; Ammon, *Monroe*, 417; Monroe Deposition, in Hamilton, ed., *Writings of Monroe*, 7:234–36.

61. Diaries of John Quincy Adams, August 30, 1831, 38:257.

62. Stenberg, "'Rhea Letter' Hoax," 485; Jackson to Van Buren, July 11, 1831, Jackson to David Burford, July 28, 1831, Henry Baldwin to Jackson, October 18, 1831, Lacock to Baldwin, February 18, 1832, Jackson to Baldwin, February 27, 1832, Lacock to Baldwin, March 12, 1832, Lacock to Jackson, June 25, 1832, Memorandum for William B. Lewis, January 1837, Bassett, ed., *Correspondence of Jackson*, 4:312–13, 319–20, 360–61, 411–13, 435, 452, 5:445.

5

Strategy, Operations, and Tactics
in the Second Seminole War, 1835–1842

JOE KNETSCH

A plan of campaign should anticipate everything which the enemy can do,
and contain within itself the means of thwarting him.
Napoleon Bonaparte

Modern military terminology has been divided into three distinct categories as a result of studying Soviet concepts immediately after the Second World War. The word *strategy* today consists of the decision on national goals and objectives in a war. The "operational" art concentrates on getting the army organized to achieve these broad goals and determining which forces should be used to conduct the campaign. It also includes the crucial study of the enemy's capabilities and how to counteract them. Logistics, in the large sense, is also included under operational art in today's nomenclature. The tactical side of the growing equation stresses the battlefield and how to maneuver the enemy into position for attack or how to defend against an assault on your own forces. The battlefield is the total focus of the tactician, and this officer is not concerned with national goals, policy, or any of the broader operational objectives. His concern is the immediate place and time of battle.[1]

In the days of the Seminole Wars, the term *strategy* covered only the planning of the campaign against the enemy; it was essentially a paper exercise until the army took the field. Tactics begins with the details of the battle plan and ascends to the generalizations and combinations necessary to carry the army into battle. According to the master of strategy at the time of the Seminole War, Antoine Henri Jomini, strategy took into account the selection of the theater of war, the decisive points to seize, the choice of lines of defense or operation, the selections of objectives, the situation of bases of operation, depots, lines of march, and points for entrenched camps or fortification and other details of planning. Tactics, in the broadest sense, took into account the movement of armies onto the field of battle and the initial disposition of the troops.[2] It is the latter, Jomini's sense of strategy and tactics, with which the following is concerned.

Almost every commander of troops in the Second Seminole War grew in military stature as a result of service in the War of 1812. Winfield Scott, Alexander Macomb, Thomas Jesup, Walker Armistead, and Zachary Taylor all served with distinction in that contest. Each learned the soldier's craft from the harsh school of experience against a determined, European-trained army. President Andrew Jackson also grew to military manhood in that war and passed much of his training on to his protégé, Richard K. Call, just as Scott did for his own student, William Jenkins Worth. The impact of this war on the thinking of these men is undeniable. Each in his own way studied the strategy and tactics of his day with special attention given to the ultimate practitioner, Napoleon Bonaparte. Combining the lessons of the war with those of Jomini, the greatest contemporary commentator on Napoleon's campaigns, gave the essential understanding of the art of war to these distinguished gentlemen.[3] There was no systematic study of guerrilla or partisan warfare available for study, thus depriving those who would meet the American masters of this type of combat on the fields in Florida and in the west. The main concern of the military leadership of the day was the potential war with Great Britain, Spain, or some other European power attempting to assert its influence in the Americas.

The immediate threat to the security of the United States was from outside invasion as it had been in the War of 1812. Little thought was given to the planning for operations against the Native Americans along the vast frontier of the United States. Rumblings in Canada would soon break out into insurgency along the border and the constant movement of insurrectionist forces along the Canadian–United States border was a major concern of the army staff.[4] The growing revolution in Texas was also diverting attention from any concentration on Indian removal from Florida and other parts of the South. Any potential warfare would most likely come from either Great Britain or Mexico. With the army covering the frontier in a long string of distant fortifications, little thought was given to planning for war with the dissatisfied Natives living so far from "civilization" or the nation's shores or the nation's vital international interests.

Unacknowledged by the relatively few planners in Washington, the Florida frontier was about to erupt into the bloodiest and most costly Indian war in American history. Despite the warnings of General Duncan L. Clinch and others in Florida, the army and the government generally were not prepared for a major Indian war in December 1835. The military establishment in Washington and a retrenchment-minded Congress were oblivious to the issue of military preparedness. The army had undergone years of reduced budgets and cuts in forces and almost constant congressional scrutiny. The election of General Andrew Jackson to the White House in 1828 did little to change or improve the military's status; indeed, the new democratic mood of the country remained distrustful of a standing military establishment, and some in Congress even cried out for the dismantling of West Point, fearing the rise of a military elite. This shortsighted view resulted in a military seeking to please the politicians yet bickering among itself for promotions and privileges caused by the reduced opportunities for advancement in a smaller army. The military establishment also still relied upon the outdated and inefficient contract procurement methods that had plagued every campaign since Washington's day. The U.S. military was in no way prepared for the outbreak of war, especially in remote, swamp-infested Florida.[5]

With the ambush and destruction of the forces under Major Francis L. Dade and the killing of Indian Agent Wiley Thompson, Lieutenant Constantine Smith and others at Fort King on December 28, 1835, the outbreak of the Second Seminole War brought a stark reality to the nation. A large military force had been annihilated, and the remaining troops under General Clinch appeared bottled up in three or four frontier posts. The Florida Militia had been defeated at the Battle of Dunlawton, which exposed the entire east coast of Florida to destruction in the wake of the retreat to St. Augustine.[6] The situation was very bleak for the army, the militia and the people of the Territory. To make matters worse, there appeared to be no prepared strategy to thwart the Seminoles and their allies. If removal was the strategy, General Clinch had less than 400 effectives to carry out the mission. It was an impossible task.

General Duncan Clinch was an upright and experienced soldier and a very well connected man. His actual military campaign experience came with the destruction of the "Negro Fort" on the Apalachicola River in 1816. There was only one battle fought in this brief campaign, and that ended when the "hotshot" from a naval howitzer hit the powder magazine, killing most of the inhabitants of the fort. The general had missed the entire War of 1812 because of unfortunate assignments and received no battle experience during those formative years. Most of his career was spent in the South at various frontier posts and none where actual combat experience could have been gained. It was probably this lack of experience and the tactical blunders of that isolated general that caused the president to send General Winfield Scott to Florida shortly after the beginning of the war, supplanting Clinch.[7]

Clinch was not supplied with adequate forces for the removal of the Seminoles and their Miccosukee and black allies. His total force in November 1835 amounted to only 536 men. The Seminoles and their allies were estimated to be nearly 5,000 people with over 1,500 warriors. Clinch had been warning the government for over a year that the Seminoles were likely to resist emigration, and he was joined in these protests by Governor John Eaton and Indian Agent Wiley Thompson. Their concerns were not shared by the government in Washington and by Secretary of War Lewis Cass. The increased number of raids upon the plantations in Florida and the bold slave raiding and land speculation by the whites moved Colonel Alexander C. W. Fanning to write the Adjutant General that unless the "cupidity of our own citizens" was ended and additional forces were sent to keep them out of Indian lands, war would soon break out.[8] Clinch's own correspondence echoed his subordinate's words.[9]

Even before he knew that one-fifth of his command had been wiped out at Dade's Battle, Clinch began making plans for his one campaign against the Seminoles. General Richard Keith Call, commanding the Florida Militia, joined Clinch near the latter's plantation in northern Marion County, called Auld Lang Syne Plantation (later Fort Drane). With a combined force of about 400 militia and over 200 regulars, Clinch and Call led their commands toward the Cove of the Withlacoochee River (today's Lake Tsala Apopka in Citrus County, Florida). The Cove was known to be the home of a large force of Seminoles, and it was hoped that the combined force would be able to quickly descend upon it and defeat the Indians in one culminating battle. Clinch and Call did not have adequate information about the territory they were entering, and their scouts could find no convenient fording place across the swift and winding river. After searching for some time, which precluded any surprise in their plans, they did locate a single old boat which could hold about five men, constantly bailing water, with which to cross the entire force. After a short conference it was decided to try and send the men across by this limited means. It was a gamble Clinch felt he had to take.

The result of his gamble was a throw of the dice that causes some controversy to this very day. Almost the entire force of regulars made it across, along with a handful of Call's mounted militia, when the Seminoles, under the able leadership of Alligator, opened fire. It was almost perfectly timed by the Seminole War leader, as the force was now only halfway across the river, isolated against his warriors and beyond the aid of any artillery. The tactical advantage lay on the side of Alligator, and he took full measure of it. The regular army men used the tactics in which they were trained and charged the hammocks where Alligator's forces were lodged. Time and again, the regulars and the few militia involved charged into the thick woods and swamps, only to find the Indians had disappeared. The results of the battle were inconclusive, but the casualties show that the Seminoles got the better of the engagement, losing only three killed and five wounded, while Clinch lost four dead and fifty-nine wounded. The force limped back to Fort Drane to ponder these results, and there began a lifelong feud between Clinch and Call over why the militia did or did not come across the river to take a more active role in the fight. The government's strategy, if it can be called such at this juncture, was stalemated, and Clinch's tactical defeat made his quick replacement by Scott more bitter. The inexperienced Clinch had divided his forces and did not consolidate them in a timely manner. Added to the division of his army at the Withlacoochee and subjecting his force to possible annihilation, the military leadership in Washington had little choice but to remove him from command. Clinch would not have an opportunity to redeem himself.[10]

The news of Dade's command did not reach official Washington until January 20, 1836. It happened that Winfield Scott was in Washington at the time and immediately volunteered his services to Secretary Cass. The very next day, Scott received his instructions to head to Florida and quell the uprising. He was not to make peace unless the Seminoles acquiesced in moving westward and gave up every slave belonging to any white man to the military authorities. The "imaginary line" between his officially assigned area of control and that of General Edmund P. Gaines, who allegedly controlled the western half of Florida, was to be ignored. This was the first time he was ever given complete command of a campaign, although he had performed admirably in all of his subordinate assignments. Scott began his preparations quickly and headed southward meeting with governors of the various states to obtain troops (militia) and supplies along the way. He was greatly handicapped by having no personal knowledge of the terrain of Florida, no adequate mapping and having no personal experience in fighting the guerrilla tactics of Native Americans. Scott was totally immersed in the knowledge of how to fight a European war and was the author of the text on infantry tactics based upon his studies of French tactics and strategy. This thorough background in European planning played a major role in his decisions during the coming campaign and was to prove totally inadequate to the needs.[11]

Scott's progress toward Florida was slowed by the conferences and the attention to details of supply he experienced. He was dismayed to find materials lacking at almost every turn and transportation for what he could find almost impossible to acquire. The lack of infrastructure in Florida also hampered the plans, and there were few forward bases from which to launch his planned attacks. Scott did learn that the Cove of the Withlacoochee had not been taken and that the Seminoles were still there in considerable strength. He quickly decided that this would be the object of his main campaign. Scott's successful work in Canada during the War of 1812 plus his intense study of European

5.1. Winfield Scott (Florida State Library and Archives).

models now played against him. In the grand tradition of Napoleon and other great European leaders, he ordered his newly forming army to be divided into three columns, which were to descend upon the Cove simultaneously. Scott believed that his strategy would bring about the conclusive battle that would end this war quickly. Even though the War Department was a bit skeptical of the overall plan, the administration saw that a quick conclusion was what they desired, and as Scott was on the ground with an "overwhelming force," he should be allowed to proceed.[12] The administration needed a quick victory in Florida, since the important election of 1836 was about to take place and Jackson's party needed the positive result to bolster its electoral chances. The political influence upon the strategy adopted is never far from the surface.[13]

Clinch had withdrawn his tattered forces to Fort Drane, his personal plantation home in Florida now surrounded by pickets, and there awaited the arrival of Scott. Scott was aware of his lack of knowledge of the Florida frontier and needed Clinch's advice and knowledge if he was to be successful. Scott tried to soften the blow of the reduced status of Clinch and wrote to him: "By letter from the Secretary of War, you will have been advised of my approach for the purpose of taking upon myself the general direction of the war in Florida. No mortification ought to be felt by you because the command has been given to me, I am your Senior & it is known that I was your friend. With very limited, & as experience has shown, inadequate resources, you have maintained you position in the enemy's country, & you have fought a battle with honor to yourself & the handful of brave men who were under you." Scott then added the following: "I shall have an overwhelming force with ample magazines & means of transportation, together with all *the benefit of your better local knowledge and personal services.*"[14] Scott enumerated the forces now at his disposal, which he planned to gather together at Picolata (on the St. Johns River) and St. Augustine. Scott also stated to Clinch: "I am unable, as yet, from the want of recent information from the theatre of war, & better topographical knowledge of that theatre, to lay down any definite plan of operations. I shall rely much on communications to be received from you, on all points necessary to the formation of such plan."[15] According to Scott biographer, Timothy D. Johnson, the general formulated his strategy en route to Florida after receiving his correspondence from General Clinch and Governor John Eaton. The latter gentleman advised Scott to attack the Seminoles from multiple points and warned: "In an open field Greek may meet Greek and contend for the palm of victory, but amidst the gloomy cover forests, where the savages can lie concealed, that sort of glory is too insecure and doubtful."[16] With the eyes of the nation upon him, this was indeed, sage advice, but could the victor of the Battle of Chippewa bring new glory to himself and the army?

Scott's grand design followed all of the dictates of the theories of Jomini. He established his bases of operations, knew roughly his lines of operation, had established with Clinch's aid the objective point of the campaign, and had secured as best as possible his bases of supply and the forward depots in which they were to be deposited. The most important thing lacking was the geographical knowledge of the campaign theater and how to get them to the objective point in fair order and on time. This lack of topographical knowledge could not be provided by Clinch or anyone under his direct command. Florida was a true frontier and much of it unexplored. River crossings were not known, nor how many such obstacles would have to be surmounted by the three columns he designed to converge upon the Cove of the Withla-coochee, which he had chosen as the objective point for the entire campaign. Another handicap to be experienced by the learned General Scott was the capabilities of his junior officers. Generals Clinch and General Abraham Eustis were well known to Scott, whereas Colonel William Lindsey, who was to lead the column from Tampa, was less understood. If successful, Scott would have met the strategic and political needs of the administration; however, if he failed, the war might drag on for years. It was a wonderful plan on paper, but as historian Allan Peskin has observed: "Rather than adapt to the unusual conditions he now confronted, the general chose to impose his view of warfare upon them. He devised an intricate plan designed to end the war at one blow. Convinced that most of the Seminoles were concentrated around the Cove of the Withlacoochee, he divided his army into three columns, each of which would converge upon the enemy from different directions, surrounding them and preventing their escape into the wilderness."[17] Scott's plan depended upon his three subordinates, the reliable delivery of the supplies, cooperation of numerous volunteer groups, and the quick execution of the plan with all three units arriving at nearly the same time. To observe that the conditions in Florida were not optimal is to state the obvious.

Scott was not comfortable in his new situation. Many of his troops would be volunteers and militia units, whom he had never trusted. Scott even once wrote that the handsome army of the War of 1812 would have been disgraced if it had admitted militia units into its ranks.[18] Scott had also written to Secretary of War Lewis Cass that the campaign would require 5,000 men, most of them mounted—a substantial addition to the burdens of supply and subsistence. The problem with a large number of militia and volunteer forces was the short term of enlistment. Most of the volunteers were signed for terms of three or six months, which did not make for a stable fighting force. Many of the militia units showed up for muster without arms, ammunition, packs, or any of the usually supplied accoutrements.[19] Because the army did not number the required strength that Scott desired, he was forced to rely upon these volunteer and militia forces, which flew in the face of General George Washington's noted dictum that "militiamen might harass but never conduct a decisive attack."[20] Militia forces are notoriously difficult to coordinate in battle, and a major three-pronged attack as that contemplated by General Scott in an unknown wilderness was asking too much from this assorted grouping of forces. Scott had weighed all of this information, but felt the need to press forward, communicating by periodic cannon blasts which negated any attempt at surprise. But for Scott there was one surprise he had not counted on: the arrival on the scene of his arch rival, General Edmund P. Gaines.

General Gaines technically had control of the western portion of the Territory of Florida. He was in New Orleans when he learned of Dade's fate and decided immediately to raise enough forces to relieve the situation. Although he would later scoff at the plan put forth by General Scott, Gaines had no set plan on how to bring about the end of the war or how to relieve Clinch. By every account he actually violated orders that awaited him in Pensacola to continue his course toward Fort Brooke at Tampa. Gaines was very much inclined to abandon Fort Brooke and put every person not going in his relief force on boats in the bay, but he soon changed his mind when the Marines arrived to augment his numbers. In a bold move, he ordered his combined forces out of the comfort of Fort Brooke, following the same primitive road Dade had taken, and set out for Fort King (today's Ocala). In short, his premature and questionable movements used up a number of supplies left by Clinch and Scott for their forces at the depots along the route to Fort Drane. Gaines sized up the situation and headed directly for the Cove of the Withlacoochee, only to become engaged with the Seminoles and their allies near the place where Clinch and Call had fought them earlier. The hastily constructed Camp Izard became a sort of entrapment for Gaines's force, and Clinch, against orders, rode to his rescue. The retreat, for the second time, back to Fort Drane was not sweetened by the presence of all three commanders, Clinch, Gaines, and Scott. To note that the air had a distinct chill would not be a comment on the weather. Scott was to blame this intrusion by Gaines for the failure of his plans.[21]

Scott faced many failures during this single campaign in Florida. His supplies were exhausted by Gaines's ill-timed intervention, and the timing of his movements had to be readjusted. The element of surprise, if it ever existed at all, was totally lost by Gaines's movements and the cannon signals and regimental band. There was a massive logistical failure in the provision of transportation and supplies of fodder for the horses. Mapping of the interior of Florida was almost nonexistent, and his columns were operating almost totally blind in the wilderness, especially those under Eustis. The performance of Colonel Lindsey with a large contingent of Alabama volunteers was very weak and resulted in a near-mutiny. The result of these problems was virtually no direct contact with the enemy, the exhaustion of the troops, and the continuation of the disastrous war. Scott did attempt to rescue some prestige with his return movements to Fort Drane and Volusia, but the Seminoles and their allies were very well aware of the superior numbers and arms of the soldiers and refused to give battle.[22]

Winfield Scott, schooled in the European style of war fashionable among the military of the day, was not prepared to fight a guerrilla war in the swamps and hammocks of Florida. Although a student of European warfare and an admirer of Napoleon, he ignored the emperor's dictum about knowing the enemy and what to expect from him. Like Jackson, before whose superior force the Seminoles and Miccosukees had retreated in the so-called First Seminole War (1817–18), Scott had underestimated the enemy. The overwhelming numbers he wished to employ would never face a united enemy force, only scattered guerrillas using hit-and-run tactics meant to discourage the enemy and prolong the war. Precision timing of the three-pronged attack could not be achieved in the swamps and mire of Florida's vast, uncharted interior. The superior knowledge of the enemy of this terrain and climate and the advantage of dictating the time and place of battle, when given at all, made Scott's strategic plan a loser from the beginning. Scott was frustrated when he left Florida to conduct a campaign in Alabama and lashed out at the citizens of Florida for their lack of intestinal fortitude in the face of the "savages" of the Territory. The citizens of the Territory demonstrated their appreciation of this display of anger by hanging the general in effigy in the territorial capitol, Tallahassee. Florida's General Leigh Read summed up the situation by noting that European tactics were used by Scott "where they could not possibly work."[23]

When Scott left Florida in May 1836, he did so with little regret.[24] His position was taken by General Richard Keith Call of the Florida Militia. Call had served with Jackson and was a trusted political ally. As he was given command at the beginning of the rainy season, Call did not take the field immediately but spent his time coordinating with General Leigh Read and the numerous volunteers from the Southern states, particularly Georgia, Alabama, Tennessee, Louisiana, and South Carolina. The regular forces remaining in Florida were placed under the command of the quartermaster general of the army, Thomas Jesup, who was second in the overall command to Call. Call was not to have the resources available to Scott and had the unenviable task of trying to coordinate the variety of forces noted above. Call did establish a number of inland posts and supply depots and ordered them to be made ready for the new campaign. However, illness of the troops, the death of his wife, an overall lack of supplies, and numerous troubles with the volunteer forces led to further aggravation and failures for Call. Again, the focus of the campaign, if such there was, centered on the Withlacoochee River basin and the lands in East Florida near Volusia, south of Lake George on the St. Johns River. Despite the best efforts of Call and Jesup, the disjointed campaign accomplished very little. On December 8, 1836, Governor Call was replaced by Jesup in command of the forces in Florida. Thomas Jesup summed up Call's misfortunes: "He has had difficulties to encounter of which no man can form an adequate idea, who has not been here. I have examined carefully the state of the service and have looked into every matter connected with the recent operations, and I am sure that no man could have done more under the circumstances."[25]

The work of William B. Skelton has laid the foundation for the understanding of how the officer class viewed conflict with Native Americans generally. As we have seen, Winfield Scott and his superiors in Washington greatly underestimated the Seminoles and their allies. By underestimating the abilities and possible strategies to be employed by the enemy, Scott and others did not develop effective counterstrategies, which became a costly error in the Second Seminole War. Skelton's work notes that the officers generally viewed the Native Americans in strictly military terms—as brave, wily, and tenacious foes. Many Indians, it was recognized, had absorbed some of the whites' habits and culture, but none were totally "civilized" or equal to whites. The "Noble Savage" ideal of American literature did not prevail in military circles. The majority of officers who served against the Seminoles and Creeks did not look favorably upon their foes and attributed to them indolence, vengefulness, and a lack of intellect. The acts of brutality and treachery viewed by these officers on the frontier became part of the mantra of the need to totally subdue the cruel savage. These same officers often overlooked similar acts by their own troops or attributed them to the militia or volunteers. The Seminoles received mixed reactions from the officers serving in Florida, but as the resistance to the military continued and the war dragged on, they became more likely to be described as cunning, duplicitous, and cruel. "To most officers," Skelton observed, "progress seemed attainable only by following white society's example." There were many who felt a bit paternal toward the Indians simply because they viewed the white frontiersman as lazy, cruel, greedy, and, for some, too willing to hunt slaves and Indians for money. Many officers opposed the concept of Indian removal because they viewed whites as the aggressors in most cases. This was true of Gaines and Colonel Josiah Vose, both of whom served in Florida. In the final analysis, however, the majority of officers felt that any show of temporizing or fraternal feelings would give the Seminoles and others the wrong message, that of weakness. The only way to counter this was to use force and to use it quickly to achieve the removal desired by the government. The fact that the army did not effectively counter the guerrilla tactics of the Seminoles and their allies and the continued criticism by the public and Congress made adopting a strategy to meet the demands of the removal more difficult for the officers and men alike. It would take a different kind of warfare to bring the brutal conflict to an end.[26]

Development of an effective strategy was made even more unlikely by the organization of the War Department and the fragmentation of power within that branch of government. The major components of the War Department were the Adjutant General's Office, the Office of the Inspector General, the Commissary Office, the Quartermaster General's Office, the Ordinance Department, the Surgeon General's Office, and the Corps of Engineers. Each department head was responsible to the secretary of war, not the commanding general of the army. Each of these departments became like little fiefdoms and guarded their turf jealously. There was no general staff within the army to coordinate these departments and make them responsible to the General of the Army. The 1836 law for governing the army called for the following: "The General Staff comprises all of the officers concerned in regulating the details of the service and furnishing the Army with the means necessary for subsistence, comfort, mobility, and action." This meaningless description did little to clarify responsibility or enforce any systematic coordination of effort. When it is understood that the secretary of war was a political appointee of the president and that the department heads reported directly to this man and not to the commanding general, one begins to see the competing sources of power that precluded effective coordination of effort or the development of effective strategies to accomplish the goals of the government. Regardless of the disastrous results of this divided authority, the United States did not rectify the situation until the reforms of 1903 and following the Spanish-American War.[27]

Thomas Jesup, another veteran of the War of 1812 and a trusted subordinate of Winfield Scott until Scott's May 1836 campaign in Alabama, received the transfer of the command from Call on December 9, 1836, only days before the term of service of the Tennessee volunteers was to expire. Jesup immediately proposed to use these volunteers to attack the strongholds of Osceola, Micanopy, King Philip, and Cooper in quick succession to prevent them from concentrating and delivering a counterblow. Although this was very unlikely, Jesup had information that they were all on the west side of the Ocklawaha River. The quickly drawn-up plan of operations was to attack in that area and then to proceed down the Withlacoochee River toward Tampa. The concept of herding the Indians in the direction of the embarkation point was convenient but not possible, given the guerrilla tactics employed by the Seminoles. Jesup also took time to inform Washington that simple removal of the Indians was not the only point of these military operations. "This, you may be assured," declared the general, "is a negro, not an Indian war; and if it be not speedily put down, the South will feel the effects of it on their slave population before the end of the next season." With this declaration, Jesup was firmly in the camp of those who recognized that not all of the overall goals of the government had been clearly stated and that his strategy would have to adjust to the new reality. Seminole strength was thought to be known, but the augmentation of this Native force with runaway slaves and others meant readjustments for the army. Once again the army was forced to attempt to strike quickly and decisively in order to prevent a possible slave rebellion and achieve the stated goal of Seminole removal. By attempting to use the Tennessee volunteers in a quick campaign, Jesup hoped to attain at least some success in reaching each goal. It was not to be.

Having served under Call's temporary command for much of 1836, Jesup soon became acquainted with the difficulties of attempting to carry out the government's removal policy in such a land. Jesup understood as those in Washington did not that the blacks aligned with the Seminoles and Miccosukees were a vital element in the resistance. As difficult as it was, Jesup also had to plan for a campaign in the Florida wilderness, and he knew that it would be very costly in men and money. Therefore, early in 1837, he attempted to persuade the Seminole leadership, as he perceived it, to come in for discussions and eventual emigration to the West. Chasing Indians through the morass of Florida's swamps and fighting sporadic engagements with a limited number of the enemy would take years and be too expensive an operation. It was politically and economically not a viable option to Washington. The talks were arranged, and the major selling point was the provision that the Seminoles and Miccosukees could keep their "property" (slaves), sell their cattle and horses at a fair market price, and be provided with subsistence for at least one year after their arrival in the West. Micanopy, Alligator, Holatoochee, Cloud, and Jumper all attended these talks in Tampa and saw the twenty-six vessels in the harbor waiting to emigrate them westward. From the middle of May, as they straggled in, until June 5, 1837, the Indians remained near Fort Brooke and consumed supplies while carrying on sputtering negotiations. Jesup was convinced that the war was at an end and so informed Washington. It was not to be, and on that night Micanopy and others left the camp under the cover of darkness and took more than 700 followers with them. Exactly what caused the failure is unknown, but it was presumed that Osceola and Coacoochee (Wildcat) had come into the camp and forced the aging "chief" to leave. This is possible, but it leaves out the role of Abiaka (Sam Jones), the elected tribal leader of both the Seminoles and Miccosukees, the only man known to whites to have been elected to lead both groups. As an ardent opponent to emigration, Abiaka's leadership must have been powerful, and it is likely that he saw some sign that led him and the others to bring about the abandonment of the emigration Jesup sought. It was a crushing blow to Jesup's relatively peaceful intentions.

Jesup was forced to develop a new strategy to bring in the fugitive Indians and end the war. Part of the overall plan was to continue negotiations while

HUNTING INDIANS IN FLORIDA WITH BLOOD HOUNDS

5.2. Taylor in Florida (Library of Congress).

he built up the force in Florida and prepared for a major campaign. When in September 1837, General Joseph Hernandez of the Florida Militia captured King Philip and Uchee Billy, two of the leaders east of the St. Johns River, the door was opened for further negotiations. King Philip was the father of Coacoochee and widely respected among the Seminole bands. When Coacoochee approached Hernandez to negotiate for Philip, he informed the General that Osceola was also willing to enter into negotiations. Following orders from Jesup, Hernandez set up the meeting for October 22, 1837, near Fort Peyton, southeast of St. Augustine. It was here that the Indians' party was surrounded by the army and Florida volunteers and forced to surrender and submit to incarceration at Fort Marion (Castillo San Marcos). Jesup and Hernandez believed that this capturing of the headmen, as they viewed it, would end the war and deprive the Seminoles of the dynamic leadership of Osceola and Coacoochee. Even Coacoochee's daring escape from the ancient fortress did not dampen the positive spirit of the army with Osceola's capture. In the end, Osceola died a martyr's death, and the issue of capturing an enemy under a white flag of truce brought condemnation upon Jesup's name. It also opened the road to additional attacks on the administration's policies to end the war.

Jesup's defense noted the military necessity of the capture and the feckless nature of negotiating with the Seminoles who kept on killing his soldiers despite truces, negotiations, and the supplying of the tribe by the army with food and clothing during these periods of relative peace. As part of the overall strategy to end the war, this phase of Jesup's plan was a failure. The war dragged on for another five years after the death of the famed Indian leader.[28]

The strategy devised by Jesup for the campaign season of 1837–38 was a marvel of planning and wishful thinking. After establishing a series of posts on some of the most strategic routes, including Fort Dade on the Withlacoochee River, and reestablishing Fort King as the center of operations in central Florida, Jesup unfolded a bold plan designed to entrap the Seminoles and their allies in the southern portion of the peninsula. Four columns of army and militia units would move in differing directions and form a vice from which there would be no escape. If they were not brought to battle and defeated, the Seminoles would be left in the Everglades, where, it was believed, they would soon starve to death or seek emigration to the West. This marvelously planned campaign depended upon the supplies of troops, boats for operating in the shallow waters of Florida's rivers, materials for the construction of a series of fortifications, rations and clothing for the men, and forage for the animals. All this required planning, massive amounts of food, fighting, building materials, and the ability to deliver these items to the areas to be fortified and defended. It was simply beyond the ability of the army of the 1830s to deliver such goods in a timely manner. The logistics of this massive operation simply could not and did not work.

The elaborate plan devised by Jesup involved simultaneous operations by as many as nine columns. The main thrust of the plan was to send four columns to the southern portion of the Territory and drive the Indians into the vastness of the Everglades and await the outcome by forcing them into battle. The object was to end the war by late March or early April 1838. To accomplish this goal meant starting the campaign in September or October 1837, the beginning of the dry season in the southern portion of Florida. As Jesup noted:

> I had desired to commence operations on the 1st of October, because, at that time, the St. Johns is navigable a greater distance than at a later period; and I could avail myself of more than two months of the services of the Florida troops, whose term of service expired in December. The regular troops, however, did not begin to arrive until the last of October, and they continued to come in until December. The principal Volunteer forces arrived about the 1st of December.[29]

The late arrivals of the regulars and main volunteer forces meant that the campaign started late in the dry season and would have to end prior to the rainy season with all of its "miasmas" and related diseases. Jesup planned to lead the main column up the St. Johns River above Lake Monroe at Fort Mellon, the main supply base for this unit. Florida Militia General Joseph Hernandez would lead his forces down the east coast between the St. Johns River and the ocean. Hernandez would be joined further down the peninsula by General Eustis regulars with the Alabama and Tennessee volunteers. Once these forces had cleared their assigned areas of the enemy, they would link up with Jesup's column and proceed further down the coast, establishing posts along the way. Included in this line of posts were Fort Pierce, Fort Jupiter, Fort Lauderdale, and Fort Dallas (Miami).[30] The only result of this portion of the campaign was the Battle of the Loxahatchee, which drove a small force of Indians from the banks of the river. The site of this battle was near that of an earlier engagement between forces under Naval Lieutenant Levin Powell and an unknown number of Seminoles. This earlier battle costs a number of casualties including Dr. Frederick Leitner.[31]

A second column under the command of Colonel Zachary Taylor was to become engaged with the Seminoles and Miccosukees at the end of his march. This phase of the operation was described by Jesup: "General Taylor was directed to proceed from Tampa Bay, open a road in nearly an eastern direction into the heart of the country, establish a post at the head of Peace Creek [River], another on the Kissimmee, and attack the enemy in that quarter."[32] Taylor's forces were very successful in creating the posts along this route. They also scouted the territory thoroughly, including the forbidding section near Lake Istokpoga. Taylor and his large force of regulars and volunteers, including those of Missouri under the command of Colonel Richard Gentry, confronted a determined force of Seminoles and Miccosukees on Christmas Day of 1837 near the northern shore of Lake Okeechobee. The defensive position of the Indians was well chosen. Tactically, Taylor had little choice but to order a full frontal assault, forcing his men to charge across an open area covered waist-deep in water and muck for a distance of nearly half a mile. The use of cavalry was out of the question, and no artillery could be drawn anywhere near the battleground. The results were devastating with 26 men and officers killed and 112 wounded. Seminole losses were minimal, and they made their escape across the lake in boats. Taylor had taken the field but at a very heavy price. Taylor established a series of posts along the shores of the lake to preclude any attempt of the Seminoles and their allies from going back northward and eastward from the vicinity.[33]

The third column of this four-pronged operation was led by Louisiana's Percifor F. Smith. Smith's group formed in Tampa and headed southward to Charlotte Harbor. Movement was delayed until late December by the lack of

5.3. Thomas Sidney Jesup
(Florida State Library
and Archives).

adequate transportation. The objective of this force was to cut off trade with the Spanish fishermen from Cuba along the southwest coast and establish posts along the western edge of the Everglades. This action would complement those of Taylor and Jesup and prevent possible penetration by the Indians into the depths of the Big Cypress. In achieving his goals, Smith established Fort Center on Fisheating Creek, the largest western tributary of Lake Okeechobee. This post would become the major supply depot for Fort Bassinger (on the Kissimmee River) and Fort McRae (on the eastern shore of the lake) and act as a stopover post for scouts along and within the vast inland lake. Smith's forces also established Fort Deynaud (near modern-day LaBelle, Florida) and Fort Keais (pronounced Keys) at the northern edge of the Big Cypress. While performing these duties, Smith's men captured 243 prisoners.[34]

The final piece of the four-pronged operation was simply a holding action at the southern edge of the Everglades. There Surgeon General Thomas Lawson took active command at Cape Sable and established Fort Poinsett, named for the new secretary of war, Joel Poinsett. Few patrols left this outpost, and their only mission was to prevent any trade by the Seminoles with the Spanish fishermen who had used the coasts of Florida for nearly 300 years to supply the Havana market with salted fish. Although many reports of whites indicated this trade was flourishing, the army and navy, which patrolled the coasts, found few active in this alleged exchange. The area northwestward of Cape Sable all the way to the mouth of the Caloosahatchee River is typically mangrove islands laced with unseen and unknown channels. The lack of success in this area is not surprising, and Lawson abandoned the post in May 1838. A later post on Cape Sable, Fort Cross, was founded during the Third Seminole War (1855–58) for the same reasons. At that post the only victors were the mosquitoes and sand flies, and it was abandoned as unhealthy.[35]

Jesup's logistical nightmare in planning this operation was again related to the need for a specific style of transportation. Boats with such designs as needed were to be built in Philadelphia and New York, but they failed to reach Florida in time for the campaign. Shallow draught steamboats capable of navigating Florida's shallow rivers and streams had to be specially designed and built, but this was beyond the capacity of most northern boat yards of the day. Great quantities of supplies ranging from caps, shoes, canteens, belts, munitions, arms, accoutrements, etc., had to be sent to Florida and advanced to the posts. Throughout the entire campaign Jesup's letters show the frustration of the commander with the constant shortage of materials. On December 29, 1837, at the very beginning of the movements, Jesup wrote to a Lieutenant Watson: "Greatly to my surprise, on my return to this post [Fort Mellon] yesterday, I ascertained that there was neither sugar or coffee here for the troops. This is a most unpardonable neglect of some officer in the Commissary's Department. Report, without delay, the cause of this neglect. . . . The beans sent to the Army are utterly unfit for issue, if you send any of them send those that are fresh."[36] In one of the more notable incidents, the forces under Jesup lacked shoes, which forced the troops under command of Colonel Benjamin Pierce to halt their operations near Jupiter.[37] Jesup clearly understood the maxim put forth by the German emperor Frederick the Great, that "the foundation of the army is the belly." Jesup also understood the famed Prussian's advice to follow rivers as the best and surest means of supplying the troops. However, Jesup could do nothing about the army's policy of using private contractors and conveyors to supply the forces in the fields. In the end, Jesup's strategy designed to bring about the end of the Florida war failed because of the lack of supplies, underestimating the enemy's abilities as guerrilla fighters, having supply lines too far extended into the unknown wilderness and the simple vastness of the theater of war. Set piece, European-style strategies will not work against guerrilla warfare, and this is the lesson here as it was to be learned again elsewhere.

Jesup was soon afterward replaced by Colonel Zachary Taylor, who soon devised a new strategy: the use of military squares or districts. Simply put, the concept was to place fortifications in twenty squares of twenty miles each out of which constant patrols would roam the area searching for the enemy. As a member of Jesup's staff and commander of the column from Tampa, he well understood the frustrations of Jesup's plan by the elusive enemy and the poor supply situation. In January 1839 he wrote, "We have not been able to bring the Indians to battle, and such is the nature of the country we can hardly hope to do so if they choose to avoid us. . . . It is as I feared a complete game of 'hide and seek.'"[38] It was to prevent the constant murders, raids, and assaults on the frontier that he began to formulate his squares strategy. He began his work by establishing posts throughout Middle and East Florida, creating a line of posts between Fort Fanning on the Suwannee River and Fort Micanopy (south of modern Gainesville). In relation to those already established along the Ocklawaha River by Colonel David Twiggs, Taylor hoped to make Alachua County one of the most secure in Florida. The goal of this plan was clearly stated in a letter to Twiggs sent in late December 1838: "I am satisfied that no county was ever better guarded than will be the County of Alachua and that the Inhabitants who had fled from their homes in said county may return without the slightest danger, provided that the officers having charge of the Posts, perform their duty properly as they should do, which I flatter myself will be the case."[39]

Taylor followed this pattern southward and began establishing a line of posts from Tampa Bay to Fort Gatlin (near modern-day Orlando). At the same time he approached the secretary of war, Poinsett, with his plan for the twenty-mile squares which he briefly described: "The whole of Florida between St. Augustine the Ocklawaha and Wacissa, and from the Georgia line to the Gulf as far as the Withlacoochee be laid off into districts of twenty miles square. That Posts be established in the center of each district or as near as health may permit, to be garrisoned by an officer and twenty men, half to be mounted." The tasks of the troops in these posts was to be on constant patrol within their assigned areas but still be close enough to reinforce each other in time of attack.[40] Taylor also reestablished the forts along the Atlantic coast that had been briefly abandoned at the conclusion of Jesup's campaign. Taylor wanted to extend a line of posts along the Gulf side of the Territory also to interdict the trade with the Cubans.[41] Colonel David Twiggs, Taylor's friend and colleague, was skeptical of this plan and wrote to Taylor, "The main body of Indians have not the least Idea of coming in, & will never under the present circumstances, willing emigrate, they *may be bought*, but years will roll over before they are caught by hunting them."[42]

Twiggs's prediction came to pass and the frustration mounted on all levels. Taylor wrote to Adjutant General Roger Jones on March 8, 1839, two months after beginning his new campaign: "It is unfortunate for the reputation of the Army in Florida that the enemy so seldom comes in collision with any portion of it; although efforts amounting to recklessness have been made unparalleled in the annals of Indian warfare. The murder of the inhabitants whenever an opportunity offers and their whole object appears to be keep out of the way of the Regulars who have unceasingly pursued them in large and small bodies penetrating their hiding-places in every direction and driving them therefrom, having lost only one individual since the opening of the campaign in October."[43] Despite the best efforts of the troops in the field, the Indians struck close to the capitol of Tallahassee in March 1839 and brought forth a call for relief from Governor Richard K. Call. Taylor's response was to send Colonel William Davenport into the area and create a new system of squares for the area west of the Suwannee River measuring eighteen miles and following the township and range lines as closely as possible. Davenport was also given authority to call on the Territory for the use of the recently created twelve companies of Florida Militia, a move opposed by Taylor with his usual distrust of such units.[44] The results of Davenport's localized operation were minimal.

The reason for the prompt response to Call's urgent message can be seen in the following letter sent by Call to Taylor: "At no period since the commencement of the War have so many murders been committed by the Indians, within the same length of time. And seldom ever in the history of savage warfare have such horrid scenes been exhibited." Call continued: "The orphan children who escaped the ferocity of the savages, were piously engaged in driving off the hogs from the mangled body of their lifeless Mother, while they witnessed the heartrending spectacle of seeing one of their brothers devoured by these animals."[45] Such scenes were not uncommon on both sides during this vicious war. Taylor's frustrations along with those of Call and others did not bring success to his campaign in 1839. A system of static posts trying to pin down a highly mobile enemy in the enemy's home territory has seldom worked in military history. Taylor's plan was doomed from the start, but it did produce some remarkable results not unrelated to the fighting. Taylor's forces, during the extent of his operations in Florida, constructed or rebuilt fifty-three fortifications, built nearly 4,000 feet of bridges, and opened almost 1,000 miles of new roads. Also the work of the topographic corps and local officers in mapping Florida's complex interior paved the way for more settlement and exploration by pioneers in the near future. However, in the words of Francis Prucha: "Yet the army could not seem to catch the elusive Indians, who fled from one swamp to another but who could not be captured or brought into open battle."[46]

Taylor had had enough of Florida and its frustrations and diseases. He requested to be relieved of command, which was granted in April 1840. Taylor was replaced by Walker K. Armistead, then a Brevet Brigadier General, who arrived in Florida on May 5, 1840. Armistead claimed he did not know of Taylor's strategy or plans and began immediately to devise his own plans of operation. He began by dividing up the Territory into two districts (north and south) and later another two districts divided on a line east and west. Armistead then centered his operations at Fort King where he amassed a force of over 900 men who were to be sent out in units numbering no more than 100 at a time. Armistead introduced the concept of attempting to attack the Seminoles and their allies during the early part of the rainy season and destroying their crops and villages before they had time to plant crops for the coming campaign season. He hoped to do this early in the rainy season before Florida's notorious heat and humidity sapped his men's strength. Armistead was fortunate to have a number of subordinates who adapted many guerrilla techniques to combat the Seminoles, among them Lieutenant Colonel Bennett Riley and Captain B. L. E. Bonneville. Famed Indian fighter Colonel William Harney also served under Armistead at this time. Harney went so far as to ask permission of Armistead to dress his men as Indians to deceive the enemy, but he was refused. These commanders were somewhat successful in finding and destroying villages and crops, but their work was not decisive. Their efforts did, however, contribute to the gradual wearing down of Seminole resistance, and increasing numbers of the Indians appeared at the posts to surrender and emigrate westward.

The best-known illustration of the loose strategy implemented by Armistead's commanders was the Everglades expedition of William Harney in early 1840. Harney had just recovered from the attack on his command on the Caloosahatchee River in 1839, and he was anxious to get back into action. He parlayed briefly with Abiaka and Chitto Tuskenugee (Snake Warrior) at Fort Lauderdale and was assured by these two that they had nothing to do with the affair on the Caloosahatchee. They indicated that the attack may have been led by the so-called Spanish Indian, Chakaika, and related bands. Harney devised a plan to attack the enemy in the fastness of their Everglades home and set out to do just that. Approaching the islands where Chakaika's bands were hiding, Harney violated orders and had some of his men in the lead canoes dress Indian style and thus caught the enemy off guard. The short battle that ensued brought Harney's men three captives and the dead body of the infamous Indian. Harney then ordered two of the men hung by the nearest tree, and he

5.4. William Jenkins Worth (Library of Congress).

strung up the corpse of Chakaika as a warning to any others who wished to continue the fight. But this was an isolated battle, and only an indication of strategy was involved. Armistead was fortunate to have innovative subordinates, but he appears to have done little in developing a strategy to end the war or bring the Seminoles to the table.[47]

Armistead did get an increase in the regular troops sent to Florida, and at the time of his departure he commanded 4,941 officers and men. An additional 1,500 militia were employed in northern Florida to control the situation in that sector. After dividing the Territory into seven districts, each with its own command, Armistead had had enough of Florida. At his own request he turned over his command to Colonel William Jenkins Worth of the Eighth Infantry.[48] Worth was a worthy opponent to anyone foolish enough to risk it. He was brash, vain, and capable. Like most of those before him, he had served in the War of 1812 and was formerly commandant of the military academy at West Point, New York. Worth's naturally aggressive personality led him to propose something totally new in Florida, a campaign that did not stop during the rainy season but continued the pressure throughout the year. Some in high places considered this an impossible strategy, but Worth maintained that as many men died in the forts from dissipation during the summer as would be killed or wounded in battle with the Seminoles. He continued to press the enemy and destroy their crops and hiding places.[49]

Worth's strategy was supplemented by the steady encouragement of settlers to return to their homesteads or migrate to the frontier. There Worth would see to it that they were armed, given guns, ammunition, flints, tents (if needed), and a year's supply of seed.[50] A number of settlements were begun under this program, and many survived to take advantage of the passage of the Armed Occupation Act of 1842, which gave settlers 160 acres of land if they would stay on it for five years, build a habitation fit for man, improve at least one acre per year, and be capable of bearing arms. Worth, Call, and many others encouraged the passage of this act, which came to fruition under the leadership of Senator Thomas Hart Benton of Missouri in August 1842.[51] The strategy Worth worked out and implemented worked very well against an already exhausted enemy who had been fighting a sustained resistance for nearly seven years. It also was more cost-effective in that it was conducted almost totally by federal troops and fewer civilian employees. The congressional urge for retrenchment necessitated such moves and dictated to some extent Worth's methodology. In the end, the Seminoles settled for emigration for some who wished to join families in the West, and the rest were confined to an area in southern Florida where few whites would want to settle at that time. However, these few remaining Seminoles and Miccosukees were still considered to be under the agreement that would force them to emigrate after a period of years. This consideration would lead to yet another war in the swamps of Florida.

At the beginning of the Second Seminole War the army did not correctly anticipate the fierce resistance that the Seminoles and their allies would offer. The military and political leadership totally underestimated the strength of the enemy and its alliances with other groups. This leadership did not know what to expect from the enemy and sent its army into battle with an almost complete lack of preparation, supplies, and knowledge of the terrain. There was a basic disregard for weather and climatic conditions, lack of proper mapping, and no knowledge of the trafficability of the terrain. The same terrain almost eliminated the practical use of artillery and in many instances forbade the use of cavalry in battle. The European-style strategies adopted by Scott, Jesup, and others was totally unfit for use against seasoned guerrilla fighters like the Seminoles and Miccosukees of Florida. The limited experience of the officers sent to Florida in fighting such a war played havoc on their ill-conceived plans. Set piece battles were not a feature of frontier warfare, and it took six severe years of experience before Worth came up with a workable solution.

What appears more remarkable to some observers is the lack of understanding of the nation's experience in fighting on other Indian frontiers. Not one leader discussed above attempted to train his troops in the fashion of George Rogers Clark or "Mad Anthony" Wayne, who taught their men the rudiments of fighting "Indian style." No European war allowed for such examples, yet the wars of Europe were all that appear to have been studied by any American officer. In the end, the refusal to learn the lessons of American Indian wars cost the army 1,466 killed and an unknown number of militia and volunteer forces lost in battle and disease. From 1836 to 1842, 41,122 men served in the army during this extended war. The money expended in fighting this war by both the army and navy was just under $70 million, and that comes during the economic crisis known as the Panic of 1837.[52] In the end, the majority of the Seminoles and Miccosukees had been emigrated or killed, but the original goal of complete removal was not met. When President John Tyler sent his message to Congress stating that "further pursuit of these miserable beings by a large military force seems as injudicious as it is unavailing," he was stating the obvious. "Yet," as Allan Millett and Peter Maslowski have written, "enough Seminoles remained to wage a comparatively minor Third Seminole War during the 1850s."[53] The strategies and political necessities of the day failed to finish the job as outlined by the leadership of the military and the political parties in power. In attempting to mold the enemy into its own vision, the army's strategies remained out of focus for seven long and bloody years.

Notes

Epigraph taken from "Military Maxims of Napoleon," in Brigadier General T. R. Phillips, ed., *Roots of Strategy* (Harrisburg: Stackpole Books, 1985), 1: 407.

1. Michael D. Krause and R. Cody Phillips, eds., *Historical Perspectives of the Operational Art* (Washington: Center for Military History, U.S. Army, 2005), v, vi.

2. Antoine Henri Jomini, *The Art of War*, trans. from the French by G. H. Mendell and W. P. Craighill (Philadelphia: J. B. Lippincott, 1862; reprint, Westport, Conn.: Greenwood Press, 1971).

3. It is important to remember that West Point was just beginning to produce significant numbers of officers at this date and that nearly 95 percent of the books in the initial library at the Academy were in French with an emphasis on Napoleonic studies. Very few of these volumes studied the Peninsula campaign of Wellington and his allied forces, and none went into depth on the partisan warfare that so sapped the strength of

the French armies in Spain and Portugal. The great commentaries of von Clausewitz were not yet translated into French and English and were not available to regular officers or West Point cadets at the time of the Seminole Wars.

4. Samuel Watson, "United States Army Officers Fight the 'Patriot War': Responses to Filibustering on the Canadian Border, 1837–1839," *Journal of the Early Republic* 18 (Fall 1998): 485–519.

5. For the best discussion of the army at this critical juncture, see William B. Skelton, "The United States Army, 1821–1837: An Institutional History," PhD diss., Northwestern University, 1968. Also see Jack K. Bauer, *Zachary Taylor: Soldier, Planter, Statesman of the Old Southwest* (Baton Rouge: Louisiana State University Press, 1985); Timothy D. Johnson, *Winfield Scott: The Quest for Military Glory* (Lawrence: University of Kansas Press, 1998); John D. Eisenhower, *Agent of Destiny: The Life and Times of General Winfield Scott* (New York: Free Press, 1997), is also useful in studying the transition of the army from an almost all volunteer group into a professional fighting force.

6. Joe Knetsch, "Benjamin A. Putnam and the Battle of Dunlawton: A Reappraisal," *Halifax Herald*, Halifax Historical Society, Daytona Beach, Fla., December 1998 and June 1999 (2 parts).

7. Patrick Rembert, *Aristocrat in Uniform: General Duncan L. Clinch* (Gainesville: University of Florida Press, 1963). Also see the author's "Duncan L. Clinch, Property, Class, and the Army: War and the Military in 1836," paper given to the Amelia Island Historical Society, Fernandina Beach, Fla., October 8, 2007.

8. Clarence E. Carter, ed., *The Territorial Papers of the United States* (Washington: National Archives and Records Service, 1960), 25: 132–33.

9. Ibid., 59: 99–100.

10. See John K. Mahon, *History of the Second Seminole War, 1835–1842,* rev. ed. (Gainesville: University Presses of Florida, 1985), 108–12. Mahon gives one of the best accounts of this battle and its aftermath.

11. Allen Peskin, *Winfield Scott and the Profession of Arms* (Kent, Ohio: Kent State University Press, 2003), 91–99.

12. Ibid.

13. For a good discussion of this perception, see Michael D. Pearlman, *Warmaking and American Democracy: The Struggle over Military Strategy, 1700 to the Present* (Lawrence: University of Kansas Press, 1999).

14. Italics are mine. Letters Received by the Office of the Adjutant General (Main Series), 1822–1860, roll 130, R 82–S 189, 1836 (Washington: National Archives and Records Service, 1964), microcopy 567, Record Group 94, letter of February 12, 1836, Scott to Clinch (hereinafter cited as AGLR, roll number, letter date, and correspondents).

15. Ibid.

16. Johnson, *Winfield Scott*, 115.

17. Allan Peskin, *Winfield Scott and the Profession of Arms* (Kent, Ohio: Kent State University Press, 2003), 92.

18. Pearlman, *Warmaking and American Democracy*, 89.

19. *The Military Policy of the United States*, 62nd Cong., 2nd sess., 1912, S. Doc. 494,

Brevet Major General Emory Upton (Washington: Government Printing Office, 1912), 165–66 (hereinafter cited as Upton and page number).

20. Pearlman, *Warmaking and American Democracy*, 78.

21. The best discussion of this fiasco is found in Mahon, *Second Seminole War*, 144–50. For Gaines at Tampa, see Joe Knetsch and Pamela Gibson, "Being continually in apprehension of an attack from the Indians . . . : Tampa Bay in Early 1836," *Sunland Tribune* 29 (2003).

22. See Mahon's chapter on Scott and the account in Upton. For a good brief summary, see Maurice Matloff, ed., *American Military History* (Conshohocken, Pa.: Combined Books, 1996), 1: 159–61.

23. Mahon, *Second Seminole* War, 161.

24. Eisenhower, *Agent of Destiny*, 160–61.

25. AGLR, roll 126, letter of December 9, 1836, Jesup to Benjamin F. Butler, Acting Secretary of War. For a summary of Call's brief tenure, see Mahon, *Second Seminole War*, 168–89. The only biography of Call is that of Herbert J. Doherty, *Richard Keith Call: Southern Unionist* (Gainesville: University of Florida Press, 1961), 93–117. Doherty's work is now dated, and it spends very little space discussing the campaign. Doherty's major interest was in Call's complicated and controversial political career. This is important to the understanding of the distrust showed to Call by the regulars in Florida who blamed him for the failure to reinforce Clinch at the Battle of the Withlacoochee.

26. William B. Skelton, *An American Profession of Arms: The Army Officer Corps, 1784–1861* (Lawrence: University of Kansas Press, 1992), 305–25.

27. J. D. Hittle, *The Military Staff: Its History and Development* (Harrisburg: Military Service, 1949), 164–67.

28. This episode of the war has been described by nearly every commentator on the conflict. The best brief summary of the capture of Osceola and condemnation of Jesup can be found in Francis Paul Prucha's classic, *The Sword of the Republic: The United States Army on the Frontier, 1783–1846* (New York: Macmillan, 1968), 284–89. The best single work on Osceola is still Patricia R. Wickman, *Osceola's Legacy* (Tuscaloosa: University of Alabama Press, 1991).

29. U.S. Senate Executive Document No. 263, 25th Cong., 2d sess., July 7, 1838, 253.

30. Ibid., 254.

31. See Mahon's *Second Seminole War*, 233–35. Also see the author's "Jesup's Strategy, the Founding of Fort Lauderdale, and the Role of Lieutenant Colonel James Bankhead," *Broward Legacy* 19 (Winter/Spring 1996).

32. Mahon, *Second Seminole War*, 253. Taylor was promoted to the rank of brevet brigadier general at the time of Jesup's report, quoted by Mahon.

33. Prucha, *The Sword of the Republic*, 291–92. Historical work by Willard Steele of the Seminole Tribe's historical office and archaeologist Robert Carr of Miami located this battle site in 1986. Their documentation and findings were published in "Preliminary Report on the Search for the Okeechobee Battlefield," Archaeological

and Historical Conservancy, Inc. of Florida, October 25, 1986 (later expanded and illustrated in booklet form). Also see J. Floyd Monk's "Christmas Day in Florida, 1837," *Tequesta* 38 (1978): 5–38.

34. Joe Knetsch, "All His Wants Should Be Promptly Supplied: Persifor F. Smith and the Caloosahatchee River Campaign of 1837–1838," *Sunland Tribune* 22 (November 1996).

35. Joe Knetsch, "Fort Cross on Cape Sable: Controlling the Trade between Cuba and the Seminoles in the Third Seminole War," *Journal of America's Military Past* 94, no. 1 (Spring/Summer 2002).

36. AGLR, roll 167, letter of December 29, 1837, to Lt. George Watson.

37. AGLR, roll 167, letter of January 28, 1838, Jesup to Lt. Lemuel Powell.

38. AGLR, roll 196, letter of January 5, 1839, Taylor to Roger Jones, Adjutant General.

39. AGLR, roll 196, December 21, 1838, Taylor to Twiggs.

40. AGLR, roll 196, letters dated January 10, 1839, Taylor to Lt. Col. Cummings, and January 5, 1839 Taylor to R. Jones.

41. AGLR, roll 196, letter of January 15, 1839, Taylor to Twiggs, and letter of January 22, 1839, George F. Griffin (Taylor's aide) to Captain John McLaughlin (a naval officer who later headed the "Mosquito Fleet" along the southern coasts of Florida).

42. AGLR, roll 197, letter of February 10, 1839, Twiggs to Taylor.

43. AGLR, roll 197, letter of March 8, 1839, Taylor to Roger Jones.

44. AGLR, roll 197, letter of March 12, 1839, Taylor to Davenport.

45. AGLR, roll 197, letter of March 6, 1839, Call to Taylor.

46. Prucha, *The Sword of the Republic*, 295.

47. Mahon, *Second Seminole War*, 274–93. Mahon's discussion of Armistead's term is the only one available at this time.

48. Upton, 186.

49. See the author's articles in *At Home,* Citrus County Historical Society, Inverness, Fla.: "The Cove Once More: The Gates Withlacoochee River Expedition of 1841" (March/April and May/June 2006); "Worth's Southern Prong and the Exploration of the Homosassa River" (May/June 2000); "Into the Cove Again: Worth's 1841 Campaign" (November/December 1999).

50. AGLR, roll 262, letter (report) of June 13, 1842, Worth to R. Jones. The author has discussed this in detail in "Colonel Sam Reid, the Founding of the Manatee Colony and the Surveying of the Manatee Country, 1841–1847," *Sunland Tribune* 21 (November 1995): 29–34.

51. James Covington, "The Armed Occupation Act of 1842," *Florida Historical Quarterly* 40 (July 1961): 41–52. This is the best discussion of the act and its contents. It is wrong on the number of people attracted into Florida because of Dr. Covington's not having the opportunity of viewing the actual permits, which would have led him to other conclusions than those found in this early article.

52. Upton, 190–92.

53. Allan R. Millett and Peter Maslowski, *For the Common Defense: A Military History of the United States of America* (New York: Free Press, 1984), 136.

6

∞∞∞∞∞∞∞∞∞∞∞∞∞∞∞∞∞∞∞∞∞∞∞∞∞∞∞

Seminole Strategy, 1812–1858

A Prospectus for Further Research

SAMUEL WATSON

Why study Seminole strategy? Readers may question whether there *was* a Seminole strategy, a question that must be addressed. But, first, why might one look for Seminole strategy? What purpose can such study serve? What insights can be gained?

In the study of warfare and national security, strategy is the level of scale at which objectives are chosen and resources are allocated to forces in the field. Modern military doctrine distinguishes between several levels of strategy, in the following descending order: coalition (sometimes called "grand") strategy, national strategy, military strategy, and sometimes campaign strategy. National strategy, sometimes confusingly referred to as policy, political strategy, or the political level of war, is normally determined by civilian leaders and includes nonmilitary objectives, but it encompasses a nation's security strategy, which is usually more holistic than its military strategy. In national security strategy, the most important decision is whether or not to go to war. In this schema, "foreign policy" and international negotiations are part of the national security strategy.

Nations do have military strategies when formally at peace. These can include, for example, action against civil unrest, peacekeeping, and deterrence, intimidation, and coercion short of war, in support of the nation's foreign policy. Historically, most military strategies have fallen into one of the following categories: strategies of annihilation, strategies of attrition, and strategies of exhaustion. A strategy of annihilation focuses on the rapid destruction of enemy combat power, or the means of armed resistance "in the field," through a series of discrete operations—campaigns, maneuver to and from battles, sieges, or other engagements—and tactical engagements (the employment of fires, or firepower, while maneuvering in the face of or close proximity to the enemy). In other words, destroying the enemy army, which is presumed to open the enemy's territory to occupation and his political system to restructuring.

A strategy of attrition focuses on doing so more gradually, usually because rapid annihilation of the enemy's military power seems unlikely. A strategy of exhaustion focuses on wearing down the enemy's resources—some form of economic warfare—or will to resist. Of course, one of the principal means of wearing down an enemy's will is to cause casualties, so a strategy of exhaustion may be put into practice through attrition, with the desired result being enemy concessions rather than the utter destruction of the enemy's ability to resist. In practice, there is often significant overlap between these "forms of strategy," but they do delineate fundamental distinctions in focus—or more bluntly put, targeting—and tempo (the expected pace of operations and timing of victory).

"Campaign planning" is variously interpreted by modern scholars and analysts. Since selecting a theater of operations is a strategic decision, usually made by civilian leaders or necessitated by their choice of enemy or national strategic objectives, some students view campaign planning as a matter of strategy, hence the term *campaign strategy*. I, like many others, view the planning, particularly the sequencing, of objectives, dispositions, and maneuver within a campaign, which is usually done by military commanders with forces allocated to them by civilian leaders, as a matter of operations and the operational level of war. The operational level is the level that connects combat, which is the tactical level—battles and engagements, conducted almost entirely by direct (line of sight) fire prior to the twentieth century—with objectives, which are set at the strategic level. Simply put, the operational level means the movement before and after combat: maneuver against an enemy force, to force it to fight, to attack its resources or supply lines, to attack or besiege population centers, etc., and to exploit success or to reposition one's forces (retreat) in case of setbacks. The decision to fight a battle, or to launch an offensive within the campaign, is an operational one.

My focus here is not Seminole battlefield tactics. It is why the Florida Indians fought: the level of national strategy. But, given substantial agreement on this point, it is even more how they hoped to employ military force to achieve their objectives: military strategy. Passing references to "guerrilla warfare" are far too vague to encompass the Seminole resistance or to assess Seminole military strategy—or any strategy, for that matter. Indeed, for most people, "guerrilla warfare" really means little more than the tactics of raid and ambush. By that criteria, the U.S. Army engaged in guerrilla warfare against the Indians of Florida, particularly after 1837, albeit much less efficiently than the Seminoles. By that standard, U.S. forces often engaged in guerrilla warfare in Vietnam and might in some cases be understood as conducting "guerrilla" operations in Iraq and certainly Afghanistan today. Though sometimes employed to hint at a lack of political support for an occupying force, the term *guerrilla warfare* obscures as much as it clarifies. The tactics of raid and ambush are not the same thing as the politics of occupation and insurgency.

The problem here is primarily in distinguishing scale and scope, between intermediate efficiency and ultimate effectiveness, or, in military terms, between tactics and strategy—the political big picture. Strategy is the forest; tactics are the trees. No one would argue that the U.S. Army was well adapted, or even sought to adapt itself, to combat on Native American terms. Facing small parties of skilled outdoorsmen, the conventionally oriented army found it difficult to deter Indian raids or to find, catch, and prevent the Indians' escape when it was on the offensive. The same was usually equally true of Florida militia and citizen-soldier volunteers. The usually inexperienced soldiers were not individual matches for native warriors; its reconnaissance, intelligence, and terrain utilization were often sorely lacking; its artillery was often unable to keep up to reach the Indians. The historic strength of American military logistics—supply systems—often became a liability, as expected logistical requirements burdened offensive columns and slowed their advance. The army usually lacked the Indians' agility and had trouble coordinating its power to gain and retain the tactical initiative.

Nevertheless, native tactical skill in skirmishes and battle did not prevent the army from winning campaigns and wars, east or west of the Mississippi. In modern wars, characterized by resource depth on at least one side, battles and tactics, the focus of much of the history written about the Indian wars, are usually less decisive than operations, campaigns, and strategy (the level of mobilization). The U.S. Army has historically been mediocre at the tactical level, but has excelled at the strategic one of synchronizing resources for persistent, gradually decisive power projection. Indeed, the army proved surprisingly, and significantly, capable at exploiting divisions within and between Seminole factions. Seminole advantages remained fundamentally tactical and military rather than strategic, political, social, or economic.[1]

We should first note that Seminole strategy has *not* been studied: most narratives of the Second Seminole War, and the Seminole Wars in general, focus on U.S. strategy or, more often, narrate U.S. operations, frequently without any attention to strategy as such.[2] The same is true of anthropological studies. Patricia Wickman provides a rare explicit discussion of Seminole (or, in her terms, Maskókî, including the Creek) warfare, and uses the term *strategy*, but her assessment is essentially tactical, in the terms set out above: Maskókî war was "a state of belligerence . . . marked by periodic . . . hit-and-run attacks." Wickman distinguishes between Maskókî and European warfare in terms of both tempo and objectives, but the distinction is unclear, except in tempo. She suggests that the Maskókî rarely launched sustained offensive campaigns—a series of battles or engagements connected by common targets and objectives—of the type that modern military theory associates with the "operational level" of warfare. Yet they did do so during the Second Seminole War, at least at its outset, when Indian military actions demonstrated a more earnest quest for decisive victory—a conclusive outcome—than a mere "state of belligerence" suggests. Nevertheless, Wickman's taxonomy of the range of Maskókî approaches to diplomacy does suggest strategic thought and a de facto national security strategy, including attacks intended at "goading . . . to take the measure of [opponents'] ability and willingness to respond," an essentially political approach that should be categorized as strategic in scope.[3]

Why has Seminole military strategy not been examined? There are few contemporary written sources that focus on Seminole objectives, and they come from whites. When historians look for strategy, they usually expect to find planning and decision documents. More significantly, many observers associate strategy with states. Given the uncertain, debatable degree of Seminole national identity and political unification in 1835, many would question whether the Seminoles, much less the Florida Indians as a whole, constituted a nation, much less a national or nation-state. Without an authoritative central authority apart from that designated by the United States, primarily as a means of communicating its will, how could "the Seminoles" have a national strategy, or even agree on a military strategy? Wickman observes that the Maskókî were "a people whose traditions of warfare did not include the concept of large-scale, unified action" under a single leader. Can there be strategy without unity of command? Beyond or underneath this question lie images of the savage Indian or the free Indian—in either case an easily romanticized individual whose loyalties and identity are assumed to be primarily local, centered in family, kin, clan, and village.[4]

Even if we reject referring to the Seminoles, or the Florida Indians more generally—including Mikasukis (whom U.S. Army officers often distinguished from, or among, the Seminole), Yuchis, Hitchiti-speakers, so-called "Spanish Indians," and former Red Stick Creeks—as a nation, with a centralized political structure, we can still recognize that they functioned as a coalition. Seminole politics did not pause for the war. If we examine Indian strategy and operations solely in military terms, we have to wonder at their logic. Why did the Seminoles not disperse their forces earlier in the 1835–42 war? Why did they continue to fight substantial engagements, battles like Wahoo Swamp and Okeechobee, for two years after the United States began to mass its forces against them? Having dispersed into smaller bands during 1837 and 1838, why did they not campaign more extensively in West Florida—west of the Suwannee, in particular from St. Marks and Tallahassee farther west—an effective distraction of U.S. forces throughout much of the conflict? In other words, why did the Indians not adopt "guerrilla warfare" more rapidly and more completely? Clearly the tactical, and even the operational and strategic, advantages of guerrilla warfare were insufficient to overcome other considerations during the first year or so of the war.

*   *   *

Why did the Seminoles initiate large-scale armed conflict in 1835? The date may be explained by the American intention to begin removal on New Year's Day in 1836. Yet saying the Seminoles began the war to resist removal ignores the variety of approaches, or strategies, employed by the other Native American groups, particularly the Cherokee: lobbying and legal maneuver, a public relations or public diplomacy campaign, preemptively moving west in 1809 and 1819, or withdrawing into the hills among those who refused removal in 1838. The Seminole lacked the acculturated leaders who enabled the Cherokee to pursue legal and political strategies or the Choctaw and Chickasaw to win substantial material concessions for elites who had adopted commercial agriculture. Nor did they voluntarily adopt a "strategy of migration," as many Shawnee and some Cherokee had done decades earlier. Indeed, with whites spreading across Missouri and Arkansas, the regions where the Shawnee and Cherokee had migrated before 1820, the threat of removal extended beyond the Mississippi, and Seminoles who "chose" emigration during the 1830s could reasonably be seen as betrayers of those who sought to remain in Florida. The result was not the amicable separation of the decentralized Shawnee, moving in three directions during the 1780s and 1790s, or the sometimes bitter but uncontested split among the Cherokee, which may have prevented civil war in 1809. The result was the execution of Charley Emathla by Osceola.[5]

On the other hand, while withdrawal from contact with whites was not a viable means of retaining political autonomy, it was employed sporadically by Native Americans across the United States from the colonial period into the nineteenth century. Creeks fled into Florida, Choctaw and Chickasaw concealed themselves to remain in Mississippi, Potawatomis, Winnebagos, and other northwestern Indians hid out or returned to the Great Lakes region after being forced westward, and Indians in similar situations remained behind in the colonial, revolutionary, and early national Northeast. The Seminoles and Mikasukis remaining in Florida after 1842 employed this approach so consistently that the necessary coordination wholly merits the term *strategic*, and some were able to avoid removal by doing so at the conclusion of the "Third Seminole War" in 1858.

6.1. Osceola
(Library of
Congress).

The Seminoles made a choice—effectively a national security decision—in 1835. Moreover, they did so collectively, through the national council, its most important decision to that date, if not in its history.[6] And their initial military operations were coordinated, not perhaps to the degree we tend to expect of a nation-state with centralized legislative, decision-making, and executive structures, but surely as much as the initial U.S. response, which featured Edmund Gaines rushing to the scene and conducting a campaign independent of, overlapping, and interfering with that assigned to his rival Winfield Scott by the War Department. Indeed, Seminole command and control was better organized, in effect if not in structure, than that of the United States during the first six months of the war, and overland communications between Indian leaders were sometimes faster than those of white messengers on horseback, to say nothing of those by steamboat to and from Washington.

The decision to strike can be examined from several perspectives. How did Seminole leaders envision the outcome of their action? Did they expect to fight for nearly seven years? Or did they hope that the United States, or white Floridians, would be sufficiently shocked and demoralized by the destruction that they would make peace on native terms? In other words, did the Seminoles expect white leaders to make a national cost-benefit analysis, which would surely, in the short term, have counseled allowing the Indians to remain in Florida, as most federal military commanders advised once they understood the difficulty and cost of compelling removal? (Indeed, army officers repeatedly observed that the land being fought over in the 1830s and 1840s was unsuitable for profitable cultivation given the existing state of technology.) Did they hope to impress white leaders, but fail to account for the growth of white democracy and its demands for racial hegemony without regard to national expense? How much of a role did people of African ancestry, whatever their precise status, play in the Seminole decision for war? From the larger perspective of U.S. history, did the Indians fail to reckon with the Slave Power?[7]

Who were the Indians targeting in the Dade ambush and their raids on the plantations of East and Middle Florida? Were they merely trying to destroy a small unit of the U.S. Army and steal some provisions? It seems indisputable that they intended to strike fear into white Floridians. But were they engaged in nothing more than terrorism, random and savage as we, like contemporary whites, tend to view it? Clearly the destruction of a hundred soldiers would not defeat the U.S. Army. Presumably the Seminoles knew that the United States could quickly replace them with reinforcements from the north and west. Nor would burning plantations defeat the United States. Instead, I would posit that the Seminoles were trying to send a message.[8] Perhaps the message was too strong for whites to swallow. By demonstrating the cost of threatening native interests, the Seminoles may have hoped to reduce pressure for their removal from the most aggressive proponents of removal in Florida, the whites who lived there. The execution of the removal treaty might have been delayed, perhaps until a new administration offered the opportunity for renegotiation, had Florida whites and their territorial representative in Congress been forced to rethink the consequences and value of the removal policy. Scholars sometimes refer to "threat-based strategies"; in this case the threat, and the U.S. center of gravity, the group most committed to compelling immediate removal, was the squeaky white wheel.

The Seminoles miscalculated, if they calculated, the effect of liberating slaves on white opinion in Florida and the South. They were forced to strike sixteen months too early; Andrew Jackson, the architect of removal, was not known for listening to Native Americans. But their initial strategy had the potential to impress northern whites, some Whigs and perhaps humanitarian reformers. It also served to force Seminoles and other Florida Indians to make a choice. Some, who had already accepted removal as inevitable, departed Florida as soon as they could do so. Yet the initiation of war, combined with the execution of Charley Emathla for advocating removal, produced a more united native stance against removal, while the assassination of U.S. Seminole agent Wiley Thompson eliminated the most familiar means of negotiation, minimizing the chance for further compromise or concessions.

Given the larger U.S. strategy—the de facto national strategy—of wearing down and exhausting native resistance to removal through economic pressure, the threat of imposing state or territorial laws, and the effects of liquor, debt, and violence by private groups and individuals, as well as military intimidation, it may be that the Florida Indians had no alternative if they sought to retain their reservation and live in substantial villages there. Remember that few Indians lived in the Everglades prior to the war. Had the Seminoles viewed that region as a viable refuge, they might have fled there rather than initiating war, or they might have fled there in 1836, after sending their message of resistance. Thus we may categorize their strategy as "objectives-based," to avoid removal, or "capabilities-based," to strike before Seminole military power had been worn down, like that of the Creeks, the Choctaw, or the Chickasaw, by the social, political, economic, and cultural effects of white intrusion.

Once the Seminoles chose to go to war, what was their military strategy? The Seminoles appear to have prepared for war by concentrating much of their population in the Cove of the Withlacoochee,[9] and then combined a sustained defense of that population center with months of raids against the plantations across the peninsula along the St. Johns River to the northeast. With one hand they held off the U.S. Army; with the other they struck at some of the wealthiest of white Floridians, threatening the system of slavery by kidnapping the slaves or inducing them to flee their bondage. Yet they also put out peace feelers to the U.S. Army officers opposing them, particularly when they appeared to hold the upper hand, as in their siege of Edmund Gaines's force along the Withlacoochee in early March 1836. After rebuffing Gaines, some of the former Red Stick Creeks may have gone north to join in the "Second Creek War," of resistance to removal, in Alabama.[10] By the fall, the army had repressed the Creek uprising and was preparing a new campaign against the Seminoles, who were reinforced by Creeks fleeing south. Many of these Indians concealed themselves in areas of Middle and West Florida no longer ranged by the Seminoles, creating new threats and tying down Florida militia and volunteers in areas whites had thought secure. Though many Creek refugees sought shelter and avoided raids and combat or coordination with the Seminoles, the outcry among whites compelled the territorial government to raise further militia and volunteers, significantly increasing the expense of the war.

Nevertheless, the army's autumn offensive into the Cove of the Withlacoochee demonstrated that that position was no longer secure, and the Seminoles fought a rearguard action at Wahoo Swamp to shield the escape of their families southward. From this point, with the exception of the battle of Okeechobee at the end of 1837, Indian forces rarely numbered more than several hundred warriors in any engagement. Recognizing the power the army was beginning to bring to bear, the Seminoles did not attempt to re-create the concentration of population and force they had temporarily amassed in the Cove of the Withlacoochee during the first year of the war. Like their predecessors in 1818, they turned to dispersion and evasion, a strategy of exhausting the United States' will to continue the struggle by protracting the war, rather than by striking sharp blows against white forces, resources, and egos. The shift had unintended benefits for the Indians: white Floridians continued to fret and panic, but the conflict no longer seemed an immediate threat to southern slavery, and volunteers from the southern states began to slow along with the publicity that had drawn them. Despite their progress in driving the Seminoles from their initial concentration area in the Cove, many American soldiers seem to have felt less urgency after 1836, and even more so after 1837, when the Indians had dispersed across central and southern Florida.

Dispersal made it much more difficult for the United States to defeat the Seminoles militarily. Although some historians maintain that Indian leaders sustained regular communications throughout the war,[11] it certainly became more difficult to assemble leaders for councils to coordinate sustained offensive action or a united negotiating strategy. Dispersion therefore made it much more difficult for the Seminoles to defeat the United States through military means or to synchronize their efforts to strike military blows to take advantage of new political opportunities. In any event, the election of Martin Van Buren hardly signaled a halt to Indian removal or the war against the Seminoles. Nor did the Panic of 1837 and the prolonged economic depression that followed. Indeed, the inauguration of a Whig president in 1841 did not make a difference for another year, and initially the Harrison and Tyler administrations supported more vigorous offensives by the army. Thus Seminole strategy came to rely on white frustration but had few means of intensifying that frustration beyond existing levels. With their strategy focused on preserving Indian strength, rather than striking against white centers of gravity, Seminole councils seem to have focused primarily on maintaining a united resistance, through coercion if persuasion failed, against the urge to negotiate. In other words, dispersion meant decentralization, of motive and effort as well as population, and Indian leaders had to counter the moral exhaustion that their more passive strategy of dispersal and protraction encouraged within their own ranks.

This exhaustion had two principal components with contradictory implications. On one hand, Seminole supplies, of food as well as ammunition, were often short, and the Indians used truces and negotiations with the army to seek presents to replenish the stocks essential to continuing their resistance. These negotiations, involving repeated trips back and forth into the wilderness, to and from many different groups of Indians, also protracted the conflict and its expense for the United States, shielding the Seminoles while the army waited on their outcome. Indeed, many soldiers were disenchanted and even demoralized by the war and preferred negotiations. It is not clear whether or how clearly the Indians understood this, but they certainly looked to federal military commanders rather than Florida territorial leaders for negotiating partners, and these negotiations repeatedly enabled them to delay American offensives for extended periods. (The willingness to stop and negotiate, on the verge or even in the midst of long-planned offensives, is a significant indicator of the army's distaste for the war.) One of the best examples was the diplomacy involving a Cherokee delegation, led by anti-removal spokesman John Ross, in the autumn of 1837: it seems probable that Ross and the Seminoles collaborated in spinning out their talks to delay the army's advance.[12]

Yet doing so also exposed the Seminoles to easy capture, when frustrated U.S. commanders treacherously seized them under flags of truce. More insidiously, the temptation to negotiate in order to secure material goods often slipped gradually into the temptation to surrender, to give up the arduous struggle to remain in Florida for a less harried life in the "Indian Territory" reserved in the west. Lacking a centralized political system with strong claims on individuals, the Seminole proved highly vulnerable to internal dissension, in the form of efforts to persuade family members to join in emigration west, which led to the surrender of as many Indians as were captured by the army. Thus "negotiating while fighting" served the Seminoles well in the short term but poorly in the long run, and those who remained in Florida when the army declared peace in 1842 would increasingly pursue a strategy of isolation from contact with whites. This approach to national security, avoiding wars and defeat by avoiding contact, reached its culmination in the decades after the Third Seminole War ended in 1858. Indeed, it is noteworthy that the Civil War among whites did not involve the Florida Seminoles.

6.2. Micanopy
(Florida State
Library and
Archives).

These Indians exhausted white will by occupying the most isolated areas, least hospitable to sustained white settlement, but it is questionable whether such an approach would have served for several thousand Seminoles in 1835, particularly given white desire to enslave the Indians' black slaves and allies. Indeed, some historians emphasize that the "post-Removal Florida Seminole provide an inappropriate model for understanding the earlier Seminole" because of their dispersion into very small groups.[13] The logic of this argument extends to the war years after 1836 or 1837, suggesting a loss of cohesion and the ability to make and execute coordinated strategic and operational decisions. Other scholars suggest that the national council continued to make decisions in the summer of 1837, particularly to depose Micanopy and break the Indians held captive at Tampa out of their confinement.[14] Historians have identified two councils in the spring of 1841, at which Seminole, Creek, and Mikasuki leaders still remaining in Florida agreed not to negotiate, and to kill any Indians who did so.[15] The Seminoles and Creeks who met in council near

Fort King that June also agreed to a defensive strategy, but Indians launched an offensive against the St. Johns River settlements later that year and into 1842. This may have been a response to the U.S. offensive in the summer of 1841 and a means of diverting growing U.S. pressure, but it, like the periodic surrender of further small groups, demonstrates the limits to authoritative political control among the Indians dispersed throughout Florida after several years of war.

Recognizing the difficulty of procuring subsistence while remaining isolated from contact with whites, and the loss of national control and cohesion that developed as the Seminoles dispersed across Florida in 1837, we can see that their initial strategy, of sharp blows to white Floridians and the U.S. Army, was a rational effort at shocking the United States into modifying its demands for removal. Whether this objective was fully calculated, and whether the later loss of control and cohesion was fully anticipated, are certainly open to debate, but surely the Indians could make cost-benefit estimates and calculations from experience. The Seminoles had defeated the first American military incursions between 1812 and 1814, cutting the line of communications between the United States and its forces besieging St. Augustine by ambushing a supply convoy in September 1812, and turning back a Georgia militia offensive (the Newnan expedition) against the Alachua towns. On the other hand, continuing white raids and Andrew Jackson's onslaught in 1818 led to the abandonment of those towns, and virtually all of those in Florida west of the Suwannee, and a general flight southward. Yet interactions during a decade of life within the reservation allotted to the Seminole in central Florida by the Treaty of Moultrie Creek may have suggested that the U.S. government was open to compromise in clashes between red and white Floridians.

The 1836 offensive exceeded anything the United States had seen since the Creek War in 1813: neither the First Seminole War, the Black Hawk War, the Winnebago War, or the Arikara War, nor the various incidents on the Missouri and northwestern frontiers between 1815 and 1836, remotely approached the devastation and panic of the first months of 1836. Indeed, the Seminoles, probably unwittingly, struck during a moment of great psychic tension in the American South, with controversy over the mailing of abolitionist tracts and a slave insurrection panic along the Mississippi in 1835. These uproars may have been known to black Seminole allies like Abraham, counselor to Micanopy, the hereditary leader of the Alachua Seminoles; even if they were not, Seminole leaders surely knew about the growing pressure for Creek and Cherokee removal, and probably reckoned on some support, or at least diversion of white military resources, from those sources.[16]

6.3. Negro Abraham (John Frost, *Pictorial Life of Andrew Jackson*, 1847).

Unfortunately, the Seminole offensive helped unite white policymakers in favor of war. Though it was probably necessary to strike at the army to show the United States they were serious, doing so angered and embarrassed military commanders, whose immediate reaction was to redeem the institution's honor and seek revenge for their soldiers' deaths through a counteroffensive. When that failed, frustration spurred the army to further efforts: army commanders would not seek peace until they had punished the Indians for their temerity.[17] The moment of negotiation between General Edmund Gaines and the Seminoles besieging him along the Withlacoochee, interrupted by the approach of another army detachment but sometimes cited as an early opportunity to end the war, was conditioned by Gaines's vulnerability. It seems highly unlikely that the U.S. government would have backed away from its demand for removal, particularly as a result of an unauthorized offensive by a general at odds with the president over the removal policy. Whites in Florida and the South were united by the Indians' raids on the St. Johns River plantations, particularly by the liberation of slaves. And it would take time for the war's expense to arouse opposition from mainstream Whigs: the war does not appear to have been an issue in the 1836 elections, which featured Whig William Henry Harrison of Tippecanoe fame running against Jackson in the South. The Jacksonians countered in kind: Richard M. Johnson of Kentucky, who claimed to have slain Tecumseh, ran as Van Buren's vice president. If anything, the war probably gave pro-removal Jacksonians an issue to whip up the racial antagonism that made American democracy white.

Ultimately, the Seminoles' effort to trade space for time, with which to exhaust the American will to continue their removal, failed in the face of white supremacist democracy and the resources the United States persistently brought to bear. Small as the regular army was, the government committed half of it to Florida. Though their effectiveness was debatable, Florida militia and volunteers from throughout the South helped prevent sustained Seminole incursions against the settlements of northern Florida. Contingents of volunteer soldiers from New York and Pennsylvania anticipated participation from those states in the war with Mexico, suggesting the sympathy many northerners felt for territorial expansion against peoples of color. The Florida Indians lost the strategic and operational initiative; U.S. depth in manpower enabled the army to sustain increasing numbers of outposts and patrols, ultimately gaining the tactical initiative in many instances.

Nor could the Seminoles continue to synchronize their offensive efforts to maximize their impact. Indeed, their capture or surrender had a snowball effect, as families were divided and those held captive sought reunification by attempting to persuade others to surrender. These Indians felt compelled to adopt a new, necessarily more accommodationist strategy for social and cultural survival and cohesion: reuniting their families, and whatever Seminole nation they believed to exist, in the west. Though Seminole did not fight Seminole, those captured or surrendered ultimately provided invaluable aid to the United States, sometimes as guides or interpreters, but above all as emotional pressure on their kin. It is unclear what role clan affiliations, so much emphasized in the literature on Seminole and Creek society, played in this process, or indeed in wartime strategy and military operations, but the dynamics of nuclear families clearly worked to draw resisters west. Operating at such a remove, our value judgments may not echo theirs, but their impact is clear.

Nor were the Florida Indians able to turn their tactical advantages into an insurgency, which is ultimately societal and political. The Seminole wars of resistance were intercultural, essentially international, fought against a polity increasingly defined along racial lines, and the United States did not face the classic counterinsurgent dilemma of losing popular support through aggressive military operations against fellow citizens. Indeed, the army proved surprisingly, and significantly, capable at exploiting divisions within and between varied Indian groups. As early as the autumn of 1836, Florida territorial governor Richard K. Call secured seventy-five Seminole men, from among those who had already surrendered or been captured and were awaiting transportation west, as guides for his campaign against the resistant Indians.[18] Seminole advantages of initiative and agility remained fundamentally tactical and military rather than strategic, political, social, or economic. Thus, even leading military historians who criticize the army's tactical and operational methods observe that economic factors—in military terms operational and strategic logistics, resource depth—most often prove decisive, in asymmetrical conflicts between simple and complex societies as well as those between symmetrical conventional opponents.[19]

The success of insurgencies and revolutionary warfare ultimately depends on persistence: depth of political will, or a lack thereof on the part of counterinsurgent and counterrevolutionary states, so that the latter prove unwilling to deploy their potential power—the depth of their economic and military logistical resources—against the militarily weaker insurgents. Tactics are not the critical distinction. The military forces of large states can adapt and employ "guerrilla warfare" and "guerrilla tactics," as the United States increasingly did toward the Seminoles once they dispersed. The key question in an insurgency is whether the status quo power can adapt its political objectives and policies, whether to compromise with and reconcile the insurgents or to undermine their popular support.

The small abolitionist minority notwithstanding, the United States was fundamentally united in support of removal. The Whigs criticized its expense but continued the war when they assumed the presidency. Indeed, army officers themselves provided most of the immediate stimulus to declare an end to the war, largely for their own reasons, as much out of personal convenience and distaste for mucking through swamps to help settlers they often detested, as from sympathy for the Seminoles. The few Indians who persisted in their resistance were able to remain, and most of these used the same strategy of exhaustion to avoid removal despite U.S. pressure (on a lower level of intensity) throughout the 1840s and in the Third Seminole War of 1855–58, but whites were able to settle Middle Florida. In this sense, both the United States and the Seminoles—some Seminoles—could claim they won the war, but the Seminoles did not do so as a nation. The United States secured its primary objectives—the conquest of Middle and central Florida, and the destruction of the major Seminole and maroon shelters for refugees from slavery—while most of the Florida Indians were forced from their homeland, at a grievous human cost that the army was paid to afford. Following the Second Seminole War, white settlement proceeded at a rate dictated more by ecology than native opposition. Ultimately, reliance on geographic isolation and climate, rather than human resistance, proved the most effective strategy for Indian survival in Florida during the nineteenth century.

I cannot know what Seminole strategy truly was, or whether there was indeed a single or unified strategy. I doubt that these things can be known with the certainty that some historians would demand if we are to speak meaningfully of Seminole strategy. Moreover, it seems probable that the coordination that connects operations to strategy, or into a strategy, diminished as the Indian bands dispersed across Florida after 1836. But asking whether the Seminoles had a strategy has value in a number of ways. First, it encourages us to think of the Florida Indians as rational actors, rather than savages, terrorists, or a doomed decentralized tribe irrationally resisting the inevitable forces of modernity, as undergraduates tend to interpret Native American resistance.

Second, thinking about Seminole strategy encourages us to think about Seminole political structure and dynamics, to think about the degree and form of Seminole political centralization (or decentralization), identity, and cohesion. In doing so we must think about the character of Seminole leadership: what was it rooted in, did it vary depending on the issue in question, and how was it maintained, transferred, or diffused? How were decisions made, communicated, and implemented? How were operations coordinated? How central were individual leaders, like Osceola or Coacoochee? What about war termination? If one crucial question is how and why the Florida Indians decided to go to war, another, of equal importance, is how decentralized polities terminate conflict, whether they can do so of their own volition, or are simply "defeated" or conquered.[20]

The question of political organization is one of the most disputed questions in Seminole historiography, often serving as a stand-in for stances on Seminole social and cultural identity and cohesion, and an element in debates over their chronological, geographic, and ethnocultural origins. Most scholars agree that prior to the twentieth century, the Seminoles demonstrated their greatest political unity in their decision for war. Those who have envisioned a more centralized model of Seminole social and political organization, derived from the Creeks, argue that the Seminole council was "transformed into a true government" once the Indians moved to the land reserved for them in central Florida under the 1823 Treaty of Moultrie Creek. Indeed, there is little firm evidence of a national council before 1821, suggesting that the council formed as a means of dealing with U.S. pressure once the United States replaced Spain in Florida.

Concentrating on the question of geographic concentration and spatial cohesion, such historians observe that "the council became progressively more unified," not only because of U.S. pressure but because of the Seminoles' close proximity to one another within the reserved area. Thus these students maintain that the period 1825–35 produced "the first emergence of a unitary Seminole identity."[21] Other historians, focused on discerning complex distinctions within and between Seminole, Muskogee, and non-Muskogee ethnies, have argued that "if the Seminole and Creek nations ever existed," it was under the pressure of war after 1834, but they maintain that the Seminoles remained "an assemblage of southeastern remnant tribes," who "did not necessarily understand one another," linguistically and perhaps culturally.[22] Perhaps the only clear agreement among scholars is that "the strongest evidence for political unity comes during the early American period, and this only under duress."[23] What then does the war tell us about the Creek elements in Seminole culture and politics? More importantly, does the evidence of the war affirm the value of precise distinctions between the many linguistic and cultural groups present in Florida, or does a scholarly "lumping" more accurately reflect the impact of growing conflict with the United States?

How did the dispersal of the Seminoles after 1836 affect their leadership and cohesion? How were these sustained, or hindered, as Indians were captured or surrendered? How was it affected by the army's use of captured or surrendered Seminoles as guides, interpreters, and emissaries seeking the surrender of their former comrades-in-arms? What was the role of the black Seminoles and maroons, and how did their capture and surrender, essentially complete by 1838, affect the Indian resistance? How did the centrality of military affairs during the war affect the character and composition of Indian leadership, of cultural criteria and parameters for leadership?

What role did religion play in motivating war and sustaining cohesion? The conflict brought new leaders, most famously Osceola, to the fore, but a religious leader, Abiákî (Abiaka, Arpeika, or Sam Jones), proved one of the most persistent and most difficult for U.S. forces to catch. This subject has received little attention among students of the Seminole, in contrast with scholars' emphasis on nativist and revitalization movements in Indian drives for political unity and the initiation of war, from Neolin (the Delaware Prophet) and Pontiac to Tenskwatawa (the Shawnee Prophet) and Tecumseh, to the Red Stick Creeks and Hillis Hadjo (Josiah Francis, the Creek or Alabama Prophet).[24] Remarkably, Arpeika is the only religious figure prominent in the literature of the Seminole resistance struggle, but he was a Mikasuki rather than a Muskogean Seminole. On the other hand, one scholar has suggested that a "Creek prophet," who escaped from a Georgia jail to Florida in 1836, led a war band, presumably largely Creek in composition, more cohesive than those of the Seminoles.[25] Why does religion seem to have played so much less significant a role in Seminole political decisions than it did among the Red Sticks, many of whom had fled to Florida after their defeat in 1814?

Students of conflict, to say nothing of history as a whole, should always examine both sides. Thinking of the 1835–42 war in terms of Indian objectives and strategy may help explain its operational trajectory, from both sides of the conflict. Historians have long periodized the war in phases, largely according to the form of U.S. operations and the campaign plans or strategies of the successive theater commanders. Thus we normally go from Clinch and Gaines launching individual thrusts into the Cove of the Withlacoochee, to Scott sending several columns to converge on the Cove and trap the Seminoles, to further advances against the Cove by Call and Jesup, calls for negotiation and an armistice followed by a multi-armed advance south toward the Everglades by Jesup in 1837, with more decentralized operations followed by negotiations early in 1838, Alexander Macomb's armistice negotiations in 1839, Zachary Taylor's "square plan" of patrols that year, and "scouts" or patrols of increasing aggressiveness and frequency, penetrating deeper into the Everglades, under Walker K. Armistead in 1840–41 and, in the summer and combined with constant negotiations with individual Indian bands, under William Worth in 1841–42.

Did the Indians merely retreat in the face of growing U.S. pressure? Did U.S. commanders think the Seminoles had a strategy? Their frequent reflections on the Indians' refusal to accept battle strongly suggest that they did, that they believed the Seminoles intended to wear down the United States by making the war protracted and expensive, though they left little evidence of conceptualizing Seminole strategy in explicitly political terms or at a political level.[26] War is a two-sided affair, and we need to restore agency to the Seminoles in their war against American aggression. Vague references to guerrilla warfare do not do justice to the rationality, vision, complexity, and dilemmas of the Seminole war effort.

Pondering Indian objectives and strategy—and divisions over them—might help us understand Seminole actions as more than a series of indistinguishable ambushes and raids, which may appear like flailing about without political purpose—the violent expression of doomed savagery. By doing so, we can enhance our understanding of Indian actions beyond the level of tactical minutiae, to refocus on political intent, indeed on political (or "national") strategy. A strategic perspective might help us understand the resumption of the war with the attack on William Harney's outpost on the Caloosahatchee in the summer of 1839, or why some bands struck out to the north, returning to Middle and East Florida and penetrating West Florida every year after 1837, while others lay low and tried to avoid contact in the Big Cypress and other southern swamps.

Many of the Indians in Middle and West Florida were Creeks, many of them refugees from the "Second Creek War" in Alabama. Indeed, some scholars have maintained that "the most obdurate Florida Seminoles were nineteenth-century Creek immigrants," reporting that Yuchi Billy, aka Billy Hicks, went to Georgia and/or Alabama and brought back more than a hundred Yuchis to fight in Florida in 1836.[27] Some Creeks returned to launch an offensive into southern Alabama in 1837,[28] and others ranged along the Georgia border, primarily in the Okeefenokee Swamp, intermittently throughout the Seminole conflict. Though it seems unlikely that they were involved in coordinated strategic planning, or even execution, with the Seminoles in central and southern Florida, what role did northern Florida, particularly distant West Florida, play in Indian military strategy and operations after the majority of Seminoles withdrew southward in 1837? More generally, anthropologists maintain that early nineteenth-century Seminole "identity owed much to the infusion of Red Stick Creeks into Florida" after 1814, observing that the Red Sticks knew that Florida was much larger than their former territory in Alabama, encouraging hopes for sustained resistance. How important was the Creek "reinforcement" in sustaining the Seminole struggle, not just in numbers or reinvigorated morale, but in military ideas, in expanding the areas of military operations within Florida and beyond?[29]

These are political, diplomatic, economic, and cultural questions as well as military ones. What was the impact of Seminole concepts of place, for a people born of migration, often flight? We know that the Seminoles often planted in one area and moved away, returning later to harvest. What role was played by such fields in Middle Florida, the Cove of the Withlacoochee, the hammocks along the western coast of the peninsula north of Tampa Bay—where U.S. officers reported extensive Indian movements in 1840, 1841, and 1842—and the Alachua (Payne's) prairie? What role did the cultural concept of "old fields" play, like the Suwannee Old Fields and those in the vicinity of Alachua, where Seminoles had lived before the first U.S. war in 1818, at which U.S. officers reported Indian planting and raids even after 1840?[30]

What about generational change, amid a conflict that continued intermittently for a full generation after 1835? Did the maturation of young Indian men, unable to secure status by performing their predecessors' cultural roles as warriors during the years of U.S. occupation between 1820 and 1835, encourage demands for military resistance to removal?[31] How did their maturation, and that of younger men during the war itself, affect Seminole society, politics, culture, and diplomacy? Why did warriors engage in corpse mutilation and attacks on women and children—as, indeed, did whites? Did the Seminoles view these acts as atrocities? Did they understand the impact they would have on white public opinion?

Attention to Indian strategy will encourage study and understanding of the Seminoles both as militarily and economically "rational actors" and as an ethnie whose cultural values and practices influenced military strategy and operations, as well as tactics. We may deny the presence of a coherent national military strategy after 1837 or 1838. But thinking in strategic terms can help us try to identify, understand, and assess their military actions and understand why they chose a particular course of action with particular targets at a particular point in time, under particular circumstances. What did the Creeks and Seminole learn from conflicts between 1812 and 1818, or the occasional clashes during the first reservation period during the 1820s?

Exploring the dynamics of Seminole strategy, particularly at the "national" rather than a solely military level, encourages us to explore Indian relationships with other actors, both in peace and war: the impact they intended for, of even if unintended may have had on, white Floridians, white southerners, northern whites, Whigs, the federal government, Congress, and the executive branch. Surely the Seminoles could envision divisions among whites, whether from experience during the reservation period or as the analogue of their own differences. Indeed, we know that individual Seminole leaders, and often individual warriors, maintained near-constant contact, effectively diplomatic relations, with their counterparts in the U.S. Army, even during periods of active operations like Zachary Taylor's advance to Lake Okeechobee in December 1837.[32] When they sought to negotiate, whether to emigrate or to delay army operations against them, the Florida Indians turned first to the closest agents of U.S. power, the officers of the army, rather than territorial civil officials.

While it seems unlikely that the Seminoles were fully aware of the Second Party System, growing and maturing during the very years of the war, and they may not have understood the significance of Congress in the American system of government, they clearly understood that some whites were more sympathetic, less eager to pursue removal, than others. And whatever they knew of whites, it would be foolish to assume that they did not hope to influence other southern Indians, particularly the Creeks and perhaps the Cherokee. Whatever role the Seminole uprising had on the origins of the Creek rebellion six months later, U.S. Army officers from Georgia to Wisconsin worried that news of the Florida conflict would stir unrest and violence, and they reported rumors of communications between northern, southern, and western Indians throughout 1836.[33]

It is important, perhaps crucial, that historians, and scholars in other disciplines, recognize the strategic dimensions of Seminole resistance to U.S. conquest: in order to understand the geographic and chronological trajectory of the resistance; in order to recognize the range of methods—economic and diplomatic as well as purely military—employed by the resistance; to better comprehend Seminole political dynamics and decision-making; to evaluate the role of cultural values and practices in political, diplomatic, and military decision-making and action. Indeed, assessments of the American wars and U.S. military operations against the Seminole would benefit almost equally from more conceptualization at higher levels of analysis, whether the analysis and evaluation is militarily focused, politically and diplomatically focused, or socially, economically, and culturally focused.

More explicit attention to the strategic level of scale would help scholars of Native American resistance identify commonalities, continuities, and trajectories across the tribal lines that still tend to divide their research. Like students of U.S. history called upon to "internationalize" and transcend American exceptionalism, they could begin to write a more comparative, synthetic history of Indian politics, diplomacy, and resistance than can be achieved through specialized tribal studies alone.[34] Indeed, we might extend our transnational comparisons to cases and patterns of resistance to European colonialism outside North America—to South and Central America, to Asia, to Africa and Oceania.[35] Even in the absence of direct written evidence, the use of white sources, oral tradition, and inference from anthropological, archaeological, military, diplomatic, political, economic, and cultural perspectives can enable students to better understand the Seminole side, in a conflict commonly depicted and understood largely from the standpoint of whites. Victors' history serves us no better here than anywhere else; exploring the conflict through the lens of Seminole strategy can help historians draw political, military, and cultural perspectives together, enhancing them all.

Notes

1. Robert M. Utley, *The Indian Frontier of the American West, 1846–1890* (Albuquerque: University of New Mexico Press, 1984), 44, 166, criticizes the army's lack of creativity and imagination in developing tactics to defeat the trans-Mississippi Indians. Utley implicitly recognizes that operational persistence was the decisive factor, observing that "when they worked, [the army's] offensives worked with a vengeance,"

167, but seems unwilling to let go of his causally secondary tactical assessment: "in the end it was not combat success but convergence, unremittingly prosecuted," that won the Red River War and ended Comanche, Cheyenne, Kiowa, and Arapaho resistance on the southern Plains (178). Utley sought to raise the analysis of the Indian Wars above the tactical level so beloved by buffs; my point would be that it was the national standing army, not settlers, that conducted these campaigns. Indeed, Utley recognizes this when he observes that the western volunteer forces of the Civil War melted away at its end, even before they might have been demobilized (77–79). The research behind the present essay was originally done for Samuel Watson, "'This thankless . . . unholy war': Army Officers and Civil-Military Relations in the Second Seminole War," in David Dillard and Randal Hall, eds., *The Southern Albatross: Race and Ethnicity in the South* (Macon, Ga.: Mercer University Press, 1999), 9–49, and David Dillard and Randal Hall, *Frontier Diplomats: The Army Officer Corps in the Borderlands of the Early Republic, 1814–1846* (Lawrence: University Press of Kansas, 2011).

2. This is true even for the works of Susan Miller, Brent Weisman, Patricia Wickman, and J. Leitch Wright, which are written from Seminole perspectives or those sensitive and favorable to the Seminoles. See Susan A. Miller, *Coacoochee's Bones: A Seminole Saga* (Lawrence: University Press of Kansas, 2003); Brent R. Weisman, *Unconquered People: Florida's Seminole and Miccosukee Indians* (Gainesville: University Press of Florida, 1999); Patricia R. Wickman, *Osceola's Legacy* (1984; rev. ed., Tuscaloosa: University Press of Alabama, 2006); and J. Leitch Wright Jr., *Creeks and Seminoles: The Destruction and Regeneration of the Muscogulge People* (Lincoln: University of Nebraska Press, 1986). Among histories of the Second Seminole War, John Missall and Mary Lou Missall, *The Seminole Wars: America's Longest Indian Conflict* (Gainesville: University Press of Florida, 2004) is most attentive to Seminole perspectives. The standard history of the Seminoles is now James W. Covington, *The Seminoles of Florida* (Gainesville: University Press of Florida, 1993); the standard history of the Second Seminole War remains John K. Mahon, *History of the Second Seminole War, 1835–1842* (Gainesville: University of Florida Press, 1967; rev. ed. 1985); Edwin C. McReynolds, *The Seminoles* (Norman: University of Oklahoma Press, 1957) provides a general history with extensive attention to the Second Seminole War. See also Joe Knetsch, *Florida's Seminole Wars, 1817–1858* (Charleston, S.C.: Arcadia, 2003); Milton Meltzer, *Hunted Like a Wolf: The Story of the Seminole War* (2d ed., Sarasota: Pineapple Press, 2004); and Virginia B. Peters, *The Florida Wars* (Hamden, Conn.: Archon Books, 1979). Even the prolific Joe Knetsch has not published on Seminole strategy.

3. Wickman, *Osceola's Legacy*, 16–17 (references to strategy), and Patricia R. Wickman, *The Tree That Bends: Discourse, Power, and the Survival of the Maskókî People* (Tuscaloosa: University of Alabama Press, 1999), 97 ("hit-and-run attacks"), table 1, 124, 129.

4. Wickman, *Osceola's Legacy*, 12. For further context, see Leroy V. Eid, "American Indian Leadership: St. Clair's 1791 Defeat," *Journal of Military History* 57 (January 1993): 71–88.

5. The most comprehensive historical analysis, at least for the eastern woodlands, is

in Stephen Warren, *The Shawnees and Their Neighbors, 1795–1870* (Urbana: University of Illinois, 2005); see also Colin G. Calloway. "'We Have Always Been the Frontier': The American Revolution in Shawnee Country," *American Indian Quarterly* 16 (Winter 1992): 39–52; John P. Bowes, *Exiles and Pioneers: Eastern Indians in the Trans-Mississippi West* (Cambridge: Cambridge University Press, 2007); and more generally Harry A. Kersey, Jr., "The Cherokee, Creek, and Seminole Responses to Removal: A Comparison," in John K. Mahon, ed., *Indians of the Lower South: Past and Present* (Pensacola: Gulf Coast History and Humanities Conference, 1975). I have drawn the phrase "strategy of migration" from Seminole tribe member Miller, *Coacoochee's Bones*, 10. This was Coacoochee's response to defeat—being captured and compelled to emigrate, rather than a voluntary preemptive strategy of trying to choose the terms of one's migration, as the Shawnee and Cherokee had done.

6. Wickman, *Osceola's Legacy*, 15, refers to "a series of calculated and daring moves orchestrated by the elders of the war council," certainly a strategic-level synchronization of effort. Comparable situations include the initiation of the "Creek Wars" in 1813 and 1836; see especially Karl Davis, "'Remember Fort Mims': Reinterpreting the Origins of the Creek War," *Journal of the Early Republic* 22 (Winter 2002): 612–36; Gregory A. Waselkov, *A Conquering Spirit: Fort Mims and the Redstick War of 1813–1814* (Tuscaloosa: University of Alabama Press, 2006); and John T. Ellisor, "The Second Creek War: The Unexplored Conflict," PhD diss., University of Tennessee, 1996.

7. People of African ancestry living with the Seminoles, under whatever status are treated in Daniel F. Littlefield Jr., *Africans and Seminoles: From Removal to Emancipation* (Westport, Conn.: Greenwood Press, 1977); Kenneth Wiggins Porter, *The Black Seminoles: History of a Freedom-Seeking People*, ed. Alcione M. Amos and Thomas P. Sutter (Gainesville: University Press of Florida, 1996), along with Porter's many articles; Kevin Mulroy, *Freedom on the Border: The Seminole Maroons in Florida, the Indian Territory, Coahuila, and Texas* (Lubbock: Texas Tech University Press, 1993); and Bruce E. Twyman, *The Black Seminole Legacy in North American Politics, 1693–1845* (Washington, D.C.: Howard University Press, 1999). The questions of their status and treatment, their relations with the Indian Seminoles, and their roles in initiating and conducting the war are probably the most hotly contested issues in the historiography of the Seminoles, particularly because American military commanders played up the role of blacks to draw attention to the war and because most people of African ancestry ultimately surrendered to the U.S. forces in return for guarantees of safe transit and freedom in the west. Most scholars have been sympathetic to them; the outstanding exception is Miller, *Coacoochee's Bones*. The other extreme is Twyman, *The Black Seminole Legacy in North American Politics*, who maintains that the Florida Indians could not have enslaved or subordinated the maroons, presumably armed (particularly by the Spanish), who sought refuge in the region beginning in the seventeenth century. Consequently, Twyman sees the blacks living outside white control as autonomous, to the point that "the Second Seminole War was a war to preserve the freedom of the black Seminoles," 121, the sort of hyperbole, to the utter neglect of Jacksonian plans for Seminole removal, that Miller rightly rejects. Similarly, Twyman

repeats older interpretations, rooted in the papers of contemporary U.S. Army officers, that blacks were "the dominant war policy negotiators with U.S. generals," 113, denying the Indian Seminoles agency in their own struggle for home and autonomy. Twyman does argue that the black leader Abraham "knew that ultimately the Seminoles could not prevail," 120, and sought to exhaust white will, in order to secure better terms for the people of African ancestry among them, which seems a reasonable conclusion, and certainly suggests strategic vision on Abraham's part. Whatever their status among the Indians, most students agree that white racism and the demands of the slave system made them crucial to the origins of the war; though primarily a scholar of Seminole culture, Brent Weisman labels their presence, and the Seminoles' undeniable refusal to surrender them to whites, "the single most important immediate cause of the Second Seminole War." Weisman, *Unconquered People*, 44. Yet, without further research into the level of white pressure for the maroons' surrender, the January 1, 1836, deadline for the Seminoles to begin removal might appear to be an equal or greater catalyst. Abolitionist perspectives are best seen in Joshua R. Giddings, *The Exiles of Florida* (1858; reprint, Baltimore: Black Classic Press, 1997); the only modern case study is John Campbell, "The Seminoles, the 'Bloodhound War,' and Abolition, 1796–1865," *Journal of Southern History* 77 (May 2006): 259–30; but see also John Stauffer, *The Black Hearts of Men: Radical Abolitionists and the Transformation of Race* (Cambridge, Mass.: Harvard University Press, 2002), ch. 6; Mary Hershberger, "Mobilizing Women, Anticipating Abolition: The Struggle against Indian Removal in the 1830s," *Journal of American History* 86 (June 1999): 25–40; and Linda K. Kerber, "The Abolitionist Perception of the Indian," *Journal of American History* 62 (September 1975): 271–95.

8. Wickman, *Osceola's Legacy*, 17, came to the same conclusion.

9. Weisman, *Unconquered People*, 52.

10. Wright, *Creeks and Seminoles*, 269–70.

11. Ibid., 261.

12. The best primary sources for army operations are the Thomas Sidney Jesup Papers, in the Generals Papers, entry 159, Records of the Adjutant General's Office, Record Group 94, National Archives, and the letterbooks of Walker K. Armistead and William J. Worth, 5 vols., Ninth Military Department (Provisional), 1838–45, Letters Sent, entry 72, Records of Continental Army Commands, Record Group 393. Similar correspondence from Zachary Taylor's period in command is mostly contained in the Adjutant General's Office, Letters Received, Registered Series, Microfilm Production 567, Record Group 94 (usually in the "T" files for each reel).

13. Richard A. Sattler, "Remnants, Renegades, and Runaways: Seminole Ethnogenesis Reconsidered," in Jonathan D. Hill, ed., *History, Power, and Identity: Ethnogenesis in the Americas, 1492–1992* (Iowa City: University of Iowa Press, 1996), 37.

14. Wickman, *Osceola's Legacy*, 22–24. However, Wickman's assertion that the council "gave war power to Abiáki" (the religious leader also known as Abiaka, or Arpeika, or among whites such as Sam Jones) is unclear. Surely he did not receive the power to terminate the war on his own, and as an elderly religious figure it seems unlikely that he was given operational military command.

15. Covington, *The Seminoles*, 102–5.

16. It seems rather less likely that the Seminoles knew about the revolution in Texas, but edgy white military commanders envisioned Indian wars stretching the length of the western frontier in 1836.

17. See the classic article by Thomas C. Leonard, "Red, White, and Army Blue: Empathy and Anger in the American West," *American Quarterly* 26 (May 1974): 176–90, for a look at the ambivalence of post–Civil War army officers toward war with the Indians. The most extensive treatment of military attitudes toward Native Americans, also focused on the post–Civil War years, is Sherry L. Smith, *The View from Officers' Row: Army Perceptions of Western Indians* (Tucson: University of Arizona Press, 1990); see also William B. Skelton, "Army Officers' Attitudes towards Indians, 1830–1860," *Pacific Northwest Quarterly* 67 (July 1976): 113–24, and Samuel Watson, *Frontier Diplomats*, for the era of the Seminole Wars.

18. Meltzer, *Hunted Like a Wolf*, 105.

19. Thus, as Robert Utley observes, the army was often more tactically successful when it did so, but institutional, psychological, and cultural considerations, rooted in the factors Utley himself emphasizes, and the variety of potential future missions, often make it difficult and undesirable over the long term for complex conventional institutions to adopt unconventional methods on an extensive or exclusive scale. See Utley, "Culture Clash on the Western North American Indian Frontier: Military Implications," in James C. Bradford, ed., *The Military and Conflict between Cultures: Soldiers at the Interface* (College Station: Texas A&M University Press, 1997). Nor did the Seminole pose a threat to U.S. national survival, so the imperative for tactical and institutional adjustment was much less urgent than it might be for a state defending itself against domestic insurgency.

20. For a thoughtful comparison, see Kingsley M. Bray, "Crazy Horse and the End of the Great Sioux War," *Nebraska History* 79 (Fall 1998): 94–115.

21. Sattler, "Seminole Ethnogenesis Reconsidered," 58–59.

22. Wright, *Creeks and Seminoles*, 245, 255.

23. Weisman, *Unconquered People*, 26.

24. Gregory Evans Dowd, *A Spirited Resistance: The North American Indian Struggle for Unity, 1745–1815* (Baltimore: Johns Hopkins University Press, 1991); Gregory Evans Dowd, "The French King Wakes Up in Detroit: 'Pontiac's War' in Rumor and History," *Ethnohistory* 37 (Summer 1990): 254–78; Gregory Evans Dowd, "Thinking and Believing: Nativism and Unity in the Ages of Pontiac and Tecumseh," *American Indian Quarterly* 16 (1992): 309–35; David R. Edmunds, *The Shawnee Prophet* (Lincoln: University of Nebraska Press, 1983); David R. Edmunds, "Tecumseh, the Shawnee Prophet, and American History: A Reassessment," *Western Historical Quarterly* 14 (July 1983): 261–76; Joel W. Martin, *Sacred Revolt: The Muskogees' Struggle for a New World* (Boston: Beacon Press, 1991).

25. Covington, *The Seminoles*, 100–101.

26. When Winfield Scott failed to catch the Seminoles in 1836, he warned that "it [will] continue . . . to be the policy of the enemy to remain scattered in small parties

and to avoid a general battle—thereby protracting the war almost indefinitely." Letter to Capt. F. M. Robertson of the Augusta Volunteers, May 26, 1836, published in *Army and Navy Chronicle* 2, no. 24 (June 16, 1836): 380. I have not found any suggestions by army officers that the Seminoles sought to take advantage of sectional or partisan divisions.

27. Wright, *Creeks and Seminoles*, 253, 255.

28. Wright, *Creeks and Seminoles*, 270.

29. Weisman, *Unconquered People*, 27, 48.

30. Cf. Gregory Waselkov, "Changing Strategies of Indian Field Location in the Early Historic Southeast," in Kristen J. Gremillion, ed., *People, Plants, and Landscapes: Essays in Paleoethnobotany* (Tuscaloosa: University of Alabama Press, 1997), 179–94, and Gregory A. Waselkov and Brian M. Wood, "The Creek War of 1813–1814: Effects on Creek Society and Settlement Patterns," *Journal of Alabama Archaeology* 32 (June 1986): 1–24.

31. Weisman, *Unconquered People*, 49.

32. See the Jesup Generals Papers, National Archives, and the John W. Phelps Papers, New York Public Library.

33. See the 1836 correspondence in the letterbooks of Brevet Brigadier General Henry Atkinson, Sixth Military Department, Letters Sent, 1834–46, entry 45, Record Group 393, National Archives.

34. See Jeffrey Ostler, *The Plains Sioux and U.S. Colonialism, from Lewis and Clark to Wounded Knee* (Cambridge: Cambridge University Press, 2004), and William H. Moore, *Chiefs, Agents, and Soldiers: Conflict on the Navajo Frontier, 1868–1882* (Albuquerque: University of New Mexico Press, 1994), for outstanding studies of patterns of resistance over time in the trans-Mississippi West; Warren, *The Shawnees and Their Neighbors*, provides an example east of the Plains, in which we can identify numerous resistance strategies short of war.

35. See especially Bruce Vandervort, *Indian Wars of Mexico, Canada, and the United States, 1812–1900* (London: Routledge, 2006); Bruce Vandervort, *Wars of Imperial Conquest in Africa, 1830–1914* (Bloomington: Indiana University Press, 1998); and James O. Gump, *The Dust Rose Like Smoke: The Subjugation of the Zulu and the Sioux* (Lincoln: University of Nebraska Press, 1994). Older and more localized case studies that extend over long chronological periods and present a sense of the strategic level of scale include James Belich, *The New Zealand Wars and the Victorian Interpretation of Racial Conflict* (Auckland, New Zealand: Auckland University Press, 1986), which is as much about the Maori as the white intruders, and Michael Crowder, ed., *West African Resistance: The Military Response to Colonial Occupation* (London: Hutchinson, 1971). There is also a growing literature on resistance to Russian expansion in the Caucasus, Central Asia, and Siberia, and to responses to European penetration in eighteenth-century India.

7

"It is a negro, not an Indian war"

Southampton, St. Domingo, and the Second Seminole War

MATTHEW CLAVIN

In 1836, a little-known writer published a sensationalistic account of a series of dramatic events that were unfolding in the Florida territory.[1] For the second time in a generation, the United States was going to war with the Seminole Indians in an effort to remove them from their land and clear the way for American expansion. In describing a series of violent clashes that sparked the conflict, Daniel F. Blanchard detailed some of the atrocities committed by Seminole warriors against white soldiers and settlers, including several massacres of defenseless white men, women, and children. The pamphlet also included an eye-catching illustration. A two-page woodcut of the carnage described in the accompanying text, it served as a pictorial summary of Seminole savagery. In spite of its graphic nature, the visual was unremarkable, something that many readers would have found cliché. Authors and editors routinely inserted similar images in Indian captivity narratives and related literary genres, which capitalized on the cruel and terrifying imagery of frontier war.

There is one significant exception to the normative character of Blanchard's image. A center panel depicts the slaying of two white civilians by armed and enraged black men, presumably slaves. It, too, was unoriginal. Blanchard copied the image from a pamphlet published four years earlier by Samuel Warner. Entitled *Authentic and Impartial Narrative of the Tragical Scene Which Was Witnessed in Southampton County*, Warner's pamphlet chronicled Nat Turner's slave revolt in southeastern Virginia in 1831.[2] In what many accept as the largest slave rebellion in U.S. history, Turner, a plantation laborer and mystic, spurred dozens of bondmen to murder nearly sixty white Virginians under the cover of darkness. In addition to describing the Southampton revolt, Warner's book also examined the unprecedented slave insurrection in the French colony of Saint-Domingue, or St. Domingo, which occurred at the turn of the century. The extraordinary slave revolution that resulted in the liberation of some 500,000 bondpeople and the birth of the new nation of Haiti came at a

7.1. Oversized engraving of atrocities committed by Native and African Americans during Second Seminole War, from Daniel F. Blanchard's *An authentic narrative of the Seminole war* (1836). Courtesy of the Collections of the Library of Congress..

tremendous price. The "horrors of St. Domingo" resulted in the deaths of tens of thousands of settlers, soldiers, and slaves, and France lost the wealthiest colony in the Americas.[3]

Blanchard's deployment of an image inseparable from the slave revolts in both Southampton and St. Domingo demonstrates how Americans drew sharp distinctions between the Seminole and the fugitive slaves, or maroons, who fought beside them. In the literature of the period, authors routinely described the threat that both Seminoles and their black allies posed to white settlement. They eagerly reported atrocities committed by both groups. Yet one detects in these works an obvious distinction. Writers often displayed both sympathy and empathy for the Seminole, whom they imagined as Noble Savages. In various published accounts they depicted the Seminole, like other native people still remaining in North America, as a noble yet disappearing race whose last days in America—as well as on earth—were numbered. The same writers who paid tribute to the vanishing Indian, however, did not wax nostalgically about the bondpeople who aided the resistance movement. While the end of Indian violence was imminent, they feared a different trajectory. For them, the course of black rebellion from St. Domingo to Southampton and ultimately the Second Seminole War was both evident and alarming.

The significant role that fugitive slaves played in the Second Seminole War fueled Americans' fear of a massive slave insurrection originating in the Florida territory. Generations of scholars have understood this role due to Kenneth Porter's pioneering work, and today, the African American character of the war also inflects the popular imagination due to a compelling Web site that is devoted to proving that "From 1835–1838 in Florida, the Black Seminoles, the African allies of Seminole Indians, led the largest slave rebellion in U.S. history."[4] The debate over whether the Second Seminole War is more deserving of the label Indian war or slave revolt is valuable, bringing much needed attention to the enduring military alliance among Native and African Americans in the antebellum South. It nevertheless does little to explain how those who lived through and experienced the war understood and interpreted the conflict. Those who first chronicled the war did so in the shadow of both Nat Turner's revolt and the Haitian Revolution. Which, as this essay illuminates, is why in the early print culture of the war they depicted bondpeople, in spite of centuries of violent Indian resistance, as the greatest and immediate threat to the republic.

The decades following American independence witnessed some of the deadliest clashes between Native and European Americans in the history of North America. Tecumseh's efforts to create a pan-Indian army in the Northwest Territory and the militant Creek response to the intrusion of American settlers on their land in the South are among the legendary episodes in the history of violent Native American resistance. While the increase in bloodshed between Americans and Indians might have portended a never-ending cycle of frontier bloodshed, shortly after the conclusion of the War of 1812, the threat to American expansion across the middle of the continent had all but subsided. The decline of violent Indian resistance resulted in a number of unintended consequences, including an outpouring of compassion for Native people who remained in the United States. It was a nostalgic and nationalistic celebration of Indian history and culture. By the time Andrew Jackson assumed the presidency in 1828 and announced his final solution to the Indian problem, many had come to see Native Americans not as a threat but as a blameless people who deserved the aid and protection of the United States.

Sympathy for the Native American plight was widespread, even among some of the nation's most eminent frontiersmen. In 1819, the Kentucky planter and politician Henry Clay recommended that Congress shift federal policy. Noting the ascendancy of the European American population, Clay remarked on the transition of military and political power from Native to European American hands. "We are powerful and they are weak," he affirmed. "The poor children of the forest have been driven by the great wave which has flowed in from the Atlantic ocean to almost the base of the Rocky Mountains, and, overwhelming them in its terrible progress, has left no other remains of hundreds of tribes, now extinct, than those which indicate the remote existence of their former companion, the mammoth of the New World!"[5] In 1826, William

Clark, half of the legendary tandem that led the Corps of Discovery across the continent in 1803, served as the superintendent of Indian affairs, and he urged Congress to aid those Indians who remained in the United States and "save them from extinction." From the American Revolution through the second war of American independence, Clark avowed that "the tribes nearest our settlements were," admittedly, "a formidable and terrible enemy"; but now "their power has been broken, their warlike spirit subdued, and themselves sunk into objects of pity and commiseration."[6]

The sentiments of Clay and Clark stretched eastward to the nation's capital. President Andrew Jackson in his famous message to Congress in 1830 on Indian removal displayed little of the fury that earned him the nickname "Indian Killer." Jackson announced munificently, "Humanity has often wept over the fate of the aborigines of this country; and philanthropy has been long busily employed in devising means to divert it." But there was no doubting the inevitable. "One by one have many powerful tribes disappeared from the earth. To follow to the tomb the last of his race, and to tread on the graves of extinct nations, excites melancholy reflections." Jackson insisted that removal was unregretful. "What good man would prefer a country covered with forests, and ranged by a few thousand savages, to our extensive republic, studded with cities, towns, and prosperous farms; embellished with all the improvements which art can devise, or industry execute; occupied by more than twelve millions of happy people, and filled with all the blessings of liberty, civilization, and religion!"[7] Supreme Court Justice Joseph Story amplified Jackson's attitude when commenting on the inescapable fate of Native Americans, given the Manifest Destiny of the American people to conquer the continent. "There is, indeed, in the fate of these unfortunate beings, much to awaken our sympathy, and much to disturb the sobriety of our judgment; much, which may be urged to excuse their own atrocities; much in their characters, which betrays us into an involuntary admiration," Story wrote. "What can be more melancholy than their history? By a law of nature, they seem destined to a slow, but sure extinction." Wherever white men approach, "they fade away. We hear the rustling of their footsteps, like that of the withered leaves of autumn, and they are gone for ever."[8]

Despite the words of these political leaders, it is perhaps in popular fiction that the construction of Native Americans as a noble and vanishing people most resonated with the American people. Though James Fenimore Cooper filled his widely read novels with lurid tales of Indian savagery, including acts of cannibalism and infanticide, they nevertheless evoke a strong sympathy for various characters like Chingachgook and Uncas, who represent the last vestiges of a once proud and honorable people. In the introduction to *Last of the Mohicans*, the most famous of the five-part frontier epic known as the *Leatherstocking Tales*, Cooper wrote of Native Americans, "the seemingly inevitable fate of all these people, who disappear before the advances, or it might be termed the inroads of civilization, as the verdure of their native forests falls before the nipping frost, is represented as having already befallen them. There is sufficient historical truth in the picture to justify the use that has been made of it." Where the story took place, Cooper noted the existence of only a "few half-civilized beings" of one tribe. "The rest have disappeared, either from the regions in which their fathers dwelt, or altogether from the earth."[9]

Not everyone was as convinced as Cooper was of the passing of the Indian threat. In the spring of 1838, a dispute rose in the House of Representatives over the government's execution of the Florida war. As had become standard, some political leaders expressed great remorse over various flawed Indian treaties and the issue of forced Indian removal. Yet for those in the Florida territory, the time to mourn the Indians' disappearance had not yet arrived. Charles Downing, a congressman from St. Augustine, took exception with those "who professed so much sympathy for the Indians." Excoriating those who "must have gotten their knowledge of Indian character from Cooper's novels," he avowed that if they went and lived among the Indians like "he had done," then "they would change their feelings." Downing asserted that he "had known a man, as honest as any in existence, in earth or heaven," who with great sympathy for the Indians had gone to live among them and had become, "in one year, as thorough an Indian hater as he was."[10] In spite of his pleading, men like Downing fought a losing battle. Outside of Florida, increasingly what most Americans knew about the Indians came from writers like Cooper.[11]

Thomas Loraine McKenney published nonfiction, but regarding Indian extinction he shared the same authorial intent as Cooper. As superintendent of Indian trade and later Indian affairs, McKenney hoped to preserve "in the archives of the Government whatever of the aboriginal man can be rescued from the destruction which awaits his race."[12] Capitalizing on the romanticization of Indian culture, he and the writer James Hall published one of the most significant illustrated books of the nineteenth century. Like a modern zoologist who photographs a rare endangered species, McKenney in *History of the Indian Tribes of North America* compiled a massive visual catalog of Native American men, women, and children. In a lengthy historical essay that provided context for the portraits, Hall lamented the fate of the Indian, yet he hoped for a charitable solution. "Could we bring back the three centuries that have elapsed since the discovery by Columbus, how much might we hope to recall of the history, tradition, and institutions of the Indians which have for ever passed away! Still much remains—and if all who have opportunities for observation would devote themselves to these researches, a race of men not more insulated in their position, than peculiar in their opinions and customs, would be rescued from that comparative oblivion in which we fear they are destined, under present circumstances, speedily to become involved."[13]

The inclusion of the Seminoles in the famous pictorial is ironic. When the book first appeared, the Second Seminole War was entering its third year. At the same time that McKenney and Hall honored the nobility of the Indians and bemoaned their disappearance, violent resistance by the Seminole to encroachment on their land gave little indication of the inevitability of Indian removal in the Florida territory. The co-authors said little about the Second Seminole War; however, they did include in their volume five biographical sketches of Seminole leaders who were either "friendly to the United States" or, like the great chief Micanopy, among those who eventually emigrated from Florida. Conspicuously absent from the publication are some of the prominent leaders of the Seminole forces during the war, including Osceola and Billy Bowlegs.[14]

The co-authors listed several causes of the war. Much responsibility lay with both the American government, which throughout the years had reneged on treaties, and lawless settlers, who committed violent depredations among the Seminole and stole their land. The Seminole also bore responsibility. "From the swamps and hammocks of Florida, they have been in the habit of annoying the frontiers of the adjacent states, and these injuries have been rendered the more galling by the protection afforded by those savages to runaway slaves, and by the ferocities practiced by the latter under the influence of revenge and the fear of recapture."[15] The quotation is instructive, highlighting the distinction that the authors drew between the Seminole and their black allies. It moreover indicates how many thought differently about Native and African American violence: while Americans dreaded Seminole attacks, ferocious assaults by fugitive slaves represented an entirely different threat. This had not always been the case. Indians and slaves had once represented great threats to European American civilization. This, however, was when events in Virginia caused the fear of slave revolt to reach its zenith.

Nat Turner was by all accounts a good slave. Born and raised in southeastern Virginia, he was with rare exception an obedient field hand who met with fair treatment from his masters and overseers. Yet there was always something extraordinary about the diminutive Turner. From an early age, he demonstrated a keen intelligence. His ability to read and write without instruction opened doors for him that for many slaves would always remain closed. Turner's religiosity also distinguished him from his peers. Turner read the Bible voraciously and preached the Holy Word to local slaves, who came to refer to him as "The Prophet." Turner saw strange visions, heard distant voices, and experienced other supernatural phenomena, all of which he interpreted as a call to lead enslaved men and women out of bondage. An American Moses, he set out to fulfill his destiny in August 1831. The revolt began on a Sunday evening, when Turner and several trusted followers mounted horses and set out toward the plantations of numerous white families. Armed with hatchets, axes, scythes, and eventually muskets, they went on a door-to-door killing spree. As most white men had gathered away from their plantations, Turner and his small army, which grew larger as the rebellion continued, murdered mostly women and children. At no other time in the history of the United States did so many white victims fall beneath the sharpened blades and blunted objects wielded by black bondmen.[16]

The revolt sent shockwaves throughout the nation, and as expected, the effect in the slave states was extraordinary. In the days and weeks after the revolt, scores of African Americans died at the hands of vigilantes. The guilt or innocence of both free and enslaved black men and women meant little to white Southerners who were intent on seeking vengeance. At the same time, the realization of the tenuousness of America's slave society led to public debate over the future of slavery. The Virginia legislature pondered both the colonization of free blacks and, for a time, the gradual abolition of slavery. Thomas Jefferson Randolph, a Virginia assemblyman who, like his famous grandfather and namesake, feared a violent clash of the races in the South, warned, "The hour of the eradication of the evil is advancing, it must come. Whether it is affected by the energy of our minds or by the bloody scenes of Southampton and San Domingo is a tale for future history." Instead of ending slavery, local and state authorities throughout the South passed laws that restricted slave literacy, mobility, and other aspects of life that suggested black autonomy. These Black Codes additionally called for the severe punishment of bondpeople who violated the regulations.[17] Nat Turner's revolt lasted just a few hours, but its impact would last for generations. In the words of one of Turner's biographers, in the aftermath of his capture and execution, the fear of slave revolts "haunted Southern whites throughout the rest of the antebellum period. In spite of all their precautions and all their resounding propaganda, they could never escape the possibility that somewhere, maybe even in their own slave quarters, another Nat Turner was plotting to rise up and slit their throats."[18]

For any publisher willing to capitalize on the horrors of slave insurrection, Turner's revolt represented a significant opportunity. In the early nineteenth century, Americans were avid readers of sensationalistic tales of murder and violence, and those of interracial carnage and bloodshed were particularly

AN
AUTHENTIC NARRATIVE
OF THE
SEMINOLE WAR;
ITS CAUSE, RISE AND PROGRESS,
AND A MINUTE DETAIL OF THE
HORRID MASSACRES
Of the *Whites*, by the *Indians* and *Negroes*, in Florida,
in the months of December, January and February.

Communicated for the press by a gentleman who has
spent eleven weeks in Florida, near the scene of the Indian depredations, and in a situation to collect every important fact relating thereto.

PROVIDENCE:
Printed for D. F. Blanchard, and others, Publishers.
1836.

7.2. Frontispiece of the first of two editions of Daniel F. Blanchard's pamphlet published in 1836. Courtesy of the Collections of the Library of Congress.

appealing.[19] The first full-length treatment of the Turner revolt appeared several weeks before Turner's capture. In the thirty-eight-page pamphlet, Samuel Warner described how Turner and his army of "blood-thirsty monsters" murdered indiscriminately, decapitating their victims and bathing in their blood. The revolt "presented a spectacle of horror the like of which we hope our countrymen will never again be called upon to witness! a spectacle from which the mind must shrink with horror, when it contemplates whole families murdered, without regard to age or sex, and weltering in their gore!"[20]

In addition to graphic descriptions of Seminole atrocities, Warner employed two additional strategies to make the threat of slave revolt more terrifying and the pamphlet more sensational. First, he included a large engraving. It was a visual representation of many Americans' worst nightmare: the murder of a white family by armed and enraged black men. In the center of the top panel, two black men with long knives hack away at Joseph Travis, Turner's master as well as his first victim. Travis falls to the ground, stunned, as he awaits the coup de grace. To the left, a black man armed with an axe stands over a kneeling white woman who shields her four children from the expected blow. To the right another black man with a hatchet is engaged in hand-to-hand combat with John Barrow, who wields a broadsword. Barrow, a veteran of the War of 1812, defends his life and that of his wife and infant in the background. The bottom panel depicts mounted dragoons pursuing Turner and two of his accomplices as they flee into a wooded area. It is an indication that as of the time of publication, numerous rebels remained free. The threat remained.

Second, Warner at great length recounted the slave revolution in St. Domingo and drew direct parallels to the Turner revolt. The pamphlet begins: "In consequence of the alarming increase of the Black population at the South, fears have long been entertained, that it might one day be the unhappy lot of the whites, in that section, to witness scenes similar to those which but a few years since, nearly depopulated the once flourishing island of St. Domingo of its white inhabitants—but, these fears have never been realized even in a small degree, until the fatal morning of the 22d of August last, when it fell to the lot of the inhabitants of a thinly settled township of Southampton county (Virginia) to witness a scene horrid in the extreme!—when FIFTY FIVE innocent persons (mostly women and children) fell victims to the most inhuman barbarity." Throughout the text, Warner referenced and at one point dedicated five pages to a narrative of the uprising. He argued that the memory of St. Domingo inspired Turner, who told fellow slaves of "the happy effect which had attended the united efforts of their brethren in St. Domingo, and elsewhere, and encouraged them with the assurance that a similar effort on their part, could not fail to produce a similar effect, and not only restore them to liberty but would produce them wealth and ease." Warner warned in closing, "Such were the horrors that attended the insurrection of the Blacks in St. Domingo; and similar scenes of bloodshed and murder might our brethren at the South expect to witness, were the disaffected Slaves of that section of the country but once to gain the ascendancy."[21]

Scholars have rightly dismissed the veracity of Warner's pamphlet, which contains numerous gaffes.[22] Indeed, the various misspellings and obvious factual errors give the text a juvenile quality. The illustration likewise lacks authenticity: the scenery, along with Travis's gentlemanly attire, is inaccurate, given that his murder occurred while he was sleeping in his upstairs bedroom in the middle of the night; there is also no evidence to suggest that at the time of the revolt Barrow and his wife had a child; lastly, a stark difference is evident in the contrary representations of the white and black subjects. Because of the relatively primitive printing technology, the lines of the rebels' faces—in contrast to those of the whites—disappear in the black ink. This has the effect of making the image more horrifying as these white men, women, and children are facing a murderous band of generic slaves, nameless and faceless black brutes. In spite of these problems, Warner's image accomplished its goal on a symbolic level. Both the pamphlet and illustration made one thing clear: a repetition of the events in Southampton and St. Domingo was possible wherever slavery existed.

The fear of Southampton and St. Domingo expanded beyond the boundaries of the southern United States, deep into the Florida territory. Evidence abounds in the numerous steps Floridians took in the months after Turner's revolt to secure their safety. In West Florida, the Board of Aldermen of Pensacola passed a resolution, requesting from the Governor "one or two Companies of Infantry to be stationed in or near Pensacola for the protection of the people of Florida against any insurrection of slaves or free negroes in this vicinity."[23] The residents of Alachua County in East Florida expressed great trepidation over the presence of more than 1,000 slaves among the Seminole, "many of whom are traversing the County night and day." In a petition to the President of the United States, they requested the deployment of a "Company of U.S. Troops" from more than 100 miles south, as "an armed force is deemed requisite to protect the Citizens of said County from aggressions by the Indians or attempts of an insurrection among the slaves."[24]

Concern over the inability of either local or federal troops to provide adequate protection led the territorial legislature to pass a series of laws to help maintain the peace. Primarily, the new regulations empowered slave patrols to increase their vigilance. In addition to meeting as least once every two weeks, patrolmen were to "take up all slaves who may be found without the limits of their owners' plantation, under suspicious circumstances, or at a suspicious distance therefrom, and to correct all such slaves by a moderate whipping with a switch, or cowskin, commonly called COWHIDE, not exceeding twenty-nine lashes." The legislature additionally gave the patrols greater authority to capture runaway slaves. In addition to being required to disperse all unsupervised gatherings of three or more slaves, patrolmen were "to enter into any disorderly house, or into any other house, vessel or boat, suspected of harboring, trafficking or dealing with negroes, whether the same be occupied by white persons, free negroes, mulattoes, mustizoes, or slaves, and to apprehend and correct all slaves found there, by whipping."[25] Displaying great faith in the deterrent effects of capital punishment, the legislature declared additionally, "if any person or persons, shall excite an insurrection or revolt of slaves, or shall attempt by writing, speaking, or otherwise, to excite an insurrection or revolt of slaves, he, she, or they, so offending, shall on conviction thereof suffer death."[26]

The presence of large numbers of African Americans among the Seminole greatly increased the likelihood of a repetition of either Southampton or St. Domingo in the Florida territory. Though the Seminole enslaved many of these people, observers saw little in Seminole bondage that resembled American slavery. Dr. William Hayne Simmons, who visited Florida and wrote an account of his experiences, testified to the unique status of the Seminole's bondpeople: "The Negroes uniformly testify to the kind treatment they receive from their Indian masters, who are indulgent and require but little labour from them. . . . The Negroes dwell in towns apart from the Indians, and are the finest looking people I have ever seen. They dress and live pretty much like the Indians, each having a gun, and hunting a portion of his time."[27] Four years later, U.S. Army Major General George A. McCall noted, "There now flourishes one of the most prosperous negro towns in the Indian territory. We found these negroes in possession of large fields of the finest land, producing large crops of corn, beans, melons, pumpkins, and other esculent vegetables. They are chiefly runaway slaves from Georgia, who have put themselves under the protection of Micanopy, or some other chief, whom they call master; and to whom, for this consideration, they render a tribute of one-third of the produce of the land, and one-third of the horses, cattle, and fowls they may raise." Unlike American slaves, these men and women were "free to go and come at pleasure, and in some cases are elevated to the position of equality with their masters. I saw, while riding along the borders of the ponds, fine rice growing; and in the village large corn-cribs well filled, while the houses were larger and more comfortable than those of the Indians themselves."[28]

There were, in addition to the Seminole's slaves, numerous free blacks who intermarried with the Seminole and held positions of authority. As Kevin Mulroy points out, these select individuals are deserving of the name *Black Seminoles*.[29] Among the most influential was Abraham, a fugitive slave from Pensacola who became an important translator and soldier. While Abraham's motives for serving as an intermediary between American agents and Seminole leaders remain fodder for historical debate, his status among both groups is undeniable. Cosmopolitan black men like Abraham, John Caesar, and John Horse served as the spokesmen for the Seminole, and in wielding their power they often gave observers a false impression of their authority over their Indian allies. Simmons, for example, wrote, "In the late war, the infamous Colonel Woodbine . . . regularly embodied and armed several hundred of these Negroes—by whom, the Indians, themselves, were kept in awe—and for a period, were placed in the worst of all political conditions, being under a dulocracy or government of slaves."[30]

The existence of substantial numbers of fugitive slaves from the southern United States and throughout Florida, coupled with the obstinacy of numerous Black Seminole leaders, spelled the onset of a violent conflagration. Both the federal government and various reform groups took steps to avoid such an outcome. Throughout the first decades of the nineteenth century, they encouraged Indian peoples to acculturate to Anglo-Americans ways and offered to assist them in migrating; however, the Seminole proved unwilling to abandon their land or adopt the language, laws, and even the clothing of Americans. Negotiations between the two sides supposedly reached a settlement in 1832, when representatives agreed to a number of treaties, which promised, among other things, cash, blankets, and shirts to the Seminole in exchange for their timely relocation. It appeared that the Seminole would follow the paths of the Cherokee, Creek, and other Indian nations to reservations west of the Mississippi, but many Seminole denounced the treaties and refused to abandon their villages. They taunted and threatened those who had signed the documents. Tensions rose as defiant Seminole stood their ground and continued to offer safe haven to bondpeople who fled American plantations on both sides of the Florida border. Nevertheless, white Floridians remained sanguine about avoiding another war with the Seminole. In May 1835, a writer in St. Augustine observed, "There is no foundation for reports which have been in circulation, of apprehended difficulties in the removal of the Seminole Indians from Florida to the west of the Mississippi. The Seminole of the present day is a different being from the warlike son of the forest when the tribe was numerous and powerful, and no trouble in the removal of the remnant of the tribe is anticipated."[31]

A petition forwarded to President Andrew Jackson from residents in East Florida indicates the primary reason why Americans needed the government to remove both the Seminole and their black allies. Many hoped to re-create in Florida the slave society that had fired the economic dreams of so many Americans throughout the Deep South. Countless acres in northern Florida were conducive to cotton production, and the rivers and harbors that linked the southeastern United States with the Gulf of Mexico and the greater Atlantic world were equally valuable to a regional economy dependent on King Cotton. The petitioners estimated that of the "more than five hundred negroes residing with the Seminole Indians," four-fifths were runaways or their descendants. These fugitives lived among the Indians, who offered them safety and protection. "It is perfectly obvious, that during the existence of such a state of things, the interests of this fertile and promising section of Florida cannot flourish, and we are constrained to repeat, that there is no rational prospect of a change for the better, so long as the Indians are suffered to remain in their present location." A unified band of defiant Native Americans and African Americans was a dangerous symbol when located so closely to a burgeoning plantation society built on the backs of enslaved people. The petitioners explained that without the government's assistance, "the owner of slaves in our Territory, and even in the States contiguous, cannot, for a moment, in any thing like security, enjoy the possession of this description of property."[32]

The existence of large numbers of fugitive slaves among the Seminole threatened the entire plantation system not just in Florida but throughout the entire South. This was something made clear by United States Army General Thomas Sidney Jesup as the timetable for removal came and passed. Undaunted, Seminole and their black allies launched a series of devastating raids across the plantations of East Florida, burning crops, farms, and homes, and liberating hundreds of slaves.[33] With a limited supply of manpower, militia groups were ineffective in stopping the insurgents. The rising tide of red and black frontier violence led Jesup to declare in an official letter, "This, you may be assured, is a negro, not an Indian war; and if it be not speedily put down, the south will feel the effects of it on their slave population before the end of the next season."[34]

In spite of Jesup's warning and the violent actions that took place, a second war with the Seminole remained avoidable until the Seminole launched two bloody attacks on the same day late in December 1835. In the first, a young warrior named Osceola turned his rage on Americans at Fort King, located in present-day Ocala, Florida, where he and a small party of warriors assassinated U.S. agent Wiley Thompson and six other Americans. Following the ambush, the victors attached the scalps of their victims to a stake, where they would remain for several years. Thompson's scalp may have survived the exhibition. It was, according to John Mahon, "cut into tiny pieces so that each participant might have a trophy."[35]

In the second attack, the Seminole routed a sizeable military contingent under the direction of Major Francis L. Dade. Known today as the Dade Massacre, the battle resulted in the deaths of 105 of 108 American soldiers, making it one of the deadliest defeats of the U.S. military in its history. The massacre became an important touchstone of the Second Seminole War, much like the Alamo in the Mexican-American War less than a decade later. It began when Dade's forces, unwisely dressed in brightly colored blue jackets and red pants, marched along a thin trail cut out of the central Florida wilderness. En route to Fort King they were led by a slave translator named Louis Pacheco, whose loyalties remain contested. On the morning of the 28th, the troops entered an opening in a heavily forested area in double-file lines. As Dade consoled his men with the promise of a belated Christmas party upon reaching the fort, the unseen enemy opened fire. According to John Mahon, "Dade and half the command dropped with the first volley." The Americans fought bravely, but they were overwhelmed by the Seminole, who soon after securing victory retired to their swamp hideout to celebrate.[36]

What came next left little doubt that this was not going to be a typical Indian war. Black men on horseback approached the battlefield. Upon dismounting, they stepped over the corpses of dead soldiers and with knives and other bladed instruments finished off the wounded. Two white men escaped but soon died. Only one white man, Ransom Clark, lived to tell the story of the massacre. It is in the various published versions of his story that we begin to see the construction of the Second Seminole War not as another Indian war but as a nascent slave revolution. That numerous versions of Clark's initial report exist makes it difficult to decipher the original report; nonetheless, the brutality of the black invaders remains consistent. In the earliest published account, Clark recalled the events that transpired following the Seminole retreat:

> Forty or fifty negroes, on horseback, galloped up and alighted, tied their beasts, and commenced, with horrid shouts and yells, the butchery of the wounded, together with an indiscriminate plunder, stripping the bodies of the dead of clothing, watches and money, and splitting open the head of all who showed the least signs of life with their taunting derisions, and with frequent cries of 'what have you got to sell.' Lieut. B, hearing the negroes butchering the wounded, at length sprang up and asked them to spare his life. They met him with the blows of their axes and their fiendish laughter. Having been wounded in five different places myself, I was pretty well covered with blood, and two scratches that I had received in my head gave me the appearance of having been shot through the brain, for the negroes, after catching me up by the heels, threw me down, saying 'd——n him he's dead enough!' They then stripped me of my clothes, shoes and hat, and left me.[37]

Clark's report soon took on a life of its own. The more it was repeated, the more brutal and savage the crimes committed by these black men became.[38] Within a year, versions of the story appeared in two separate accounts written by soldiers. While Myer M. Cohen, a South Carolina militiaman, copied the report verbatim, Captain James Barr, a Louisiana volunteer, embellished. "When they [Seminoles] had quit the field, a body of negroes fifty or sixty in number, came up on horseback, entered the enclosure, and commenced hacking and cutting the wounded, in a most savage manner. They approached Lieutenant Bassinger, he sprang on his feet and begged them to spare his life, but they knew not the voice of mercy; they struck him down with a tomahawk, cut open his breast and tore out his heart and lungs." Barr described the thefts in detail: "They proceeded in the same brutal manner with the rest of the wounded, stripping them all of their clothes. At length they approached Mr. C. and stripped off his jacket, in the pocket of which he had one hundred and twenty dollars; they also took off his hat and boots and felt for his watch." At last, "One of the ruffians remarked that he was alive and proposed to drive a bayonet through him but was overruled by one of his comrades, who observed that the wound in his head would certainly kill him, and that they should let him suffer as much pain as possible before death. This saved him. The negroes soon departed laden with plunder.[39]

Other soldier authors added to the list of atrocities committed by the Seminole's black allies. John Lee Williams underscored the racial character of the attackers, writing, "Soon after the Indians had retired, about fifty negroes galloped up on horseback; when they reached the breast-work they alighted, and tied their horses. Then commenced a horrible butchery. If any poor fellow on the ground shewed the least signs of life, the thick lipped savages sank their tomahawks in their brains, and with their knives stabbed and mutilated them amid yells and blasphemies."[40] Woodburne Potter added sexual violence to the crimes committed by the black marauders. "Sometime after the Indians left, the negroes came inside of the breastwork and began to mutilate the bodies of those who showed the least signs of life, when Bassinger sprang upon his feet and implored them to spare him; they heeded not his supplications, but struck down with their hatchets, cut open his breast and tore out his heart and lungs; such is the report of Clark, the only survivor." Potter, who was among the soldiers who came upon the battlefield shortly after the massacre, continued, "I must confess that the appearance of the body on the 20th of February did not seem to indicate that such violence had been committed on *him*, although one of the slain (a private) was found in a truly revolting condition—a part of his body had been cut off and crammed into his mouth!"[41]

Clark reentered the literary fray in 1839, with a singular publication entitled *Narrative of Ransom Clark, the Only Survivor of Major Dade's Command in Florida.* Perhaps spurred by the increasingly shocking descriptions in rival texts, he further explained the actions of the black rebels who came upon Lieutenant Bassinger and the other wounded American soldiers during the infamous massacre. "They commenced stripping him of his clothes—when one of the renegade *negroes* stamped upon his body with his foot, saying in Seminole—"*I este chattee tamockusche!*" (This is one of the d——d officers!) Lieut. B. then jumped up from the ground, and begged them to spare his life—when one of the inhuman monsters struck him over the head with his battle-axe, severing it in twain—and they then cut open his breast, and tore out his heart and vitals, scattering them upon the ground."[42] The comparison of rebel slaves with monsters was a standard trope in the literature of the early national period.[43] In this case it indicates the depth of the shadows of both Southampton and St. Domingo, which towered over the United States during the Second Seminole War.

Daniel Blanchard's pamphlet offered yet another version of the Dade Massacre, which the author suggested marked a turning point. "It stands without an example in the annals of Indian warfare!" Black horsemen bore the greatest responsibility for the savagery, Blanchard explained. "Many negroes were in the field, but no scalps were taken by the Indians, but the negroes, with hellish cruelty, pierced the throats of all, whose loud cries and groans showed the power of life to be yet strong."[44] As we have seen, an oversized illustration in Blanchard's pamphlet evoked the horrors of slave insurrection.[45] The image on the frontispiece of Blanchard's did likewise, and it too came from the engraving of Nat Turner's revolt in Samuel Warner's pamphlet. In it, a black man with an axe towers over a white woman and her four small children. The mother is Mrs. Mary Godfrey, a Florida settler whose husband had left his family to fight the Seminoles. In the text, Blanchard describes the confrontation between Mrs. Godfrey, her children, and a black ally of the Seminole, who after discovering the fugitives and preparing to murder them, "dropped his axe, and after contemplating the melancholy spectacle for a few moments, appeared much affected, and broke silence by assuring Mrs. G. that she had nothing to fear, that neither herself or her children should be hurt."[46] The contrast between the sympathetic black figure described in the text and the one represented in the visual is extreme. The frontispiece gives no indication that this man saved the lives of the women and girls he threatened; to the contrary, the image leads the viewer to conclude that these defenseless females met the same fate as many of their white counterparts in Southampton and St. Domingo. For an audience accustomed to graphic tales of murderous slaves, the link between Southampton, St. Domingo, and the Second Seminole War was unmistakable.

Blanchard's pamphlet tells a terrible story of black violence, and given the way in which Americans had come to imagine Indians, it comes as no surprise that as the Second Seminole War progressed, accusations of black responsibility for the conflict increased. Throughout the war, writers laid responsibility for the war squarely at the foot of the Seminole's black allies, who refused to accept the role reserved for them on Southern plantations as pliant and submissive unfree laborers. A commentator in the *New Orleans Bulletin* doubted a timely conclusion of the war, explaining that "the Indians themselves are determined to hold out, and are encouraged and sustained by the gang of

7.3. Likely the earliest published visual of Nat Turner's revolt, from Samuel Warner's *Authentic and impartial narrative of the tragical scene which was witnessed in Southampton County* (1831). Courtesy of the Collections of the Library of Congress.

sable banditti nominally their slaves, but who are really their chief counselors, and in effect their masters." Demonstrating the resonance of General Jesup's opinion of the war, he concluded, "It is a negro, not an Indian war."[47]

At the U.S. Military Academy at West Point, New York, Lieutenant Benjamin Alvord addressed a group of cadets on the virtue of military service and the great sacrifice of the men who were presently engaged in fighting the Seminole in Florida. Alvord considered Indians a "feeble, misguided, and uncivilized race" whose demise was preordained. He nonetheless justified this outcome, writing that "the fate of the red man of the forest, melancholy though it is, appears to have been inevitable and arranged for the best of purposes by the hand of Divine Providence." The outbreak of war made little sense, given the state of Indian resistance. Continued Alvord, "Do you ask why they were induced to violate such solemn engagements?" The answer was clear. "I believe that the influence of the negroes, who were afraid of detection by the whites, and therefore opposed to removal, has been all powerful in creating and fomenting their hostile acts. Many of those negroes were arch-fiends in their race. Obtaining great influence over their self-styled masters, by their talents and acuteness, as well as by their superior knowledge of the whites,—they were cunning enough to excite the war, and make the red man push forward and conduct operations while they pulled the wires in the back-ground."[48]

In addition to placing the blame for the war on the Seminole's black allies, writers commented on their extraordinary savagery. A writer in the *Pennsylvania Sentinel* admitted that "the present is not an Indian, so much as a negro war. The Indian force is made up principally by blacks. Most of the atrocities which have reddened the frontier settlements with blood, have been committed by them." If not for their involvement, "the Indians would long since have been subdued." The success of these fugitive slaves, "whom accident has enabled to escape from the whites," forced the writer to wonder, "If such are the consequences of peace, what would be the result of war? If, in a season of tranquility, the runaways of the South should defy the whole energies of the nation—what would be the consequence of united effort? If a large force of the blacks should escape into the swamps of Florida, how could they be subdued?" Such a force, "constantly increased by runaways, would be found truly formidable." The conclusion, therefore, was simple: "It is apparent that the present military force of the country is inadequate to its necessities. It is necessary, imperatively necessary, that our army should be reorganized, and quadrupled."[49]

Army Lieutenant John T. Sprague shared the same fear of an insurgent black army. "The negroes, from the commencement of the Florida war, have, for their numbers, been the most formidable foe, more blood-thirsty, active, and revengeful, than the Indian. To surrender or to be captured, was to them slavery and punishment; while victory gave them plunder, and added confidence to the already excited feelings of their [Seminole] masters." Florida was their ideal homeland. Its terrain "could, for years, be made safe retreats from bondage, where, without labor or expense, they might defy the efforts of armed men. It would require blood and money to besiege them, and when forced out, they could remove unseen to other strong-holds, which nature has so abundantly provided. Ten resolute negroes, with a knowledge of the country, are sufficient to desolate the frontier, from one extent to the other." Noting the tumultuous and violent history of Florida, Sprague suspected that the imperial struggle for control over the valuable territory was not yet complete. "Florida, from its discovery, has been the battle ground of carnage and discord. . . . Its position, in a national point of view, should be regarded. It may yet be the strong-hold of a powerful foe, who might increase his strength, by inducing the blacks from neighboring states, to join his standard." Sprague noted the ease with which a steamship could deliver from the West Indies to Florida "a black force, well calculated to perfect the work."[50]

The fear of a revolutionary black army from the West Indies landing on Florida's shores was widespread during the Second Seminole War.[51] A committee report forwarded to the Senate requesting a parcel of land for development in southern Florida listed a number of justifications for the land grant. "Hence, when the Indians shall be expelled from the pestilential swamps and impregnable morass of southern Florida, they may again become the impregnable fortresses for fugitive negroes and piratical out-laws, who will be still more dangerous enemies to the tranquility of our southern States than the actual savage Seminoles." Without white settlement and development of the land, the petitioners argued that "southern Florida will become a solitary desert, or will be occupied by a still worse race than the Seminoles. Its pestilential swamps and impenetrable morasses will become the fortresses of the worst portions of the black and piratical inhabitants of the adjoining West Indian islands."[52] With the question of Florida's admission to the Union confronting the nation, a writer using the pseudonym Vindex worried about the future of the territory given the rising abolitionist movement in the North. "We have spoken of Florida in relation to the abolition question. Are Southern gentlemen aware that the fanatics have already their eye upon this devoted land?" Abolitionists were sanguine about the prospects of the territory for some of their wild schemes. Florida had numerous advantages, among them that it was "already surrounded by negro communities, all of which, most probably, will, ere long, be reduced to the condition of St. Domingo. Its separation from the Bahamas is so narrow and shoal, that fishing boats habitually cross over. The war which desolates the territory is carried on by negroes as well as Seminoles, and their number might be formidably increased by the accession of runaways from the Southern States and outlaws or emissaries from the West Indies." Florida was "peculiarly favorable to a maroon war. The Abolitionists, we repeat, are alive to all their advantages. They have already established a nest or nursery in East Florida. . . . Constant communication is kept up with Hayti, by a regular trading vessel, belonging to a gentleman who has lately published a pamphlet, in which he celebrates the charms of the fair daughters of that dingy democracy or ragamuffin republic."[53]

The "gentleman" was most likely Zephaniah Kingsley, the wealthy English-born planter who lived in St. Domingo during the revolution and who, after spending several decades in East Florida, returned to the black republic with his African wife, members of their extended multiracial family, and numbers of their slaves. An independent and eccentric thinker, he published between 1826 and 1834 multiple versions of a radical tract in which he championed both slavery and its amelioration. He moreover promoted racial mixing. Kingsley denied the likelihood of a second Haitian Revolution taking place in the United States, insisting that, "under a just and prudent system of management, negroes are safe, permanent, productive and growing property, and easily governed; that they are not naturally desirous of change but are sober, discreet, honest and obliging, are less troublesome, and possess a much better moral character than the ordinary class of corrupted whites of similar condition." Still, he seemed to admire the rebel slaves who under the leadership of the former bondman Toussaint Louverture nearly returned the colony to its former prosperous condition. Kingsley offered, "In short, when we consider the massacres and bloodshed necessarily attending such a horrid revolution, where a vast number of slaves were forced into a state of licentious anarchy, and led on by partisans blinded by revolutionary fury, who gave no quarter on either side, it is astonishing that the slaves now liberated should have so soon returned to a peaceable and quiet state of domestic order."[54]

Kingsley was not an abolitionist. Yet his liberalism led his proslavery peers to place him in the same category as the predominately northern radicals who were—slave owners insisted—allegedly seeking a violent end to the institution of slavery in Florida. A writer in the *Jacksonville Courier* lashed out at those who encouraged slave revolt through the distribution of incendiary literature. "The abolitionists declare that they send none of their publications to other than the most respectable citizens, when to our limited knowledge, one has been sent for a long time to a molatto, which we are informed, is read to his dark acquaintances, both free and slaves. How many such will it require, to blaze every house in the South? Shall we wait till the tragic scenes of Hayti are commenced, before we act, and act efficiently?"[55]

The expected alliance of abolitionists, slaves, and Seminoles prompted a brigadier general of the East Florida Militia to petition the territorial governor for hundreds of muskets and ammunition, as well as the authority to arm an additional 200 men. "Much apprehension is already manifested by the community at large on this subject," Joseph M. Hernandez explained, "particularly as there are a large number of Negroes amongst the Indians, who may be under the influence of the Abolitionists of the North, whose machinations, are now endangering our safety."[56] Sentiments like these reinforced the idea that East Florida was the most likely starting point of a slave insurrection. In Congress, Hopkins Holsey criticized those who took the government to task for treating the Seminole too harshly. According to the Georgia representative, any military successes were remarkable given the limited support the federal government had shown for the war. Responding to the charge by Massachusetts congressman Caleb Cushing that the actions of the U.S. military toward the Seminole were "disgraceful," Holsey retorted, "As well . . . may we call the action at Thermopylae disgraceful, as the campaigns in Florida, which had covered the army there with imperishable glory." Few understood the grave threat that the United States faced in Florida, especially in East Florida, a region Holsey described as "the St. Domingo of America: impregnable from its situation, and the facilities of concealment and escape."[57]

The equation of the Second Seminole War with a slave rebellion struck some in the North as ironic, given white Southerners' staunch defense of slavery. A writer in the *New York Transcript* opined, "The recent efforts of the American arms against the savages of the South, have developed the existence of a new and more dangerous and daring foe than the Indians themselves, and one whose strength can be continually increased, and, whose numbers and resources can be instantly augmented by almost endless thousands who could be rallied to their relief. . . . No longer under the eyes of those whom they considered only as their tyrants, and whom they served through fear rather than love, they evinced a disposition to destroy the lives and property of the whites, surpassing that of even the Seminoles themselves." Slaves "were frequently more bold and daring, and also more cruel than most of their Indian allies. And from the ferocity with which they fought—the atrocity with which they perpetrated murders on the bodies, and the skill with which they massacred and tore off the scalps of those who fell wounded in battle, in the sanguinary destruction of the force of Major Dade, and in almost every subsequent battle; it became apparent that the United States had more to dread from the black, than from the red savages, with which they fought." The writer wondered what would be the result upon the advent of a slave war. "Then a terrible desolation would soon sweep with the fierceness of the tornado, over many of the finest fields of the south. Then the earth and the air would be vocal with the fires, and bathed in the blood of the inhabitants of the southern states. Then a terrible storm of wrath would be let loose to devastate, to butcher and destroy." This was no imaginary scenario. "Many of those negroes have now, as Indian allies, been enabled to obtain a taste of blood. Many of them have gained a fearful knowledge of their physical and martial strength." For a long time, they had "been enabled to keep so large an enemy of white men in check, and occasionally to carry death and destruction through their ranks, owing to the density of the forests, and the almost impregnable strength of the natural fastnesses of the country," that unless actions were taken, the time was fast approaching when Northerners would be called on to intervene. "We confess we fear for the worst, and anticipate some great commotion, at no distant day to be produced, by the lessons the negroes have learned. Let the South look to it then in time, or all their boasted chivalry, and superior wisdom and courage will not save them. When these negroes fight the fight of desperation and despair, hecatombs must bleed, and humanity will weep in tears of gore."[58]

In spite of the shared expectations of Northerners and Southerners, the slave revolt modeled on the insurrections in Southampton and St. Domingo that so many Americans anticipated during the Second Seminole War never materialized. A revolutionary black army never landed on Florida's coast, and the Seminole's black allies never swarmed across the Florida border seeking vengeance on the farms and plantations of Southern landowners; instead, with federal assistance, they, along with the Seminole, relocated to the Oklahoma territory. In a surprising irony, what many acknowledge as a crushing defeat for the Seminole is at the same time considered a triumph for these black freedom fighters. This dichotomous view is a testament to the resiliency of the divergent views of the Seminole and their black allies who between 1835 and 1842 violently resisted removal from the Florida territory. Despite the absence of a slave revolt, the second war between the U.S. government and a combined force of Seminole and their African American allies was a terrible conflict. The campaign cost the U.S. government $20 million and the lives of more than 1,500 soldiers, making it arguably the costliest Indian war in American history.[59]

Adam Rothman has described the triple threat that the free citizens of the southern United States faced in the wake of American independence. It was "the southern citizenry's ultimate nightmare," Rothman writes, "a triple alliance of British soldiers, Indian warriors, and slave rebels."[60] For more than a generation, British soldiers and their Indian and slave allies remained a thorn in the side of American expansionism. American victory in the War of 1812 secured the removal of the British threat from the Gulf Coast, at the same time it placed tremendous pressure on Indians who remained on land east of the Mississippi River. The destruction of the Negro Fort on the Apalachicola River and the resultant First Seminole War spelled the end of Indian civilization in Florida. Ultimately, however, it was Andrew Jackson's election as president of the United States that ensured Indian removal from both Florida and the entire South.

With that, only one threat remained to the United States' expanding slave society. But nothing in the early history of the republic assured or even suggested the end of violent slave resistance. Looking back from the vantage point of two centuries, it is easy to assume that the widespread fear of slave revolt throughout the antebellum period was a product of the overactive imaginations of Northern abolitionists and Southern slave owners alike. However, for those who witnessed, read, or heard about the events in Southampton and St. Domingo, there was good reason to expect revolutionary black violence wherever enslaved people lived, worked, and ran away. Indeed, the recent memory of Nat Turner's revolt combined with the more distant memory of the Haitian Revolution gave the American people good reason to believe that slave insurrection would be a permanent feature of life in the slave states. It was the pervasiveness of this fear that helps explain why those who lived through and experienced the Second Seminole War recognized from the outset that the conflict would be something other than an ordinary Indian war.

Notes

1. Two slightly different versions of Daniel F. Blanchard's pamphlet appeared in the same year. The first, used here, was entitled *An Authentic Narrative of the Seminole War; Its Cause, Rise and Progress, and a minute detail of the horrid massacres of the whites, by the Indians and Negroes, in Florida, in the months of December, January, and February. Communicated for the press by a gentleman who has spent eleven weeks in Florida, near the scene of the Indian depredations, and in a situation to collect every important fact relating thereto* (Providence: D. F. Blanchard, 1836); the second, updated version was *An Authentic Narrative of the Seminole War; and of the Miraculous Escape of Mrs. Mary Godfrey, and Her Four Female Children. Annexed is a Minute Detail of the HORRID MASSACRES of the* Whites, *by the* Indians *and* Negroes, *in Florida, in the months of December, January and February* (New York: D. F. Blanchard, 1836).

2. Samuel Warner, *Authentic and Impartial Narrative of the Tragical Scene Which Was Witnessed in Southampton County (Virginia) on Monday the 22d of August Last, When FIFTY-FIVE of the Inhabitants (mostly women and children) were inhumanly MASSACRED BY THE BLACKS! Communicated by those who were eye witnesses of the bloody scene, and confirmed by the confessions of several of the Blacks while under Sentence of Death* (New York: Warner & West, 1831).

3. C. L. R. James, *Black Jacobins: Toussaint L'Ouverture and the San Domingo Revolution*, 2nd ed. (New York: Vintage Books, 1989), 126; Laurent Dubois, *Avengers of the New World: The Story of the Haitian Revolution* (Cambridge: Belknap Press, 2004).

4. See http://www.johnhorse.com/black-seminoles/black-seminole-slave-rebellion. htm#1.

5. *Annals of Congress*, 15th Cong., 2nd sess., 1819, 639.

6. House Committee on Indian Affairs, *Civilization of the Indians: Letter from the Secretary of War to the Chairman of the Committee on Indian Affairs; Transmitting a Report of General Clark, Superintendent of Indian Affairs, in Relation to the Preservation and Civilization of the Indians*, 19th Cong., 1st sess., 1826, H. Rept. 124, 4.

7. "The President's Message," *Abridgment of the Debates of Congress, from 1789 to 1856*, 21st Cong., 2nd sess., 1830, 118–19.

8. Joseph Story, *The Miscellaneous Writings, Literary, Critical, Juridical, and Political* (Boston: James Munroe, 1835), 78.

9. James Fenimore Cooper, *Last of the Mohicans* (Ann Arbor: Ann Arbor Media Group, 2004), 5.

10. *Congressional Globe*, 25th Cong., 2nd sess., 1838, 408.

11. Cooper was, in the words of biographer Alan Taylor, "the single most influential American writer of the early nineteenth century. In particular, Cooper created the stock characters—the noble but doomed Indian, the resourceful frontiersman, and the loyal slave—as well as the favorite settings, especially the violent frontier, that characterized most historical romances throughout the nineteenth century and into the twentieth." *William Cooper's Town: Power and Persuasion on the Frontier of the Early American Republic* (New York: Vintage Books, 1995), 7, 412.

12. James B. Finley, *History of the Wyandott Mission, at Upper Sandusky, Ohio, under the Direction of the Methodist Episcopal Church* (Cincinnati: J. F. Wright and L. Swornstedt, 1840), 272–73.

13. Thomas L. McKenney and James Hall, *The Indian Tribes of North America, with Biographical Sketches and Anecdotes of the Principal Chiefs* (Edinburgh: J. Grant, 1933–34), 3: 1. This reprint, with the exception of the inclusion of Osceola and other prominent combatants in the Second Seminole War, is an exact replica of the original publication, a copy of which is housed in the Special Collections at the University of West Florida: *History of the Indian Tribes of North America, with biographical sketches and anecdotes of the principal chiefs* (Philadelphia: E. C. Biddle, 1836–44).

14. McKenney and Hall, *Indian Tribes of North America*, 2: 320. Later editions of the volume would include portraits and biographical sketches of both men.

15. Ibid., 2: 262.

16. Stephen B. Oates, *The Fires of Jubilee: Nat Turner's Fierce Rebellion* (New York: Harper & Row, 1975).

17. John W. Cromwell, "The Aftermath of Nat Turner's Insurrection," *Journal of Negro History* 5, no. 2 (April 1920): 208–34.

18. Oates, *The Fires of Jubilee*, 145.

19. Karen Halttunen, *Murder Most Foul: The Killer and the American Gothic Imagination* (Cambridge: Harvard University Press, 2000); Matthew Clavin, "Race, Revolution, and the Sublime: The Gothicization of the Haitian Revolution in the New Republic and Atlantic World," *Early American Studies: An Interdisciplinary Journal* 5, no. 1 (Spring 2007): 1–29.

20. Warner, *Authentic and Impartial Narrative*, 12–13.

21. Ibid., 5–6, 28–32.

22. Herbert Aptheker wrote, "This pamphlet is almost wholly inaccurate." *Nat Turner's Slave Rebellion: Together with the Full Text of the So-Called "Confessions" of Nat Turner Made in Prison in 1831* (New York: Humanities Press, 1966), 116. Henry Irving Tragle notes that Warner "quite obviously culled largely from newspaper accounts. . . . No sources are identified." *The Southampton Slave Revolt of 1831: A Compilation of Source Material* (Amherst: University of Massachusetts Press, 1971), 280–81.

23. Clarence Edwin Carter, ed., *The Territorial Papers of the United States,* vol. 24, *The Territory of Florida* (Washington: Government Printing Office, 1959), 581.

24. Ibid., 24: 643–45.

25. "Laws of Florida," *Liberator,* 5 May 1832.

26. Aptheker, *Nat Turner's Slave Rebellion,* 77–78.

27. William Hayne Simmons, *Notices of East Florida* (Charleston: A. E. Miller, 1822; reprint, Florida: State of Florida, 1973), 76.

28. George A. McCall, Hillsborough Bay, *Letters from the Frontiers: Written during a Period of Thirty Years' Service in the Army of the United States* (Philadelphia: J. B. Lippincott, 1868), 160.

29. The term *Black Seminoles* conflates the Seminole and their black allies into a distinct people and implies a relationship that did not, in fact, exist. The clearest enunciation of the generally bifurcated relationship between the Seminole and their black allies is Kevin Mulroy, *Freedom on the Border: The Seminole Maroons in Florida, the Indian Territory, Coahuila, and Texas* (Lubbock: Texas Tech University Press, 1993). Mulroy writes, "Whether runaways, captives, or slaves of the Seminoles, these blacks preferred to live beyond the pale and ally with Europeans and Native Americans rather than remain enslaved on Southern plantations. Of major significance to their ethnohistory, the maroons' early and close association with the Seminoles would contribute strongly to the development of their identity. Yet these people would go on to establish a culture and history of their own and in so doing define themselves, and be defined by others, as a separate and distinct entity" (10–11). Examples of the misuse of the term *Black Seminole* is Kenneth W. Porter, *The Black Seminoles: History of a Freedom-Seeking Peoples,* rev. and ed. by Alcione M. Amos and Thomas P. Senter (Gainesville: University Press of Florida, 1996), and Bruce Edward Twyman, *The Black Seminole Legacy and North American Politics, 1693–1845* (Washington: Howard University Press, 1999).

30. Simmons, *Notices of East Florida,* 75.

31. "Miscellaneous," *Niles' Weekly Register,* 12 May 1835; John K. Mahon, *History of the Second Seminole War, 1835–1842* (Gainesville: University of Florida Press, 1967), 69–103; Joe Knetsch, *Florida's Seminole Wars, 1817–1858* (Charleston, S.C.: Arcadia, 2003), 60–62, 69.

32. Petition to President Andrew Jackson, January 1834, *Seminole Hostilities. Message from the President of the United States, A supplemental report respecting the causes of the Seminole hostilities, and the measures taken to suppress them* (3 June 1836), 24th Cong., 1st sess., H. Doc. 271, 30–32.

33. The best account of these raids remains Kenneth Porter, "Florida Slaves and Free Negroes in the Seminole War, 1835–1842," *Journal of Negro History* 28, no. 4 (October 1943): 390–421.

34. In the coming years, Jesup would embark on a desperate quest to remove the Seminole's black allies from Florida and, as Kenneth Porter has shown, play a key role in the emancipation of numbers of them: *Black Seminoles,* 95–96, 106, 115–16. Edwin

C. Reynolds writes of Jesup's liberal treatment of the Seminole's black allies: "While he took no stand against slavery—it would not have been remarkable if he had, considering his background—he insisted upon the human rights of Negroes, gave full respect to their talents as guides and interpreters, and recognized the bravery of Negro warriors." *The Seminoles* (Norman: University of Oklahoma Press, 1957), 229–30.

35. Mahon, *History of the Second Seminole War*, 104.

36. Ibid., 102–6; Knetsch, *Florida's Seminole Wars*, 104–6.

37. *Portland Daily Advertiser*, in Frank Laumer, *Dade's Last Command* (Gainesville: University Press of Florida, 1995), 235–37.

38. Frank Laumer suggests that it was Clark who embellished "with each telling of the story" in order to "justify harsh retribution." *Dade's Last Command*, 235–36.

39. Myer M. Cohen, *Notices of Florida and the Campaigns* (1836; reprint, Gainesville: University of Florida Press, 1964), 72–73; James Barr, *A Correct and Authentic Narrative of the Indian War in Florida, with a Description of Maj. Dade's Massacre, and an Account of the Extreme Suffering, for Want of Provision, of the Army—Having Been Obliged to Eat Horses' and Dogs' Flesh, &c. &c.* (New York: J. Narine, 1836), 10–11.

40. John Lee Williams, *The Territory of Florida; or, Sketches of the Topography, Civil and Natural History, of the Country, the Climate, and the Indian Tribes, from the First Discovery to the Present Time, with a Map, Views, &c.* (1837; reprint, Gainesville: University of Florida Press, 1962), 218.

41. Woodburne Potter, *The War in Florida: Being an Exposition of Its Causes, and an Accurate History of Its Causes, and an Accurate History of the Campaigns of Generals Clinch, Gaines, and Scott. By a Late Staff Officer* (Baltimore: Lewis and Coleman, 1836), 106.

42. Ransom Clark, *Narrative of Ransom Clark, the Only Survivor of Major Dade's Command in Florida; Containing Brief Descriptions of what befel him from his enlistment in 1833, till his discharge, in 1836; with an account of the Inhuman Massacre, by the Indians and Negroes, of Major Dade's Detachment* (Binghamton: Johnson & Marble, 1839), 15.

43. See above for Samuel Warner's use of the trope in describing Nat Turner's revolt. For the use of the trope in the literature of the Haitian Revolution, see Clavin, "Race, Revolution, and the Sublime," 21–25.

44. Blanchard, *Authentic Narrative of the Seminole War*, 12–13.

45. Blanchard employed a standard publishing strategy of the time. By purchasing or borrowing existing woodcuts of Indian war, he saved both time and money. In this case, six of the eight panels Blanchard employed, which did not come from the Warner pamphlet, appeared previously in an Indian captivity narrative entitled *Narrative of the massacre, by the savages, of the wife and children of Thomas Baldwin, who, since the melancholy period of the destruction of his unfortunate family, has dwelt entirely alone, secluded from human society, in the extreme western part of the state of Kentucky* (New York: Martin and Wood, 1835).

46. Blanchard, *Authentic Narrative of the Seminole War*, 9–10.

47. "From the New Orleans Bulletin," *Army and Navy Chronicle* 4 (2 February 1837): 80.

48. Benjamin Alvord, *Address before the Dialectic Society of the Corps of Cadets, in Commemoration of the Gallant Conduct of the Nine Graduates of the Military Academy, and Other Officers of the United States' Army, Who Fell in the Battles Which Took Place in Florida* (New York: Wiley & Putnam, 1839), 20–21, 29–30.

49. "Slavery," *Pennsylvania Sentinel*, in *Philanthropist*, 17 March 1837.

50. John T. Sprague, *The Origin, Progress, and Conclusion of the Florida War* (New York: D. Appleton, 1848), 309–10.

51. Shortly after Turner's revolt, the governor of Virginia received a mysterious letter from a former slave writing under the pseudonym Nero. In the letter, Nero describes an imminent invasion of the South, led by an army of black men trained for insurrection in St. Domingo. Fantastic though the letter may be, it reinforces the widespread belief in the possibility of a massive slave rebellion taking place in the United States on the heels of the Turner revolt. Ira Berlin, "After Nat Turner: A Letter from the North," *Journal of Negro History* 55, no. 2 (April 1970): 144–51.

52. Senate Committee on Agriculture, *Report to Accompany Bill S. No. 241*, 25th Cong., 2nd sess., 1838, S. Doc. 300 (Serial 317), 2, 11.

53. "'Vindex' on Abolitionism!" *The Crisis. Devoted to the Support of the Democratic Principles*, 18 April 1840.

54. Kingsley wrote of racially mixed persons: "The intermediate grades of color are not only healthy, but when condition is favorable, they are improved in shape, strength and beauty, and susceptible for every amelioration." Zephaniah Kingsley, *A Treatise on the Patriarchal, or Co-Operative System of Society as It Exists in Some Governments, and Colonies in America, and in the United States, under the Name of Slavery, with Its Necessity and Advantages*, 2nd ed. (1829), 8, 10.

55. "Effects of the Fanatics," *Jacksonville Courier*, 8 October 1835.

56. Carter, *Territorial Papers of the United States*, 25: 189–90. An even less credible abolitionist conspiracy involved the notorious outlaw John A. Murrell, who stole horses and slaves for a living. He was also reputedly the mastermind behind a massive slave insurrectionist plot. Why this frontier bandit intended to lead slaves to revolt is unknown; however, slave owners took any possible threat to the slave system seriously. A fantastic pamphlet on Murrell published upon his arrest in 1835 revealed that Murrell traveled extensively throughout the South, including Florida, where he established emissaries for his incendiary plot. Murrell hoped to light the fire of revolt among American slaves by offering the Haitian Revolution as a model of black rebellion, explaining, "We tell them that all Europe has abandoned slavery, and that the West Indies are all free, and that they got their freedom by rebelling a few times, and slaughtering the whites; and convince them that, if they will follow the example of the West India negroes, they will obtain their liberty, and become as much respected as if they were white." The *Jacksonville Courier* took a special interest in the conspiracy, publishing the names of more than fifty men from Georgia and Florida who "were

concerned with that desperate outlaw, in exciting slaves to insurrection." While much of the hysteria surrounding Murrell's arrest seems preposterous, the paper reported the arrest of a foreigner in September 1835, which legitimized these fears. "Murrell, the Insurrectionist," *Jacksonville Courier*, 27 August 1835; "Arrest" and "Public Meeting," *Jacksonville Courier*, 3 September 1835. H. R. Howard, *The History of Virgil A. Stewart: And His Adventure in Capturing and Exposing the Great "Western Land Pirate" and His Gang, in Connexion with the Evidence; Also of the Trials, Confessions, and Execution of a Number of Murrell's Associates in the State of Mississippi During the Summer of 1835, and the Execution of Five Professional Gamblers by the Citizens of Vicksburg, on the 6th July, 1835* (New York: Harper & Brothers, 1836), 53–60.

57. "Causes of Failure of Florida Campaigns," *Albany Evening Journal*, 23 September 1837.

58. "Indian and Negro War," *New York Transcript*, in *Liberator*, 18 March 1837.

59. Mulroy, *Freedom on the Border*, 29.

60. Adam Rothman, *Slave Country: American Expansion and the Origins of the Deep South* (Cambridge: Harvard University Press, 2005), 122.

8

South Carolina Volunteers
in the Second Seminole War

A Nullifier Debacle as Prelude to
the Palmetto State Gubernatorial Election of 1836

JAMES M. DENHAM AND CANTER BROWN JR.

The South Carolina General Assembly on December 10, 1836, elected as governor thirty-eight-year-old Pierce Mason Butler, heralded as a Nullifier in the state's recent clash with President Andrew Jackson over enforcement of tariff law. A committee of notables, including Butler's friend Robert Howell Goodwyn, quickly notified him of the honor. At the time Goodwyn served as state senator from St. Matthew Parish, but within the year he had acted, in the capacity of regimental colonel of mounted South Carolina volunteers, as the newly elected governor's immediate superior in Florida's recently commenced Second Seminole War. In a matter of weeks after taking office on December 21, Butler would appoint Goodwyn to the powerful position of cashier of the Columbia branch of the Bank of the State of South Carolina. Butler had launched himself into state affairs in 1830 from that position and had ascended from it to the presidency of the bank in 1833.[1]

Butler's climb to the governor's office had come amidst controversy regarding his and Goodwyn's roles in the Second Seminole War. This fact drew national attention just as he was savoring his election victory and organizing his administration. Four hundred miles to the north a far different, though not unrelated, process then was underway. At Frederick, Maryland, a court of inquiry had convened on November 7, 1836, to examine the conduct by Major Generals Winfield Scott and Edmund P. Gaines during the opening stages of the Florida war. In the ten days prior to Butler's election, Brigadier General Abraham Eustis stood out as the star figure at those proceedings. Testifying in defense of General Scott, Eustis found occasion to mention Butler's name. In so doing he intimated that certain actions taken by Butler and others associated with him, rather than ones taken by Scott, had contributed to the failure of the Florida campaign.[2]

The events of that Florida campaign during the early months of 1836—and their aftermath—form an integral part of the story of Pierce M. Butler's election as governor of South Carolina and of the persistence of the Palmetto State in its willingness to confront and to disobey federal authority. A review of those events discloses a tale of bravado and promise, of courage, sacrifice, and tragedy. They portray a very human disappointment projected upon a canvas of personal ambition and national controversy. They help us to understand how and why the early history of that war came to be written, and they suggest how South Carolina's commitment to the intertwined philosophies of states' rights and nullification was hardened by Butler's personal and political needs.

Since Butler's actions were to figure so prominently in the early dynamics of the Florida conflict, a quick review of his life up to that point seems in order. The future governor began his professional career in 1819 as a U.S. Army officer, a position that he obtained through the intercession of South Carolina congressman Eldred Simkins and the encouragement of Simkins's law partner George McDuffie. Butler served in the Arkansas Territory before leaving the service in 1829 upon his marriage to Miranda Julia DuVal of Washington. Upon his return to civilian life in the Palmetto State, he soon found himself politically at McDuffie's side as a delegate to the 1832 Nullification convention. Both men acted as leaders, and Butler went so far as to urge secession in the event of any federal military coercion directed at the state. Butler's extreme views were circulated in part through a series of letters written to prominent Nullifiers during and after the crisis. "There is only one question among our party," he wrote to James H. Hammond, "& I wonder that it is a question— which is to the time of the application of this act of Nullification—*I say without further delay*—in the name of *God*[,] Hammond, why pause longer."[3]

A sidelight of the Nullification Crisis saw political conflicts infused into the South Carolina state militia as never before. This took on special significance because nowhere was the importance of the state militia as a social and political institution greater than in South Carolina. Vernon Burton, in his seminal study of Edgefield, has noted that a "military ethos pervaded South Carolina's culture." He added: "All white males were required to be members of the state militia. Drills, parades, and even week-long bivouacs and maneuvers regularly occupied militia troops[, and] local militia officers always made speeches at celebrations, such as Fourth of July gatherings." Once the militia was politicized, Unionists and Nullifiers competed for dominance within its ranks, a contest that continued well into the 1830s. Butler further infused himself into this conflict after his appointment as lieutenant colonel of the South Carolina Regiment of Mounted Volunteers in January 1833. When compromise of the Nullification controversy removed the threat of federal attack on the state, however, he found himself outside the direct flow of politics. His efforts nonetheless brought their reward, as mentioned, in the form of the presidency of the Bank of the State of South Carolina. In 1834 he toyed with the idea of running for Congress, but abandoned it upon the advice of friends. Soon he was expressing disappointment at the performance of his old ally George McDuffie, who in December 1834 had been elected governor. It required only an easy step thereafter for him to join with others committed to breaking the grip on state politics enjoyed by McDuffie and John C. Calhoun. Walter Edgar has noted a more general dynamic of the same sort. Nullification, he insisted, "attracted men who had been outside the state's power structure but who saw an opportunity to become part of it." This application would have fit Pierce Mason Butler snugly.[4]

Butler and his Nullifier associates, many of whom were future Seminole War campaigners, became convinced that their strong stand—especially their efforts at military mobilization—had forced federal capitulation. They continued to stress the imminent danger of expanding federal authority, ever mindful that President Jackson's use of the patronage system threatened to undercut their party unless they kept citizens aroused to the danger of submission to the national government. By late summer 1834, however, Butler sensed a growing public apathy. Expressing his frustrations to James Henry Hammond, he declared, "[I]t is like a clear spring trying to purify a large putrid river or controlling its current—the patronage is too abundant and the servile spirits too acrid." He added, though, "Our safety, Hammond, is in the arming and training of our volunteers, it should be looked at with more importance. . . . Bring the subject more to view in any way your judgement or opinion dictates—we must hold some stimulants to the volunteers and the Privates."[5]

Thus by 1835 Butler had involved himself in the dynamics of South Carolina politics, taken to active criticism of the state's then current powerbrokers, and perhaps already begun to have thoughts of how much better he might handle the governor's duties than did the incumbent. Then as the year progressed and South Carolina politics approached factional clash, the Second Seminole War exploded onto the scene. The conflict immediately offered an ambitious young politician the opportunity for positive exposure statewide and the kinds of political rewards a share of the glory derived from such a conflict might offer. Moreover, Butler and his Nullifier colleagues were quick to grasp the opportunity to stir public enthusiasm or, as Robert Hayne put it, "[I sense] a slight impulse of feeling on the Florida business." Within days,

Butler and his allies were alerting South Carolina's residents to the emergency, which they blamed, not surprisingly, on an incompetent administration in Washington. South Carolinians and other brave Southerners, they asserted, must come to the rescue.[6]

The scene toward which they cast their eyes indeed was a terrible one. Spain had transferred Florida to the United States only in 1821. Various individuals, many of them protégés of Andrew Jackson, had opted to cast their lot with the new territory, aiming to make their fortunes from government, land speculation, and cotton planting. Settlement began in the counties located at the heart of Florida's Panhandle region, with a new town called Tallahassee hosting the capital. This region came to be known as Middle Florida, as opposed to the old settled Spanish areas of East Florida, with its center at St. Augustine, and West Florida, focused on Pensacola. Additionally, Key West emerged in the 1820s as a shipping and commercial center, while Jacksonville slowly grew with the timber industry, port activities, and steamboating on the St. Johns River. The types of cotton plantations envisioned by Middle Florida planters required gang-type slavery, and even smaller plantations and farms often utilized the labor of one or two black families.[7]

The obstacle that loomed before these would-be cotton magnates appeared in the form of Florida's Indian population of 5,000 or so, including Seminoles, Creeks, Miccosukees, and others, as well as their maroon allies—increasingly called Black Seminoles—in numbers estimated at 1,500 and up. To counter the threat they posed to securing slaves and protecting white family members, Florida's officialdom by 1823 had concluded a treaty that limited settlement by these persons to a reservation in the peninsula's interior. Fort Brooke, at present-day Tampa, rose as a central focus for military strength and supplies in the vicinity. An Indian agency and outpost called Fort King, near today's Ocala, provided additional support services. Andrew Jackson's presidency then brought the infamous Indian Removal Act of 1830, designed to facilitate relocation of eastern Indians to west of the Mississippi. Florida's planters enthusiastically endorsed the measure as a means for ridding themselves completely of the danger they faced in building their fortunes. A substantial portion of the Indian population, especially Red Stick Creeks under the influence of the war chief Osceola, and maroons led by Abraham, Harry, and others, decided to resist. Through 1835 Osceola, Harry, and their followers attempted to provoke war, finally realizing their goal in late December. By early 1836, the peninsula had been overrun by the combatants, as white settlers succumbed to attacks or else fled in fear of their lives. The conflict would be remembered in history as the Second Seminole War.[8]

While many South Carolinians no doubt held genuine feelings of concern for their neighbors in the Territory of Florida, the conflict's overtone as a slave rebellion inflamed passions further. For one year or more before open hostilities commenced, the Black Seminole leader Abraham and his associates had organized slaves living adjacent to the reservation for war. No one knows how many slaves rebelled, but estimates suggest between 750 and 1,500. As General Thomas Jesup declared, "This is a negro and not an Indian War." Plus, initial reports of widespread violence attendant upon the outbreak of the conflict no doubt exacerbated the fears held not only by white Floridians but also by white South Carolinians. As John T. Sprague, a veteran of the war and one of its early historians, wrote, Florida "was a scene of devastation, murder, sorrow, and distress."[9]

Reaction from South Carolinians to the outbreak of hostilities in Florida came quickly. Meetings were held in Charleston as early as January 1, 1836, to hear pleas for assistance from citizens of St. Augustine. At the assemblies, "the most elevated spirit" was manifested for the distressed. Subscriptions were raised, food and supplies were forwarded, and by the end of the month four companies of volunteers had organized, departed South Carolina, and arrived at the Ancient City. On January 20 Brigadier General Abraham Eustis, then stationed in Charleston, requested that Governor McDuffie raise for Florida service a detachment of 600 men, a figure that Eustis's superior, Major General Winfield Scott, soon raised to 740 organized as a regiment of ten companies. As reports of desolation and destruction increased, Scott on January 31 also asked McDuffie for a regiment of mounted men to rendezvous with other forces on the lower Savannah River and then marched into Florida. Amidst the furor, the *Charleston Courier*, echoing their calls, demanded that "a respectable number of our militia should volunteer their services . . . in numbers sufficient to scour the territory and extirpate *red-skins* from the soil they savage."[10]

Responding to the requests of Eustis and Scott, McDuffie ordered a draft. This was to come from South Carolina militia brigades representing the districts of "Abbeville, Edgefield, and of the middle and lower Districts, from whence the transportation could be soonest made to Florida in vessels." When the governor received on February 2 the summons of a regiment of mounted men, he turned to the districts of "Anderson, Laurens, Abbeville and some others of the upper districts." To exercise overall command of the two regiments, McDuffie designated militia brigadier general and former lieutenant governor William A. Bull of Abbeville. Colonel Abbot H. Brisbane was named commander of the regiment of foot, and command of the mounted men was placed in the hands of state senator and former U.S. Army officer Robert H. Goodwyn.[11]

Pierce Mason Butler soon chose to enter the picture as most of the militia companies quickly were filled with volunteers and even though in some districts men sought exemption through the provision of substitutes. One mounted company that needed no substitutes was organized at Columbia on February 11. The men quickly elected Butler as their captain, but no sooner had the action been taken than word was received that Governor McDuffie had designated Butler as second-in-command of the mounted regiment with the rank of lieutenant colonel. In that capacity Butler delivered an "animating address" to the volunteers as they gathered for departure. Before taking their leave, the men elected Benjamin T. Elmore as their new captain.[12]

As Captain Elmore's company prepared for its overland journey to Florida, other of the required mounted companies began to gather. The "M'Duffie Fairfield Volunteers" appeared at Columbia by February 11, as did Captain John Chesnut's "Kershaw Volunteers." Captain Paul Quattlebaum and his Lexington Volunteers arrived in Charleston by train on February 9. Captain Denny's Edgefield Company attached to Gen. Bull's brigade reached Charleston about the same time and embarked by boat for St. Augustine on February 11. Delays beset some units, though, while others headed to Florida via Savannah. It took nearly two weeks for Major Richard F. Simpson's "Laurens Volunteers" to reach that city, and Captain S. C. Hargrove's volunteers from Newberry did not rendezvous with the combined forces under Colonels Goodwyn and Butler at Jeffersonville, Georgia, until February 29.[13]

The call for volunteers fulfilled the wishes of the Nullifiers such as Butler by rekindling partisan fires in the state, and many observers believed that the Nullifiers were more eager to volunteer than Unionists—a fact deplored by some who thought their efforts would have been better made at home. "This Florida War," one man wrote, "has swept off all of our most inflammable spirits; and, indeed, we have scarcely a [Nullifier] left, to whom, in public assemblies, the people are accustomed to look. We are without an orator." Another associate of Butler confided to a friend, "Your friend Butler has gone to the wars, as you have doubtless heard, and the rest of us must double our licks and strike harder." The press soon picked up the partisan nature of volunteerism. The Unionist *Charleston Courier* deplored this situation but could not escape the fact that Nullifiers more enthusiastically answered the call.[14]

Good press, however, did not mean there were not problems for Nullifier Volunteers. Delays in the departure of Goodwyn's mounted regiment particularly frustrated South Carolina and army officials. Governor McDuffie complained to General Bull, for instance, that he simply could not understand why it took so long for the mounted men to get to Florida. The foot regiment under Colonel Brisbane—which had traveled by water—had completed its arrival at

St. Augustine by February 17, but not until early March were the mounted men able to enter that town.[15]

Considering that the Florida war had continued to build in intensity through February, the frustration of these officials easily is understood. It can only be assumed, though, that this frustration was more than matched by that of Colonels Goodwyn and Butler. Their moods at the time their regiment organized likely involved expectations of quick action and glory. One of General Bull's friends summed up the prevailing atmosphere: "I wish you great sport in your Florida Hunt. If you cant get Indian scalps load a Steam Boat with Aligators, Possums & *Bull* frogs." In the event, the colonels found little or no sport on the road to Florida.[16]

The fact was that, although Goodwyn and Butler formerly had been officers in the U.S. Army, they had not properly prepared for the journey. To begin with, the road itself posed difficulties enough for anyone. A correspondent of the *Charleston Mercury* writing in 1837 described the travails of the journey: "If, however, they are mounted men, they must go by land to Savannah, thence to the Altamaha, thence to St. Mary's, Jacksonville, and Picolata or St. Augustine." He continued, "This march can not be accomplished in less than four weeks, and it will be performed through a country, in which their ingenuity will be severely taxed, in devising plans to avoid starvation, and where, in some nights, they will sleep upon the comfortable bed of several poles laid horizontally in the mud, to keep themselves dry." As the mounted men slogged onward they ran low on provisions, and their commanders desperately sought food and transportation. One observer at Darien, Georgia, reported on February 27 that the South Carolina Mounted Troops had "swept all the Corn in the place, and I may add neighborhood. Three thousand dollars were offered to the agent in Savannah" for the use of a steamer to Picolata, but it was refused.[17]

They faced other problems in addition to bad roads. Some companies left South Carolina without proper provisions, and a lack of discipline encouraged incidents sure to cause delays. One such incident occurred when several Newberry volunteers wandered into the town of Jeffersonville, Georgia, where they found an old cannon lying in the street. "They got some powder," one veteran remembered, "and charged the piece quite heavy—took an old empty hogshead and laid before it and fired off the piece into the hogshead, which bursted all to pieces and wounded one of the boys on the foot." Coupled with human failings, the hand of nature also played its role. Time and again the journal keeper for the volunteers from Newberry laced his account with phrases such as "it rained all night," "it set in to raining," and "went through a cold rain." The hard road to Florida proved to be "nothing but mud and water."[18]

Despite the rigors of the journey, hopes remained high for Butler and among the men of the mounted regiment upon their arrival at St. Augustine on March 5. One local citizen reported on that day that the 750 mounted men from South Carolina "made a stirring scene of din and bustle [in our town]." At least they did not arrive seasick as had many of the men belonging to the regiment of foot. While they were ordered to camp "in the worse thicket that ever was seen," during their short stay they still could revel in the quaintness and beauty of the town. Its charms were enhanced for them by its location so near the wild and exotic frontier. "St. Augustine," wrote one South Carolinian, "was like another Santiago in Cuba, on the occasion—a stopping place of civilization, previous to an entry into the savage wilderness." However savage that wilderness might be and whatever dangers it might hold, the volunteers could take comfort that their intended deeds of valor would be properly recorded. Numerous newspapers had arranged for volunteers or others to send firsthand reports from the field directly to Charleston and Columbia.[19]

As it happened, even the most optimistic reports from the field could not hide the fact that delays were not the only problems encountered by the volunteers. Some could have been anticipated. For instance, a typical report might read, as did one from Captain Paul Quattlebaum, "A bad night too we had of it as it rained & our blankets & cloaks were on the Boat & no chance to get them before day.—the musketoes too annoyed us very much." Other occurrences spoke of a continued lack of discipline and a growing anxiety about confrontation with the hostiles. One such incident occurred at St. Augustine when a sleepy guard mistakenly gave an Indian alarm. A visitor later recalled:

> There were five hundred Charleston volunteers in the city, ready for the first show of fight or frolic; and in half an hour every man in town who had a musket or rifle, was on his way to do battle against—nobody knew what. There was much tramping, and shouting of "Where are the rascals?" "Which way?" "Clear the track for the big gun!" "Down with the red devils!" etc.; all which passed over, after a little, and the people went back again, with a keen relish for hot suppers, and a highly exhilarating sense of their increased importance.[20]

The above account exemplifies the volatile nature of the South Carolina volunteers and the degree to which their high-spirited antics unsettled the St. Augustine community. By early March when Butler's mounted men arrived on the scene, citizens has already endured two months of raucous activity of the volunteers and their officers. The troopers were wearing out their welcome. A regular army officer, Lieutenant Samuel Peter Heintzelman, witnessed this ebb and flow of public opinion. Casting an ever-ambivalent eye toward the volunteers, Heintzelman admitted that while some "were fine looking men" and "performed tolerably well," they were for the most part rough and undisciplined. The indignant West Pointer was appalled at the condition of their barracks when they departed the town, recording in his diary that the Charleston volunteers had "become a nuisance. The barracks they occupied are very much defaced & damaged & furniture destroyed. They carried off mattresses & such things as ladies had furnished to make them comfortable. For some days before they left a female could scarcely walk the street at dark without being insulted." Officers' accommodations at the Florida House were equally disgraceful. On February 24, Heintzelman noted that Colonel Brisbane and his officers had "left this morning," leaving his rooms at the Florida House "very much defaced, windows & chairs broken & the floor of the room occupied by the men as dirty as I ever saw."[21]

As the South Carolinians, including Butler's regiment, fanned out to isolated posts between St. Augustine and Volusia, a trading center on the St. Johns River some sixty-five miles south of the old Spanish capital, two additional problems evidenced themselves. First, the command structure of the army in Florida stood in disarray. Major Generals Scott and Gaines, not to mention General Duncan L. Clinch, engaged through March in a not-too-delicate contretemps as to who, in fact, was in charge. The confusion extended to the immediate command of the Carolina forces. "Scott is Major General of our Division, Eustis Brigadier," wrote one officer, "but Bull has come on with an appointment from the Gov. & how the matter will be arranged I do not now know." Although Scott eventually emerged as overall army commander, confusion continued to trouble the Carolinians, a situation complicated beginning March 24, if not before, when General Bull appears to have taken to a serious and steady recourse to "ardent spirits."[22]

While command confusion could prove dangerous to army efficiency, another problem presented its ranks with a more direct—and potentially deadly—threat. No sooner had Butler and the South Carolina regiments arrived in Florida than disease broke out among the volunteers. Particularly, within days of their landing at St. Augustine, members of the regiment of foot had been struck by disease. "Parker's Company," Paul Quattlebaum noted, "in this time had been severely visited with the measles & consequently could not march with us." Though the mounted regiment arrived weeks later than the foot, they proved no more immune to the disease. By March 25 the chronicler of the Newberry Volunteers recorded, "Went back to the old camp at Spring Garden; R. Dugan and W. Allen both sick with the measles; saw some signs of Indians; rained all night and all got wet to the skin." Three days earlier, Captain Thomas Parker had notified General Bull that, of the men located at

Camp McRae on the Tomoka River near present-day Daytona Beach, seventy-six were sick and should be released from active operations. Idle troops became restless, and news of the volunteers' plight began to trickle back to South Carolina. Complaints were leveled against mismanagement of the U.S. War Department.[23]

One disillusioned South Carolina trooper related conditions in some depth. He wrote from Camp McRea on March 8:

> We have only five Companies of Brisbane's Regiment here, the others are scattered over the country. Some of them complaining of hunger—we have never had full rations since we left St. Augustine. I do not know what detains us—we never have more than two days rations at a time in Camp—you never heard of such bad management they have not a wagon large enough to carry a dozen pair of Turkies. I fear we will spend our three months in doing nothing, and that when the sickly season arrives they will expect us to remain longer, but we have been so badly treated to remain one hour over the time.

Four days later General Bull arrived at Fort McRae in advance of the entire body of the mounted South Carolinians, and the men reorganized as best they could for the thirty-five-mile march to Volusia.[24]

As disease, privation, and confusion began to take a toll on the South Carolinians, General Scott finally found himself in a position to implement his grand strategy for driving the hostiles into a trap. To effect the plan, he divided his combined forces—comprising some 5,000 men—into three wings referred to as the left, center, and right. The three columns were to converge on the area presently known as Lake Tsala Apopka but which then was called the Cove of the Withlacoochee, a remote region that lay deep in the peninsula a considerable distance north of Tampa Bay. The Left Wing, to which the Carolinians were attached, was placed under the command of Brigadier General Eustis. Its orders involved crossing the St. Johns River from east to west at Volusia, traversing the entire width of the peninsula and, in the process of its "rapid movement of advance," occupying the key Indian town of Pelaklikaha, the prewar home of the Seminole chief Micanopy and subsequently that of the Black Seminole leader Abraham and his closest followers. The plan was far too ambitious.[25]

General Scott's plan envisioned the arrival of the Left Wing at Pelaklikaha by March 25. On that day, however, the column had yet to complete its formation, and General Eustis was left wondering just where Colonel Pierce Butler was. Multiple reports of Indian sightings in the vicinity of Volusia had

8.1. South Carolina Troops at the Withlacoochee (Library of Congress).

been received in the several preceding days. Due to what Eustis later called "a *misunderstanding* of my orders on the part of Brigadier General Bull," on the morning of the twenty-second, Butler had taken the wing's best guides and 200 men of the mounted regiment to scout to the southeast. When he had not returned by the following morning, a worried Eustis dispatched a volunteer detachment with two additional guides. They found no sign of Butler or his men, and after a brief and unsuccessful skirmish with a small party of hostiles, the search party was forced to return to Volusia empty-handed.[26]

General Eustis and the greater part of the Left Wing enjoyed no option but to await Butler without word, and not until the twenty-sixth did his force make its way to Volusia. Butler indicated at the time that the guides had lost their way. As a private account disclosed, "It seems that they got lost on the way to Orange Grove, the guides not knowing the way perfectly, and on Wednesday, March 23d, the men became so much displeased that they threatened to shoot the guides if they did not find the way." Whatever the reason for Butler's absence, crucial time had been lost in a delicately coordinated operation that allowed for no such delays.[27]

The Left Wing launched itself across the St. Johns River on March 26 and, having done so, almost immediately bogged down. The heavy military wagons intended as transport for much needed supplies proved far too heavy a load for the primitive water-logged trails of the area. In two days the force advanced a mere seven miles toward Pelaklikaha. Thereafter, the pace picked up, but the problems continued. Lieutenant W. W. Smith described the situation this way:

> On the way, the army was much encumbered with the wagons which they had to lighten, by throwing away some of the provisions, the pork, beans, candles, soap, &c. were scattered on the road, and rations issued every day. There were many sick, who suffered severely; some who could hardly support themselves, being compelled to walk for want of transportation. Expecting to return in ten days they carried very little clothing—many only one shirt. Each horseman carried a bushel of corn in his saddle bag, which he had to drop when any Indians made their appearance, as he could not charge with such an encumbrance. In this way, once or twice they lost their corn, for while they would be dashing far ahead after a few scattering Indians, the greater body of them would sneak up behind, and carry off the corn. . . . They found before they had proceeded half way, that they had not brought corn enough.[28]

Those horsemen "dashing far ahead" primarily were South Carolinians commanded by Goodwyn and Butler. On several occasions they engaged in sharp skirmishes with parties of Indians and blacks, and in at least one of them, Butler came under fire. Despite the valor shown by the Carolinians, however, their actions came at great expense. Remaining supplies, particularly forage for the horses, were consumed at an alarming rate, and the ordeal exhausted the force's animals. Although they occupied and burned an abandoned Pelaklikaha on April 1, the dearth of supplies and increasing rates of illness among the men forced Eustis to cancel the proposed juncture with the Right and Center Wings and to order his men to march south directly to Fort Brooke on Tampa Bay. Seemingly the operation had ended in fiasco.[29]

The march to Tampa Bay took the better part of five days. On the first of those days, Captain S. C. Hargrove noted in his journal: "Now out of rations for our horses, and had not had any since we left Fort Volusia, but what we carried on our horses. Much dissatisfaction on account of it—the men murmuring." By April 5 the volunteers were reduced to eating "flour made into dough, and salt pork." Morale had plummeted. One of the men soon expressed the general state of despair to readers of a Columbia newspaper. "From this succinct history, you will perceive that the expedition, so far, is a failure," he asserted. "The measles continue to prevail." The paper's columns also disclosed that Captain Elmore's company had been reduced by sickness from 115 to 78 men, and that among the numerous officers "returning home on account of bad health" was Colonel Butler.[30]

A reporter vividly described for readers of the *Key West Inquirer* the desperate condition of many of the volunteers and their officers upon arrival at Tampa Bay, having seem them on that island as they made their way home. "When they landed here," he wrote, "they were objects of compassion. Among them were men of wealth, of character, and intelligence who had been reared on ease and luxury, and were the hope and pride of their families, and who had been brought to the brink of the grave by exposure, hardships, and STARVA-TION. They had gallantly marched to our defense expecting that their government would give them soldier's fare. In this, it seems, they have been miserably disappointed."[31]

For those who remained at Tampa Bay, Winfield Scott prepared to assign them one more chore. News obtained from a Spaniard who was captured while running arms to the hostiles indicated that Osceola, his men, and their black allies—together with their women, children, and supplies—had gathered at a town on Peace River, some fifty miles east from Fort Brooke. Desirous of acting upon the intelligence and anxious to redeem the campaign, Scott conceived a plan whereby those South Carolinians fit for duty would directly approach the refuge, called Talakchopco (today's Fort Meade), while a regiment of Louisiana volunteers ascended the river from Charlotte Harbor. Initially Scott planned to lead the Carolinians on the foray, but on April 14 he decided to leave the responsibility solely to Colonel Goodwyn and his mounted regiment.[32]

When Bob Goodwyn received "an intimation" that his men would be ordered to Peace River, he hastened in alarm to General Eustis. As Eustis later testified, "He came to me to request my intercession with General Scott that they should be excused from that duty, expressing great doubt whether his horses would be able to accomplish it, and the extreme reluctance of his men to go upon the expedition, assuring me, however, that if they were ordered they would obey." When approached on the matter by Eustis, Scott refused the request. At Eustis's suggestion, Goodwyn then confronted the commanding officer directly, though the results were the same. Eustis later claimed that "it was only with great difficulty, by an urgent appeal to the patriotism and State pride of the South Carolina brigade, that I could induce them to obey the order, the terms of service having nearly expired, and all being anxious to return home."[33]

As events occurred, Scott and Eustis might just as well have granted Goodwyn's request; the expedition proved little but an embarrassment. To begin with, shortly after the regiment left Fort Brooke on April 15, it found itself involved in a hapless incident during which elements of the regiment opened fire upon other Carolinians, mistaking them for Indians. It then took the force almost two days to travel the forty or so additional miles to the river settlement. "The men were required to take eight days provisions in their haversacks," protested one man, "to put two bushels of corn on the backs of their horses, and to *lead* them two days—thus making, it will be remarked, pack-asses of the men and camels of their horses: and all this to accomplish—nothing!"[34]

Forced to lead, rather than ride, their mounts, the Carolinians' slow progress allowed ample time for their opponents to fade away to the prairies and swamps to the south and east of Peace River. The volunteers did discover Talakchopco and, upon Goodwyn's orders, burnt its two or three hundred log houses to the ground. After scouring the surrounding country "for some other Indian villages which were supposed to be in the neighborhood," they turned back to the north and west toward a rendezvous with Scott, Eustis, and their fellow Carolinians at the ford over the Hillsborough River north of Fort Brooke. They arrived at the site, Fort Alabama, on April 18.[35]

The campaign had failed, and along with it had come an ignominious end to the South Carolinians' efforts. A frustrated Winfield Scott had conceded by the time of Goodwyn's arrival at Fort Alabama "that he would not be able to win the war during the present Campaign," a fact that he attributed at the time to "the sickly season coming on, and the indisposition of his men." The remains of the Left Wing of the Army of Florida were ordered to recross the peninsula by foot to St. Augustine. The force, composed primarily of Carolina volunteers and led by Scott and Eustis, departed on the ordeal within a day of Goodwyn's rendezvous at the Hillsborough.[36]

The trip home afforded little more comfort to the South Carolinians than had the campaign. "We amounted to more than a thousand men," remembered one veteran of the journey, "the horse constituting the larger portion, as many who had been unwell, or worn down on the march, provided themselves with the horses of the mounted men, who were sick and went in the steam boat." Morale, already fragile, further was strained, and resentment came increasingly to be focused upon the officers of the regular Army. One Carolinian reported, "An occasional murmur and complaint of the unmannerly treatment of Uncle Sam's officers in sending the Carolina troops by land a long and tedious route, while the pet regulars were to be transported at their ease in steam boats." Another noted that "[e]ven an officer of the grade of Col. Brisbane, [led] his heavy leaden horse the entire way from Camp Shelton to Camp Sidney, while the very attendants of superior U.S. officers (superior on grade, I mean) rode all the while, carrying little or no corn."[37]

The Carolinians did not reach Volusia until April 25 and not without further trouble. On the way they received fire and engaged in heated skirmishes on several occasions. While Scott and the South Carolinians made their way to the St. Johns, the general requested that the volunteers make one more excursion against the Indians. He did so to no avail. As noted in his official report, "[on May 7 and 8] application was made for volunteers from the South Carolina foot," but only seven men of the entire number complied. "No more would volunteer," Scott recorded, "either to go by water, on foot, or horseback. On inquiry, it was found useless to issue an order, as Colonel Brisbane could not pledge that it would be obeyed. Brisbane was, to the contrary, certain that it would be disregarded. By that time Goodwin's regiment already had crossed the river, and the cause was lost. At Volusia, Scott boarded a steamer for Jacksonville. Eustis and Bull, "both being much indisposed," accompanied him. Goodwyn's force ultimately reached St. Augustine on the last day of the month.[38]

The end of the campaign and the proximity of home seem to have cheered the men and restored somewhat their sense of bravado. An observer watching them enter the Ancient City reported, "The men in general look much jaded and in a wretched plight; for they have undergone great fatigue, privation, encountered dreadful weather and bad roads, but they are in high spirits, only regretting that they were not ordered, when opportunities offered, to give the Indians a good drubbing." He additionally remarked, "They complain very much of the treatment received of Gen. Eustis." Yet an officer from Brisbane's staff quickly recognized the "good cheer and kind treatment of the good people here [in St. Augustine]." He continued, "It is well for us that we have had the opportunity for shaking the dust off, before arriving in our city, for a more ill-looking set you have never seen collected in any one place."[39]

Eustis, for his part, attempted soothe over the dissensions with lavish praise. His orders disbanding the South Carolina brigade spoke eloquently of their "spirit and promptitude," "the cheerfulness and alacrity with which they sacrificed all personal interests to the public service," and "the patience with which they have endured privations and hardships." Sensing that kind words were not enough to heal the wounds, he added, "He hopes and trusts that this cordiality of feeling may continue through life among all his present associates and that wherever we may meet, we may recognize each other as fellow soldiers and comrades of the Left Wing of the Army of Florida." As will be seen, the "cordiality of feeling"—if it ever existed—dissolved immediately.[40]

The South Carolina brigade officially disbanded at Jacksonville on May 6, confronted with the challenge of making their way home from there. General Eustis managed to take care of the problem for some by arranging steamboat transportation for field officers and fifty of the sick and wounded. The vessel

Santee returned them to Charleston three days later. The bulk of the force proceeded overland to their homes as best they could.[41]

Pierce Butler had preceded Goodwyn to Charleston. An ailing Butler appears to have left Tampa Bay, along with John Chesnut and several others, for Pensacola on April 15 or 16. Soon he was back in South Carolina and engaging himself in discussions about his possibilities in the upcoming gubernatorial election. Events thereafter hint that he—or friends on his behalf—quickly undertook efforts to shift all blame for the Florida fiasco away from Butler and onto the backs of federal military officers. Such an effort, if successful, would have fitted quite well with Butler's political philosophy of antagonism for federal authority and a passionate defense of states' rights to the point of secession.[42]

That Butler's thoughts centered on the gubernatorial election appear clear. Almost immediately upon their return to South Carolina, he and his associates made the rounds of welcome-home banquets and public events. By July, his gubernatorial candidacy was being talked about openly. The *Charleston Courier* reported, "Co. Pierce M. Butler is toasted at numerous 4th of July celebrations in this state as the next governor of South Carolina." The *Pendleton Messenger* endorsed his candidacy but expressed doubts as to whether Butler would "relinquish his present lucrative [bank] office for the political dignity in question." Then, in late July Butler essentially announced his candidacy. "I hold this to be an office," he proclaimed in a letter to the editor of the *Pendleton Messenger*, "no citizen has a right to decline, provided the people think him qualified." He added, "At the same time, it *should not be sought in the remotest degree*." Despite his claim that the office should seek the man, Butler was working behind the scenes to ensure support for his candidacy. U.S. Senator William Preston loomed as his chief rival, and the backstage maneuvering proved complex. Early in August, insider Francis Pickens offered a political appraisal. "Butler has been . . . nominated in the *Mercury*," Pickens wrote a friend. "I believe Preston let it be understood that he would not run, but at a dinner that some of our citizens honored him with [they] nominated him, expressly desiring (I rather think) that he would run against Butler, but of this I cannot speak certainly, as nothing was said on the subject. Some say that Butler will be elected Adjt. General with a salary of $3,000 and that Preston will be governor and Judge [Andrew Pickens] Butler will go to the Senate."[43]

Pickens's reference to Butler's interest in the office of adjutant general had some foundation. The candidate was hedging his bets, likely—as will be seen—pending the outcome of certain public relations efforts. On August 26, for example, he wrote that "if I can get the Adj. General's office organized as I like it, I do not want to be gov [and would] only accept as a point of honor."

But few of Butler's contemporaries believed this. As one observer summed matters up in late October, "[H]e still keeps trying." By the end of the month, even Butler, despite a continuing coyness, admitted, "I believe . . . I am looked to now certain almost."[44]

Butler's coyness throughout the summer and fall of 1836 arose, at least in part, from the disasters endured as a result of the Florida campaign. That the effort had been a fiasco could not be denied, and Butler's political future depended upon the blame being placed on someone other than him. Where better could fault be found to suit a Nullifier's purpose than with the officer corps of the U.S. Army? The problem lay, however, in the credibility of men such as Scott and Eustis and their ability to command national attention. That they would be defending their actions seemed certain by May 1836. Floridians were hanging Scott in effigy, newspapers were denouncing him, and Florida's congressional delegate Joseph M. White had demanded the general's removal from command. If Scott and Eustis attempted to shift any responsibility for the mess onto the South Carolinians, as they subsequently did, their case certainly could be damaging.[45]

Any objective assessment would have judged Butler's record in the Florida to be mixed, at best. He and his friend Bob Goodwyn both were experienced officers of the U.S. Army and, as such, should have been prepared to deal with the problems common to a military operation. Nonetheless, their progress to Florida—however difficult—was marked by a lack of discipline, a want of supplies, and costly delays. Butler, in particular, may be singled out for criticism of his scout of March 22–26, a move that had thrown the operations of the Left Wing seriously behind schedule and hampered the coordinated execution of Scott's plan of operations. To their credit, both men displayed a tenacity in the field and courage in combat. Goodwyn saw the entire mission through, and Butler cannot be blamed for succumbing to illness.

Curiously, in light of Butler's experience in the Florida war, one of his actions after his return to South Carolina involved a claim that Scott had urged him to accept a regular army position. He supposedly intended for this to be in the Washington office of the Adjutant General. Inexplicably Butler also suggested that he had spent most of the war "as commandant over a munitions depot at Tampa Bay." The truth of the matter, of course, was something else entirely.[46]

If the incident illustrates an attempt by Butler to color the nature of his Florida service, broader attempts already were underway—ones likely instigated by or else involving Butler—to do the same for the service of all South Carolinians in the conflict. An opening salvo in that direction was fired on May 18, 1836, in the columns of the *Charleston Mercury*. Prominently displayed was a "Review of the Campaign," which, the journal assured, was "impartially written." The author, a veteran of the effort, declared: "Whether the neglect to provide the necessary comforts of any army, such as Tents, Baggage, Waggons, ample supply of Provisions, &c., is referable to Gen. Scott, or to the contracted policy of the Government, I cannot say." He continued, "In either event, however, the injustice to the troops was not the less flagrant; and forms, of itself, an admirable commentary upon the *parental* care usually bestowed by Government upon the troops that have been once unadvisedly entrapped into her power." He added to his charges the allegation that federal authorities had made no effort "to discover the location of the negroes carried off from plantations by the enemy" and further declared, "The campaign should never have been abandoned without a discovery of the kind." Thus the national government was painted as favoring black runaways over South Carolina's valiant volunteers.[47]

The article seemingly spurred a public relations effort that involved a rewriting of history to suit the purposes of Nullifiers and of Butler's candidacy. The facts are these. Several days after the article's appearance, unnamed individuals approached state assemblyman Myer M. Cohen of Charleston, commanding officer of Colonel Brisbane's "pioneers" and possible author of the piece. They proposed that he "undertake a work on that country [Florida], and the recent campaign therein." At virtually the same time W. W. Smith, also a lieutenant in Brisbane's regiment, received similar encouragement. Cohen and Smith quickly fell to work and produced substantial memoirs of the campaign. Cohen's reached publication in June, and Smith's followed in August. A central theme of both books concerned the ill-treatment of the South Carolinians at the hands of federal officials. Cohen faulted Scott's plan of operation but reserved his most stinging criticisms for Eustis. He included within the general's shortcomings even "his citizen's dress, and total disuse of sword, or other badge of office." Smith stressed the suffering and sacrifices of the Carolinians, but found ample opportunity as well to criticize the regular Army generals and their subordinate officers.[48]

These books offered South Carolina and the nation the first comprehensive treatments of the conduct of the war. Their significant impact was enhanced during the summer and fall of 1836 in numerous ways. In those days before the advent of photography, engraved or lithographed illustrations offered a way for the public to conceive of and remember events occurring at a distance. That summer the *Charleston Mercury* helped publicize a series of renderings of the Florida campaign drawn by J. F. Gray, a volunteer in Captain Elmore's company. The scenes treated by Gray—including "Attack of the Seminoles on the Block House," "Carolina Mounted men fording the Withlacoochee," and

"Burning of the Town of Pilaklikaha"—conveyed a romantic, and even heroic, perspective on the Carolinians' wartime service.[49]

Additional accounts of the war, sharing perspectives not far different from those of Cohen and Smith, also received widespread attention. In late July, for example, the *Mercury* ran South Carolinian James W. Simmons's "Recollections of the Campaign in East Florida," which had been serialized in the *New York Evening Star*. The release of Woodburne Potter's book, *The War in Florida,* added more credence to the effort to place blame away from the actions of South Carolina's native sons. Potter, a regular Army officer during the campaign, frankly declared, "The author does not hesitate to transfer a large share of the 'glory,' in producing this war in Florida, to the officers of the War Department."[50]

These and other attacks upon Generals Scott, Gaines, and Eustis appear to have resulted from a coordinated effort based in South Carolina without parallel with respect to any other geographical region of the nation. Meanwhile, they contributed to a national controversy over the conduct of the war. On their part, Scott and Gaines added to the impression that they and other regular Army officers were responsible for failure to properly prosecute the conflict by trading charges against each other. Ultimately, a court of inquiry assessed their allegations. It was scheduled to commence its proceedings on November 7. Meanwhile, by the end of the summer of 1836, any clouds hovering over the head of Pierce Butler as to his conduct in the war virtually had dissipated.[51]

If Butler and his allies helped to create this climate of opinion, their efforts proved very successful. One incident occurred, however, that could have reopened what would have been some very delicate matters. In September, a captain in the service of Colonel Brisbane's regiment, David Denny of Edgefield, charged General Bull with "unofficerlike conduct." Specifically, Denny alleged that "the said Wm. A. Bull was intoxicated with ardent spirits on the twenty-fourth day of March last and on divers days and times between that day and the twenty-fifth day of April last, to wit, in the Territory of Florida." Governor McDuffie had no recourse but to order a court-martial, although he did not include Colonels Goodwyn and Butler on the list of witnesses authorized for the prosecution. In the end, any anxieties for Pierce Butler that might arise out of Bull's court-martial proved groundless. Upon his appearance, Bull pleaded that the court had no jurisdiction over him as he was acting at the time of the alleged intoxication as a United States officer, rather than one of South Carolina. The argument carried the day, the witnesses were dismissed, and the court sustained his plea.[52]

Roughly coincident with Bull's court-martial, Butler managed to remove the last obstacles to his gubernatorial election. In October, he received the endorsement of Senator Preston. He also secured the neutrality of John C. Calhoun, perhaps by agreeing to the election of Calhoun's supporter William Dubose of Charleston as lieutenant governor. With that accomplished, he proceeded to his own election and inauguration in December.[53]

The sense of camaraderie gained among those who participated in the mobilization during the Nullification Crisis created political bonds that by 1836 had weakened but remained very strong. Nullifiers dominated the militia organization of the state, and the yearly musters provided an opportunity to renew and revitalize political friendships. The Second Seminole War provided a means for these activities on a far wider scale. Nullifiers volunteered with profusion, and the war rejuvenated them politically. Only a few months before the crisis in Florida, many of the leaders had sensed that the movement was losing its edge. The conflict offered a great opportunity to revitalize the movement through active service in an arena where patriotism, honor, and a readiness to risk life and limb for the good of the distressed victims of depredations could be displayed on the battlefield. Shortly, the entire conflict was being blamed on the mismanagement, incompetence, and even corruption of the federal government. What could be more suitable to the political ends of the South Carolina Nullifiers and their leadership? The bungling of the federal government, the corruption of its bureaucrats, the incompetence of its army—all provided fruitful political ammunition to be used in the future political struggles in South Carolina. It seemed that only chivalrous sons of South Carolina could rescue a distressed, mismanaged Southern territory from a corrupt, inept, and bungling federal government.

These are the circumstances under which Butler's participation in the Second Seminole War and his eventual candidacy for governor must be seen. He and his supporters succeeded in using the war—at least their version of the otherwise vainglorious conflict—as a vehicle to resurrect their movement. They succeeded, at least temporarily. The military action had provided a needed forum, perhaps the best available. And finally, though the campaign lasted only three months, it gave Butler's compatriots the opportunity to show those inside and outside the state that the Nullifiers were ready not only to defend their own state from the federal authority from the outside, but also defend fellow Southerners from an Indian menace that the federal government was incapable of snuffing out. A constant theme throughout was the incompetence of federal forces in Florida. Although South Carolina forces were no more successful against the Seminoles than the federal forces and maybe less so, reports flowing back into the state were manipulated in such a way as to construct two specific points of view: (1) to discredit South Carolina Unionists as less than stouthearted in the defense of its state's honor at home and abroad and (2) to create favorable conditions for a political resurgence of Nullifiers that would be achieved with the ascension of Butler into the governor's office.

South Carolina Unionists and supporters of President Andrew Jackson during the Nullification Crisis were fond of portraying Nullifiers as discouraged office seekers, who trumped up Nullification as a method by which they could secure election. If this description fits, Pierce Mason Butler would offer an illustrative example. James Hammond, an ally of Butler during the movement's early years, though prone to a chronic sense of paranoia, portrayed Butler, especially in his post-gubernatorial years, as not only an incessant office seeker but someone ready to foment any discord among his friends for his own personal or political advantage. For example, on February 25, 1841, Hammond recorded: "Butler has spent the evening with me. He starts to Washington *office hunting*. He has three strings in his bow: the Charleston Collectorship, the governorship of Florida, and the General Indian Agency in Arkansas. . . . He is a shrewd man, overshrewd." He added, "It makes me unhappy to be with him long."[54]

Hammond clearly had grown tired of his old political ally's machinations. He noted after a visit from Butler on April 28, 1841, for instance, "Butler was here yesterday and said a great deal, but I cannot place implicit reliance on anything he says." And later, he asserted: "[Butler] is well known now to be a rascal in every way and no one can venture to endorse for him by bringing him forward. What a fule [*sic*] is he. He . . . has been an extraordinary actor. . . . He is now a cynic." It was not long before Hammond's dislike for Butler, a sentiment he shared with others, had matured into a virulent hatred. On June 24, 1841, he recorded: "Butler delights in setting people by the ears and by lying insinuations to keep up constant warfare. He is also a fool and a bungler who mismanages every thing." As those words did not entirely convey the depths of his sentiments, Hammon continued, "He is a bad man, who has been very intimate with us all and who forces himself so upon us that we cannot absolutely banish him from Society, tho' he is partially excluded. I wish he would go away." When Hammond learned that Butler would be appointed Indian agent and would have to relocate to Fort Gibson in the Indian Territory, Hammond was relieved to "be rid of him at last."[55]

Butler, it seems, had become a political vagabond. On January 5, 1847, Hammond noted that his former friend had volunteered and would lead a regiment of South Carolinians to fight in the Mexican War, where, claimed Hammond, "he will do nothing creditable to himself or the State. . . . I have thought him a scoundrel utterly devoid of principle, yet have weakly sustained him because (tho' justly) he was abandoned by most of his former friends."

Nevertheless, Butler died a hero's death while gallantly leading the famed Palmetto Regiment in the Mexican War. This act, along with his service against the Seminoles, would make him a hero in the annals of the state.[56]

It seems that Butler and his followers had succeeded brilliantly in their attempt to rewrite history. In 1892, for example, a well-known chronicler of men of mark in South Carolina could write of Butler's service in the Second Seminole War:

> It was a trying field where the immutable climate of the Florida glades, as well as the subtle attacks of the savages had to be met, but Col. Butler bore his part with valor and intrepidity which fully established his soldierly qualities, and brought into full play the equipments of his early education. He distinguished himself in many a sanguinary contest with the wily savages, and remained in the field till the enemy was thoroughly conquered . . . a better or braver soldier never fought and fell on the battlefield.[57]

These remarks, though certainly erroneous, by 1892 had become historical fact.

The Seminole War background to the story of Pierce Mason Butler's election as governor of South Carolina suggests much about the man. Certainly he was intelligent and possessed personal courage and determination. On the other hand, his actions displayed at times a lack of discipline bordering on rashness. The record also reveals a man who felt himself no servant of truth; who perhaps envisioned his political philosophy not in terms of principle but in terms of his own ambition. He was a man who did not hesitate to rewrite the record when it stood in his way, and in so doing he added another stone in the foundation of South Carolina's monument to states' rights and the implications of the doctrine of nullification. Understanding these very human traits and actions may allow us to appreciate that South Carolina's progress to secession at least in part was propelled by the needs and ambitions of individuals, and that the great principles they espoused sometimes were voiced for purposes other than that of the public good.

Notes

1. South Carolina *Senate Journal* (1836): 78–79; *Acts and Resolutions of the General Assembly of the State of South Carolina Passed in December 1836*, 40, 43; Miles S. Richards, "Pierce Mason Butler: The South Carolina Years, 1830–1841," *South Carolina Historical Magazine* 87 (January 1986): 16–17, 24; N. Louise Bailey, Mary L. Morgan,

and Carolyn R. Taylor, *Biographical Directory of the South Carolina Senate, 1776–1985,* 3 vols. (Columbia: University of South Carolina Press, 1986), 1: 585–86; *Columbia* (S.C.) *Southern Times and State Gazette,* February 12, 1836; Pierce M. Butler to James H. Hammond, January 13, 1837, James H. Hammond Papers, Library of Congress; available on microfilm at South Carolina Library, University of South Carolina, Columbia, hereinafter cited as SCL.

2. *Proceedings of the Military Court of Inquiry, in the Case of Major General Scott and Major General Gaines,* 24th Cong., 2d sess., S. Doc. 224, 9; Richards, "Butler," 37–38.

3. Carolyn Thomas Foreman, "Pierce Mason Butler," *Chronicles of Oklahoma* 30 (Spring 1950): 8; Richards, "Butler," 15, 18; Butler to Hammond, November 20, 1832, Hammond Papers. On the South Carolina Nullification Controversy, see William W. Freehling, *Prelude to Civil War: The Nullification Controversy in South Carolina, 1816–1836* (New York: Oxford University Press, 1992); William W. Freehling, *The Road to Disunion: Secessionists at Bay, 1776–1854* (New York: Oxford University Press, 1990); Richard Ellis, *The Union at Risk: Jacksonian Democracy, States' Rights, and the Nullification Crisis* (New York: Oxford University Press, 1987); Lacy Ford, *Origins of Southern Radicalism: The South Carolina Upcountry, 1800–1860* (New York: Oxford University Press, 1988), 120–38; Drew Faust, *James Henry Hammond and the Old South: A Design for Mastery* (Baton Rouge: Louisiana State University Press, 1982), 40–58, 137–48; John Edmunds, *Francis and the Politics of Destruction* (Chapel Hill: University of North Carolina Press, 1986), 3–20; Charles Wiltse, *John C. Calhoun: Nullifier, 1829–1839* (Indianapolis: Bobbs-Merrill, 1949), 86–153, 169–204; James Brewer Stewart, "'A Great Talking and Eating Machine': Patriarchy, Mobilization, and the Dynamics of Nullification in South Carolina," *Civil War History* 27 (1981): 198–220. An excellent brief summary also may be found in Walter Edgar, *South Carolina: A History* (Columbia: University of South Carolina Press, 1998), 330–40. Additionally, see Irving H. Bartlett, *John C. Calhoun: A Biography* (New York: W. W. Norton, 1993).

4. Orville Burton, *In My Father's House There Are Many Mansions: Family and Community in Edgefield, South Carolina* (Chapel Hill: University of North Carolina Press, 1985), 98; Edgar, *South Carolina,* 334; Richards, "Butler," 20–22.

5. Two of these Nullifiers were Robert H. Goodwyn and Paul Quattlebaum. Butler to Hammond, August 4, 1834, Goodwyn to Hammond, January 15, 1833, and Quattlebaum to Hammond, March 20, 1833, Hammond Papers.

6. Robert Hayne to Hammond, January 14, 1836, Hammond Papers.

7. On Florida's evolution during the Territorial Period, see Sidney Walter Martin, *Florida during the Territorial Days* (Athens: University of Georgia Press, 1944). On the rise of cotton planting and gang slavery in Middle Florida, see Julia Floyd Smith, *Slavery and Plantation Growth in Antebellum Florida* (Gainesville: University of Florida Press, 1973); Larry E. Rivers, *Slavery in Florida: Territorial Days to Emancipation* (Gainesville: University Press of Florida, 2000); Edward E. Baptist, *Creating an Old South: Middle Florida's Plantation Frontier before the Civil War* (Chapel Hill: University of North Carolina Press, 2002).

8. The principal source for the Second Seminole War is John K. Mahon, *History of the Second Seminole War, 1835–1842* (Gainesville: University Press of Florida, 1967). See also Joshua R. Giddings, *The Exiles of Florida; or, The Crimes Committed by Our Government against the Maroons, Who Fled from South Carolina and Other Slave States, Seeking Protection under Spanish Law* (Columbus, Ohio: Follett, Foster, 1858; reprint, Gainesville: University of Florida Press, 1964); Virginia Bergman Peters, *The Florida Wars* (Hamden, Conn.: Archon Books, 1979); Kenneth W. Porter, *Black Seminoles: A History of a Freedom-Seeking People*, rev. and ed. by Alcione M. Amos and Thomas P. Senter (Gainesville: University Press of Florida, 1996); Joe Knetsch, *Florida's Seminole War, 1817–1858* (Charleston, S.C.: Arcadia, 2003); John and Mary Lou Missall, *The Seminole Wars: America's Longest Indian Conflict* (Gainesville: University Press of Florida, 2004). Also helpful are Rivers, *Slavery in Florida*, 189–209; Canter Brown Jr., *Florida's Peace River Frontier* (Orlando: University of Central Florida Press, 1991); Canter Brown, "Race Relations in Territorial Florida, 1821–1845," *Florida Historical Quarterly* 73 (January 1995): 287–307; Canter Brown, *African Americans on the Tampa Bay Frontier* (Tampa: Tampa Bay History Center, 1997).

9. Porter, *Black Seminoles*, 39–52; Rivers, *Slavery in Florida*, 189–205; Sprague, *Florida War*, 93.

10. Woodburne Potter, *The War in Florida, Being an Exposition of Its Causes and an Accurate History of the Campaigns of Generals Clinch, Gaines, and Scott* (Baltimore: Lewis and Coleman, 1836), 125–26; *Charleston Courier*, January 13, 20, 21, 1836; *St. Augustine Florida Herald*, January 13, 1836; *Charleston Southern Patriot*, January 1, 12, 19, 21, 22, 23, 29, 30, 1836; *Proceedings*, 24th Cong., 2d sess., S. Doc. 224, 215–17, 220–21.

11. W. W. Smith, *Sketch of the Seminole War, and Sketches during a Campaign* (Charleston, S.C.: Dan J. Dowling, 1836), 111, 118; George McDuffie to William Bull, February 16, 1836, Bull Papers, SCL; David Duncan Wallace, *The History of South Carolina* (New York: American Historical Society, 1934), 3: 3, 497; Bailey, Morgan, and Taylor, *Biographical Directory of the South Carolina Senate, 1776–1985*, 1: 585; *Charleston Southern Patriot*, February 7, 1836.

12. Elmore had been associated with Butler in the leadership of the mounted militia forces raised in 1833. Smith, *Sketch of the Seminole War*, 112; "The War with the Seminoles, 1836," in John Belton O'Neall and John A. Chapman, *The Annals of Newberry, in Two Parts* (Newberry, S.C.: Aull and Houseal, 1892), 799–803; *Columbia Southern Times and State Gazette*, February 12, 1836; "Journal of the Volunteer Company from Columbia: Feb. 11, 1836–May 12, 1836, Benjamin T. Elmore, Captain," South Carolina Department of Archives and History, Columbia; Richards, "Butler," 20.

13. *Columbia Southern Times and State Gazette*, February 12, 26, 1836; *Charleston Southern Patriot*, February 10, 11, 1836; O'Neall and Chapman, *Annals of Newberry*, 800.

14. Edward W. Johnston to James Hammond, February 20, 1836, and Thomas Harrison to James Hammond, February 16, 1836, Hammond Papers; *Charleston Courier*, February 14, 1836.

15. George McDuffie to William A. Bull, March 25, 1836, George McDuffie Papers, SCL; *Columbia Southern Times and State Gazette,* February 26, 1836; *St. Augustine Florida Herald,* March 9, 1836; *Greenville Mountaineer,* March 5, 1836; O'Neall and Chapman, *Annals of Newberry,* 800.

16. J. J. Whitten to William A. Bull, February 15, 1836, letters to Bull from various military personnel, February 14–September 21, 1836, Bull Papers, P. K. Yonge Library of Florida History, University of Florida, Gainesville, hereinafter cited as PKY.

17. *Charleston Mercury,* September 19, 1837; *Charleston Southern Patriot,* March 2, 1836.

18. O'Neall and Chapman, *Annals of Newberry,* 800–801.

19. *Jacksonville Courier* quoted in *Charleston Southern Patriot,* March 14, 1836; Paul Quattlebaum to James Hammond, February 29, 1836, Hammond Papers; O'Neall and Chapman, *Annals of Newberry,* 801; Smith, *Sketch of the Seminole War,* 117.

20. Quattlebaum to Hammond, February 29, 1836, Hammond Papers; "Sketches of East Florida. Number Two. My Last Night on Guard," *Knickerbocker Magazine* 22 (November 1843): 448.

21. Samuel Peter Heintzelman Diary, January 28, February 3, 23, 24, 1836, reel 2, p. 17, 19, 32, 33, Library of Congress. Also, on the conditions of St. Augustine during the war, see Joe Knetsch, "St. Augustine and the Second Seminole War: A Time of Trouble and Need," *El Escribano: The St. Augustine Journal of History* 42 (2006): 47–62.

22. Mahon, *Second Seminole War,* 150; charges filed by Captain David Denny against Brigadier General William A. Bull accompanying the letter of J. W. Wimbish to Bull, September 21, 1836, Bull Papers, PKY.

23. Quattlebaum to Hammond, February 29, 1836; O'Neall and Chapman, *Annals of Newberry,* 802.

24. Thomas Parker to Bull, March 19, 1836, Bull Papers; *Charleston Southern Patriot,* March 23, 25, 1836.

25. Mahon, *Second Seminole War,* 143; *Proceedings,* 24th Cong., 2d sess., S. Doc. 224, 294–296.

26. *Proceedings,* 24th Cong., 2d sess., S. Doc. 224, 303; *National Banner and Nashville Whig,* April 20, 1836; *St. Augustine Florida Herald,* March 25, 1836; *Charleston Southern Patriot,* April 4, 5, 1836.

27. *National Banner and Nashville Whig,* April 20, 1836; O'Neall and Chapman, *Annals of Newberry,* 801. For more on this episode, see *Charleston Courier,* April 6, 1836; *Army and Navy Chronicle,* April 14, 1836, 232–33. Samuel Heintzelman noted in his diary that "Col. Butler has returned. He went off from Volusia to have a fight with the Indians on his own hook." See Heintzelman Diary, March 27, 29, 1836, reel 2, p. 40.

28. *Proceedings,* 24th Cong., 2d sess., S. Doc. 224, 316; *Charleston Courier,* April 6, 1836; Smith, *Sketch of the Seminole War,* 290.

29. O'Neall and Chapman, *Annals of Newberry,* 802; *Columbia Southern Times and State Gazette,* April 29, 1836; *Charleston Courier,* April 30, 1836; *Proceedings,* 24th Cong., 2d sess., S. Doc. 224, 317.

30. O'Neall and Chapman, *Annals of Newberry*, 803; *Charleston Mercury*, April 28, 1836; *Columbia Southern Times and State Gazette*, April 29, 1836; *Charleston Courier*, April 30, 1836; *Charleston Southern Patriot*, April 30, 1836.

31. *Key West Inquirer*, May 7, 1836.

32. *Charleston Mercury*, April 28, 1836; *Morning Courier and New-York Enquirer*, May 3, 4, 1836; "Map of the Seat of War in Florida, 1836," Map No. 4343, record group 75, Cartographic Division, National Archives, Washington, D.C.; Brown, *Florida's Peace River Frontier*, 44–45; Canter Brown Jr., *In the Midst of All That Makes Life Worth Living: Polk County, Florida, to 1940* (Tallahassee: Sentry Press, 2001), 16; Thomas L. McKenney and James Hall, *The Indian Tribes of North America: With Biographical Sketches and Anecdotes of the Principal Chiefs* (Philadelphia, 1836–44), 2: 2, 367. Precise information as to the Indians' whereabouts was uncertain. On the day before he embarked on the campaign, a South Carolina officer explained, "There is home but nothing like a sanguine expectation of meeting the Indians." Scott had been told that a large body of Indians had collected at Charlotte Harbor. "Other sources of information promise that the Indians will be found in the path we will pursue. Other sources again pronounce that the whole body of Indians have separated and retired in small bodies to the glades. The latter conjecture seems to be the one most generally received and in my opinion the most probable. . . . Great hardships are anticipated in this march—the heat is now fast becoming oppressive and the men will no doubt suffer as much from the exhaustion of the severe heat, as they have hitherto done from the severe cold." *Charleston Southern Patriot*, April 27, 1836.

33. *Proceedings*, 24th Cong., 2d sess., S. Doc. 224, 36.

34. *New York Evening Star, for the Country*, July 23, 1836; *Charleston Mercury*, May 18, 1836.

35. Brown, *Florida's Peace River Frontier*, 45; "Journal of the Volunteer Company from Columbia: Feb. 11, 1836–May 12, 1836, Benjamin T. Elmore, Captain," 54, South Carolina Department of Archives and History; *Tampa Morning Tribune*, July 25, 1897; John Lee Williams, *The Territory of Florida* (New York, A.T. Goodrich, 1837; reprint, Gainesville, University of Florida Press, 1962), 234. The Louisianans never reached Talakchopco. Their adventures and misadventures are detailed in James Barr, *A Correct & Authentic Narrative of the Indian War in Florida with a Description of Dade's Massacre and an Account of the extreme suffering for want of provisions of the Army—having been obliged to eat horses' and dogs' flesh &c &c.* (New York: Narine, 1836); *Tampa Morning Tribune*, July 25, 1897; Williams, *The Territory of Florida*, 234. See also Canter Brown Jr., "Persifor F. Smith, the Louisiana Volunteers, and Florida's Second Seminole War," *Louisiana History* 34 (Fall 1993): 389–410.

36. *Charleston Mercury*, April 30, 1836; *Columbia Southern Times and State Gazette*, May 6, 1836; *Charleston Courier*, April 30, 1836; *Army and Navy Chronicle*, May 12, 1836, 294.

37. Smith, *Sketch of the Seminole War*, 293–94; Myer M. Cohen, *Notices of Florida and the Campaigns* (Charleston, S.C.: Burgess and Honour, 1836; reprint, Gainesville: University of Florida Press, 1964), 208.

38. Cohen, *Notices of Florida*, 209–217; *Columbia Southern Times and State Gazette*, May 6, 1836; *Charleston Courier*, May 4, 1836; *Charleston Southern Patriot*, May 3, 1836; letter of Winfield Scott, May 11, 1836, from *Washington Globe*, quoted *Greenville Mountaineer*, June 11, 1836; 25th Cong., 2d sess., H. Doc. 78, 439; *Charleston Mercury*, May 10, 1836; *Army and Navy Chronicle*, May 12, 1836, p. 294.

39. *Daily Savannah Republican*, May 7, 1836; *Charleston Courier*, May 9, 1836.

40. Orders, Head Quarters of the Left Wing of the Army of Florida, St. Augustine, May 1, 1836, Bull Papers; *Army and Navy Chronicle*, June 2, 1836, 349.

41. *Charleston Southern Patriot*, May 10, 1836; *Charleston Courier*, May 6, 9, 10, 1836.

42. Butler, John Chesnut, and fifty other disabled soldiers arrived in Pensacola on April 23, 1836, on board the USS *Motto*. *Army and Navy Chronicle*, May 12, 1836, 293; John Chesnut to Mrs. John Chesnut, April 21, 1836, James Chesnut Papers, SCL; Discharge of Pierce Mason Butler, Butler Papers; Richards, "Butler," 23.

43. *Charleston Courier*, May 16, July 20, 1836; Paul Quattlebaum to Butler, June 20, 1836, Butler Papers; *Pendleton Messenger* quoted in *Charleston Courier*, July 22, August 19, 1836; Pickens to Hammond, August 6, 1836, Hammond Papers.

44. Butler to Hammond, August 26, October 30, 1836, James L. Clark to Hammond, October 22, 1836, Hammond Papers.

45. Mahon, *Second Seminole War*, 161–63.

46. Richards, "Butler," 23.

47. *Charleston Mercury*, May 18, 1836.

48. Cohen, *Notices of Florida and the Campaigns*, 5, 224–28; Smith, *Sketch of the Seminole War*, iii–iv, 77–78, 281–82, 294.

49. *Charleston Mercury*, July 11, 1836.

50. *Charleston Mercury*, July 28, 1836; Potter, *The War in Florida*, vii.

51. Mahon, *Second Seminole War*, 164–165.

52. In a little more than two years, Bull was dead, "injustly, cruelly and horribly murdered by his own servants." Wimbish to Bull, September 21, 1836, Bull Papers; *Aiken Telegraph* quoted in *Charleston Courier*, October 14, 1836, January 14, February 5, 1839; *Army and Navy Chronicle*, November 10, 1836, 300; Henry H. Cawley, "Inscriptions from Cemetery, Old Presbyterian Church Willington, S.C.," *South Carolina Historical & Genealogical Magazine* 28 (October 1927): 249.

53. Although the official balloting in the South Carolina Senate was secret, one participant divulged to a friend the results: "Nine of P's [Preston's] little partisans had no more tact than to make his purposes apparent by voting for him today on the Ballot for Governor, to which Butler is elected in the very handsomest style and will be sustained by the highest influences." Thomson T. Player to James Hammond, December 12, 1836, Hammond Papers; Richards, "Butler," 23–24.

54. Carol Bleser, ed., *Secret and Sacred: The Diaries of James Henry Hammond, a Southern Slaveholder* (New York: Oxford University Press, 1988), 36.

55. Ibid., 54, 55, 61–62, 75.

56. Ibid., 178–19; Jack Allen Meyer, *South Carolina in the Mexican War: A History of*

the Palmetto Regiment of Volunteers, 1846–1917 (Columbia: University of South Carolina Press, 1996), 88–91; Edgar, *South Carolina*, 341; Foreman, "Pierce Mason Butler," 25–28; Richards, "Butler," 28.

57. Edward McCrady and Samuel Ashe, *Cyclopedia of Eminent and Representative Men of the Carolinas of the Nineteenth Century with a Brief Historical Introduction on South Carolina*, 2 vols. (Madison, Wis.: Brant and Fuller, 1892), 1: 643–45.

9

Forgotten Struggle

The Second Creek War in West Florida, 1837–1854

BRIAN RUCKER

Residents of the Florida Panhandle thought they had escaped the ravages that befell the rest of the territory during the Second Seminole War. However, in the spring of 1837, West Florida's fortunes changed when Creek refugees from Alabama descended into the thick woods and swamps of the region. The Second Creek War had come to Florida, a forgotten struggle that would convulse the Panhandle for the next year and lead to unrest that would stretch to 1854.

In the decades prior to this conflict, only a small group of natives resided in the Panhandle. The Apalachicola Indians were the largest group, but smaller bands lived along the shores of St. Andrew's, Choctawhatchee, Blackwater, and Escambia bays. Indians and half bloods often visited Pensacola, the major city of the region. They came into the area to hunt and fish, to find pasture for their cattle, and to obtain supplies in town.[1] Many white residents of West Florida were suspicious of these Indians, regarding them as cattle and horse thieves, drunks, and "rascals."[2] Even George Catlin, the celebrated painter of Native Americans, saw them in a less than favorable light. While visiting Pensacola in 1835, he painted a family catching and drying redfish on Santa Rosa Island. He observed, "The sum total that can be learned or seen of them (like all others that are half civilized) is, that they are to be pitied."[3]

Friction and mistrust grew between whites and remaining Indians throughout the 1820s and the early 1830s. The natives were considered a threat, especially by slaveholders who believed they helped slaves to escape and also harbored runaways. Such presumptions were reinforced when runaway slaves actually were found in local camps.[4] Henry M. Brackenridge, caretaker of the government-owned Naval Live Oaks Plantation on Santa Rosa peninsula, was concerned merely because "a few poor Indian families" had made the peninsula their hunting ground. He felt such activities increased the chances of destructive fires among the live oak stands. "The straggling Indians must be driven off," Brackenridge urged the secretary of the navy. "This has been their

9.1. Richard Keith Call
(Florida State Library
and Archives).

hunting ground, and unless they be ordered away, the fires will be continually breaking out from their camps."[5]

Roaming bands of Indians also inhibited development of the region's resources. Pensacolian Juan de la Rua had problems building a water-powered sawmill on Pond Creek in present-day Santa Rosa County. Indians reportedly frightened away de la Rua's laborers, and by 1828 he had sold the site and left others to worry about dependable labor.[6] Cattlemen in the area were alarmed as well. Small bands of natives frequently raided American cattle holdings and made use of the beeves for their own purposes.[7] In 1829 a number of irate settlers from the Pensacola area, concerned about the cattle raids, petitioned the government to take decisive action against the Indians.[8]

The increasing push to remove all of Florida's Indians to the west reached a crisis point in November and December 1835. Sugar plantations throughout central and south Florida were destroyed by the natives, and Major Francis

9.2. Hix Chijo, Lower Creek in Pensacola in 1834, by George Washington Sully (Special Collections, John C. Pace Library, University of West Florida).

Dade and more than 100 American troops were massacred in Sumter County. The Second Seminole War officially had begun.[9] The outbreak of war prompted Pensacola-based troops to prepare for action. The navy organized a force for use against the Seminoles, composed chiefly of men from the *Vandalia* under the command of Lieutenant Louis M. Goldsborough.[10] Governor Richard Keith Call also ordered the formation of militia regiments in Escambia and Walton counties, asking the counties to furnish sixty and twenty volunteers, respectively, for a term of six months' service. The troops were to form as soon as possible at San Pedro, Madison County. These developments caught the inhabitants of northwest Florida by surprise, and the regiment was not organized for quite some time.[11]

In the spring of 1836, settlers living in the Florida Panhandle received additional incentives to organize militias. Alabama volunteer companies, stopping at Pensacola on their way to the "Indian Wars," no doubt inspired many residents to join the crusade. Newspaper accounts detailed the violent Creek resistance that had erupted near Columbus, Georgia, and in south Alabama. The Second Creek War had begun in this region, fueled by tribal factionalism and the growing fear of white removal. The rage of the Lower Creeks resulted in plantation raids, burned bridges, and deadly attacks on mail stages, steamboats, and pioneer families. Panic spread from Columbus to Apalachicola. West Florida settlers feared that the "renegade" Creeks, fleeing removal, would travel south to join forces with the Florida Seminoles. Such fears, accentuated by the outbreaks of violence, intensified concerns of Panhandle residents about the Indian presence.[12]

Volunteer companies finally were raised and organized in Escambia County in June 1836. Jackson Morton, who owned a large brickyard on Blackwater River and recently had been elected to Florida's legislative council, was designated colonel of the First Regiment, Florida militia.[13] Fifty-seven volunteers appeared at the battalion muster on the west side of the Escambia River, and more than thirty volunteers gathered at the Black Water settlement (the present-day Milton area).[14] Local inhabitants enthusiastically supported the volunteers. Addressing the militia, Colonel Morton noted that "even the 'lasses of the woods' had caught the contagion of patriotic feeling—that even their bosoms glowed with enthusiasm in the cause of our suffering fellow-citizens of the east." Morton was referring to some thirty women from the Black Water settlement who were raising funds to equip their "gallant sons, brothers, and sweethearts" for the upcoming struggle against the hostiles.[15]

The Escambia volunteers boarded the cutter *Washington* destined for St. Marks on July 9 and were encamped near Tallahassee a few weeks later. By September they were on duty near the Suwannee River, where they were divided into three detachments—one stationed at Charles' Ferry on the Suwannee, one at a plantation in the neighborhood, and a third about six miles from the San Pedro settlement.[16] Coincidentally, Escambia County officials received orders for more volunteers, and by October thirty new militiamen had departed for Tallahassee.[17] By then, the war was beginning to affect the inhabitants of northwest Florida. The *Pensacola Gazette*'s editor reflected that the people of Escambia County were too remote to have experienced the more unfortunate aspects of the war, but he also recognized the pressure the war had exerted upon the county, pointing out that, of less than 300 Escambia men eligible for military duty, close to one-third already were in the field.[18] The difficulty of bringing the war to a speedy and decisive conclusion led to further fears and concerns among West Floridians, and in January 1837, the legislative council called for more militia troops from the area.[19]

Events soon transpired which brought the reality of war directly to the white inhabitants of the Panhandle, not from the threat of the Seminoles but from the Second Creek War in Alabama. For nearly a year, a large number of Creeks along the Alabama and Georgia sides of the Chattahoochee River had been opposing removal. Friction in the southeast between Red Stick Creeks and Creeks friendly to the United States had existed for decades. The rivalry earlier had resulted in the Creek War, and recent federal removal efforts had precipitated a new outbreak of violence. Beset by economic and social woes, usually caused by unscrupulous whites and an unsympathetic federal government, the fragile "Creek nation" fell prey to the old factionalism. Renegade Creeks who opposed removal attacked isolated farmhouses, steamboats, frontier settlements, and travelers in the area from Columbus, Georgia, to Eufaula, Alabama. These marauding Indians began moving westwardly to the upper reaches of the Pea River where they were defeated in February and March 1837 near Hobdy's Bridge and along the Pea River by Alabama militiamen under the command of Brigadier General William Wellborn. Following these losses, the renegade Creeks broke up into smaller bands and moved southwesterly along the courses of the Choctawhatchee River into Walton County, Florida, murdering and pillaging as they traveled. General Wellborn, commanding the Barbour County [Ala.] Rangers, wanted to pursue the Creeks into Florida as far as Blackwater Bay and the camp of the Escribano Indians, who were allegedly aiding the fugitives.[20]

Archibald Smith, United States agent to the Apalachicola Indians, learned in late February that renegade Creeks were moving south down the Choctawhatchee River, stealing canoes and plundering as they went. On February 28, the members of the Alberson family, living on the Alabama-Florida border, were murdered, and several other families were reported as missing, presumably murdered. Smith heard reports that the Creek women were killing their own children to facilitate their flight and were fighting as savagely as the men. He also was informed that 125 to 400 renegade Creeks had entered Florida and were traveling toward Yellow River and the Pensacola area. He believed they were seeking a haven in the unpopulated forests that stretched from Pensacola to the Apalachicola Rivers and they would likely prey off the outlying farms for subsistence. Smith also received the disquieting news that the Creeks were heading for a settlement of friendly Indians at Escribano Point on Blackwater Bay. According to reports, the Creeks had been obtaining supplies and ammunition from the Escribano Indians and were intent on reaching their camp. Realizing the urgency of the situation, Smith set out hurriedly in an effort to warn settlers and to reach the Escribano Indians before the renegades did. He also managed to send a letter to Pensacola requesting the suspension of the sale of powder and lead to Indians and to white men suspected of selling to the Indians.[21] Smith's report to the commissioner of Indian Affairs details his frantic overland journey to Blackwater Bay and his encounter with the Escribano Indians:

I was told that . . . it would probably cost me my life to make the trip but having then traveled two days I did not wish to return, wishing to see the black Water if possible before the arrival of the Runaway Creeks. . . . We pushed in bringing the sad news to every settlement on our way untill we arrived at the head of black Water bay. . . . [The Escribano Indians] are 41 in number, besides two very old Spaniards who are intermarried with them. They informed me that their fathers emigrated to that spot about the time of the Revolutionary War, . . . that they came from the old Tuckabatchie Town, near where the Town of Montgomery in Alabama now stands. . . . There are 9 or 10 men and all have families. Some have children & others have not. . . . They speak english tolerable well most of them and make a support by catching Fish and oysters for the Pensacola market, which I was told is 20 miles distant. They have [diverse] little sail boats, and travel wherever they please. I was much pleased with their conduct and told them I was sent there by the Government to inform them that the Creek Indians had broke away . . . committed several murders, & were then I thought not far from them. . . . They then told me that one of their women was out in the woods some few miles back perhaps the day before and saw two Indian boys who informed her they belonged to 4 Camps of Coweta Indians who were a few miles back, that they were resolved to die rather than emigrate to Arkansas, that a great many more would come down shortly and endeavor to live on the Coast from there to the mouth of Choctawhatchie. From what I have seen I am fearful that distress will pervade the most part of West Florida for some time. . . . I told the Indians on Black Water that their future happiness now depended on their own Conduct. . . . They assured me they should Keep a vigilant watch, that should [the Creeks] attempt to come near them they should remove their families to Pensacola, and assist the whites in subduing them. In this I greatly encouraged them, and took my leave.[22]

Northwest Floridians immediately took action. A meeting of Pensacola citizens was called to raise a militia force to defend the frontier settlers. Commodore Alexander J. Dallas of the Pensacola Navy Yard agreed to send men and boats to guard the provisions depots that would be established. Colonel Jackson Morton took control of the volunteer company, and on March 8 a mounted company was sent to the Black Water settlement where they were joined by local volunteers. Joseph Bonifay, a local citizen familiar with the area, traveled east as a scout to obtain information on Indian activities.[23] A military supply depot named Camp Dallas quickly was established at the head of East

Bay, and a United States military force, comprised of thirty-six mounted men, made its way up Yellow River, then eastward to Shoal River, and finally back to Camp Dallas. Wet weather and inhospitable swamps hindered their progress, and the forces returned having found only an abandoned camp.[24]

Military spies and agents soon made contact with a band of thirty-five Creeks who agreed to come in peacefully. In Pensacola, Army Major Henry Wilson waited to conduct them to Mobile Point, Alabama, where nearly 3,000 Creeks were being assembled for their western relocation. Excitement in the Pensacola area gradually subsided as it appeared that the majority of the renegades had dissolved into the wilderness north of Choctawhatchee Bay. The *Gazette* began to downplay the danger by noting that the Indians would do no injury except perhaps stealing their cattle for food.[25]

Optimism proved premature. The renegade Creeks soon appeared in the area, and settlers in Walton and Escambia counties again were alarmed. Several bands appeared at Mallett's Landing on the northern shore of Choctawhatchee Bay. One settler attempted to employ them as laborers on his farm as a ruse to entrap them, and another settler actually captured four Indians. The Mallett's Landing settlers were eager for troops to be sent to their community, but they expressed no fear of being murdered by the Indians. To them, the natives sought only concealment. Nevertheless, the whites were concerned with the Indians killing their cattle.[26]

The situation deteriorated rapidly. On April 15, a party of eight to ten fugitive Creeks arrived in Lumberton (present-day Milton) on the Blackwater River to purchase supplies, but after they finished trading, a number of whites attempted to detain them. The Indians fled, but not before the whites shot one in the leg. The wounded Indian drew a knife, cut his own throat, and then, reportedly, threw the knife to his son and ordered him to do the same. The youth, about ten years of age, began to do so, but the whites wrested the knife from him. The locals then took the father, tied a rope around his neck, and dragged him under a raft of lumber lying in the river until he was dead. An Indian woman and a boy (likely the son of the slain Indian) also were seized at this time but were not harmed.[27]

Editor Benjamin Drake Wright of the *Pensacola Gazette* condemned the actions at Black Water. Commodore Dallas was alarmed at the incident and feared the Indians would retaliate by raiding frontier settlements in the area. The commodore sent a party of men under the command of Lieutenant Neil M. Howison to protect the Black Water community. Howison used an Indian woman captured at Black Water, along with two friendly natives, to communicate with the camp of fugitive Creeks. The two friendly Indians returned the next day and reported that the Creeks threatened to shoot them and would not let the woman return. They also stated that the renegades had been informed of the Black Water incident and were "very much exasperated."[28]

Dallas was correct when he predicted retaliation; on April 23 the renegades struck. A party of seven Walton County men, who had been traveling along the upper Shoal River searching for their cattle, suddenly were attacked in their camp on Gum Creek at dawn. Five members of the party were shot and clubbed to death, but two who were apart from the others managed to hide in the thick cover of the nearby swamp. These two eventually made their way back to some of the Walton County settlements, and word of the attack soon spread. Settlers appealed for help, and plans were made for constructing a community fort. The inhabitants feared for their lives as well as their crops and livestock, since sparsely populated Walton County was unable to raise a force sufficient to defend the widely dispersed settlements.[29]

The editor of the Pensacola paper reacted to the Indian attack with considerable insight. While recognizing the plight of Walton County settlers, he also observed that the incident probably was sparked by the earlier savage conduct of the whites toward the Indian party at Black Water. In a stance uncharacteristic of a newspaper in an area being threatened by Indians, Benjamin Drake Wright voiced this view:

> These misguided savages were seeking concealment. They were not disposed to shed blood of the white man, but the outrage committed at Black Water, has exasperated them to the last degree, and we may now look for a savage war with all its attendant horrors. The Indians are incapable of discriminating. They imagine that the outrage . . . shews the disposition of the white man, generally, toward them, and the unhappy consequence, that before they can be driven from their present hiding places, many valuable lives will be sacrificed. On whose head rests the blood of these victims?[30]

This editorial opinion is considerably more favorable to the Indians than earlier ones in the paper. Quite different in tone, it reflects the moral ambiguity that the Indian problem often presented to the thoughtful and conscientious segments of the white population.[31] Others, however, believed in a different policy. Forty miles north of the Shoal River attack, Creeks had returned to Dale County in Alabama and attacked several farms. Seven members of the Hart family were massacred, and in response Captain Arch Justice from Dale County led a force of thirty-five men in pursuit of the raiders. Justice had previously fought the Creeks in Alabama, and he located the Creek trail down to Florida and followed it to the Shoal River, where local citizens joined

Justice's expedition. There on Shoal River, below the Cawthon ford, they came across the Creek camp and attacked it. Fourteen Creeks were killed, and the rest were captured and sent to Pensacola. Justice wanted to press further down the Shoal, but his men were exhausted and running low on provisions. General William Wellborn from Alabama (who had earlier defeated the Creeks at Hobdy's Bridge in Alabama) arrived with his battalion to relieve Justice. But by that time, the Creeks had escaped deeper into the Panhandle.[32] Wellborn petitioned Alabama's governor Clement Clay asking for permission to raise 200 troops to pursue the Indians into Florida. Wellborn was afraid that the work of federal authorities to bring in the Indians peacefully would just allow the warriors to regroup, and he felt the only way to victory was to relentlessly pursue them until they gave up unconditionally. Some Alabama citizens believed that the Creeks would move their families into removal camps temporarily just to feed and arm themselves at government expense, and then go on the warpath again. Governor Clay denied Wellborn's request, which did prevent the Alabama troops from possibly driving more of the refugees into armed violence against the whites.[33]

The Black Water incident and the outbreak of violence in Walton County already were hampering efforts to induce the fugitive Creeks to come in peacefully. Major Wilson and Marine Lieutenant John G. Reynolds were sent to Escribano Point and along the shores of Blackwater Bay in attempts to persuade the Indians to join the emigrating Creeks at Mobile Point. Using friendly natives as interpreters, Reynolds established communications with several Indian groups, and by the end of May, despite the heightened tensions, seventy Indians had come in, including the Escribano Indians. Reynolds arranged for them to be fed and protected, and they were then transported by boat to Mobile Point.[34]

In May, Indians attacked and killed at least twelve Walton County settlers, and Governor Call urged an immediate organization of the county's militia. Because of the violent conflict then under way in the rest of the territory, federal troops in the South could not be diverted for service in West Florida. Walton County citizens constructed a blockhouse in the central portion of the county, and Colonel John L. McKinnon organized a company of militiamen. To protect the frontier settlements east of Pensacola, Colonel Morton was authorized to raise new militia forces in Escambia County. Morton was ill and unable to lead any forces at that time, however, and the local militia consequently remained in "total want of organization." The governor accordingly dispatched 73 Jackson County volunteers westward to aid in the removal of the renegade Creeks, and their commander, Colonel Leavin Brown, was placed in charge of the campaign. Morton, who soon recovered his health, also raised a company at Black Water, and by June 1 troops were scouring the countryside from Yellow River to the Choctawhatchee River. But despite the presence of militiamen, Walton County settlers were in a state of panic.[35]

Pensacola residents were kept informed of the latest activities from the "seat of the war" in Walton County, and among the news items they received were accounts of several atrocities. The first incident occurred in early May at Mallett's Landing on Choctawhatchee Bay. A friendly Indian named Jim, who had served as a guide and interpreter for the whites, was murdered by a group of drunken whites. Wright once more became indignant at the treatment of the Indians and railed against the white attackers:

> These *heroes* are supposed to have been drunk when they perpetrated this outrage—they are the very last persons to go out with their neigh-bors against the hostile Indians, and expend their heroism upon those who are inoffensive and friendly! It is high time that these unprincipled wretches should be made to pay with their lives, the penalty of thus violating the laws of the land, and shedding human blood. The Indian, when friendly and peaceable, is as much entitled to the protection of our laws, as the best man in the community.[36]

A more sordid incident occurred shortly thereafter near Alaqua. Colonel Brown's Jackson County militiamen, while searching the Alaqua Creek area, killed twelve Indians. No whites were injured. Reportedly, though, the mur-dered Indians had been prisoners, one man and the rest women and children. Various accounts of this "massacre" began to spread.[37] Brown's own report was as damning as the rumors. He stated that only nine women and children were killed, along with a male prisoner. The male prisoner had been recruited as a guide by Captain Stephen Daniel, a company commander, with the promise that he would be killed if he misled the troops on their way to an Indian camp. Brown's report reveals the outcome:

> We followed him for some distance through swamps, hammocks and lakes until daylight when, finding he had no idea of conducting us to the camp, I ordered the command to turn back to where we had left the other prisoners. We returned to the [Alaqua Creek] about one hour after sunrise, Capt. Daniel's company having charge of the prisoners in the rear, when Capt. Daniel and nearly all his companions fired on the Indian prisoner who had led us through so many difficulties during the night. . . . The women and children, taking fright at this, started to run, when they were all shot down and left on the ground. I then crossed the

river and found . . . that one of the [other] Indian prisoners had poisoned himself and died. I then marched to this place [Lagrange] with the remainder of the prisoners to obtain supplies.[38]

Lieutenant John G. Reynolds's report of the incident differed from Brown's. Shortly after the massacre, Reynolds had traveled along the north shore of Choctawhatchee Bay on his way to visit some Indians reported to be at Escribano Point. On the way, the lieutenant stopped at the massacre site and inspected it. What he found appalled him:

The spot was not more than fifteen feet in diameter. I minutely examined the place, and am firmly of the opinion, that the poor devils were penned up and slaughtered like cattle and such was the opinion of the friendly Indians in company. The shrieks of the poor children were distinctly heard at a house distant, I should think a quarter of a mile. Several were scalped, and all who had earrings, had their ears slit with knives, in order to possess themselves of the silver. I do think this one of the most outrageous acts civilized men could be guilty of.[39]

Though condemned strongly at the time, the Alaqua incident soon was forgotten by the *Gazette*. Brown's report of the affair was accepted and never investigated, and Reynolds's subsequent efforts at rounding up the fugitives were hampered by the incident. The lieutenant reported that the Indians "are so frightened by the worse than savage cruelty and treachery which they have met with from the whites, that they will be sure either to fight or fly, whenever they are approached by the whites in numbers." Public attention meanwhile was focused on the continuing attempts to defeat and remove the renegade Creeks from northwest Florida. Colonel Brown's hard-driving and successful campaign against the natives soon won him local respect.[40]

Indians were still seen during the summer of 1837 as far west as the shores of Blackwater Bay. John Hunt, who operated a brickyard on the eastern shore of the bay, reported that the renegades were in the area and that his slaves saw them and conversed with them frequently. There were threats of Indians near the white settlements along Yellow River, and reports were received of parties of six to twenty Indians in the countryside between Blackwater River and Yellow River. Finding the natives in the area's swamps and forests, however, proved to be next to impossible. Morton's volunteer force at Black Water scoured the Yellow River and Blackwater River areas for a week in June without sighting any Indians.[41]

Colonel Brown requested the transfer of Morton's volunteers for service in Walton County, but the request was rejected because the men were needed to protect Escambia's eastern frontier settlements. Instead, volunteers from St. Joseph and Apalachicola arrived at Pensacola and were sent to Black Water in order to form a sizable force. Brown intended for this force to move eastward while his own men pushed westward from Alaqua, thus catching the Indians in a pincer movement.[42]

By early July, Escambia County citizens had organized a new Escambia militia regiment. The *Gazette* encouraged this move and noted that an efficiently organized militia was imperative at the present state of crisis. The editor observed that not only was the threat of the renegade Creeks to the east a problem, but the disquieting presence of 3,000 Creeks assembled for deportation at Mobile point, only a short distance west of Pensacola, also had to be considered.[43]

News from Colonel Brown at Lagrange shortly thereafter served to fuel the fears of West Florida residents—the largest engagements to date were being fought in Walton County. On May 19, a band of Walton County militiamen had cornered a party of Creeks near the "Cow Pens," west of the Choctawhatchee River (near present-day Bruce). The natives retreated into a thick swamp, but the whites followed them, and a sharp skirmish ensued. A number of Indians and whites were killed or wounded.[44]

Subsequently, on July 4, Colonel Brown's troops had a heated engagement with approximately 125 Indians on Shoal River. The natives were routed, and they fled across the river. Three militiamen were wounded; eight to ten Indians were killed, and several were wounded. The exact number of Indians killed was in question, since the Creeks "immediately bore them off and threw many of them into the river as soon as they fell." In their retreat, the Creeks threw off many of their packs. The militiamen discovered a gold watch and $263 among the Indians' belongings, plunder from previous raids. The watch belonged to William Flournoy, whose murder in early May 1836 had opened the Creek War in Georgia and Alabama.[45]

Brown's forces attacked the Creeks again on July 19 on Alaqua Creek in Walton County. The Indian force was estimated to be about seventy warriors. Captain G. S. Hawkins of St. Joseph led the attack into the swamp, but while cheering his men and waving his hat Hawkins was hit by three shots, seriously wounding him. After a brisk fight of twenty minutes, the Indians fell back. Five Creeks were killed, one militiaman was killed, and five others were wounded. The steamboat *Marion* was sent to Lagrange, and a number of wounded and sick militiamen were brought to Pensacola for medical treatment.[46]

Brown's persistent attacks on the Creeks proved successful. By August the Indians were becoming dispirited, and many were surrendering on their own accord. Major Henry Wilson, using friendly Indians, succeeded in persuading a number of the Indian bands to give themselves up, and it was anticipated that his efforts soon would net the entire Indian population without any further loss of life.[47] Cosapinia, one of the principal chiefs, surrendered at Lagrange on August 28 and was persuaded to bring in other Creeks. The chief set out with several runners westward along the north shore of Choctawhatchee Bay, and he was asked to talk with as many fugitives as possible and induce them to come in at Escribano Point.[48]

The panic began to subside some in the western area of the Panhandle as individual Indians and bands of renegade Creeks surrendered. One detriment to a speedy resolution was the incessant pursuit of the Creeks by the whites over the course of the summer. The militia movements, skirmishes, and accounts of the Alaqua massacre dispersed many Creeks into smaller parties that fled into the more remote sections of the countryside. Major Wilson's attempts at peaceful inducement, therefore, were regarded suspiciously by the Indians. Colonel Brown temporarily suspended hostilities in late summer in order to facilitate a more peaceful atmosphere for Wilson's efforts. Forces were stationed along East Bay to take in any fugitives who appeared there, and by September militia patrols could locate no Indians in the immediate vicinity of Pensacola.[49]

By October, conditions eased in Walton County, as the remaining bands of Creeks made their way eastward. Walton County had suffered several months of panic and mayhem, accented by raids and skirmishes. The U.S. Superior Court failed to hold its regular session in the county because of the disturbances, and the economy was seriously disrupted. The severe hardships of settlers in Walton and Washington counties led Governor Call in October to order rations to be supplied to those inhabitants most in need.[50]

The main body of the Creeks was moving eastwardly. In late 1837, a large band of the Creeks operating between the Chipola and the Apalachicola rivers harried Jackson County inhabitants, killing cattle and harboring runaway slaves. In late December approximately eighty fugitives were brought in near the Choctawhatchee River, and several weeks later ninety more were captured west of the Apalachicola River. Military and governmental authorities estimated that 100 more were still free and making their way toward the Seminoles in the eastern section of Florida.[51]

Even though the largest bands of Creeks made their way to the Seminoles in Central Florida, a number of fugitive Creeks still remained in the Panhandle. Brickyard owner John Hunt on Blackwater Bay complained in the fall of 1837 that a sizable number of his cows, oxen, and hogs had been stolen, presumably by Indians still in the area.[52] In October, a camp of Creeks numbering between sixty and seventy was located "near the Chipola swamp on the west side of the Apalachicola." The Indians fled when discovered. The following month, a party of thirteen were captured north of Apalachicola, possibly members of the same band.[53] Later in November, Governor Call learned that a sizable group of refugees had appeared on the Choctawhatchee River, and he hoped to persuade them to move peaceably to the west. A party of three appeared in a canoe and boarded a keelboat on the Choctawhatchee. The Creeks purchased corn and other provisions, paid in cash, and left peacefully. The Creek "requested the captain of the boat to bring them powder, for which they offered one dollar per pound in specie: their intention, they stated, was to remain quiet, but if fired upon by the whites, to resist to the last."[54] In January 1838, a barge on the Choctawhatchee River was robbed by Creeks, and in March of the same year Governor Richard Keith Call visited Lagrange on Choctawhatchee Bay in another attempt to bring in Indians still frequenting the area.[55]

By the summer of 1838, the Indian threat in the area had disappeared almost completely. The major concern of West Floridians turned instead to the issue of reimbursement for their militia service. The Escambia County volunteers that had been in service in 1836–37 were never paid for their time, and Colonel Jackson Morton even petitioned Governor Call for relief for the volunteers. The Escambia volunteers had never been paid because of financial problems and bureaucratic paperwork. Morton, who had earlier pledged responsibility for the payment of his troops, had already been forced to pay out some $500 to $600 from his own resources. Governor Call promised that payment would faithfully be made to the volunteers as soon as possible.[56]

One casualty of the Second Creek War was the Apalachicola Indians. Though some had helped Governor Call track down the fugitive Creeks, most whites viewed them with suspicion, citing instances where the Apalachicolas had taken in Creek warriors. Federal authorities then threatened to cut off their annuities and leave them to the jurisdiction of the Florida laws, and the Apalachicolas subsequently agreed to surrender their lands and emigrate. On October 28, 1838, the entire group of Apalachicola Indians and a number of other Indians left Florida for the West aboard three ships.[57]

Not all of the Native Americans had been removed, however. In fact, during the Florida Constitutional Convention at the West Florida town of St. Joseph during the winter of 1838–39, reports of large bands of Indians at nearby St. Andrew's Bay filtered into the convention hall, leading to nervous delegates.[58]

Some of the Indians definitely had escaped removal, and small bands continued to make their presence known throughout the Panhandle. Along Santa Rosa Sound, near present-day Mary Esther (Okaloosa County), a U.S. mail carrier reported two Indians camped at one of the remote station houses. There were also complaints of cattle being killed between Yellow River and East Bay, possibly by roaming bands of Indians.[59]

Farther to the east were more violent incidents, with settlers being murdered by fugitive Creeks along the Apalachicola River and in Holmes Valley. Just south of present-day Wewahitchka, Thomas Richards built a two-story enclosed blockhouse known as Fort Place. On January 14, 1838, a band of Creeks came up the river by canoe and launched an attack on the fort that lasted all night. Richards himself was killed in this incident. The hostile Creeks attacked settlements in Calhoun County in early 1840; several people were killed in a raid at Rowlett's Mills seven miles north of Fort Gadsden. Even a military patrol on the Apalachicola was fired at; several mules were killed, the soldiers fled, and the Creeks made off with their baggage. Following this, another raid occurred at the Harlan residence west of Ricko's Bluff, where several family members wee killed. A military post was established on the river near Blountstown, but in May three more families fell victim to the Creek depredations. In September 1840 Wiley Jones's wife and two children were killed, along with another individual, in the Econfina community (north Bay County.) By mid-October of that year, a militia company was raised in Marianna (Jackson County) to pursue Indians spotted in that vicinity.[60]

On August 14, 1842, Brigadier General William J. Worth, in charge of the U.S. forces in Florida, issued a proclamation which officially ended the Second Seminole War. Two weeks later, though, a band of about fifty renegade Creeks murdered the Perkins family near Orange Hill in Washington County. The Creeks had presumably not received word of the peace agreement. Local settlers quickly appealed to the government for protection. Secretary of War John C. Spencer ordered two U.S. infantry companies to Washington County and also authorized the officer in charge to employ some fifty local settlers to act as guides and assistants. Spencer also authorized a reward of $200 for every warrior taken and $50 for every other Indian. The Washington County settlers, however, did not wait for the army detachment to arrive. A mounted company was organized, with Stephen Daniel elected captain, and the whites quickly began searching the countryside for the Creeks.[61]

Instead of sending the soldiers, General Worth sent another messenger to the renegade Creeks to inform them that hostilities had ceased. Worth had no intention of stirring up further fighting, believing it was now easier to bring in the Indians without a display of force. But the Washington County volunteers were already scouting the countryside and eagerly anticipating the arrival of the regular troops and payment for their services. In late November, Spencer finally informed the local settlers that the soldiers would not be sent because of the end of hostilities. Spencer also reported that the volunteers would not be paid for their services because they were acting without proper authorization.[62]

According to local tradition, Daniel's Washington County volunteers were incensed at the failure of the government to provide protection and payment for their services. The company supposedly renewed their campaign and killed a wounded Indian near Falling Waters Hill. Learning that the main group of Creeks was moving to the northwest, Daniel's mounted force followed them and launched a surprise attack on them as they were camped on Wright's Creek. Twenty-two Indians were killed in an assault that was more or less a massacre. One local authority believes that the Indians were so quickly defeated because they had just been given solemn assurances by a messenger from General Worth that hostilities had ceased. If the episode is true, the "rogue company" violated peace terms that had been agreed upon by General Worth and Florida's Indian leaders.[63] It is interesting to note that the officer in charge of this volunteer company, Captain Stephen Daniel, appears to be the same officer who was intimately connected with the "Alaqua massacre" of 1837. If the account is true, it is only further evidence of the intolerance and the violence so characteristic between Panhandle whites and the Indians during the antebellum period.

Nor was the violence at an end. Henry A. Nunes, a citizen of Pensacola, was bound for Apalachicola aboard his barge *Emperor* in late 1843. Nunes's barge wrecked along the Gulf coast eighteen miles west of St. Andrew's Bay on December 31, 1843, and he and his crew of five set up a temporary camp to await aid. While hunting and fishing for food, the whites stumbled upon four Indians—two men, a woman, and a child. They appeared friendly, and Nunes gave them some pork, peas, and salt. On January 8, 1844, the Indians came to the camp and Nunes gave them breakfast. Later that afternoon, after Nunes and two others left the camp, the Indians suddenly attacked. The whites scattered in confusion, and Nunes managed to make his way to a nearby settlement. The next day Nunes raised a group of men and returned to the site, finding his property either destroyed or carried away, his female slave killed, and one of his employees, a Mr. Sayres, missing and presumably killed. The other members of the expedition appear to have escaped to safety in the same manner as Nunes.[64]

Nunes quickly reported the incident to Major Jacob Brown, Seventh Infantry, who was in command of the army post at Fort Barrancas, Pensacola. After a slight delay because of military channels, Brown ordered Lieutenant A. Montgomery and some twenty soldiers of the Seventh Infantry to examine the region between Choctawhatchee Bay and St. Andrew's Bay for any signs of

Indians, specifically the ones that attacked and robbed the Nunes party. Nunes served as a guide for the expedition. Using the U.S. sloop *Caroline*, the expedition sailed for St. Andrew's Bay in late February. The expedition found an Indian site near the location of the attack complete with huts, cornfields, and beehives. This could have been the motive behind the attack—the Indians may have feared Nunes telling of their presence in the area. While exploring the St. Andrew's Bay area, the U.S. troops spotted the Indians who had attacked Nunes and promptly gave chase. The Indians escaped, though, and the expedition returned to Pensacola after destroying all the Indian sites found.[65]

Lieutenant Montgomery recommended another expedition that would operate simultaneously from Choctawhatchee Bay eastward and from St. Andrew's Bay westward. In April, Montgomery led an expedition of forty men to search the Choctawhatchee and St. Andrew's Bay region. A similar expedition was launched in November, but no Indians were located.[66]

Such accounts alarmed frontier settlers in West Florida who knew that Indians were indeed lurking in the nearby woods. At the same time as the November 1844 expedition to the east, there had also been reports of several unidentified individuals seen near the head of East Bay in Santa Rosa County. Some surmised that they were runaway slaves, but it is also quite possible that these individuals were roaming Creek refugees. Two years later, Indian violence struck in that same area. In February 1846, a party of three men were hunting about ten miles from East Bay. Indians fired upon the men, killing a Mr. Pitts instantly. Pitts's brother was seriously wounded, but with the aid of Mr. Silcox, the other member of the party, the two managed to escape. The attack was quickly reported to Colonel Crane in charge of the military forces at Pensacola, and a detachment of soldiers under the command of Lieutenant Donaldson was dispatched. The troops went up Santa Rosa Sound in an effort to cut off the Indians, but after a week of searching, the detachment returned, having found no trace of the Indians. Once again, the swamps and forests of northwest Florida swallowed up the shrinking remnant of the Creek fugitives.[67]

In 1847 two Indians attacked Micajah King in the vicinity of St. Andrew's Bay. One of the Indians was "Old Joe," a Creek warrior who had led a small but notorious band of Indians in the area for years. During the struggle, King killed "Old Joe" with a knife blow; the second Indian subsequently fled into the woods. And finally, seven years later, the remaining Creeks continued to be a problem for the settlers of Washington County. The roaming Creeks had raided so many corn crops in the area that in 1854 the Florida legislature was forced to make a special appropriation for the relief of Washington County farmers.[68]

The majority of the Indians remaining in West Florida at this time began assimilating into white or even black society. To avoid removal, Indian families and individuals increasingly concealed their Indian ancestry and abandoned much of their culture. In 1853 a Florida law made it illegal for an Indian to remain within the state, and this provided a further impetus for the remaining Creeks to assimilate. Fear of removal and predominant racial attitudes led to a transformation of the remaining Indians. These isolated people slowly took on the lifestyles of rural southern farmers, including dress, housing styles, diet, religious beliefs, and even a penchant for square dancing. Often they would intermarry with whites (or African Americans, depending on their skin color), and this further diluted their Indian heritage. By 1900 most Creeks and half bloods had forgotten practically all of their Indian ancestry. Not until the mid-twentieth century did pride in Indian ancestry make a resurgence, and today several groups of West Florida Creeks have come forward in celebration of their Native American heritage. Communities with significant Indian blood can be found in Escambia, Santa Rosa, Walton, and Calhoun counties.[69]

The Second Creek War in West Florida, overshadowed by the larger conflict of the Second Seminole War in the rest of Florida, reflects the classic and often repeated frontier conflict—the struggle between the white settlers and the Indians, a struggle which involved land, cattle, racial bigotry, and the inability to compromise. For the white frontiersmen, it was a tragic episode—families were brutally murdered, property was destroyed and stolen, and communities were terrorized with fear. For the Creeks it was a more lasting tragedy. Many were killed, often unjustly; hundreds were deported to the West; and the remnant sank into poverty and lost their heritage and culture. There were atrocities on both sides; there were both white and red savages. There were voices of reason as well. Benjamin Drake Wright, editor of the *Pensacola Gazette*, offered at times rather enlightened views of the Native Americans. Major Wilson and Lieutenant Reynolds of the U.S. military were instrumental figures in conducting a peaceful removal of many West Florida Indians. And Archibald Smith risked his life to warn settlers and attempted to stop a dangerous collision of cultures. There were also noteworthy friendly Indians who served as vital guides, interpreters, messengers, and peacekeepers, Indians who often risked their lives and were eventually deported themselves. And the few who remained, who managed to escape detection, who managed to stay on lands they chose, who managed to blend into the natural and cultural landscape of West Florida—they were the true victors.

Notes

1. Lucius F. Ellsworth and Jane E. Dysart, "West Florida's Forgotten People: The Creek Indians from 1830 until 1970," *Florida Historical Quarterly* 59 (April 1981): 422–23.

2. Jane E. Dysart, "Another Road to Disappearance: Assimilation of Creek Indians in Pensacola, Florida, during the Nineteenth Century," *Florida Historical Quarterly* 61 (July 1982): 37–42.

3. George Catlin, *North American Indians, Being Letters and Notes on Their Manners, Customs, and Conditions, Written during Eight Years' Travel amongst the Wildest Tribes of Indians in North America, 1832–1839*, 2 vols. (Edinburgh: John Grant, 1926), 2: 36–40.

4. Dysart, "Another Road to Disappearance," 42; Leora M. Sutton, *Pensacola Personalities, 1781–1881* (Pensacola, 1981), 4: 35.

5. *American State Papers: Naval Affairs*, 4 vols. (Washington, D.C., 1860), 3: 924–25.

6. C. H. Overman, "After 111 Years, Bagdad Reaches the End," *Southern Lumber Journal and Building Materials Dealer* 43 (March 1939): 16.

7. *A. Gaylor v. J. Gaylor*, file 1830–2686, Circuit Court Records, Escambia County Judicial Building, Pensacola; *Pensacola Floridian*, 20 December 1823; and *Pensacola Gazette*, 29 April 1826, 10 March 1829.

8. *Pensacola Gazette*, 10 March 1829.

9. Joe Knetsch, *Florida's Seminole Wars, 1817–1858* (Charleston: Arcadia, 2003), 70–72; John K. Mahon, *History of the Second Seminole War, 1835–1842*, rev. ed. (Gainesville: University of Florida Press, 1992), 87–113; and John K. Mahon and Brent R. Weisman, "Florida's Seminole and Miccosukee Peoples," in *The New History of Florida*, ed. Michael Gannon (Gainesville: University Press of Florida, 1996), 193–94.

10. Edward W. Callahan, ed., *List of Officers of the Navy of the United States and the Marine Corps from 1775 to 1900* (New York: L. R. Hamersly, 1901), 222; and *Pensacola Gazette*, 2 January 1836.

11. *Pensacola Gazette*, 23 January, 18 June 1836.

12. Dysart, "Another Road to Disappearance," 43; Ellsworth and Dysart, "Forgotten People," 424; Grant Foreman, *Indian Removal: The Emigration of the Five Civilized Tribes of Indians* (Norman: University of Oklahoma Press, 1953), 140–51; Sean Michael O'Brien, *In Bitterness and in Tears: Andrew Jackson's Destruction of the Creeks and Seminoles* (Guilford, Conn.: Lyons Press, 2003), 235–37; and *Pensacola Gazette*, 5 March, 28 May 1836. A masterful account of the Second Creek War can be found in John Thaddeus Ellisor, "The Second Creek War: The Unexplored Conflict," PhD diss., University of Tennessee, Knoxville, 1996.

13. *Pensacola Gazette*, 18, 25 June 1836; and Brian R. Rucker, *Jackson Morton: West Florida's Soldier, Senator, and Secessionist* (Milton, Fla.: Patagonia Press, 1990), 3–5.

14. *Pensacola Gazette*, 25 June 1836.

15. *Pensacola Gazette*, 25 June, 2 July 1836.

16. *Pensacola Gazette*, 9, 30 July, 3 September 1836.

17. *Pensacola Gazette*, 1, 8, 15 October 1836.

18. *Pensacola Gazette*, 29 October 1836.

19. *Pensacola Gazette*, 14 January 1837.

20. Ellisor, "Second Creek War," 307–8; Elba Wilson Carswell, *Holmesteading: The History of Holmes County, Florida* (Tallahassee: E. W. Carswell, 1986; reprint, Bonifay, Fla.: Holmes County Public Library, 2003), 31; Foreman, *Indian Removal*, 140–51, 179–81; O'Brien, *In Bitterness and in Tears*, 237–39; and Anne Kendrick Walker, *Backtracking in Barbour County: A Narrative of the Last Alabama Frontier* (Richmond: Dietz Press, 1941), 38–58. For a comprehensive account of the political factionalism within the Creek nation and its impact on removal, see Michael D. Green, *The Politics of Indian Removal: Creek Government and Society in Crisis* (Lincoln: University of Nebraska Press, 1982).

21. Carswell, *Holmesteading*, 31–32; *Niles' Weekly Register*, March 18, 1837, 33; *Pensacola Gazette*, 11 March 1837; Archibald Smith to C. A. Harris, March 12, 1837, Letters Received by the Office of Indian Affairs, 1824–80, Florida Superintendency Emigration, 1828–1838, microfilm publication no. 234, roll 290 (mf 752), National Archives (available at John C. Pace Library, University of West Florida, Pensacola).

22. Smith to Harris, March 12, 1837, Office of Indian Affairs, 1824–80, Florida Superintendency Emigration, 1828–38.

23. *Pensacola Gazette*, 11 March 1837.

24. *Pensacola Gazette*, 18 March 1837.

25. J. G. de Roulhac Hamilton, ed., *The Papers of William Alexander Graham*, 6 vols. (Raleigh: North Carolina Department of Archives and History, 1961), 4: 151–52; and *Pensacola Gazette*, 25 March, 8 April 1837. Mobile Point was at the tip of the eastern peninsula located at the mouth of Mobile Bay (the site of present-day Fort Morgan).

26. *Pensacola Gazette*, 18 March, 8, 15 April 1837. Mallett's Landing, on Lafayette Bayou, was most likely in the modern Freeport area of Walton County, though some sources show it in the area of present-day Valparaiso-Niceville in Okaloosa County. See *American State Papers: Naval Affairs*, 4: 222; John L. McKinnon, *History of Walton County* (Atlanta, 1911; reprint, Gainesville: Palmetto Books, 1968), 8, 44; "Map of the Western Part of Florida" in John Lee Williams, *A View of West Florida* (Philadelphia, 1827; facsimile ed., Gainesville: University Presses of Florida, 1976), endpiece; and John Lee Williams, *The Territory of Florida* (New York, A.T. Goodrich, 1837; facsimile ed., Gainesville: University of Florida Press, 1962), 127.

27. *Pensacola Gazette*, 22 April 1837.

28. *Pensacola Gazette*, 22, 29 April 1837.

29. McKinnon, *History of Walton County*, 109–17; and *Pensacola Gazette*, 29 April, 13 May 1837. The whites killed by the Indians near Gum Creek reportedly were scalped. Accounts differ as to how many whites were involved in the incident. According to available information, "Big" John Anderson, Michael Elliot, Joseph Nelson, William

Nelson, John Porter, and Michael Vaughan were killed, and Bill Caswell and Thomas Broxton survived.

30. *Pensacola Gazette*, 29 April 1837.

31. Wright was editor of the *Pensacola Gazette* from 1834 to 1845. He owned the paper and wrote most of the editorials. See Horance G. Davis Jr., "Pensacola Newspapers, 1821–1900," *Florida Historical Quarterly* 37 (January–April 1959): 424–25.

32. Ellisor, "Second Creek War," 313–14; McKinnon, *History of Walton County*, 110–17, and *Pensacola Gazette*, 29 April, 13 May 1837. The attack on Shoal River by Justice's men was at a tributary creek of Shoal River, later named "Battle Creek" because of this engagement.

33. Ellisor, "Second Creek War," 317–18.

34. *American State Papers: Military Affairs*, 7 vols. (Washington, D.C.: Gales and Seaton, 1861), 7: 838; and *Pensacola Gazette*, 29 April, 3 June 1837. The Escribano Indians presumably were relocated along with the other Indian groups to reservation lands beyond the Mississippi River. Lieutenant Reynolds earlier had been an agent to the Creeks living in southern Alabama and Georgia. See Foreman, *Indian Removal*, 180; Mahon, *History of the Second Seminole War*, 251; and Walker, *Backtracking in Barbour County*, 57.

35. Carswell, *Holmesteading*, 32–33, 35; McKinnon, *History of Walton County*, 110, 116, 118–20; *Pensacola Gazette*, 13, 20, 27 May, 3 June 1837; *Tallahassee Floridian*, 1 July 1837; and Margaret H. Wooten, ed., *Henderson Chips* (privately printed, 1983), 3 (copy in John C. Pace Library, UWF). Washington County and Franklin County volunteers later joined the militiamen operating in Walton County. During this period, McKinnon's company captured a band of Creeks on Black Creek, sixteen miles from La Grange, Walton County. See Ellisor, "Second Creek War," 313.

36. *Pensacola Gazette*, 13 May 1837.

37. *Pensacola Gazette*, 27 May, 3 June 1837; and *Tallahassee Floridian*, 1 July 1837. The Indians were originally captured ca. May 22 at the J. J. Harrison home near Alaqua Creek.

38. Carswell, *Holmesteading*, 33–35.

39. *Pensacola Gazette*, 10 June 1837.

40. Carswell, *Holmesteading*, 33–35; and *Pensacola Gazette*, 10 June, 1 July 1837. There were unsubstantiated rumors of whites intent on murdering Reynolds and his party, perhaps because he was exposing the massacre.

41. *Pensacola Gazette*, 17 June 1837.

42. *Pensacola Gazette*, 17, 24 June, 1 July 1837.

43. *Pensacola Gazette*, 1, 8 July 1837.

44. McKinnon, *History of Walton County*, 118–19; and *Pensacola Gazette*, 27 May 1837. This action took place near the community of Antioch, and the swamp where the skirmish occurred is still known as "Battle Bay."

45. Ellisor, "Second Creek War," 323; *Pensacola Gazette*, 15 July 1837; and *Tallahassee Floridian*, 15 July, 16 September 1837. A battalion under Colonel Wood of St. Joseph at

the time was encamped on Santa Rosa Sound near present-day Fort Walton Beach. It was dispatched northward in pursuit of the retreating Indians.

46. *Pensacola Gazette*, 22, 29 July, 5 August 1837; and *Tallahassee Floridian*, 5 August 1837. Colonel Wood and his force had arrived to participate in this battle with Brown's forces. Corporal Stephen H. Clark was killed; Captain Hawkins, Lieutenant Myers, Corporal Whaley, Patrick Keenon, and a Mr. Marrina were wounded. The whites acquired a pony, two rifles, and a large quantity of provisions the Creeks left behind.

47. *Pensacola Gazette*, 22 July, 26, 30 August 1837. The Creeks had been removed to Pass Christian, Mississippi, by August. Lieutenant Reynolds was later in charge of removing these Creeks to the West.

48. *Pensacola Gazette*, 2, 6, 9 September 1837.

49. Hamilton, *Papers of William Alexander Graham*, 4: 151–52; and *Pensacola Gazette*, 26 August, 2 September 1837. The *Tallahassee Floridian* of September 9, 1827, reported that "a party of about twenty warriors, besides women and children, have stopped near St. Andrew's Bay, supposed to be on their way to the Seminole country, having been visited by a party of five Euchee warriors. The Indians have succeeded in visiting the Creeks unmolested, having crossed the Apalachicola river below the Indian towns. They state that in the Seminole country they can always keep out of the way of the whites, and offer this as an inducement of the Creeks to join them." Colonel Wood's company from St. Joseph (consisting of seventy men) were only enlisted for two months, and their term of service expired in August. Colonel Leavin Brown's Jackson County troops were also "much fatigued and worn out from several marches, and their horses many of them broke down by hard scouts." Brown believed that Captain McKinnon's Walton County company of about fifty men was sufficient to protect the Walton County area since the Creeks were reduced in number and heading eastward. See *Tallahassee Floridian*, 5 August 1837.

50. Carswell, *Holmesteading*, 35; and *Pensacola Gazette*, 21 October 1837.

51. Ellisor, "Second Creek War," 325–27; *Niles' National Register*, January 27, 1838, 338; *Pensacola Gazette*, 2, 30 December 1837, 20 January 1838; Jerrell H. Shofner, *Jackson County, Florida: A History* (Marianna, Fla.: Jackson County Heritage Association, 1985), 91; and *Tallahassee Floridian*, 9 September, 7, 14 October 1837. Ellisor argues that the fleeing Creeks added a significant component to the Second Seminole War when they joined the Seminoles. See Ellisor, "Second Creek War," 332–54.

52. *Pensacola Gazette*, 25 November 1837.

53. *Tallahassee Floridian*, 28 October, 18 November 1837. The Creeks were captured on the Apalachicola River, near the head of Lake Wimico.

54. *Tallahassee Floridian*, 2 December 1837.

55. *Tallahassee Floridian*, 27 January, 24 March 1838.

56. *Tallahassee Floridian*, 19 May, 2 June 1838.

57. James W. Covington, "Federal Relations with the Apalachicola Indians: 1823–1838," *Florida Historical Quarterly* 42 (October 1963): 140–41; Ellsworth and

Dysart, "Forgotten People," 424; *Pensacola Gazette* 3 November 1838; and Shofner, *Jackson County*, 91–92. An investigation of the Apalachicola Indian reservation revealed Indian agent Archibald Smith as being a disruptive element. Smith, who had traveled through West Florida in 1837 warning the settlers of the approaching renegade Creeks, was accused of setting up a liquor shop among the Apalachicolas. Evidence seemed to indicate that Smith was selling hard liquor and ammunition to the Indians and was also discouraging the removal to the West. See Ellisor, "Second Creek War," 330.

58. F. W. Hoskins, "The St. Joseph Convention: The Making of Florida's First Constitution," *Florida Historical Quarterly* 16 (October 1937): 108–9.

59. McKinnon, *History of Walton County*, 124–25; and *Pensacola Gazette*, 1 February 1840.

60. Florida, *Territorial Florida Journal of Senate*, 6th session beginning 1 January 1844, 168–79; *Niles' National Register*, 30 May 1840, 200; *Pensacola Gazette*, 19 September, 6, 24 October 1840; Shofner, *Jackson County*, 92–93; Marlene Womack, *The Bay Country . . . of Northwest Florida* (Apalachicola: New Hope Press, 1998), 19, 42; Marlene Womack, *Along the Bay: A Pictorial History of Bay County* (Norfolk: Heritage, 1994), 33; Marlene Womack, "Out of the Past: Settlers Family Tells Tale of Indian Unrest," *Panama City News Herald*, 27 July 2003; and Marlene Womack, "Out of the Past: Indian Marauders Made Desperate, Violent Raids," *Panama City News Herald*, 3 August 2003.

61. Elba Wilson Carswell, *Tempestuous Triangle: Historical Notes on Washington County, Florida* (Chipley, Fla.: Washington County School Board, 1974), 60–62; Elba Wilson Carswell, *Washington: Florida's Twelfth County* (Tallahassee: Rose Printing Company, 1991), 45–49; Charlton W. Tebeau, *A History of Florida* (Coral Gables: University of Miami Press, 1971), 168; and U.S. Congress, House Document, *Indians Remaining in Florida*, 28th Cong., 1st sess., H. Doc. 253, serial 444, 2–4.

62. Carswell, *Tempestuous Triangle*, 60–63; Carswell, *Washington*, 45–49; and U.S. Congress, *Indians Remaining in Florida*, 2–4.

63. Carswell, *Tempestuous Triangle*, 63–64; and Carswell, *Washington*, 45–49.

64. *New American State Papers: Indian Affairs*, 11 vols. (Wilmington, Del.: Scholarly Resources, 1972), 11: 444–45; and *Pensacola Gazette*, 13 January, 24 February 1844.

65. *New American State Papers*, 11: 443–53; and *Pensacola Gazette*, 24 February, 30 March 1844.

66. Clarence Edwin Carter, ed., *The Territorial Papers of the United States*, 28 vols. (Washington, D.C.: Government Printing Office, 1960), 26: 898; *New American State Papers*, 11: 451–53; *Niles' National Register*, 4 May 1844, 160; and *Pensacola Gazette*, 20 April, 30 November 1844.

67. *Pensacola Gazette*, 30 November 1844, 14, 21 February 1846.

68. Carswell, *Holmes Valley*, rev. ed. (Chipley, Fla.: E. W. Carswell, 1983), 6; McKinnon, *History of Walton County*, 125–28; *Pensacola Gazette*, 20 November, 27 December 1847; Womack, *Along the Bay*, 33, 35; and Womack, *Bay Country*, 19–20.

69. Dysart, "Another Road to Disappearance," 37–48; and Ellsworth and Dysart, "Forgotten People," 422–39. During the latter part of the nineteenth century, Creeks from south Alabama and south Georgia migrated into West Florida, adding to the small Indian population already present. As late as 1900 there were still reports of Indians stealing horses and cattle from neighbors around the Horse Branch Islands, a remote and swampy section of land on present-day Eglin Air Force base in southern Okaloosa County. See interview with Perry L. Fortune, by Claire N. Bradberry, August 27, 1977, typed transcript in Santa Rosa County Vertical File, Pensacola Historical Society Resource Center, Pensacola, Fla.

For Further Reading

Alden, John R. *John Stuart and the Southern Colonial Frontier: A Study of Indian Relations, War, Trade, and Land Problems in the Southern Wilderness, 1754–1775*. Ann Arbor: University of Michigan Press, 1944.

Bauer, K. Jack. *Zachary Taylor: Soldier, Planter, Statesman of the Old Southwest*. Baton Rouge: Louisiana State University Press, 1985.

Bice, David A. *The Original Lone Star Republic: Scoundrels, Statesmen, and Schemers of the 1810 West Florida Rebellion*. Clanton, Ala.: Heritage Pub. Consultants, 2004.

Boyd, Mark F. *Florida Aflame: The Background and Onset of the Seminole War, 1835.* Tallahassee: Distributed by Florida Board of Parks and Historic Memorials, 1951.

Boyd, Mark F., Hale G. Smith, and John W. Griffin. *Here They Once Stood: The Tragic End of the Apalachee Missions*. Gainesville: University of Florida Press, 1951; reprint, Gainesville: University Press of Florida, 1999.

Braund, Kathryn E. Holland. *Deerskins and Duffels: The Creek Indian Trade with Anglo-America, 1685–1815*. Lincoln: University of Nebraska Press, 1993.

Braund, Kathryn E. Holland, and Gregory Waselkov, eds. *William Bartram on the Southeastern Indians*. Lincoln: University of Nebraska Press, 2002.

Brooks, Philip C. *Diplomacy and the Borderlands: The Adams-Onis Treaty of 1819*. Berkeley: University of California Press, 1939.

Buchanan, John. *Jackson's Way: Andrew Jackson and the People of the Western Waters*. New York: John Wiley & Sons, 2001.

Buker, George E. *Swamp Sailors: Riverine Warfare in the Everglades, 1835–1842*. Gainesville: University Presses of Florida, 1975.

Clark, Thomas D., and John D. W. Guice. *The Old Southwest, 1795–1830: Frontiers in Conflict*. Norman: University of Oklahoma Press, 1996.

Cline, Howard F. *Notes on Colonial Indians and Communities in Florida, 1700–1821*. New York: Garland, 1974.

Coe, Charles H. *Red Patriots: The Story of the Seminoles*. Cincinnati, 1898; reprint, Gainesville: University Presses of Florida, 1974.

Coker, William S. *Indian Traders of the Southeastern Spanish Borderlands: Panton, Leslie & Company and John Forbes & Company, 1783–1847*. Gainesville: University Presses of Florida, 1986.

Corkran, David H. *The Creek Frontier, 1540–1782*. Norman: University of Oklahoma Press, 1967.

Cotterill, R. S. *The Southern Indians: The Story of the Civilized Tribes before Removal.* Norman: University of Oklahoma Press, 1954.

Covington, James W. *The Billy Bowlegs War, 1855–1858: The Final Stand of the Seminoles against the Whites.* Cluluota, Fla.: Mickler House, 1981.

———. *The British Meet the Seminoles: Negotiations between British Authorities in East Florida and the Indians, 1763–68.* Contributions of the Florida State Museum, Social Sciences, 7. Gainesville: University of Florida, 1961.

———. *The Seminoles of Florida.* Gainesville: University Press of Florida, 1993.

Crane, Verner W. *The Southern Frontier, 1670–1732.* Durham: Duke University Press, 1928.

Cusick, James G. *The Other War of 1812: The Patriot War and the American Invasion of Spanish East Florida.* Gainesville: University Press of Florida, 2003.

De Vorsey, Louis. *The Indian Boundary in the Southern Colonies, 1763–1775.* Chapel Hill: University of North Carolina Press, 1966.

Doherty, Herbert J. *Richard Keith Call: Southern Unionist.* Gainesville: University of Florida Press, 1961.

Doster, James F. *The Creek Indians and Their Florida Lands, 1740–1823.* New York: Garland, 1974.

Elder, John L. *Everlasting Fire: Cowokoci's Legacy in the Seminole Struggle against Western Expansion.* Edmond, Okla.: Medicine Wheel Press, 2004.

Ellsworth, Lucius F., ed. *The Americanization of the Gulf Coast, 1803–1850.* Pensacola: Historic Pensacola Preservation Board, 1972.

Ethridge, Robbie. *Creek Country: The Creek Indians and Their World.* Chapel Hill: University of North Carolina Press, 2003.

Fairbanks, Charles H. *The Florida Seminole People.* Phoenix: Indian Tribal Series, 1973.

———. *Ethnohistorical Report of the Florida Indians. Commission Findings.* New York: Garland, 1974.

Foreman, Grant. *The Five Civilized Tribes.* Norman: University of Oklahoma Press, 1934.

———. *Indian Removal: The Emigration of the Five Civilized Tribes of Indians.* Norman: University of Oklahoma Press, 1932.

Frank, Andrew. *Creeks and Southerners: Biculturalism on the Early American Frontier.* Lincoln: University of Nebraska Press, 2005.

Fretwell, Jacqueline K., and Susan R. Parker, eds. *Clash between Cultures: Spanish East Florida, 1784–1821.* St. Augustine, Fla.: St. Augustine Historical Society, 1988.

Frost, John. *Pictorial Life of Andrew Jackson.* Hartford, Conn.: Belknap and Hamersley, 1847.

Fuller, Hubert B. *The Purchase of Florida: Its History and Diplomacy.* Gainesville: University of Florida Press, 1964.

Gifford, John C., ed. *Billy Bowlegs and the Seminole War.* Coconut Grove, Fla.: Triangle, 1925.

Green, Michael D. *The Politics of Indian Removal: Creek Government and Society in Crisis.* Lincoln: University of Nebraska Press, 1982.

Griffin, Charles C. *The United States and the Disruption of the Spanish Empire, 1810–1822: A Study of the Relations of the United States with Spain and with the Rebel Spanish Colonies.* New York: Columbia University Press, 1937.

Griffith, Benjamin W., Jr. *McIntosh and Weatherford: Creek Indian Leaders.* Tuscaloosa: University of Alabama Press, 1988.

Heidler, David, and Jeanne T. Heidler. *Old Hickory's War: Andrew Jackson and the Quest for Empire.* Mechanicsburg, Pa.: Stackpole Books, 1996.

Hitchcock, Ethan Allen. *Fifty Years in Camp and Field: Diary of Major-General Ethan Allen Hitchcock, U.S.A.* Edited by W. A. Croffut. New York: G. P. Putnam's Sons, 1909.

Horsman, Reginald. *Expansion and American Indian Policy, 1783–1812.* East Lansing: Michigan State University Press, 1967.

Hudson, Charles M. *The Southeastern Indians.* Knoxville: University of Tennessee Press, 1976.

Kieffer, Chester. *Maligned General: The Biography of Thomas Sydney Jesup.* San Rafael, Calif.: Presidio Press, 1979.

Kirk, Cooper. *William Lauderdale: General Andrew Jackson's Warrior.* Fort Lauderdale: Manatee Books, 1982.

Knetsch, Joe. *Fear and Anxiety on the Florida Frontier: Articles on the Second Seminole War, 1835–1842.* Dade City: Seminole Wars Foundation Press, 2008.

———. *Florida's Seminole Wars.* Charleston, S.C.: Arcadia, 2003.

Lancaster, Jane F. *Removal Aftershock: The Seminoles' Struggles to Survive in the West, 1836–1866.* Knoxville: University of Tennessee Press, 1994.

Laumer, Frank. *Dade's Last Command.* Gainesville: University Press of Florida, 1995.

Lewis, James E. *The American Union and the Problem of Neighborhood: The United States and the Collapse of the Spanish Empire, 1783–1829.* Chapel Hill: University of North Carolina Press, 1998.

Littlefield, Daniel. *Africans and Seminoles: From Removal to Emancipation.* Westport, Conn.: Greenwood Press, 1977.

Mahon, John K. *History of the Second Seminole War, 1835–1842.* Gainesville: University Presses of Florida, 1967.

McReynolds, Edwin C. *The Seminoles.* Norman: University of Oklahoma Press, 1957.

Meltzer, Milton. *Hunted Like a Wolf: The Story of the Seminole War.* New York: Farrar, Straus and Giroux, 1972.

Milanich, Jerald T., and Samuel Proctor. *Tacachale: Essays on the Indians of Florida and Southeastern Georgia during the Historic Period.* Gainesville: University Presses of Florida, 1978.

Missall, John, and Mary Lou Missall. *The Seminole Wars: America's Longest Indian Conflict.* Gainesville: University Press of Florida, 2004.

———, eds. *This Miserable Pride of a Soldier: The Letters and Journals of Col. William*

S. Foster in the Second Seminole War, 1836–1839. Tampa: University of Tampa Press and Seminole Wars Historic Foundation, 2005.

Moore-Willson, Minnie. Osceola: Florida's Seminole War Chieftain. Palm Beach, Fla.: Davies, 1931.

Motte, Jacob Rhett. Journey into Wilderness: An Army Surgeon's Account of Life in Camp and Field during the Creek and Seminole Wars, 1836–1838. Edited by James F. Sunderman. Gainesville: University of Florida Press, 1953.

Mowat, Charles L. East Florida as a British Province, 1763–1784. Berkeley: University of California Press, 1943.

Murdoch, Richard K. The Georgia-Florida Frontier, 1793–1796: Spanish Reaction to French Intrigue and American Designs. Millwood, N.Y.: Kraus Reprint, 1974.

Neill, Wilfred T. The Story of Florida's Seminole Indians. St. Petersburg, Fla.: Great Outdoors, 1973.

O'Brien, Sean M. In Bitterness and Tears: Andrew Jackson's Destruction of the Creeks and Seminoles. Westport, Conn.: Praeger, 2003.

O'Donnell, James H. Southeastern Frontiers: Europeans, Africans, and American Indians, 1513–1840. Bloomington: Indiana University Press for the Newberry Library, 1982.

Owsley, Frank L., Jr. Struggle for the Gulf Borderlands: The Creek War and the Battle of New Orleans, 1812–1815. Tuscaloosa: University of Alabama Press, 1981.

Owsley, Frank L., Jr., and Gene A. Smith. Filibusters and Expansionists: Jeffersonian Manifest Destiny, 1800–1821. Tuscaloosa: University of Alabama Press, 1997.

Patrick, R. W. Florida Fiasco: Rampant Rebels on the Georgia-Florida Border, 1810–1815. Athens: University of Georgia Press, 1954.

Peters, Virginia B. The Florida Wars. Hamden, Conn.: Archon Books, 1979.

Porter, Kenneth W. The Black Seminoles: History of a Freedom-Seeking People. Gainesville: University Press of Florida, 1996.

Potter, Woodburne. The War in Florida: Being an Exposition of Its Causes, and an Accurate History of the Campaigns of General Clinch, Gaines, and Scott. Baltimore: Lewis and Coleman, 1836.

Prince, Henry. Amidst a Storm of Bullets: The Diary of Lt. Henry Prince in Florida, 1836–1842. Ed. Frank Laumer. Tampa: University of Tampa Press, 1998.

Prucha, Francis P. The Sword of the Republic: The United States Army on the Frontier, 1783–1846. New York: Macmillan, 1969.

Remini, Robert V. Andrew Jackson and His Indian Wars. New York: Viking, 2001.

Rivers, Larry E. Slavery in Florida: Territorial Days to Emancipation. Gainesville: University Press of Florida, 2000.

Satz, Ronald N. American Indian Policy in the Jacksonian Era. Lincoln: University of Nebraska Press, 1975.

Saunt, Claudio. A New Order of Things: Property, Power, and the Transformation of the Creek Indians, 1733–1816. New York: Cambridge University Press, 1999.

Shaw, Helen Louise. British Administration of the Southern Indians, 1756–1783. Lancaster, Pa.: Lancaster Press, 1931.

Sheehan, Bernard W. *Seeds of Extinction: Jeffersonian Philanthropy and the American Indian.* New York: W. W. Norton, 1973.

Smith, Hale G. *The European and the Indian: European-Indian Contacts in Georgia and Florida.* Gainesville: Florida Anthropological Society, 1956.

Sprague, John T. *The Origin, Progress, and Conclusion of the Florida War.* Gainesville: University of Florida Press, 1964.

Swanton, John R. *Early History of the Creek Indians and Their Neighbors.* Bureau of American Ethnology Bulletin 73. Washington, D.C.: Government Printing Office, 1922.

———. *The Indians of the Southeastern United States.* Bureau of American Ethnology Bulletin 137. Washington, D.C.: Government Printing Office, 1946.

Twyman, Bruce E. *The Black Seminole Legacy and North American Politics, 1693–1845.* Washington, D.C.: Howard University Press, 1999.

Waciuma, Wanjohi. *Intervention in Spanish Floridas, 1801–1813: A Study in Jeffersonian Foreign Policy.* Boston: Branden Press, 1976.

Wallace, Anthony F. C. *Jefferson and the Indians: The Tragic Fate of the First Americans.* Cambridge, Mass.: Belknap Press, 1999.

Walton, George. *Fearless and Free: The Seminole Indian War, 1835–1842.* Indianapolis: Bobbs-Merrill, 1977.

Weisman, Brent R. *Like Beads on a String: A Culture History of the Seminole Indians in Northern Peninsular Florida.* Tuscaloosa: University of Alabama Press, 1989.

———. *Unconquered People: Florida's Seminole and Miccosukee Indians.* Gainesville: University Press of Florida, 1999.

Whitaker, Arthur P. *The Spanish-American Frontier, 1783–1795: The Westward Movement and the Spanish Retreat in the Mississippi Valley.* Lincoln: University of Nebraska Press, 1927.

Wickman, Patricia. *Osceola's Legacy.* Tuscaloosa: University of Alabama Press, 1991.

Wright, J. Leitch. *Anglo-Spanish Rivalry in North America.* Athens: University of Georgia Press, 1971.

———. *Creeks & Seminoles: The Destruction and Regeneration of the Muscogulge People.* Lincoln: University of Nebraska Press, 1986.

———. *Florida in the American Revolution.* Gainesville: University Presses of Florida, 1975.

———. *The Only Land They Knew: The Tragic Story of the Indians of the Old South.* New York: Free Press, 1981.

———. *William Augustus Bowles, Director General of the Creek Nation.* Athens: University of Georgia Press, 1967.

Contributors

William S. Belko is the executive director of the Missouri Humanities Council. He is formerly associate professor of History at the University of West Florida, and is the author of *The Triumph of the Antebellum Free Trade Movement* (winner of the 2013 Phi Alpha Theta Best Subsequent Book Award) and *The Invincible Duff Green: Whig of the West*. He has a forthcoming biography entitled *Philip Pendleton Barbour, 1783-1841: An Old Republican in King Andrew's Court*.

Canter Brown Jr. is executive vice president and chief legal officer, as well as professor of history, at Fort Valley State University, Fort Valley, Georgia. He has authored numerous works in Florida and southern United States history, including *Florida's Peace River Frontier* (1991); *Ossian Bingley Hart: Florida's Loyalist Reconstruction Governor* (1997), and *Florida's Black Public Officials, 1867–1924* (1998). He has served as historian of the Supreme Court of Florida and, with Larry E. Rivers, has written works on the origins and development of African American religious denominations in Florida. His most recent work, edited with Rivers, is *The Varieties of Women's Experiences: Portraits of Southern Women in the Post–Civil War Century*, published by the University Press of Florida. His work has been recognized with a variety of awards and prizes, including the Rembert W. Patrick Book Award, the Harry T. and Harriette V. Moore Book Prize of the Florida Historical Society, and the American Association for State and Local History's Certificate of Commendation.

Matthew Clavin is assistant professor of history at the University of West Florida. His teaching and research interests focus on slavery and abolition in early America and the Atlantic world. He is the author of *Toussaint Louverture and the American Civil War* (2009), and he has published articles in the *Encyclopedia of the Nineteenth Century, Early American Studies, Civil War History,* and *Slavery and Abolition*.

James Cusick is curator of the P. K. Yonge Library of Florida History at the University of Florida and serves on the executive board of the Florida Historical Society. He is the author of *The Other War of 1812: The Patriot War and the American Invasion of Spanish East Florida* (2003) and writes and consults with organizations throughout the state on Florida history.

James M. Denham is professor of history and director of the Lawton M. Chiles Center for Florida History at Florida Southern College. He is the author of *Echoes from a Distant Frontier: The Brown Sisters' Correspondence from Antebellum Florida* (2004), with Keith Huneycutt, *Florida Sheriffs: A History, 1821–1945* (2001), with William W. Rogers, *Cracker Times and Pioneer Lives: The Florida Reminiscences of George Gillette Keen and Sarah Pamela Williams* (2000), with Canter Brown Jr., and *"A Rogue's Paradise": Crime and Punishment in Antebellum Florida, 1821–1861* (1997), and he has published numerous articles on Southern and Florida history. Denham was awarded the Florida Historical Society's Arthur W. Thompson Prize in 1992, and in 2002 he and Rogers were awarded the society's James J. Horgan Book Prize for *Florida Sheriffs*.

David S. Heidler teaches in the Department of History at Colorado State University–Pueblo. Jeanne T. Heidler is professor of history at the U.S. Air Force Academy. Together they have written numerous books and articles dealing with the history of the early American republic, the antebellum period, and the Civil War, including *The War of 1812: An Encyclopedia* (1997) and the *Encyclopedia of the American Civil War: A Social, Political, and Military History* (2000), which received the Society for Military History's Distinguished Book Award in 2003. They are the authors of *Old Hickory's War: Andrew Jackson and the Quest for Empire (1996), The War of 1812 (2002), Manifest Destiny (2003), Daily Life in the Early American Republic: Creating a New Nation, 1790–1820* (2004), and *The Mexican War (2006).* The Heidlers are also general editors for several series of monographs examining U.S. civil-military relations, American soldiers' lives, and life on the home front. Their biography of Henry Clay was published in 2010.

Joe Knetsch is a government analyst for the Bureau of Survey and Mapping of Florida's Department of Environmental Protection. He is the author of *Florida's Seminole Wars, 1817–1858* (2003), *Faces of the Frontier: Florida Surveyors and Developers in the Nineteenth Century* (2006), and *Fear and Anxiety on the Florida Frontier: The Second Seminole War, 1835–1842* (2008). He has edited two other books and published well over 100 articles on Florida history and the Seminole Wars.

Susan Richbourg Parker holds a PhD in colonial history and has taught at the University of Florida, the University of North Florida, and the University of South Florida. She is executive director of the St. Augustine Historical Society and has served as a historic preservation consultant with the Florida Department of State. She is the co-editor of *Clash between Cultures: Spanish East Florida, 1784–1821* (1988) and the author of several articles on Southern and Florida history. In 2009 she was selected as the Outstanding Woman in Florida History by the Florida Historical Society.

Brian Rucker is full professor in the Department of History, Languages, and Philosophy at Pensacola Junior College and an adjunct professor of history for the University of West Florida. His teaching and research interests include the Old South, Florida history, and the Gulf South Borderlands, among others. His extensive publications include *Timothy Twitchell: New England Entrepreneur on the West Florida Frontier* (2006), *Arcadia: Florida's Premier Antebellum Industrial Park* (2005), *Floridale: The Rise and Fall of a Florida Boom Community* (2001), *Brick Road to Boom Town: The Story of Santa Rosa County's "Old Brick Road"* (1993), *Encyclopedia of Education in Antebellum Pensacola* (1999), and *Jackson Morton: West Florida's Soldier, Senator, and Secessionist* (1990). He has also published nearly three dozen articles on Florida and Southern history.

Samuel Watson is associate professor of history at the U.S. Military Academy. He is the editor of *Warfare in the USA, 1784–1861* (2005) and the author of *Frontier Diplomats: The Army Officer Corps in the Borderlands of the Early Republic, 1815–1846* (2008). His research interests are the U.S. Army between 1784 and 1861, particularly civil-military relations and the army's role in state formation.

Index

CPSIA information can be obtained at www.ICGtesting.com
Printed in the USA
LVOW08s0222180615

442561LV00008B/3/P